D0187545

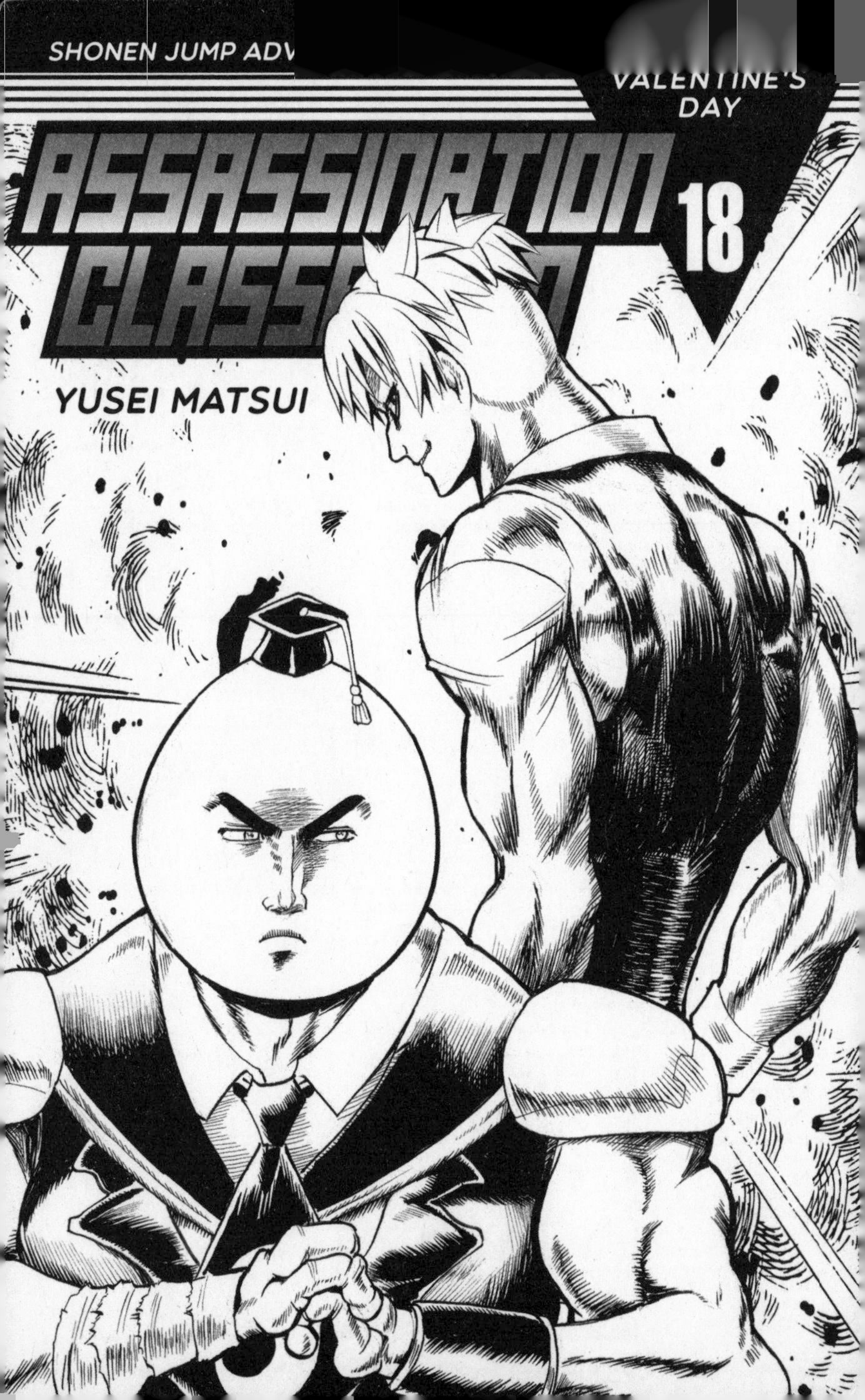
SHONEN JUMP ADV
VALENTINE'S DAY
ASSASSINATION
CLASS
18
YUSEI MATSUI

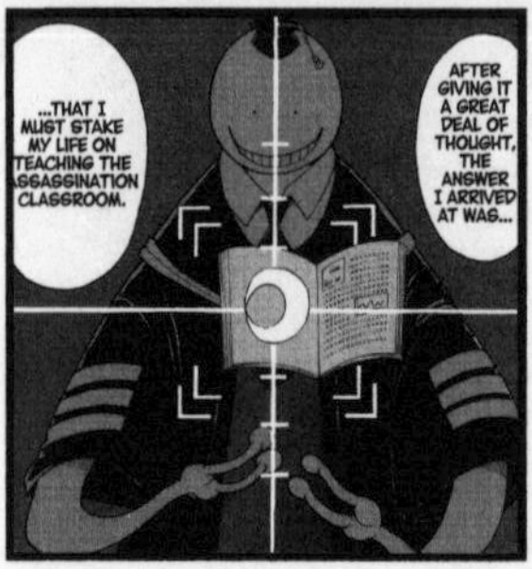
AFTER GIVING IT A GREAT DEAL OF THOUGHT, THE ANSWER I ARRIVED AT WAS...
...THAT I MUST STAKE MY LIFE ON TEACHING THE ASSASSINATION CLASSROOM.

Story Thus Far

Kunugigaoka Junior High Class 3-E is taught by a monster who even the armies of the world with all their state-of-the-art technology can't kill. That monster, Koro Sensei, is fated to self-destruct and take the planet Earth with him, so...

Koro Tribune

February Issue

Published by: Class 3-E Newspaper Staff

Off we go into outer space and beyond in search for a way to save Koro Sensei!!

...a bounty has been placed on his head. It comes down to his students in 3-E, the so-called "End Class." Once looked down upon by the rest of the school, this class of misfits is now respected for the athleticism and powers of concentration they have developed thanks to the dedicated instruction of Koro Sensei and Mr. Karasuma of the Ministry of Defense. A strong bond has formed between the students and Koro Sensei, transcending their relationship as assassins and targets. After learning the truth about Koro Sensei's past, the students split into two groups (led by Karma and Nagisa, respectively) which either advocated killing or saving their teacher. After settling their differences in a grand battle, Class E committed to finding a way to save Koro Sensei. Their first step is to infiltrate the International Space Station to steal research...

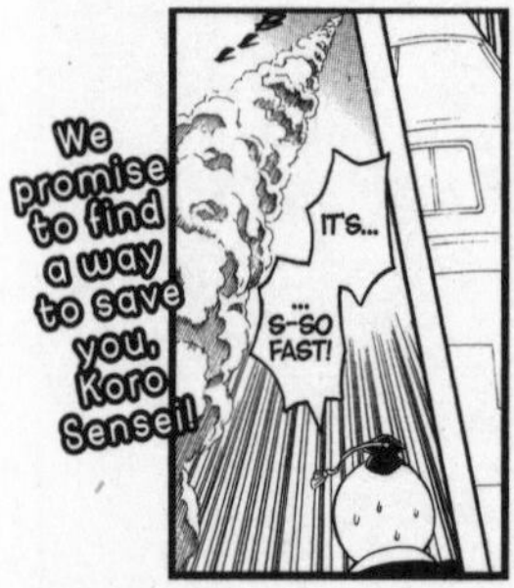
We promise to find a way to save you, Koro Sensei!
IT'S...
...S-SO FAST!

Koro Sensei

A mysterious, man-made, octopus-like creature whose name is a play on the words "koro senai," which means "can't kill." He is capable of flying at Mach 20 and his versatile tentacles protect him from attacks and aid him in everyday activities. He followed in the footsteps of Aguri, the woman who saved his humanity, by becoming the teacher of Class 3-E.

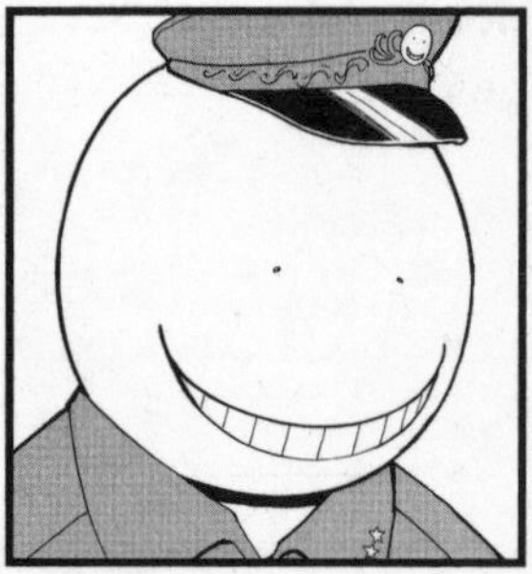

Kaede Kayano

Class E student. She enrolled in Class E to avenge her sister's death by killing Koro Sensei. Her tentacles have since been removed. Does she have special feelings for Nagisa now...?!

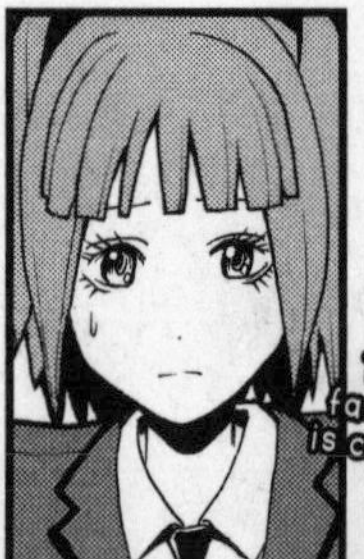

Nagisa Shiota

Class E student. He has a hidden talent for assassinations and decides to hone those skills to help others. He's a good kisser too.

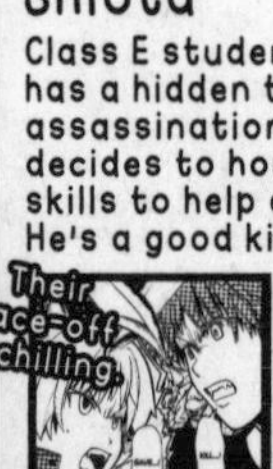
Their face-off is chilling.

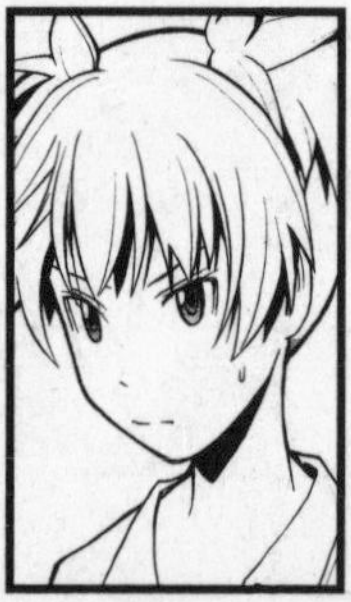

Itona Horibe

pick up!

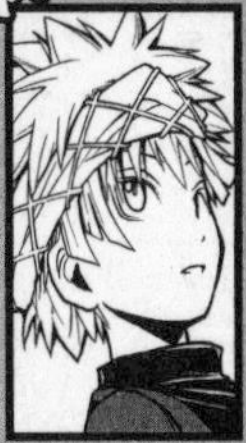

He lost some hair on his scalp where the tentacle used to grow out of his head, but Koro Sensei swiftly transplanted some of his hair follicles to fill the gap. Koro Sensei's talent is a middle-aged man's dream!

Karma Akabane

Class E student. He learned to take his studies a bit more seriously after some initial failures and earned first place in the overall school scores on the second semester midterm.

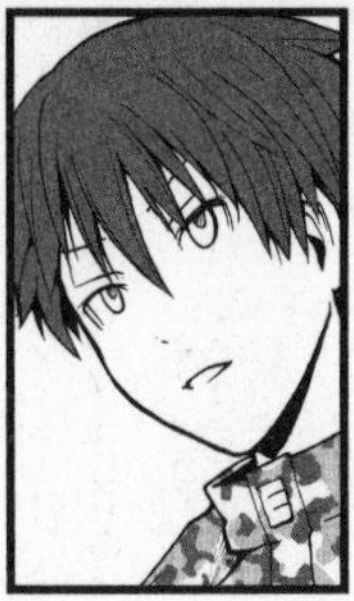

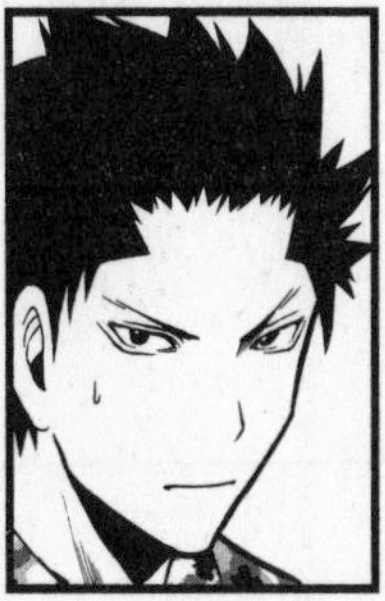

Tadaomi Karasuma

Member of the Ministry of Defense and the Class E students' P.E. teacher. Though serious about his duties, he has successfully built good relationships with his students.

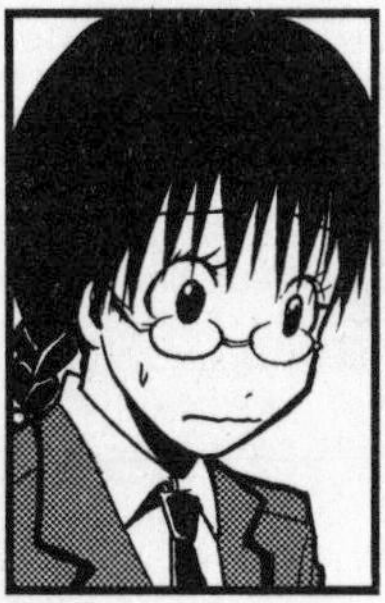

Manami Okuda

Class E student. The class's mad scientist, whose concoctions include deadly poisons. Her knowledge of chemistry might be vital to saving Koro Sensei.

After a storm comes fair weather!

The bond between the Class E students has only grown stronger since this conflict has been resolved. So strong, in fact, that I sense something suspicious is going on between some of them! We must root out those traitors!!

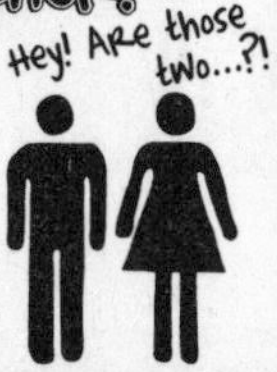
Hey! Are those two...?!

Irina Jelavich

A sexy assassin hired as an English teacher. She's known for using her "womanly charms" to get close to a target, but she's totally hopeless when it comes to flirting with Karasuma.

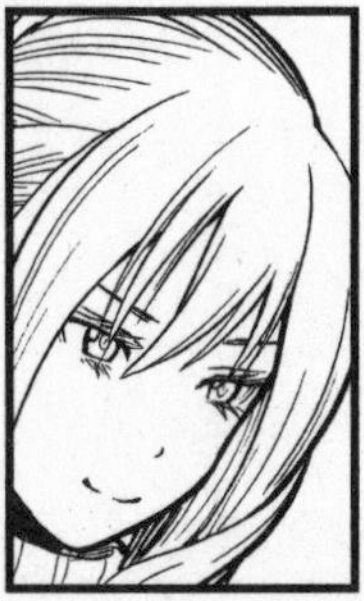

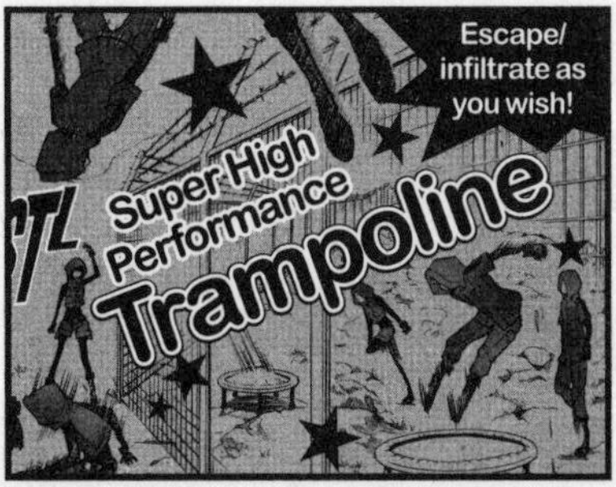
Escape/ infiltrate as you wish!
Super High Performance Trampoline

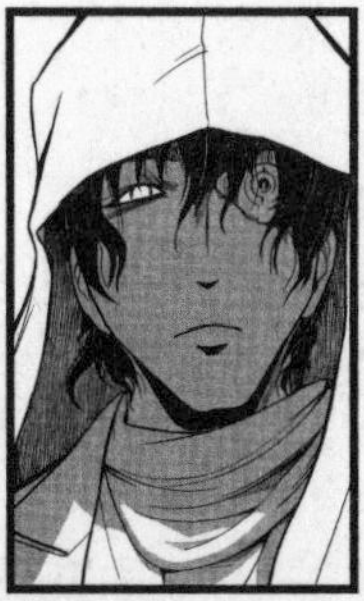

Kotaro Yanagisawa

The scientific genius who created Koro Sensei. He hates his experimental subject for stealing everything from him and has vowed revenge.

Teacher
Koro Sensei

Teacher
Tadaomi
Karasuma

Teacher
Irina
Jelavich

Assassination Class Roster

E-4 Hinata Okano

E-2 Yuma Isogai

E-10 Hinano Kurahashi

E-9 Masayoshi Kimura

E-17 Rio Nakamura

E-23 Koki Mimura

E-25 Toka Yada

E-14 Kotaro Takebayashi

E-19 Rinka Hayami

E-3 Taiga Okajima

E-8 Yukiko Kanzaki

E-26 Taisei Yoshida

E-5 Manami Okuda

E-15 Ryunosuke Chiba

E-18 Kirara Hazama

E-24 Takuya Muramatsu

E-1 Karma Akabane

E-16 Ryoma Terasaka

Always assassinate the target with a method that brings a smile to your face.

I am open for assassinations at any time. But don't let them get in the way of your studying.

I won't harm students who try to assassinate me. But if your skills are rusty, expect a good scrubbing.

Individual Statistics

E-22 Hiroto Maehara

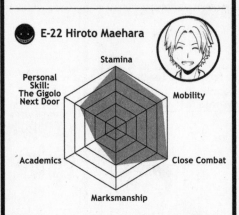

Stamina

Mobility

Close Combat

Marksmanship

Academics

Personal Skill: The Gigolo Next Door

E-23 Koki Mimura

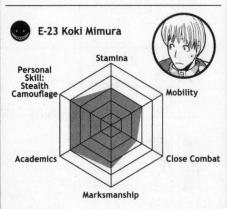

Stamina

Mobility

Close Combat

Marksmanship

Academics

Personal Skill: Stealth Camouflage

E-24 Takuya Muramatsu

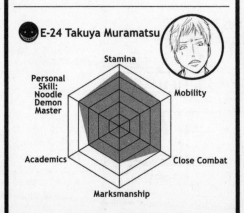

Stamina

Mobility

Close Combat

Marksmanship

Academics

Personal Skill: Noodle Demon Master

Kunugigaoka Junior High
3-E
Koro Sensei Class
Seating Arrangement

 E-6 Meg Kataoka

 E-22 Hiroto Maehara

 E-7 Kaede Kayano

 E-11 Nagisa Shiota

 E-21 Yuzuki Fuwa

 E-13 Tomohito Sugino

 E-20 Sumire Hara

 E-12 Sosuke Sugaya

 E-27 Autonomous Intelligence Fixed Artillery

 E-28 Itona Horibe

ASSASSINATION

CLASSROOM 18 CONTENTS

(Question 1): Write the pronunciation fo the underlined kanji

(1) 執拗な攻撃

(2) 暗殺方法を示

(4) 野暮なことを好む

(5) 憂さを

(Question 2): Write the kanji for the following words in katakana

(1) 律がコショウする

(2) バッと

(3) 遺伝子をソウサする

(4) 暗殺に

(5) 決死のカクゴ

(Question 3): Choose the correct parts of speech for the following sentences

(1) ああ、いい触手だ。

(2) 授業を受けながら暗殺する。

(3) こんな攻撃もあるのか。

(4) 標的は殺せんせーだ。

A: Verb B: Adjective
C: Adjectival D: Noun
E: Adverb F: Abnominal Adjective
G: Conjunction H: Interjection
I: Auxiliary V

(Question 4): Read the following Chinese poem and answer the following question

River Snow

Koro Zongyuan

A thousand mountains,
but no flying birds.
Ten thousand paths,
but no sign of
tentacle tracks.
A lone boat with an old
man in a straw raincoat
and straw hat.
Fishing alone in the
cold snowy river.

(ANSWER SHEET)

Grade	3	Class	E	Name	CONTENTS	Score	

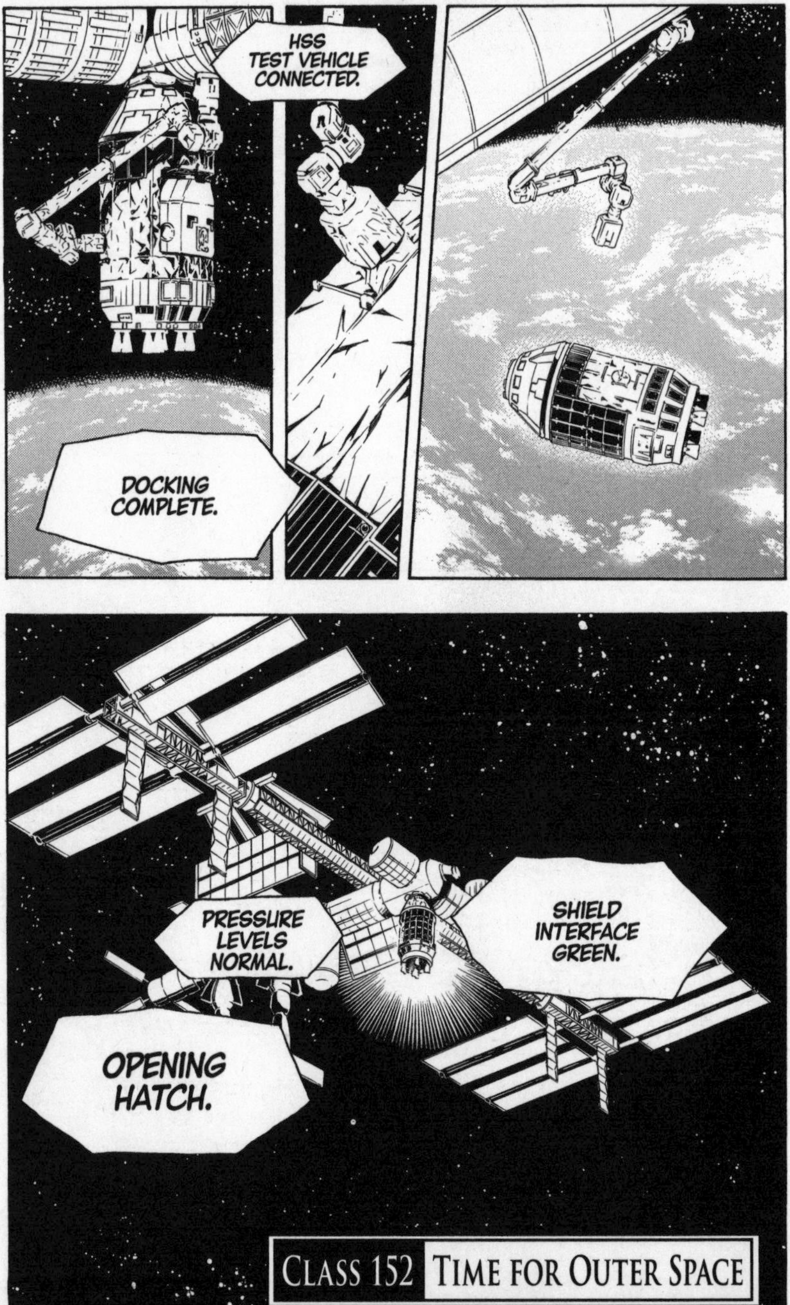
HSS TEST VEHICLE CONNECTED.
DOCKING COMPLETE.
SHIELD INTERFACE GREEN.
PRESSURE LEVELS NORMAL.
OPENING HATCH.
CLASS 152 TIME FOR OUTER SPACE

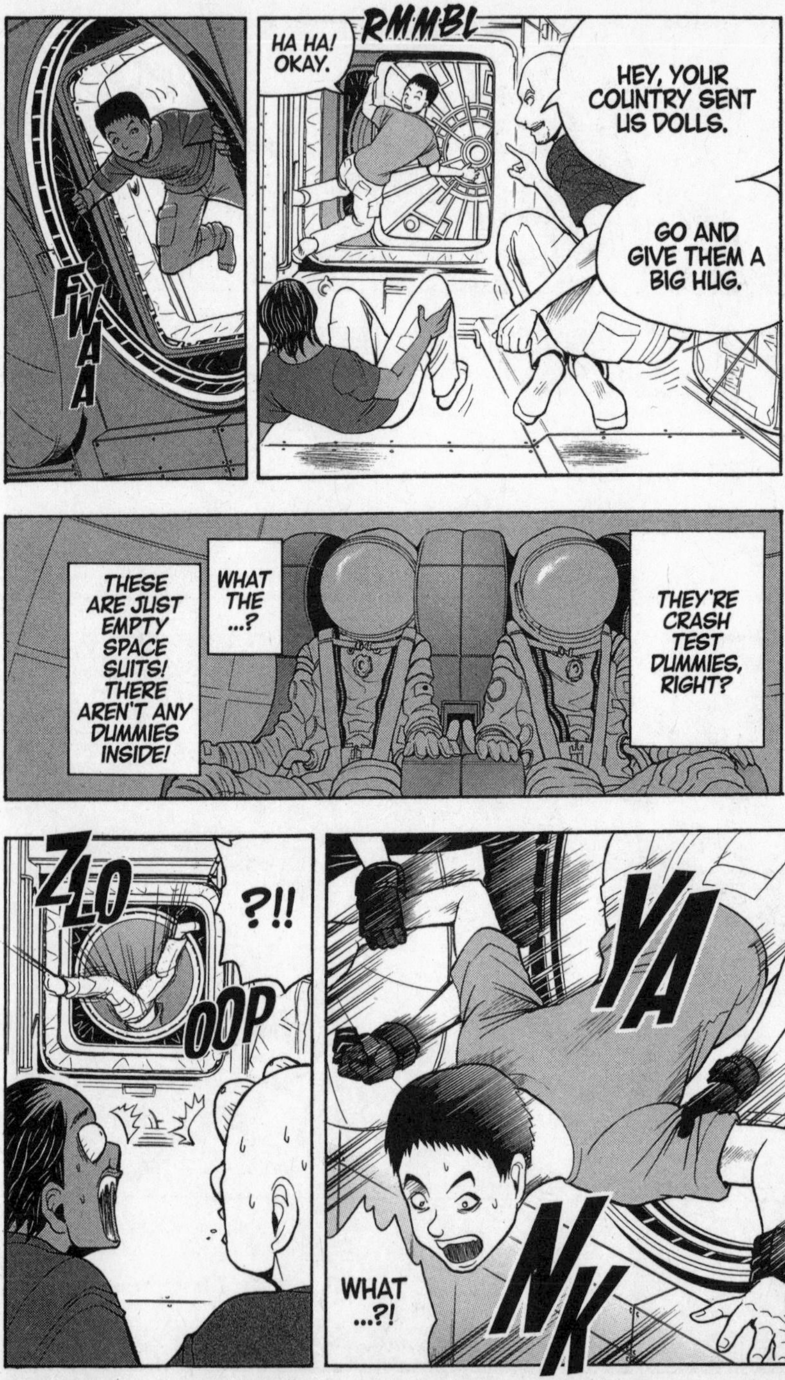
RMMBL
HEY, YOUR COUNTRY SENT US DOLLS.
GO AND GIVE THEM A BIG HUG.
HA HA! OKAY.
FWAAA
THEY'RE CRASH TEST DUMMIES, RIGHT?
WHAT THE ...?
THESE ARE JUST EMPTY SPACE SUITS! THERE AREN'T ANY DUMMIES INSIDE!
YANK
WHAT ...?!
ZLOOP
?!!

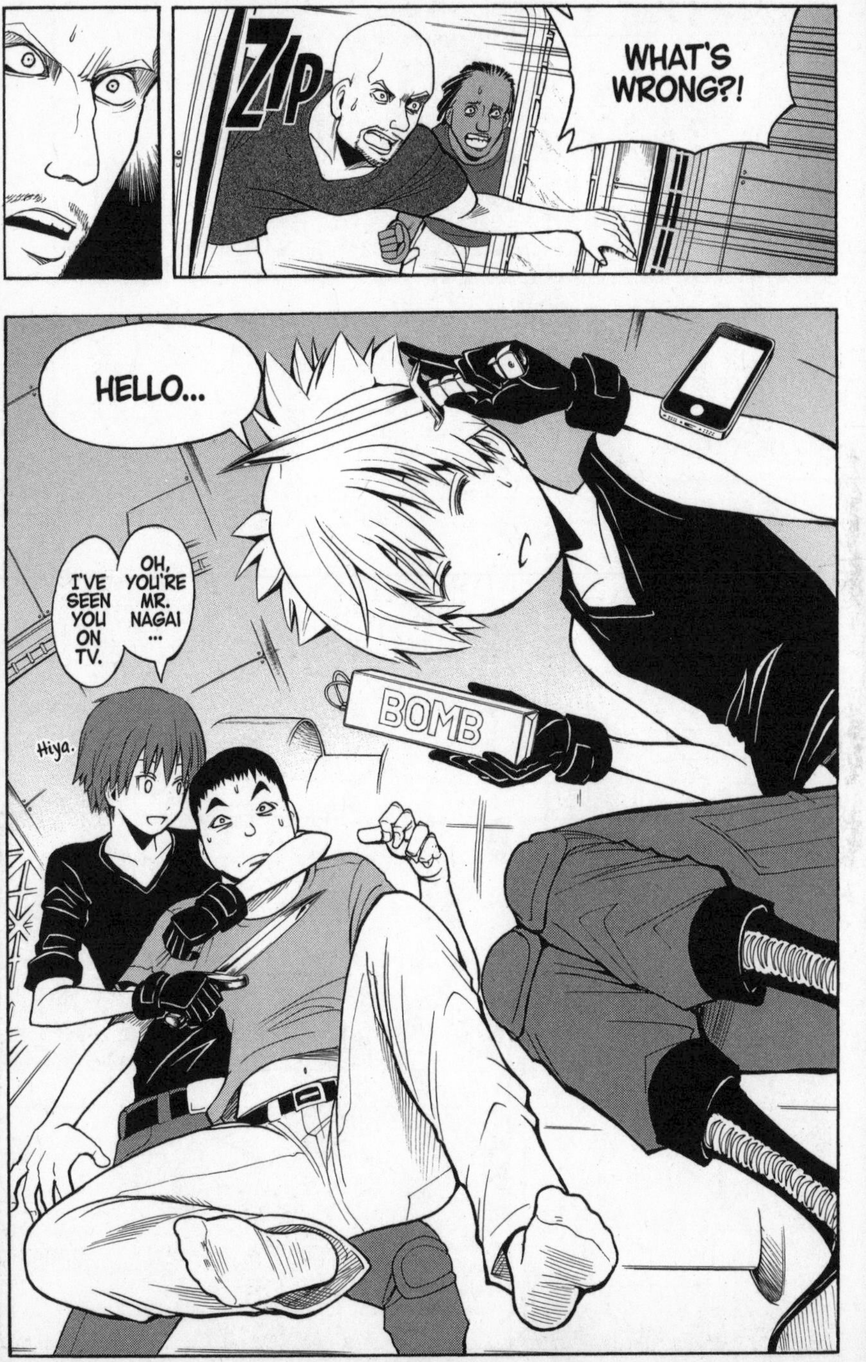
WHAT'S WRONG?!
ZIP
HELLO...
OH, YOU'RE MR. NAGAI...
I'VE SEEN YOU ON TV.
BOMB
Hiya.

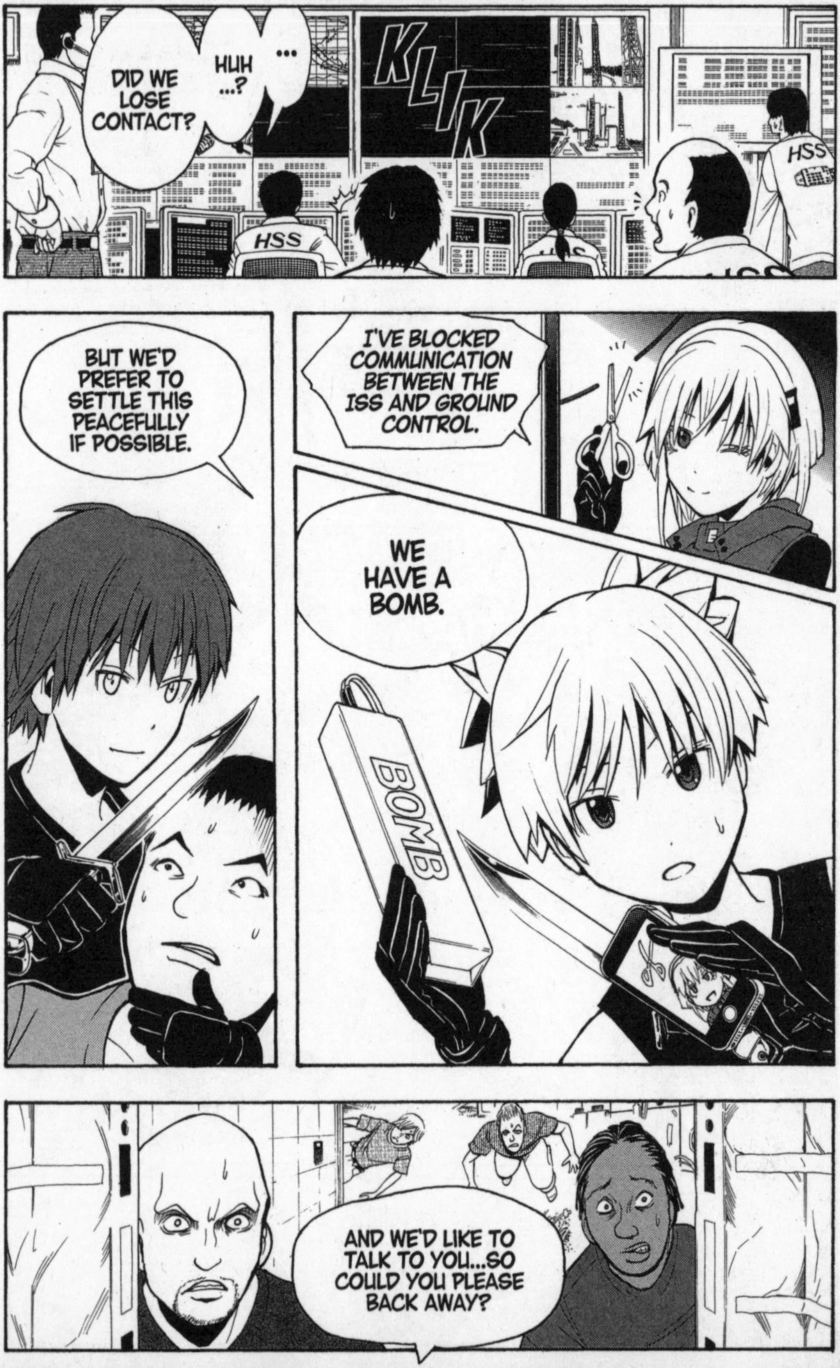
KLIK
...
HUH ...?
DID WE LOSE CONTACT?
I'VE BLOCKED COMMUNICATION BETWEEN THE ISS AND GROUND CONTROL.
WE HAVE A BOMB.
BOMB
BUT WE'D PREFER TO SETTLE THIS PEACEFULLY IF POSSIBLE.
AND WE'D LIKE TO TALK TO YOU...SO COULD YOU PLEASE BACK AWAY?

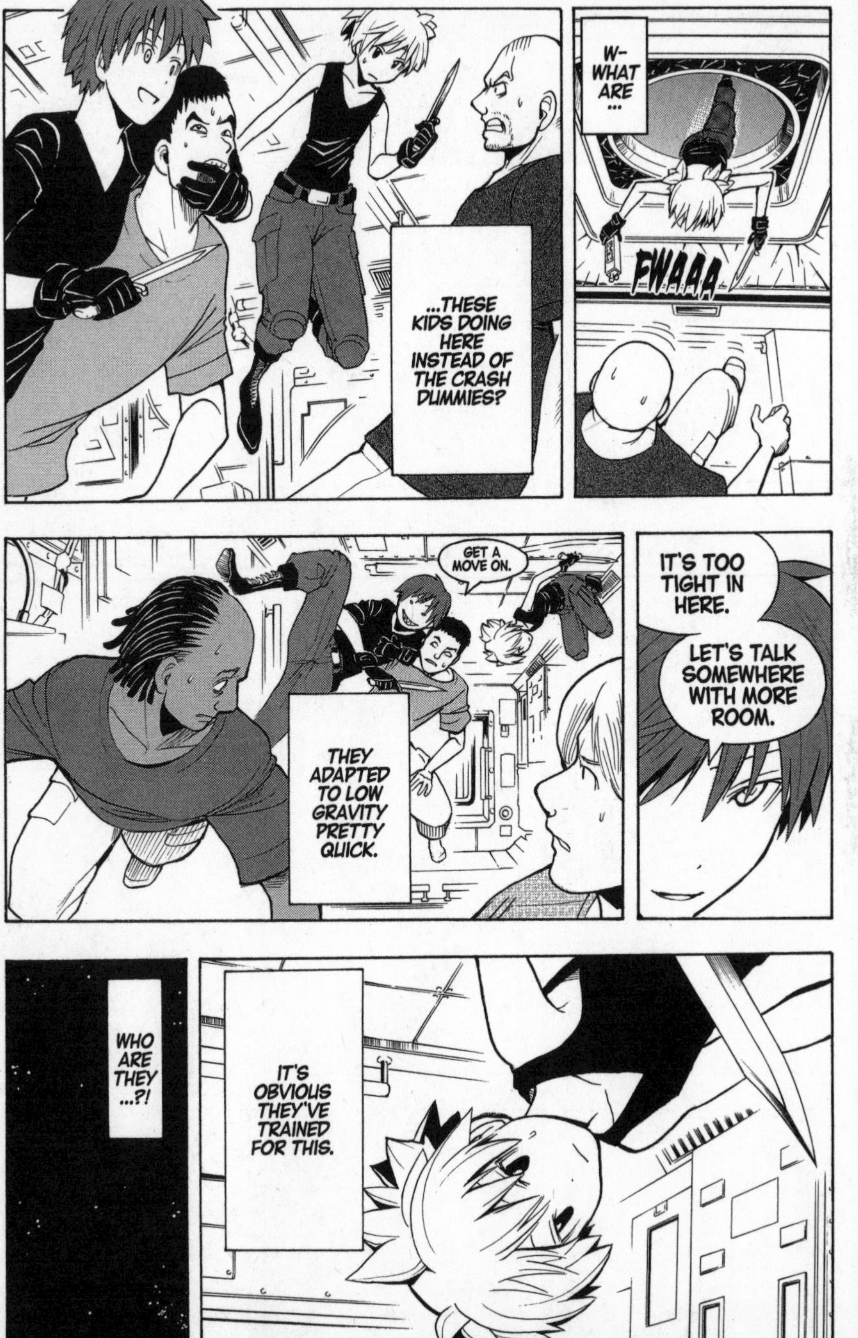
W-WHAT ARE ...
FWAAA
...THESE KIDS DOING HERE INSTEAD OF THE CRASH DUMMIES?
IT'S TOO TIGHT IN HERE.
LET'S TALK SOMEWHERE WITH MORE ROOM.
GET A MOVE ON.
THEY ADAPTED TO LOW GRAVITY PRETTY QUICK.
IT'S OBVIOUS THEY'VE TRAINED FOR THIS.
WHO ARE THEY ...?!

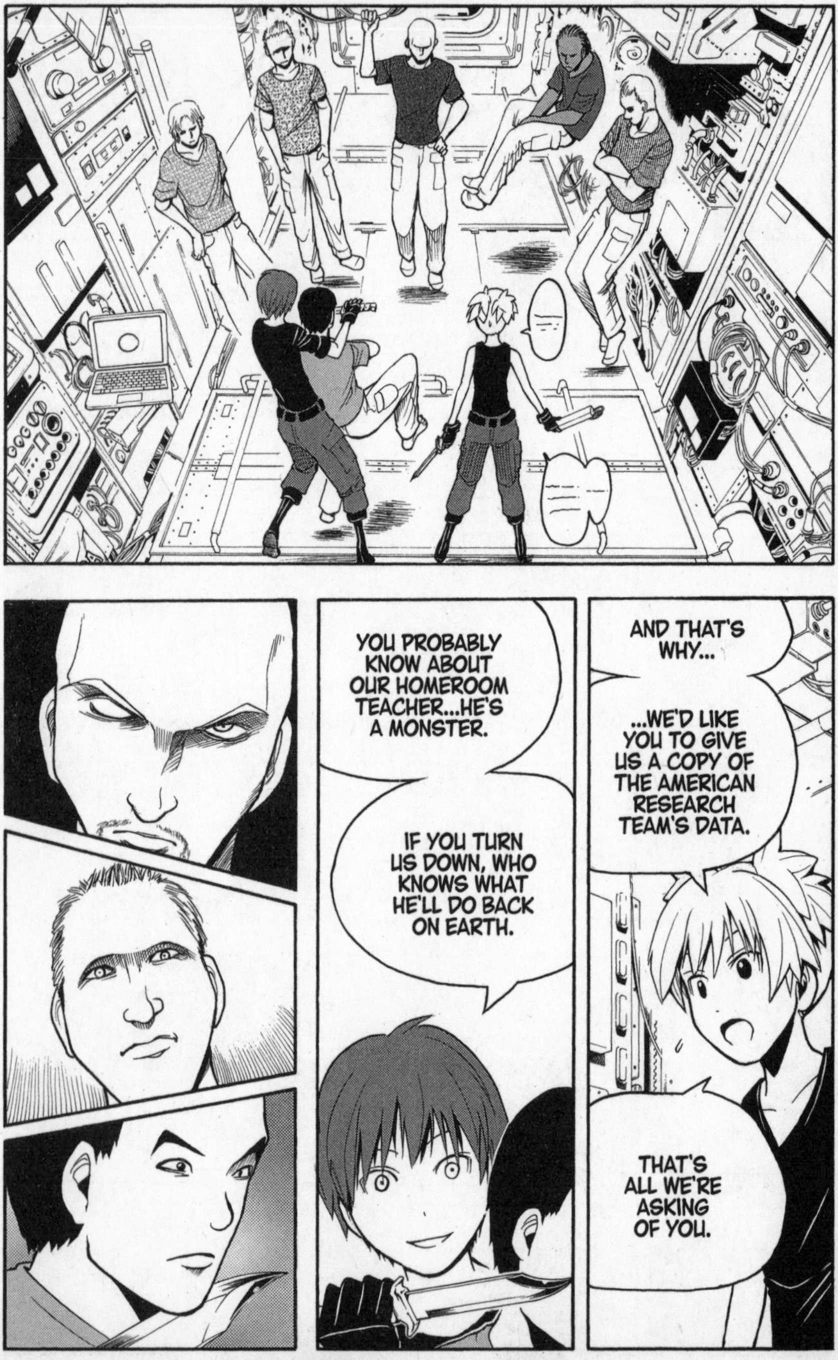
AND THAT'S WHY...
...WE'D LIKE YOU TO GIVE US A COPY OF THE AMERICAN RESEARCH TEAM'S DATA.
THAT'S ALL WE'RE ASKING OF YOU.
YOU PROBABLY KNOW ABOUT OUR HOMEROOM TEACHER...HE'S A MONSTER.
IF YOU TURN US DOWN, WHO KNOWS WHAT HE'LL DO BACK ON EARTH.

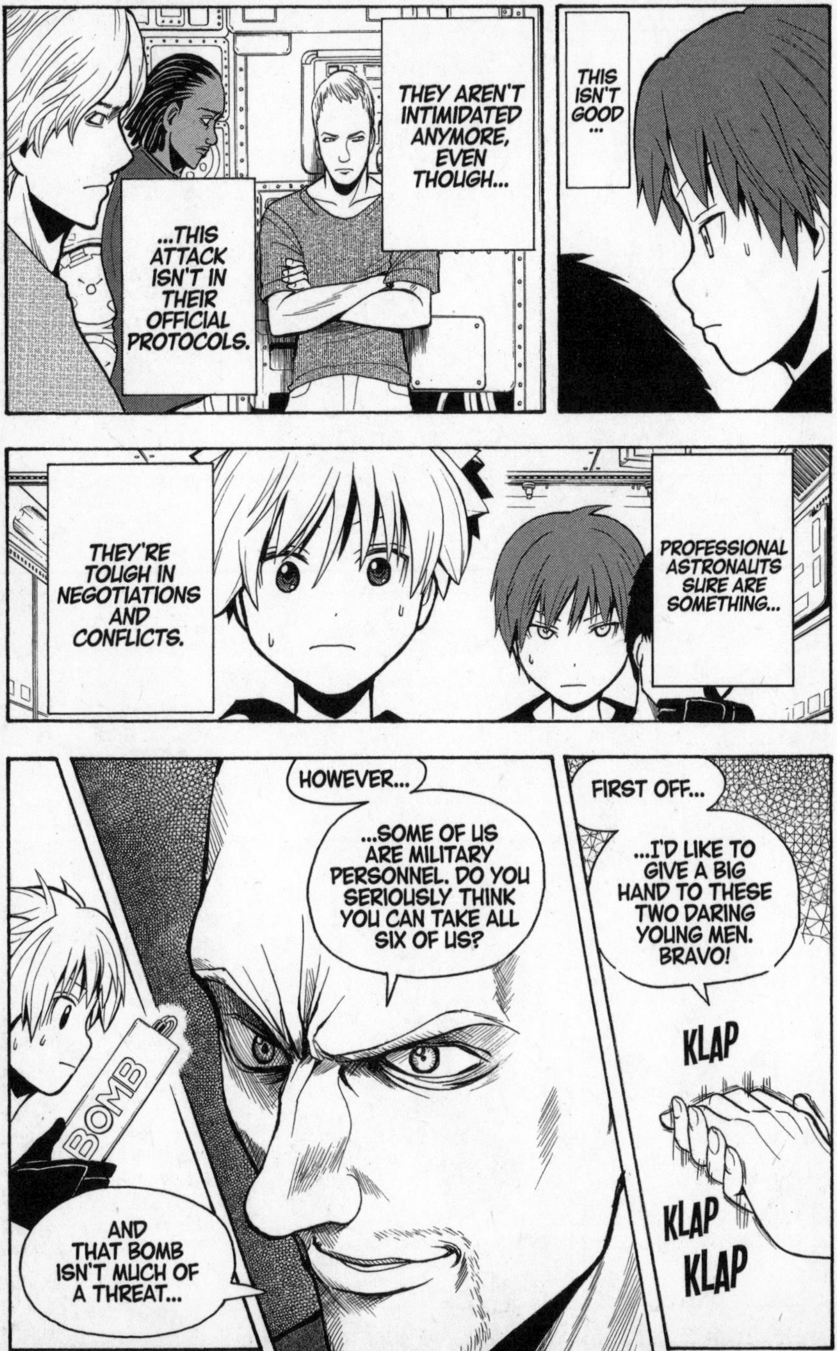
THIS ISN'T GOOD...
THEY AREN'T INTIMIDATED ANYMORE, EVEN THOUGH...
...THIS ATTACK ISN'T IN THEIR OFFICIAL PROTOCOLS.
PROFESSIONAL ASTRONAUTS SURE ARE SOMETHING...
THEY'RE TOUGH IN NEGOTIATIONS AND CONFLICTS.
FIRST OFF...
...I'D LIKE TO GIVE A BIG HAND TO THESE TWO DARING YOUNG MEN. BRAVO!
KLAP
KLAP
KLAP
HOWEVER...
...SOME OF US ARE MILITARY PERSONNEL. DO YOU SERIOUSLY THINK YOU CAN TAKE ALL SIX OF US?
AND THAT BOMB ISN'T MUCH OF A THREAT...
BOMB

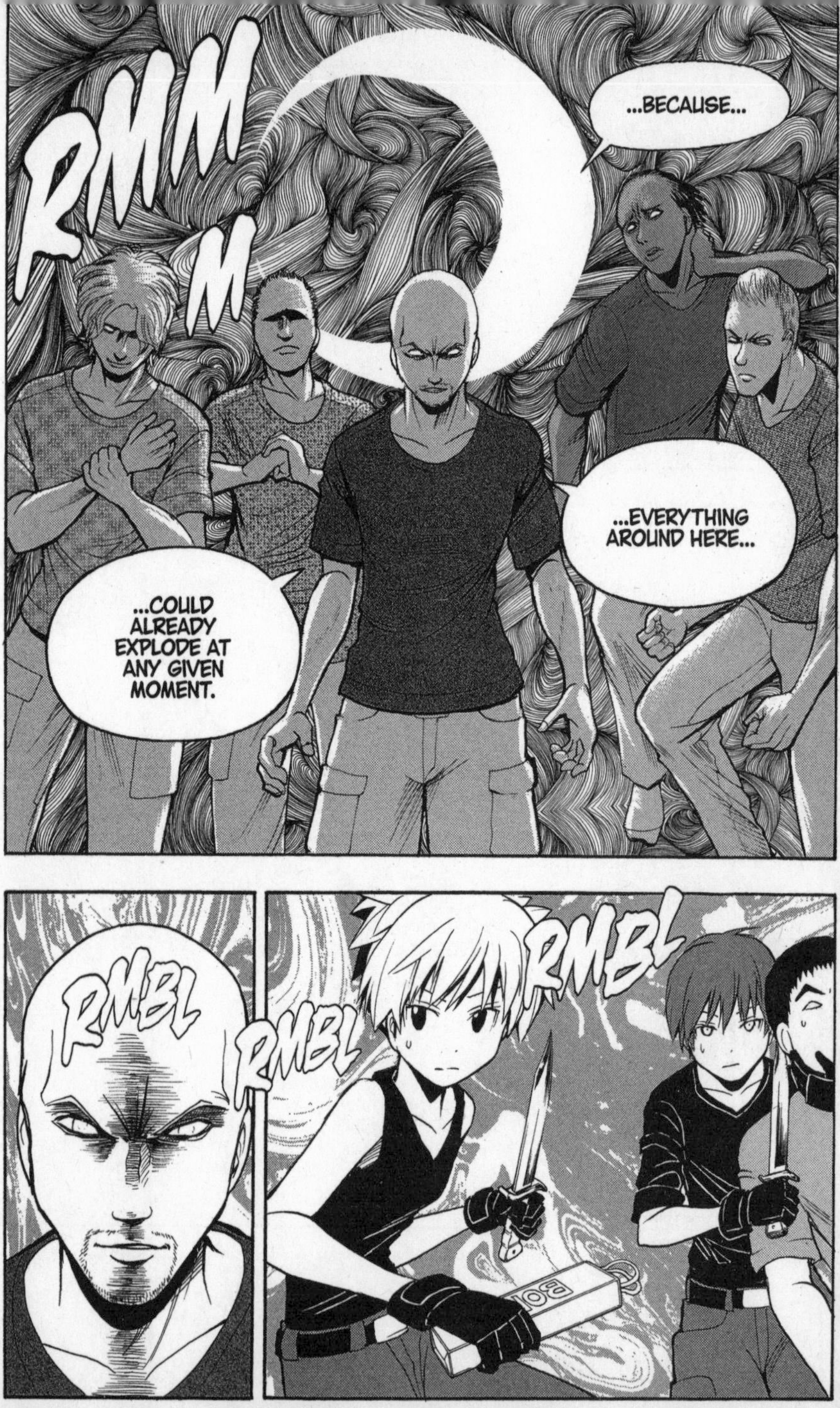
...BECAUSE...
RMMM
M
...EVERYTHING AROUND HERE...
...COULD ALREADY EXPLODE AT ANY GIVEN MOMENT.
RMBL
RMBL
RMBL

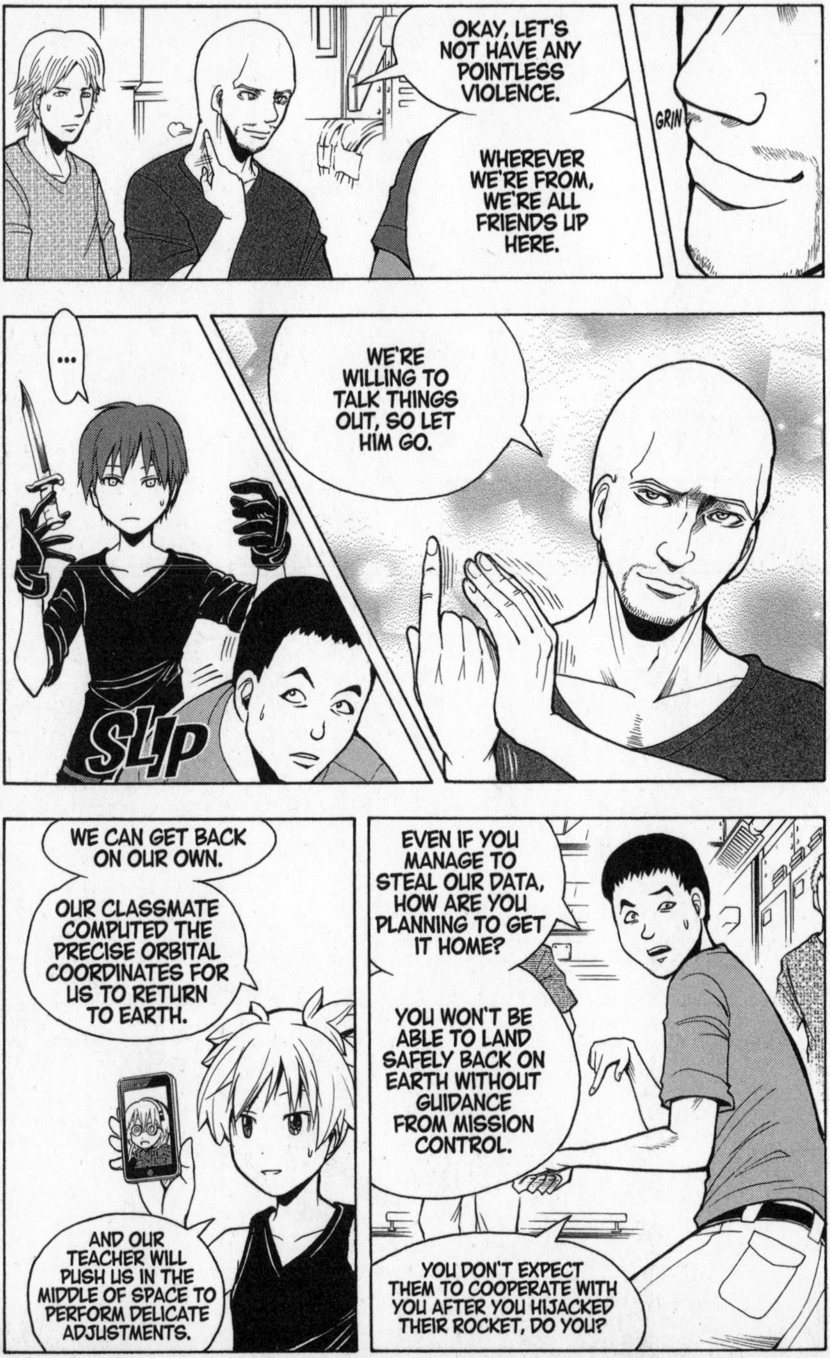
GRIN
OKAY, LET'S NOT HAVE ANY POINTLESS VIOLENCE.
WHEREVER WE'RE FROM, WE'RE ALL FRIENDS UP HERE.
WE'RE WILLING TO TALK THINGS OUT, SO LET HIM GO.
...
SLIP
EVEN IF YOU MANAGE TO STEAL OUR DATA, HOW ARE YOU PLANNING TO GET IT HOME?
YOU WON'T BE ABLE TO LAND SAFELY BACK ON EARTH WITHOUT GUIDANCE FROM MISSION CONTROL.
YOU DON'T EXPECT THEM TO COOPERATE WITH YOU AFTER YOU HIJACKED THEIR ROCKET, DO YOU?
WE CAN GET BACK ON OUR OWN.
OUR CLASSMATE COMPUTED THE PRECISE ORBITAL COORDINATES FOR US TO RETURN TO EARTH.
AND OUR TEACHER WILL PUSH US IN THE MIDDLE OF SPACE TO PERFORM DELICATE ADJUSTMENTS.

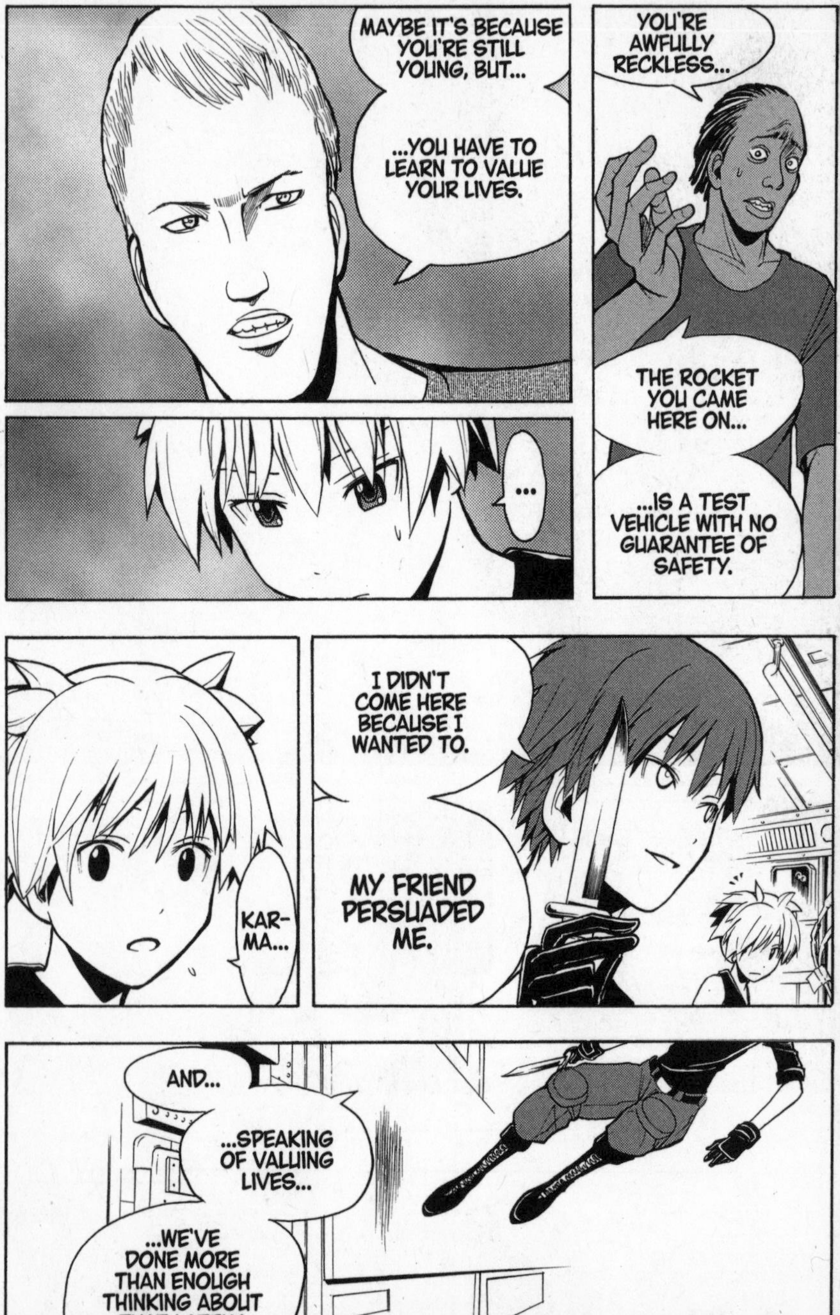
YOU'RE AWFULLY RECKLESS...
THE ROCKET YOU CAME HERE ON...
...IS A TEST VEHICLE WITH NO GUARANTEE OF SAFETY.
MAYBE IT'S BECAUSE YOU'RE STILL YOUNG, BUT...
...YOU HAVE TO LEARN TO VALUE YOUR LIVES.
...
I DIDN'T COME HERE BECAUSE I WANTED TO.
MY FRIEND PERSUADED ME.
KAR-MA...
AND...
...SPEAKING OF VALUING LIVES...
...WE'VE DONE MORE THAN ENOUGH THINKING ABOUT THAT LATELY, BELIEVE ME.

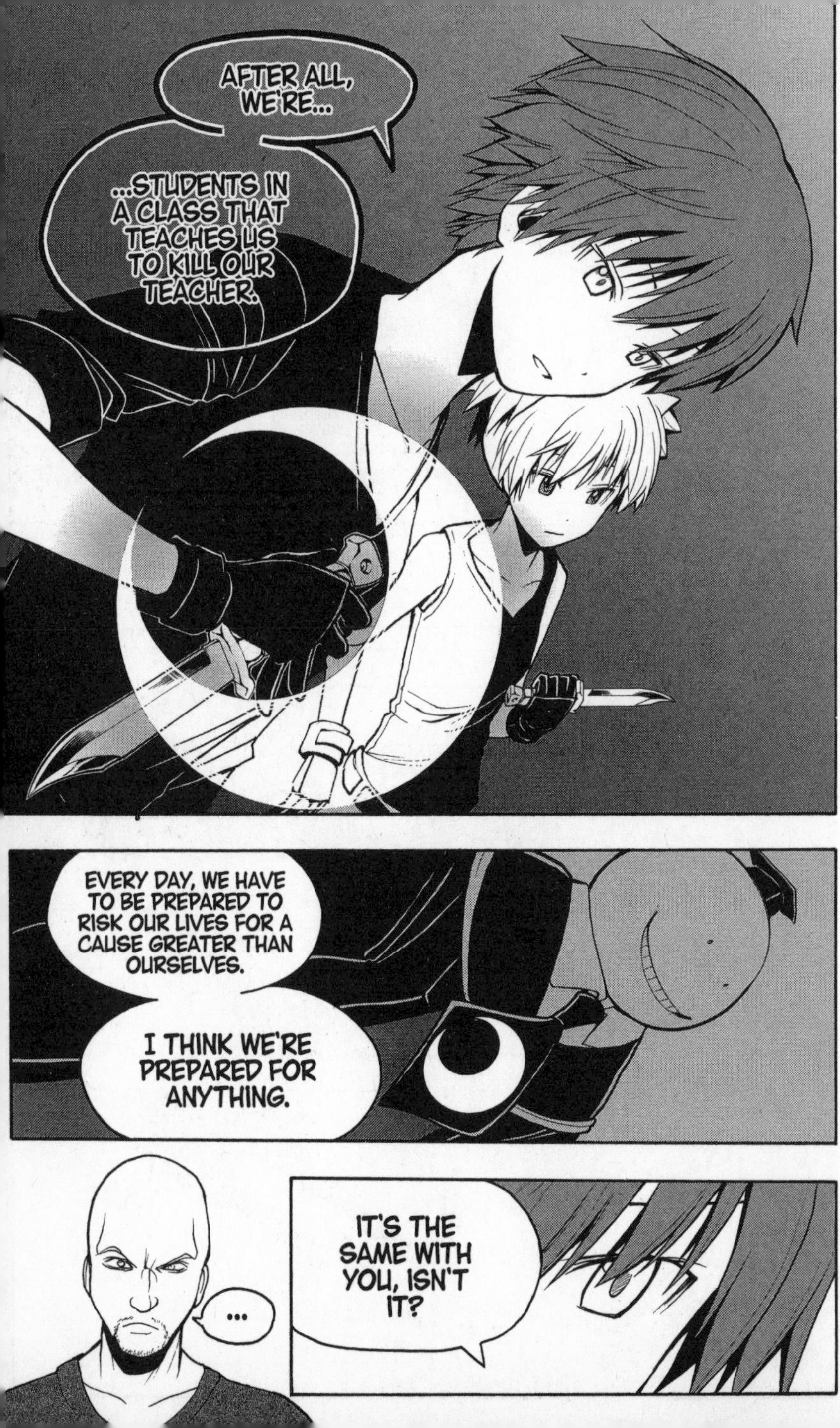
AFTER ALL, WE'RE...
...STUDENTS IN A CLASS THAT TEACHES US TO KILL OUR TEACHER.
EVERY DAY, WE HAVE TO BE PREPARED TO RISK OUR LIVES FOR A CAUSE GREATER THAN OURSELVES.
I THINK WE'RE PREPARED FOR ANYTHING.
IT'S THE SAME WITH YOU, ISN'T IT?
...

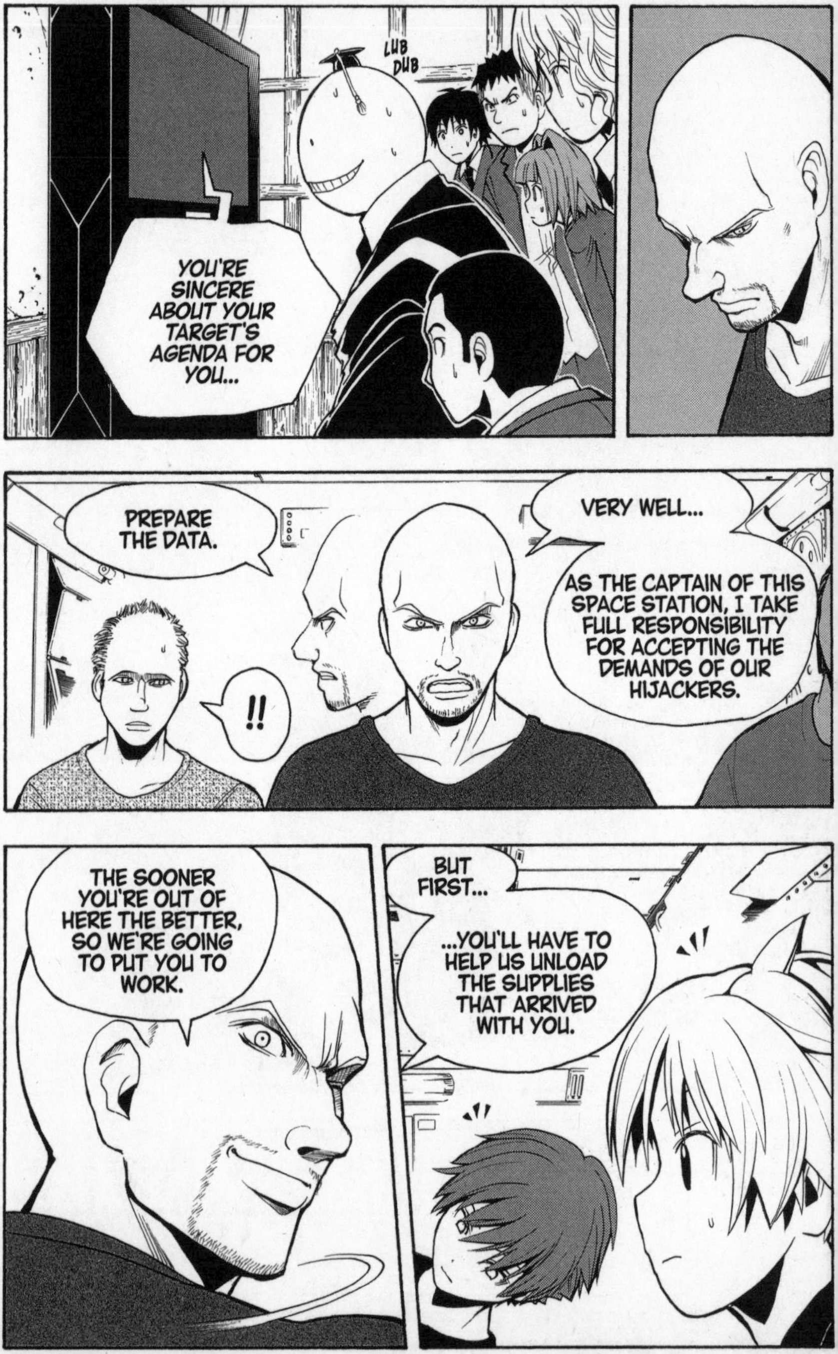
LUB DUB
YOU'RE SINCERE ABOUT YOUR TARGET'S AGENDA FOR YOU...
VERY WELL...
AS THE CAPTAIN OF THIS SPACE STATION, I TAKE FULL RESPONSIBILITY FOR ACCEPTING THE DEMANDS OF OUR HIJACKERS.
PREPARE THE DATA.
!!
BUT FIRST...
...YOU'LL HAVE TO HELP US UNLOAD THE SUPPLIES THAT ARRIVED WITH YOU.
THE SOONER YOU'RE OUT OF HERE THE BETTER, SO WE'RE GOING TO PUT YOU TO WORK.

THEY'RE GIVING US JUNIOR HIGH STUDENTS THE EXPERIENCE OF A LIFETIME.

JUST TO BE NICE.

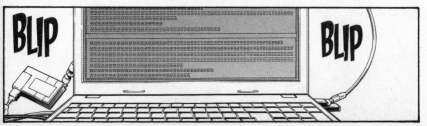

BLIP

BLIP

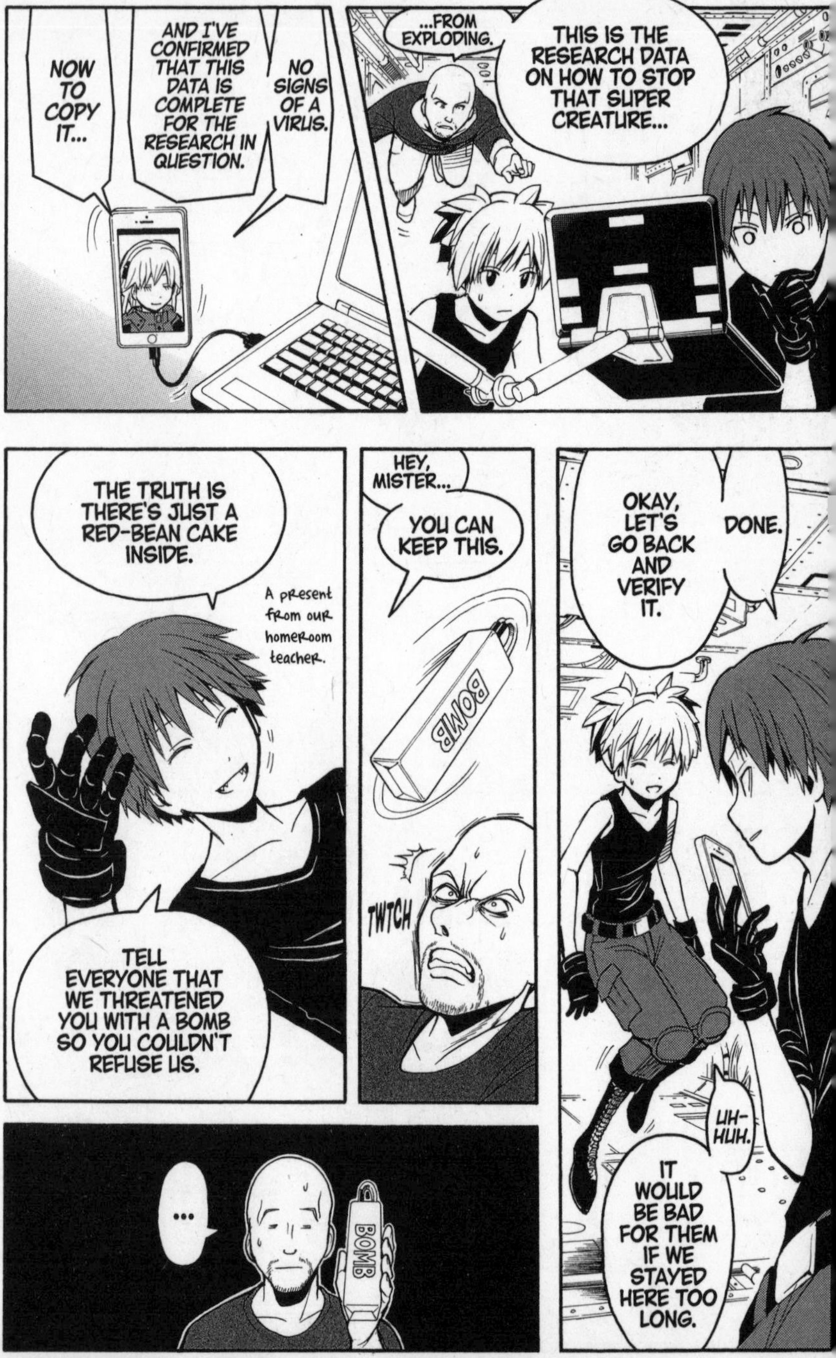
THIS IS THE RESEARCH DATA ON HOW TO STOP THAT SUPER CREATURE...
...FROM EXPLODING.
NO SIGNS OF A VIRUS.
AND I'VE CONFIRMED THAT THIS DATA IS COMPLETE FOR THE RESEARCH IN QUESTION.
NOW TO COPY IT...
DONE.
OKAY, LET'S GO BACK AND VERIFY IT.
UH-HUH.
IT WOULD BE BAD FOR THEM IF WE STAYED HERE TOO LONG.
HEY, MISTER...
YOU CAN KEEP THIS.
BOMB
TWTCH
THE TRUTH IS THERE'S JUST A RED-BEAN CAKE INSIDE.
A present from our homeroom teacher.
TELL EVERYONE THAT WE THREATENED YOU WITH A BOMB SO YOU COULDN'T REFUSE US.
...
BOMB

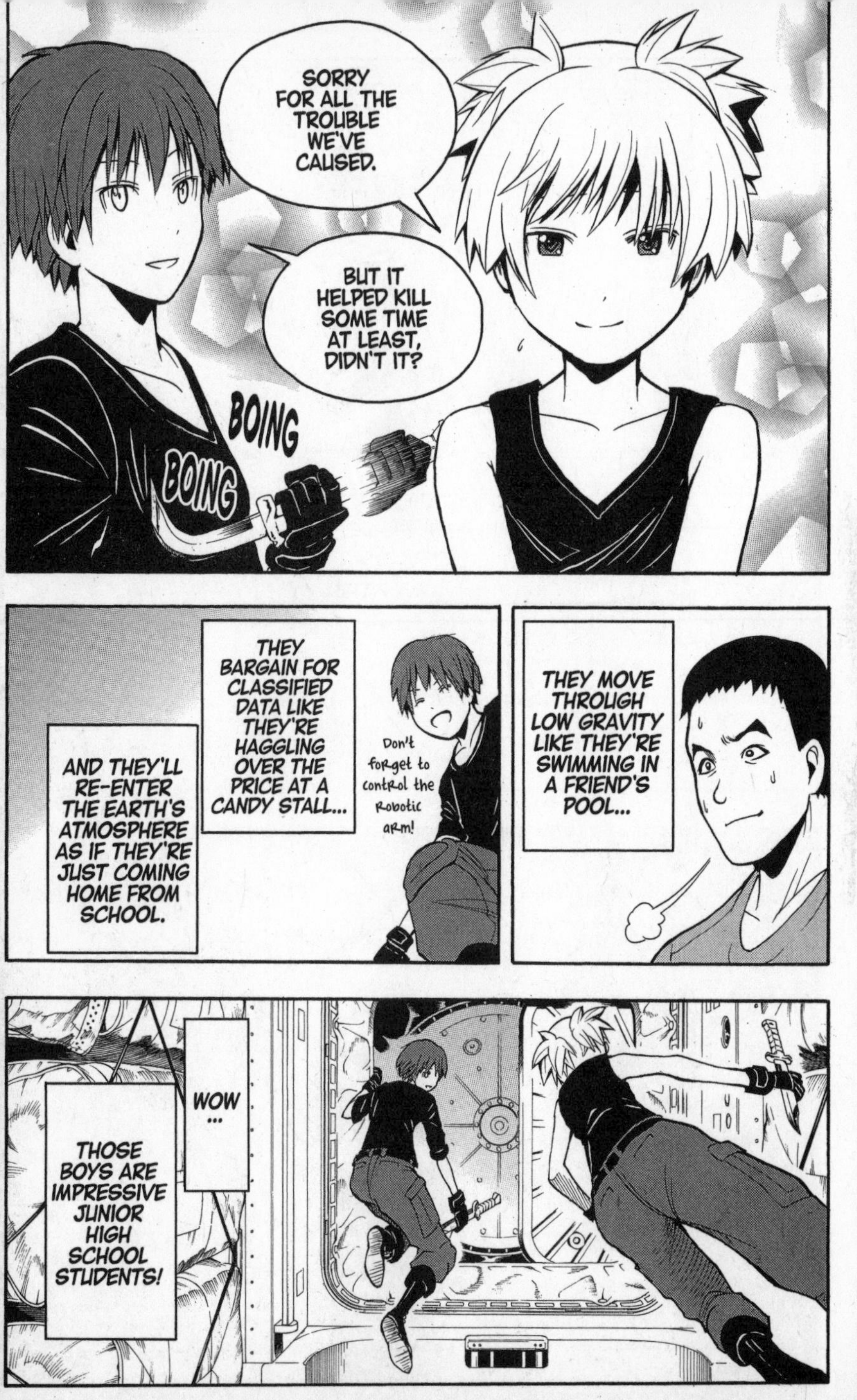
SORRY FOR ALL THE TROUBLE WE'VE CAUSED.
BUT IT HELPED KILL SOME TIME AT LEAST, DIDN'T IT?
BOING
BOING
THEY MOVE THROUGH LOW GRAVITY LIKE THEY'RE SWIMMING IN A FRIEND'S POOL...
THEY BARGAIN FOR CLASSIFIED DATA LIKE THEY'RE HAGGLING OVER THE PRICE AT A CANDY STALL...
Don't forget to control the Robotic arm!
AND THEY'LL RE-ENTER THE EARTH'S ATMOSPHERE AS IF THEY'RE JUST COMING HOME FROM SCHOOL.
WOW ...
THOSE BOYS ARE IMPRESSIVE JUNIOR HIGH SCHOOL STUDENTS!

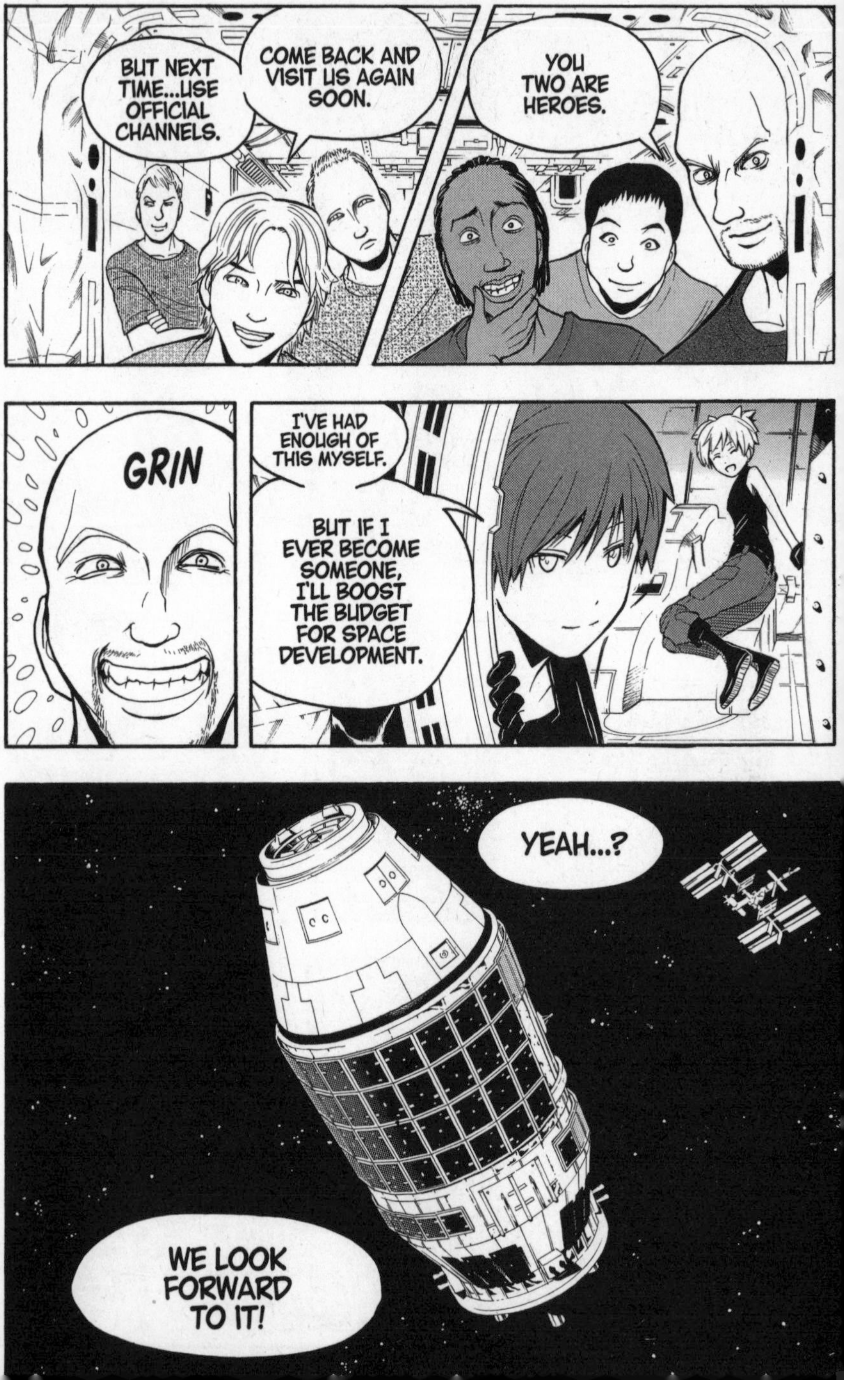
YOU TWO ARE HEROES.
COME BACK AND VISIT US AGAIN SOON.
BUT NEXT TIME...USE OFFICIAL CHANNELS.
I'VE HAD ENOUGH OF THIS MYSELF.
BUT IF I EVER BECOME SOMEONE, I'LL BOOST THE BUDGET FOR SPACE DEVELOPMENT.
GRIN
YEAH...?
WE LOOK FORWARD TO IT!

RMMMBL
...
THAT WAS A SHORT TRIP...
...INTO OUTER SPACE.
YEAH.
NOW THE QUESTION IS WHETHER WE CAN GET BACK TO EARTH IN ONE PIECE...
RITSU...
...
RITSU?
...
LEAVE IT TO ME.
I'VE BEEN WORKING ON NUMEROUS ORBITAL CALCULATIONS TO LAND YOU SAFELY BACK ON EARTH.
THIS ROCKET IS LIKE MY OWN BODY NOW.

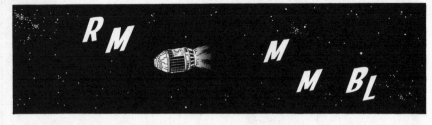

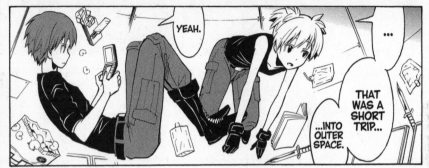

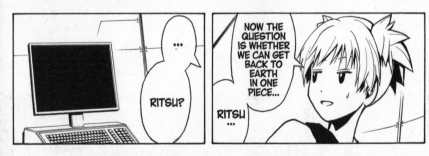

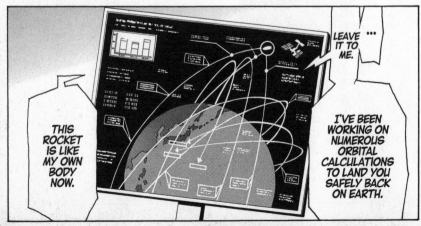

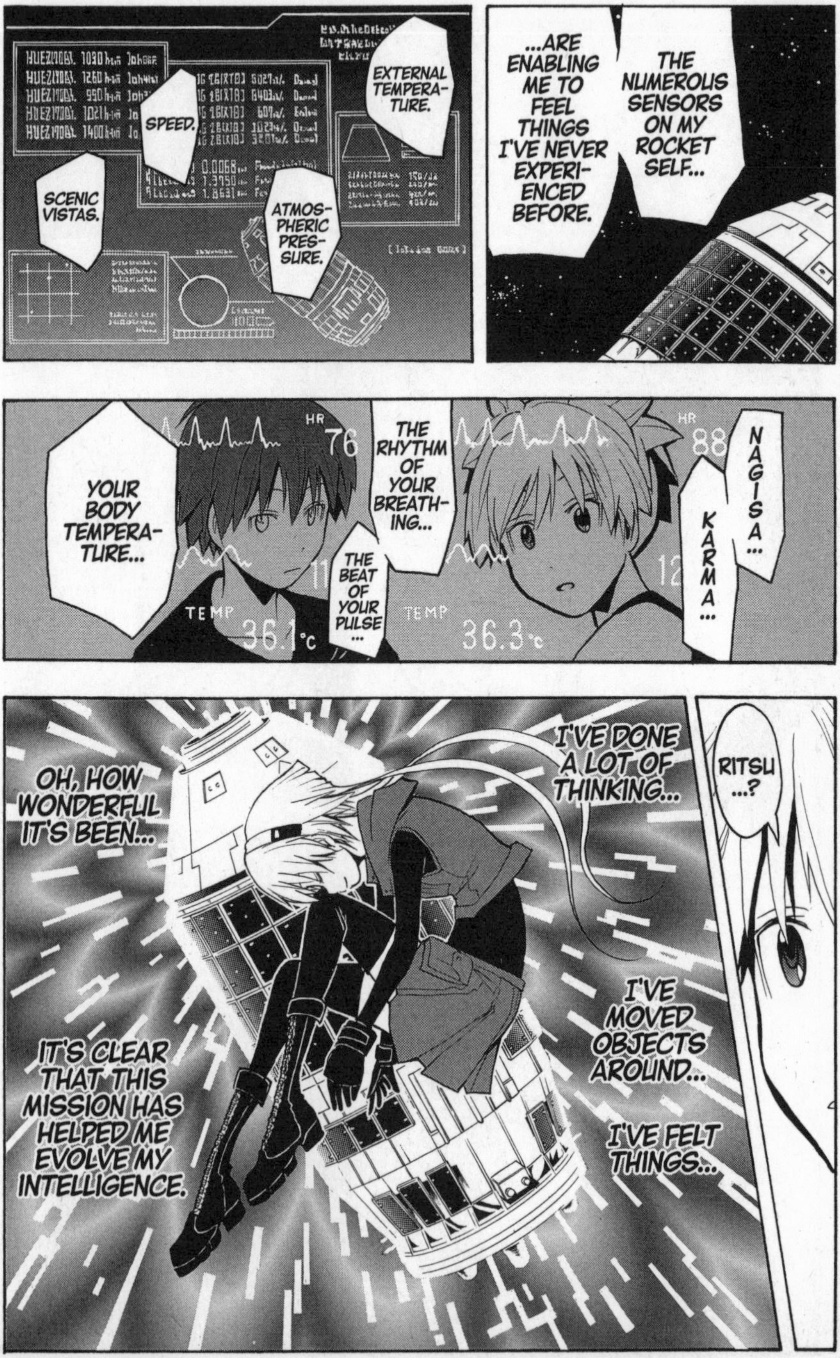
THE NUMEROUS SENSORS ON MY ROCKET SELF...
...ARE ENABLING ME TO FEEL THINGS I'VE NEVER EXPERIENCED BEFORE.
EXTERNAL TEMPERATURE.
SPEED.
ATMOSPHERIC PRESSURE.
SCENIC VISTAS.
NAGISA...
KARMA...
HR 88
12
TEMP 36.3°c
THE RHYTHM OF YOUR BREATHING...
THE BEAT OF YOUR PULSE...
HR 76
11
TEMP 36.1°c
YOUR BODY TEMPERATURE...
RITSU...?
I'VE DONE A LOT OF THINKING...
OH, HOW WONDERFUL IT'S BEEN...
I'VE MOVED OBJECTS AROUND...
I'VE FELT THINGS...
IT'S CLEAR THAT THIS MISSION HAS HELPED ME EVOLVE MY INTELLIGENCE.

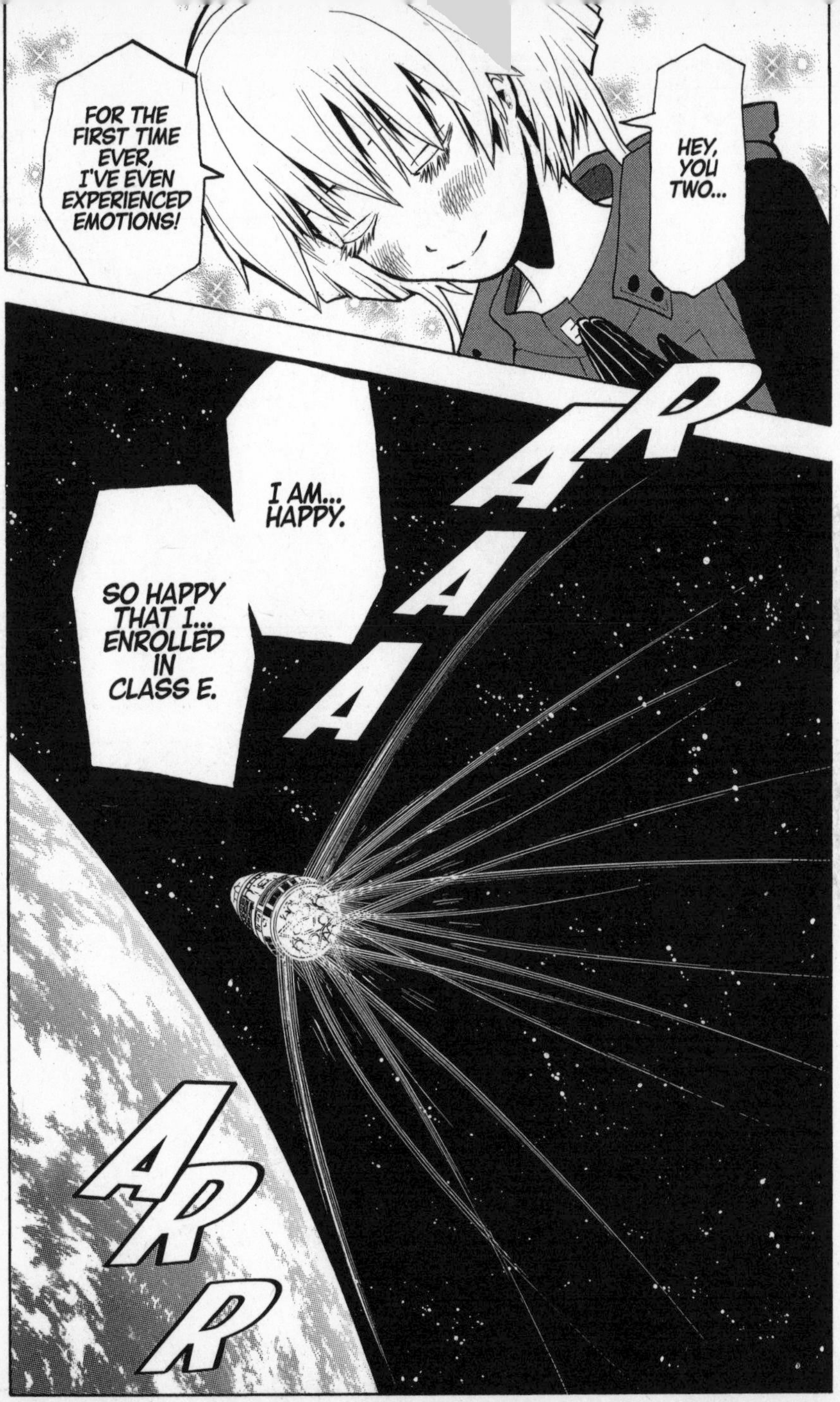
HEY, YOU TWO...
FOR THE FIRST TIME EVER, I'VE EVEN EXPERIENCED EMOTIONS!
RAAA
I AM... HAPPY.
SO HAPPY THAT I... ENROLLED IN CLASS E.
ARR

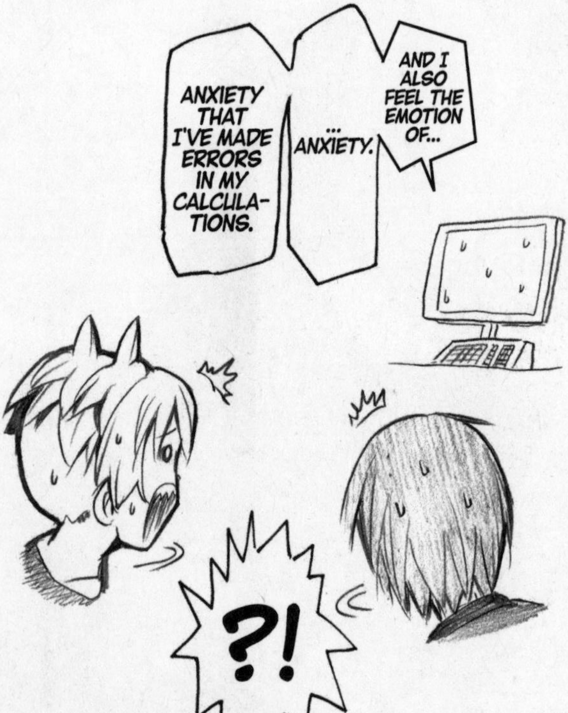
AND I ALSO FEEL THE EMOTION OF...
...ANXIETY.
ANXIETY THAT I'VE MADE ERRORS IN MY CALCULATIONS.
?!

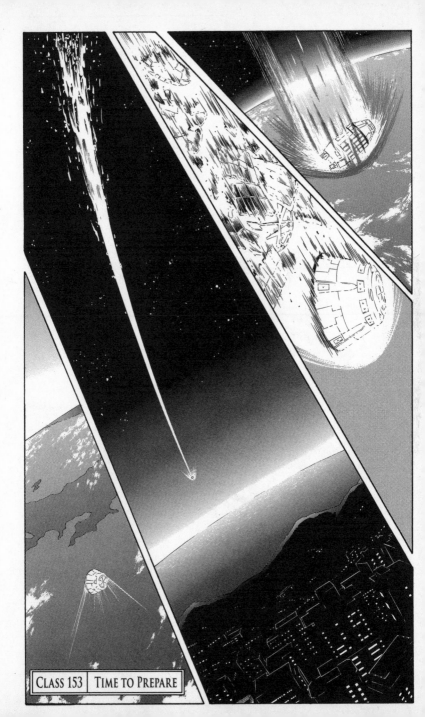

CLASS 153 | TIME TO PREPARE

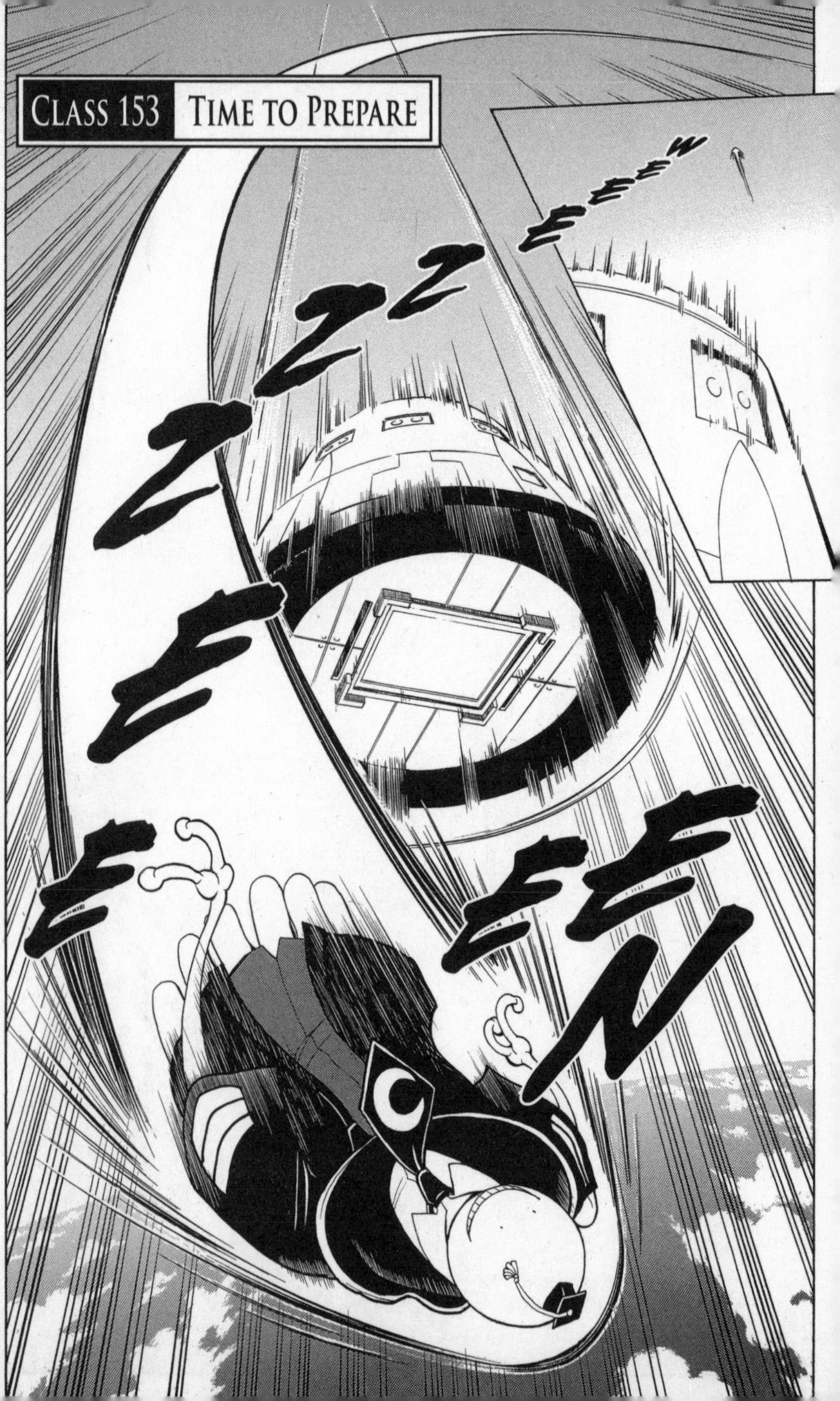
Class 153 Time to Prepare

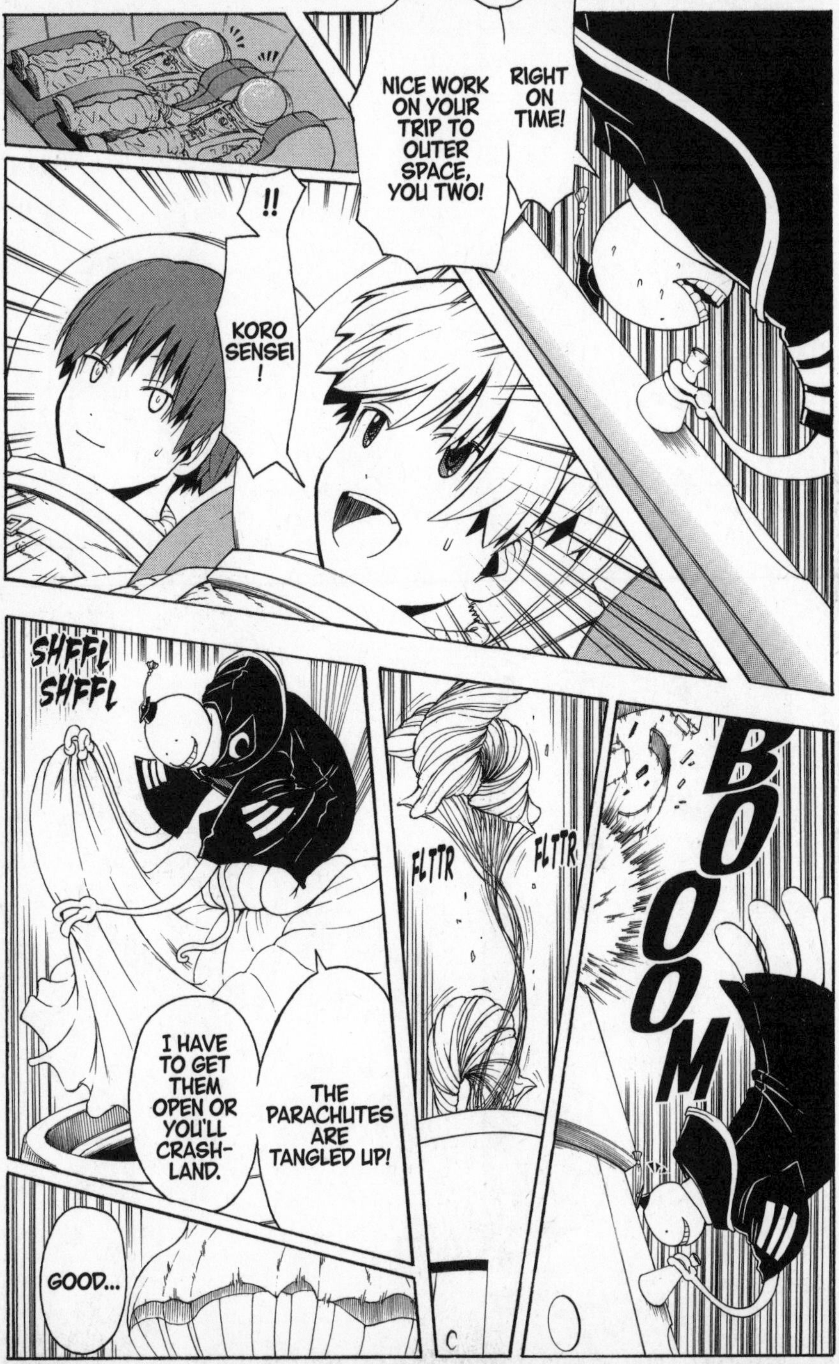
RIGHT ON TIME!
NICE WORK ON YOUR TRIP TO OUTER SPACE, YOU TWO!
!!
KORO SENSEI!
BOOOOM
FLTTR
FLTTR
THE PARACHUTES ARE TANGLED UP!
SHFFL SHFFL
I HAVE TO GET THEM OPEN OR YOU'LL CRASH-LAND.
GOOD...

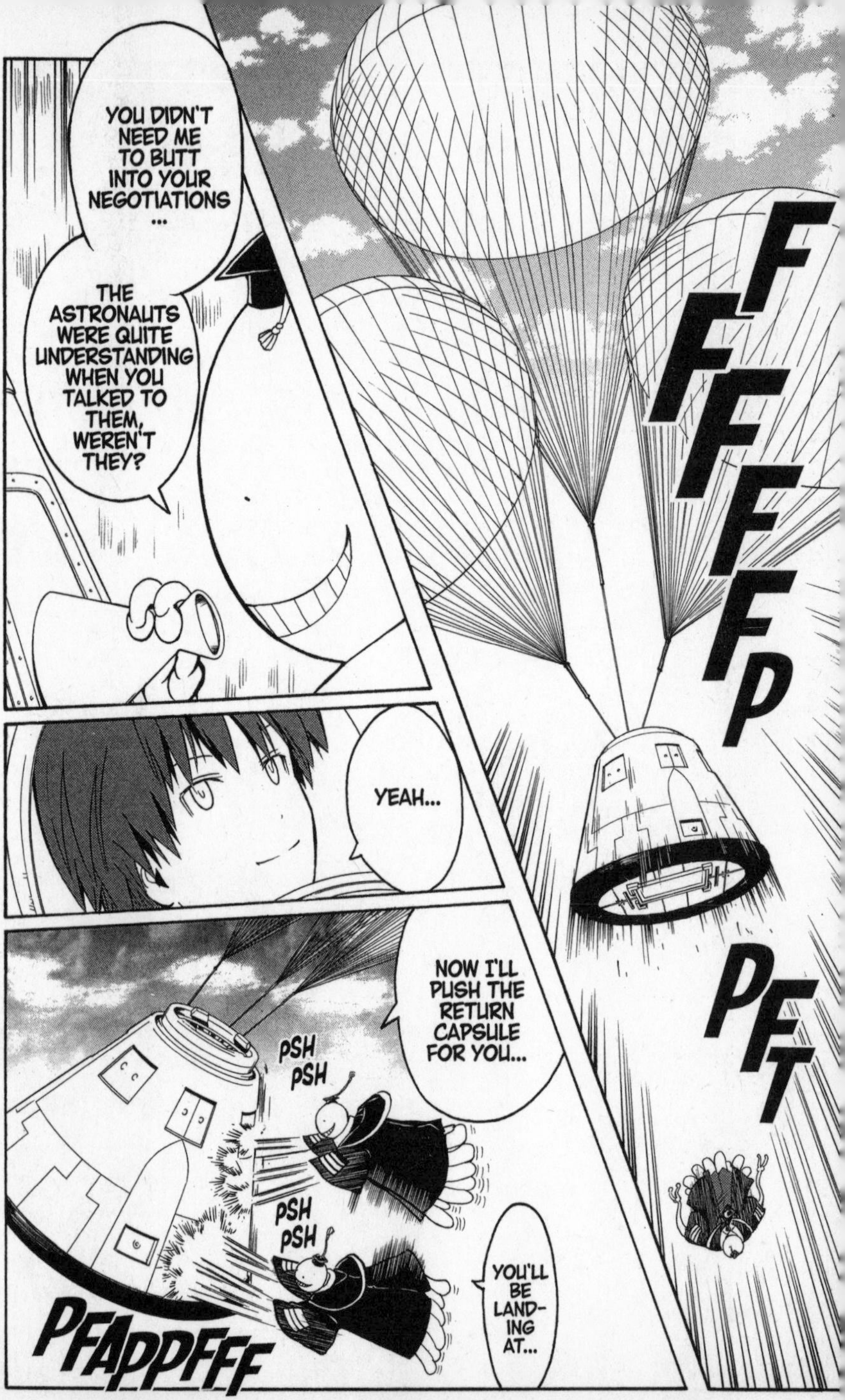
FFFFFP
PFFT
YOU DIDN'T NEED ME TO BUTT INTO YOUR NEGOTIATIONS ...
THE ASTRONAUTS WERE QUITE UNDERSTANDING WHEN YOU TALKED TO THEM, WEREN'T THEY?
YEAH...
NOW I'LL PUSH THE RETURN CAPSULE FOR YOU...
PSH PSH
PSH PSH
YOU'LL BE LAND-ING AT...
PFAPPFFF

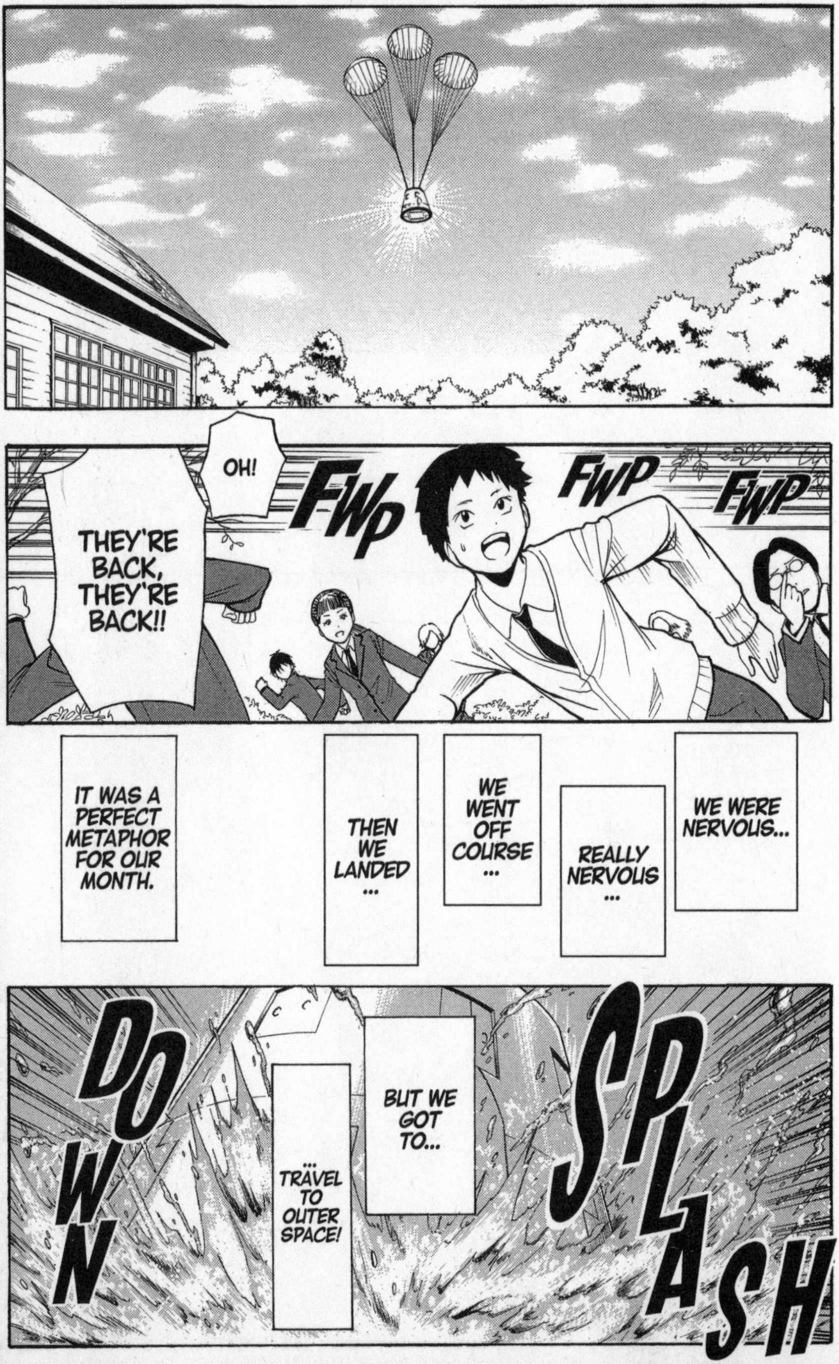
FWP
FWP
OH!
FWP
THEY'RE BACK, THEY'RE BACK!!
WE WERE NERVOUS...
REALLY NERVOUS...
WE WENT OFF COURSE...
THEN WE LANDED...
IT WAS A PERFECT METAPHOR FOR OUR MONTH.
SPLASH
BUT WE GOT TO...
...TRAVEL TO OUTER SPACE!
DOWN

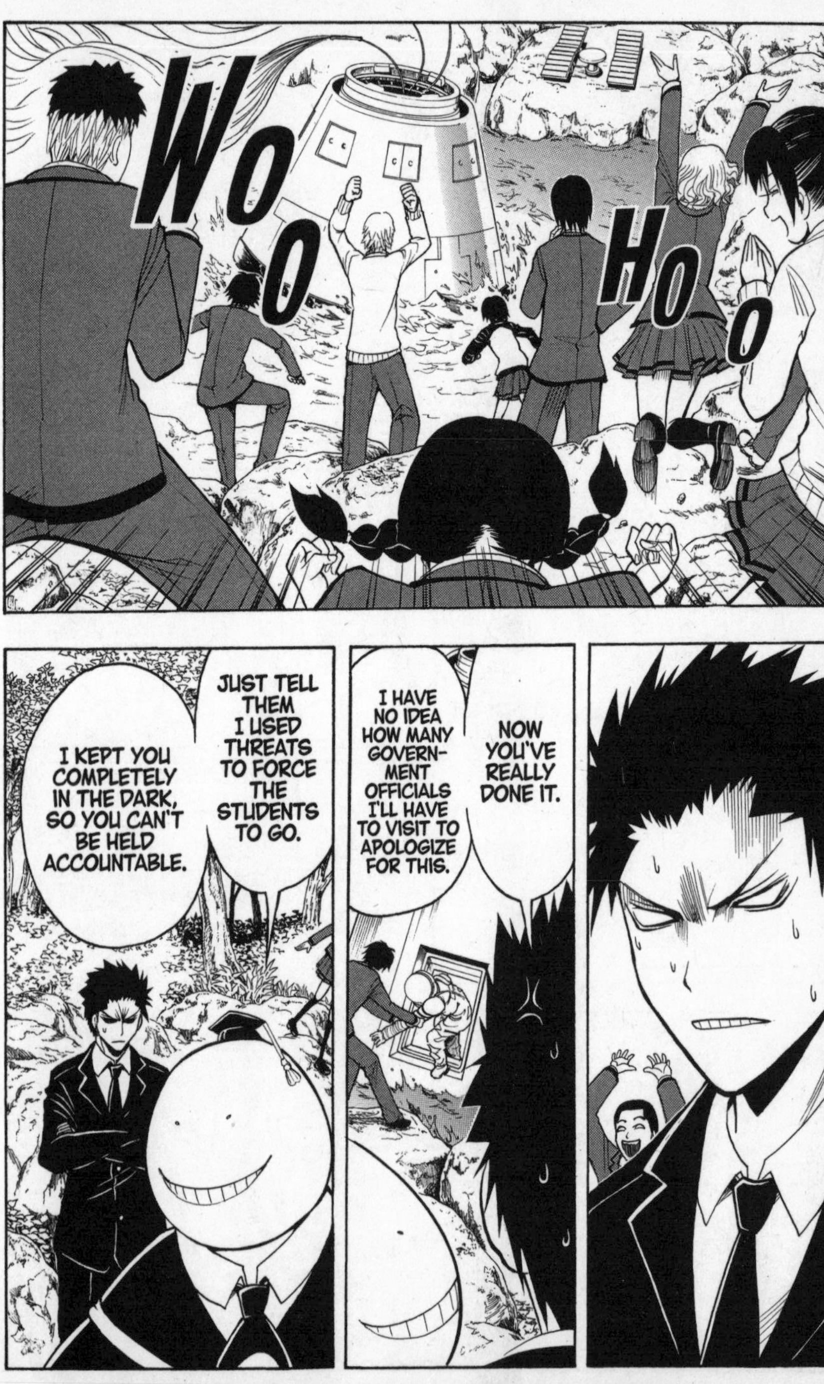
WOOHOO
NOW YOU'VE REALLY DONE IT.
I HAVE NO IDEA HOW MANY GOVERNMENT OFFICIALS I'LL HAVE TO VISIT TO APOLOGIZE FOR THIS.
JUST TELL THEM I USED THREATS TO FORCE THE STUDENTS TO GO.
I KEPT YOU COMPLETELY IN THE DARK, SO YOU CAN'T BE HELD ACCOUNTABLE.

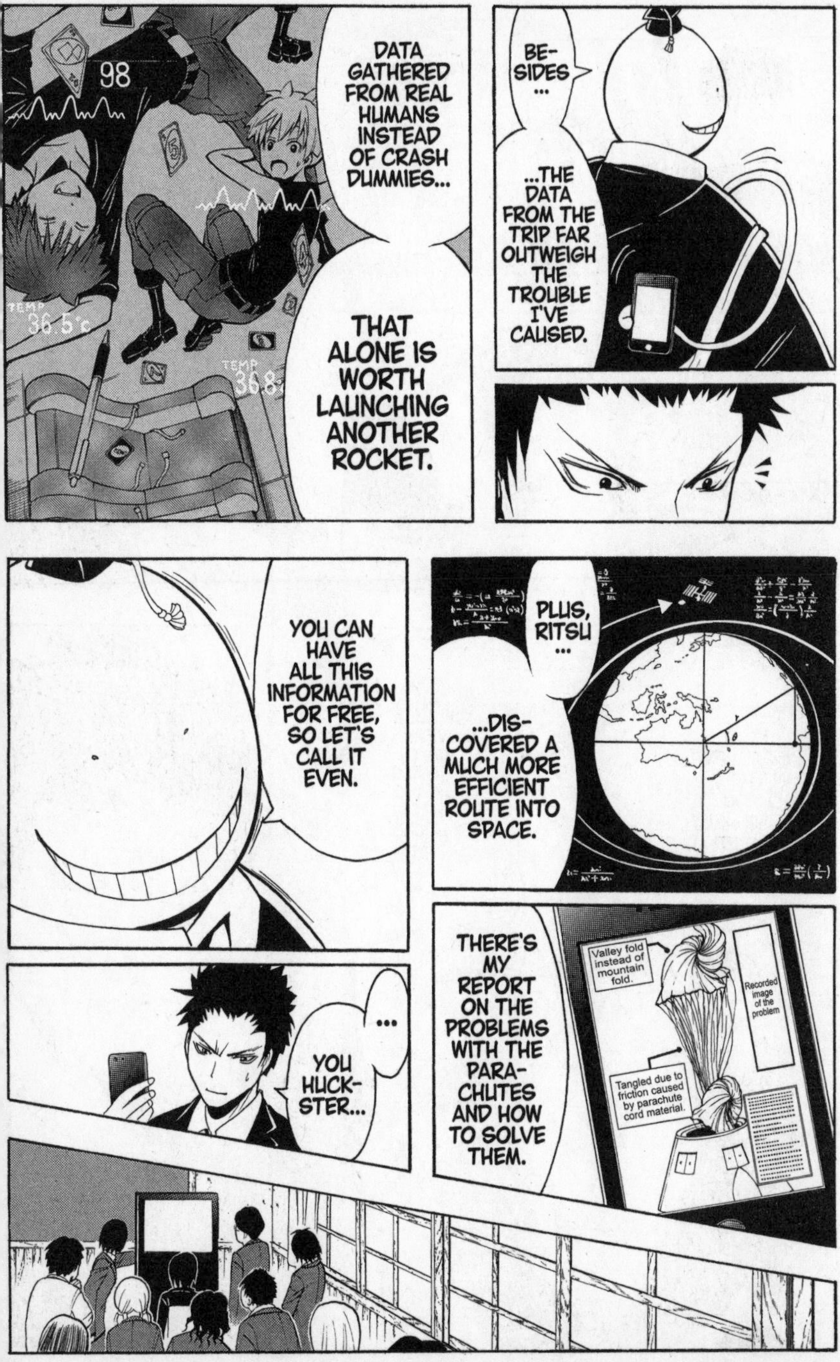
BESIDES...
...THE DATA FROM THE TRIP FAR OUTWEIGH THE TROUBLE I'VE CAUSED.
DATA GATHERED FROM REAL HUMANS INSTEAD OF CRASH DUMMIES...
THAT ALONE IS WORTH LAUNCHING ANOTHER ROCKET.
98
TEMP 36.5°c
PLUS, RITSU...
...DISCOVERED A MUCH MORE EFFICIENT ROUTE INTO SPACE.
YOU CAN HAVE ALL THIS INFORMATION FOR FREE, SO LET'S CALL IT EVEN.
THERE'S MY REPORT ON THE PROBLEMS WITH THE PARACHUTES AND HOW TO SOLVE THEM.
Valley fold instead of mountain fold.
Recorded image of the problem
Tangled due to friction caused by parachute cord material.
...
YOU HUCKSTER...

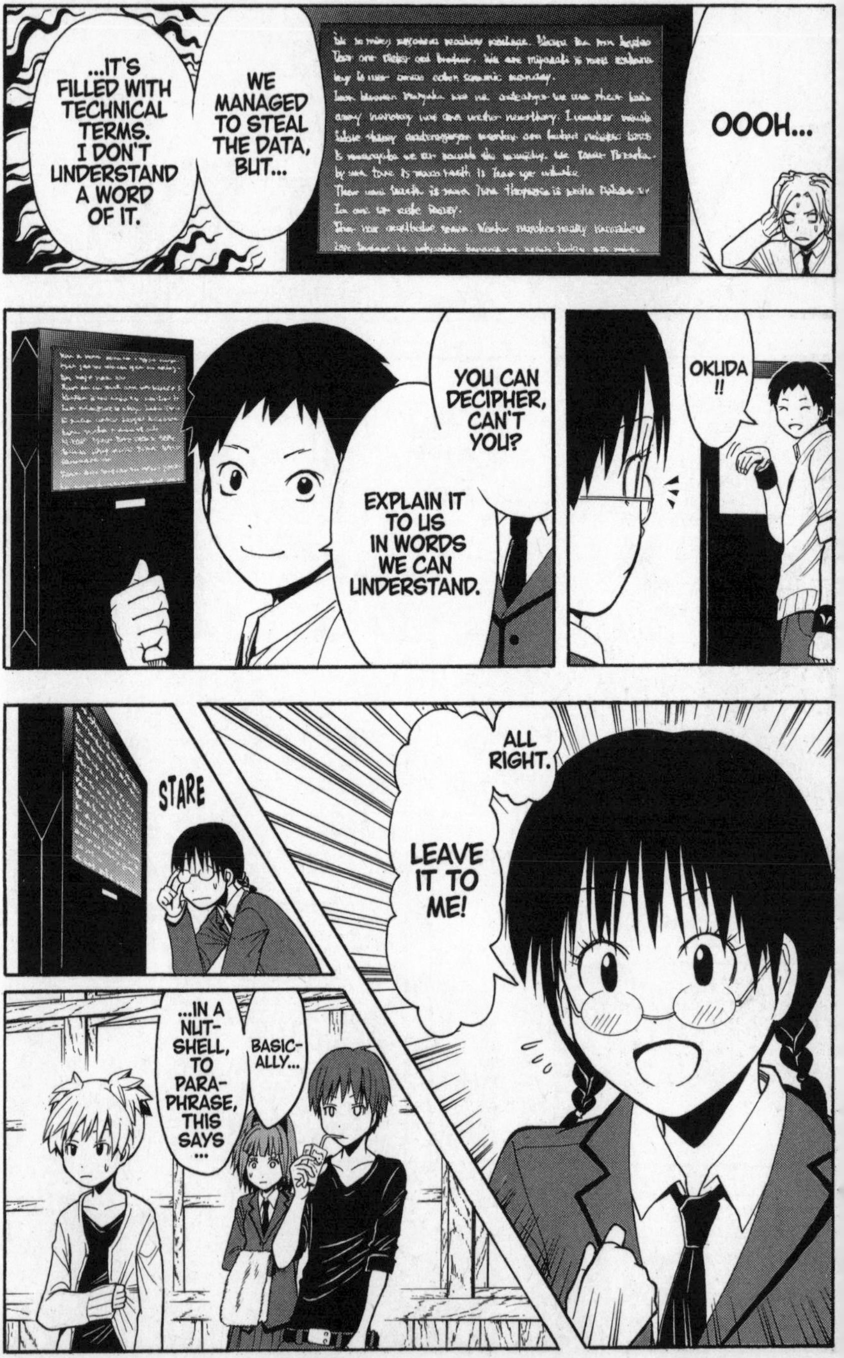
OOOH...
WE MANAGED TO STEAL THE DATA, BUT...
...IT'S FILLED WITH TECHNICAL TERMS. I DON'T UNDERSTAND A WORD OF IT.
OKUDA!!
YOU CAN DECIPHER, CAN'T YOU?
EXPLAIN IT TO US IN WORDS WE CAN UNDERSTAND.
ALL RIGHT.
LEAVE IT TO ME!
STARE
BASIC-ALLY...
...IN A NUT-SHELL, TO PARA-PHRASE, THIS SAYS...

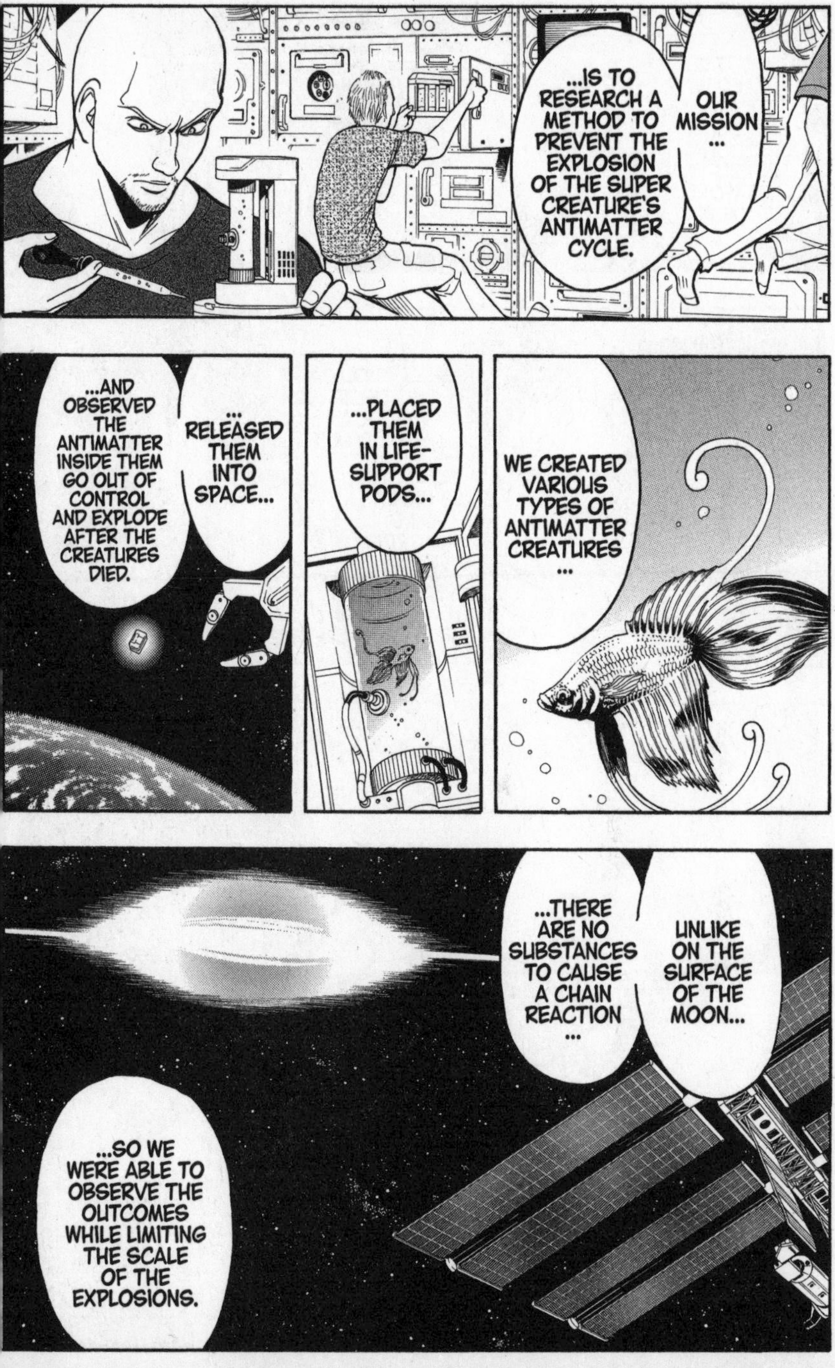
OUR MISSION...
...IS TO RESEARCH A METHOD TO PREVENT THE EXPLOSION OF THE SUPER CREATURE'S ANTIMATTER CYCLE.
WE CREATED VARIOUS TYPES OF ANTIMATTER CREATURES...
...PLACED THEM IN LIFE-SUPPORT PODS...
...RELEASED THEM INTO SPACE...
...AND OBSERVED THE ANTIMATTER INSIDE THEM GO OUT OF CONTROL AND EXPLODE AFTER THE CREATURES DIED.
UNLIKE ON THE SURFACE OF THE MOON...
...THERE ARE NO SUBSTANCES TO CAUSE A CHAIN REACTION...
...SO WE WERE ABLE TO OBSERVE THE OUTCOMES WHILE LIMITING THE SCALE OF THE EXPLOSIONS.

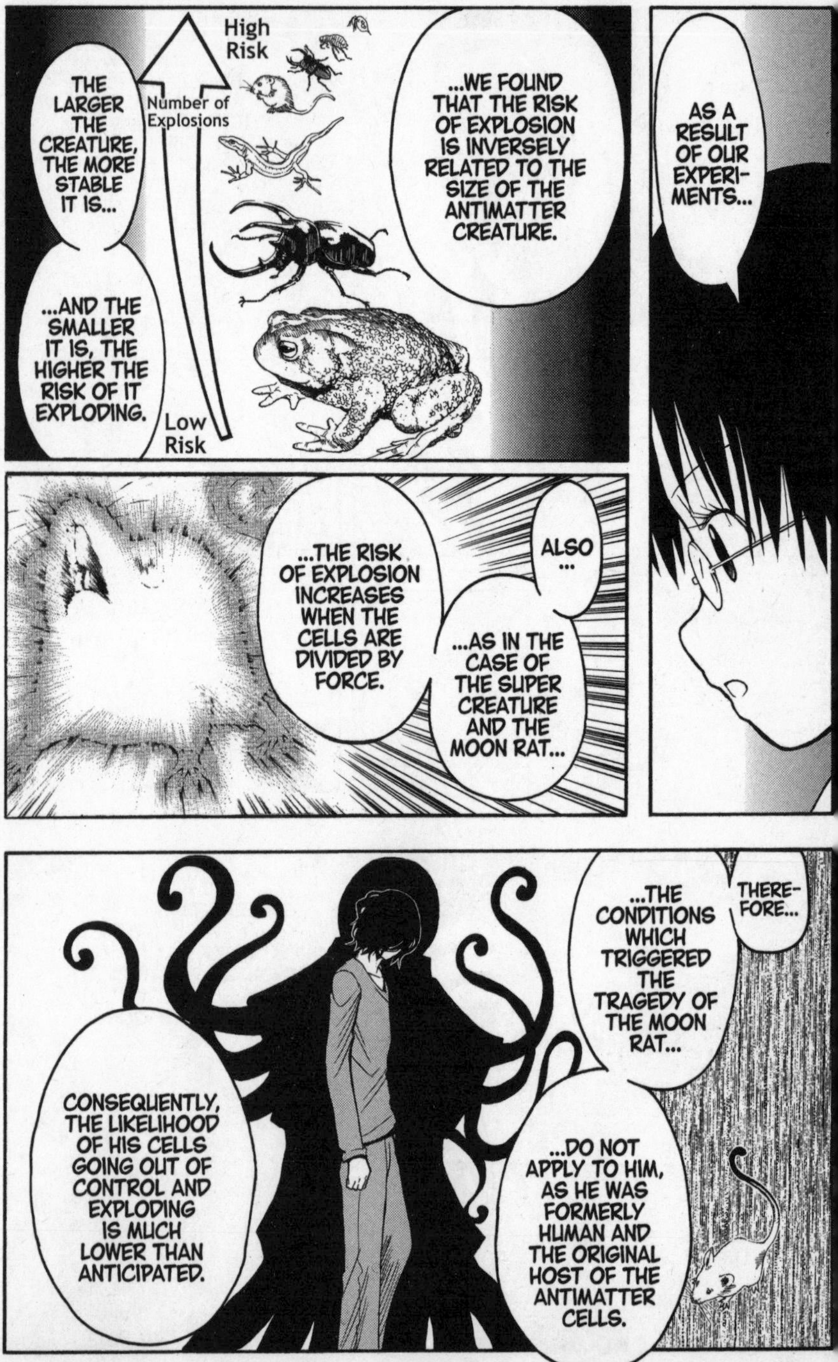
AS A RESULT OF OUR EXPERIMENTS...
...WE FOUND THAT THE RISK OF EXPLOSION IS INVERSELY RELATED TO THE SIZE OF THE ANTIMATTER CREATURE.
High Risk
Number of Explosions
Low Risk
THE LARGER THE CREATURE, THE MORE STABLE IT IS...
...AND THE SMALLER IT IS, THE HIGHER THE RISK OF IT EXPLODING.
ALSO ...
...AS IN THE CASE OF THE SUPER CREATURE AND THE MOON RAT...
...THE RISK OF EXPLOSION INCREASES WHEN THE CELLS ARE DIVIDED BY FORCE.
THERE-FORE...
...THE CONDITIONS WHICH TRIGGERED THE TRAGEDY OF THE MOON RAT...
...DO NOT APPLY TO HIM, AS HE WAS FORMERLY HUMAN AND THE ORIGINAL HOST OF THE ANTIMATTER CELLS.
CONSEQUENTLY, THE LIKELIHOOD OF HIS CELLS GOING OUT OF CONTROL AND EXPLODING IS MUCH LOWER THAN ANTICIPATED.

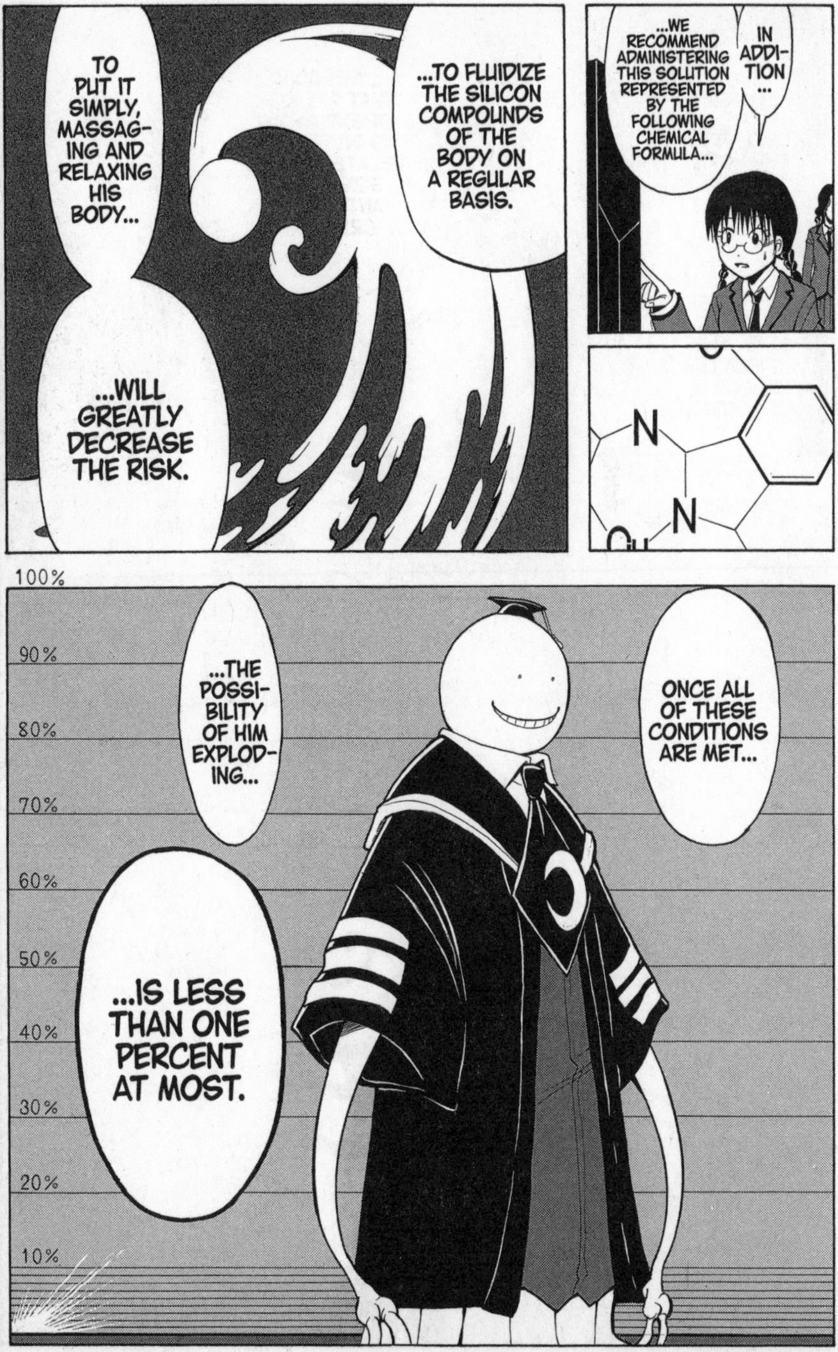
IN ADDITION...
...WE RECOMMEND ADMINISTERING THIS SOLUTION REPRESENTED BY THE FOLLOWING CHEMICAL FORMULA...
N
N
...TO FLUIDIZE THE SILICON COMPOUNDS OF THE BODY ON A REGULAR BASIS.
TO PUT IT SIMPLY, MASSAGING AND RELAXING HIS BODY...
...WILL GREATLY DECREASE THE RISK.
100%
90%
80%
70%
60%
50%
40%
30%
20%
10%
ONCE ALL OF THESE CONDITIONS ARE MET...
...THE POSSIBILITY OF HIM EXPLODING...
...IS LESS THAN ONE PERCENT AT MOST.

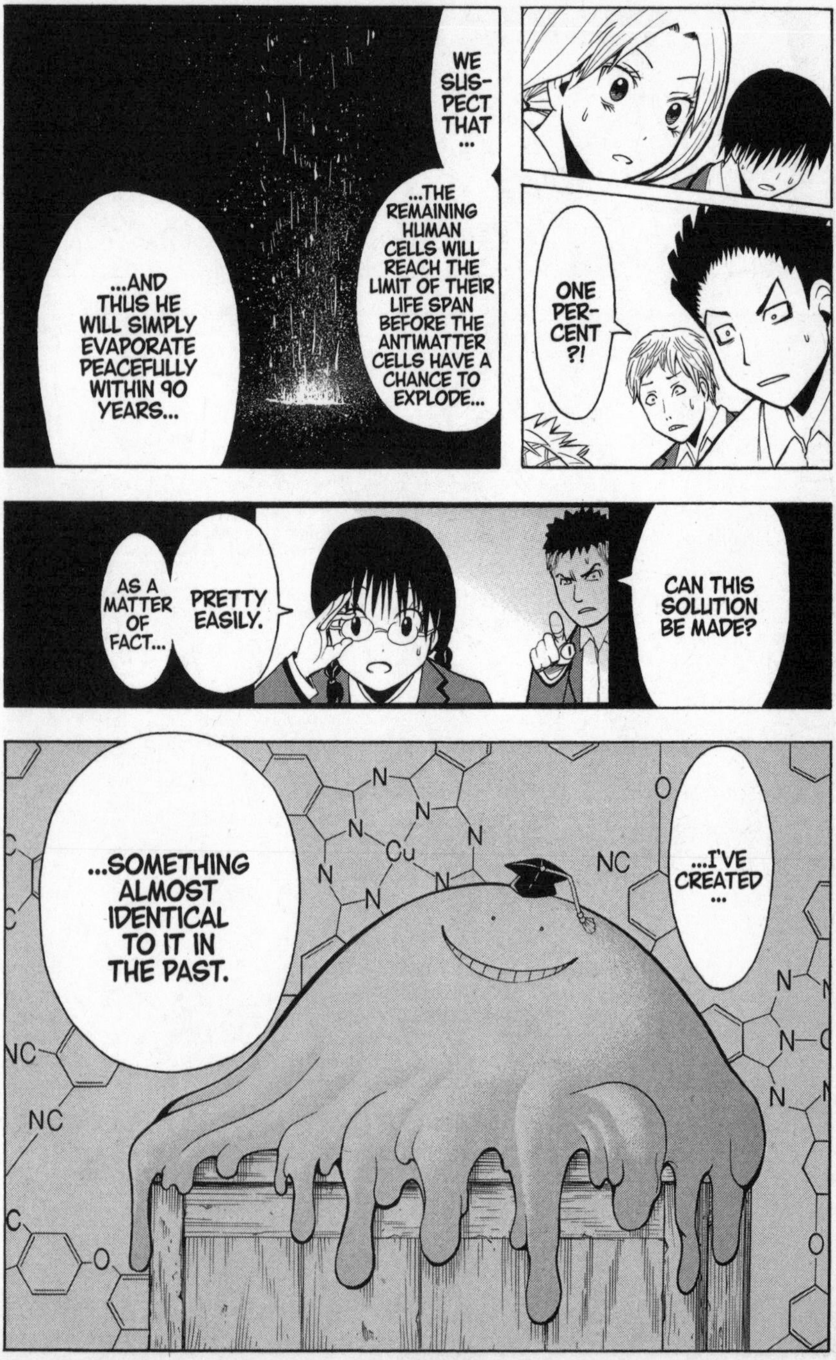
ONE PER-CENT?!
WE SUS-PECT THAT...
...THE REMAINING HUMAN CELLS WILL REACH THE LIMIT OF THEIR LIFE SPAN BEFORE THE ANTIMATTER CELLS HAVE A CHANCE TO EXPLODE...
...AND THUS HE WILL SIMPLY EVAPORATE PEACEFULLY WITHIN 90 YEARS...
CAN THIS SOLUTION BE MADE?
PRETTY EASILY.
AS A MATTER OF FACT...
...I'VE CREATED...
...SOMETHING ALMOST IDENTICAL TO IT IN THE PAST.

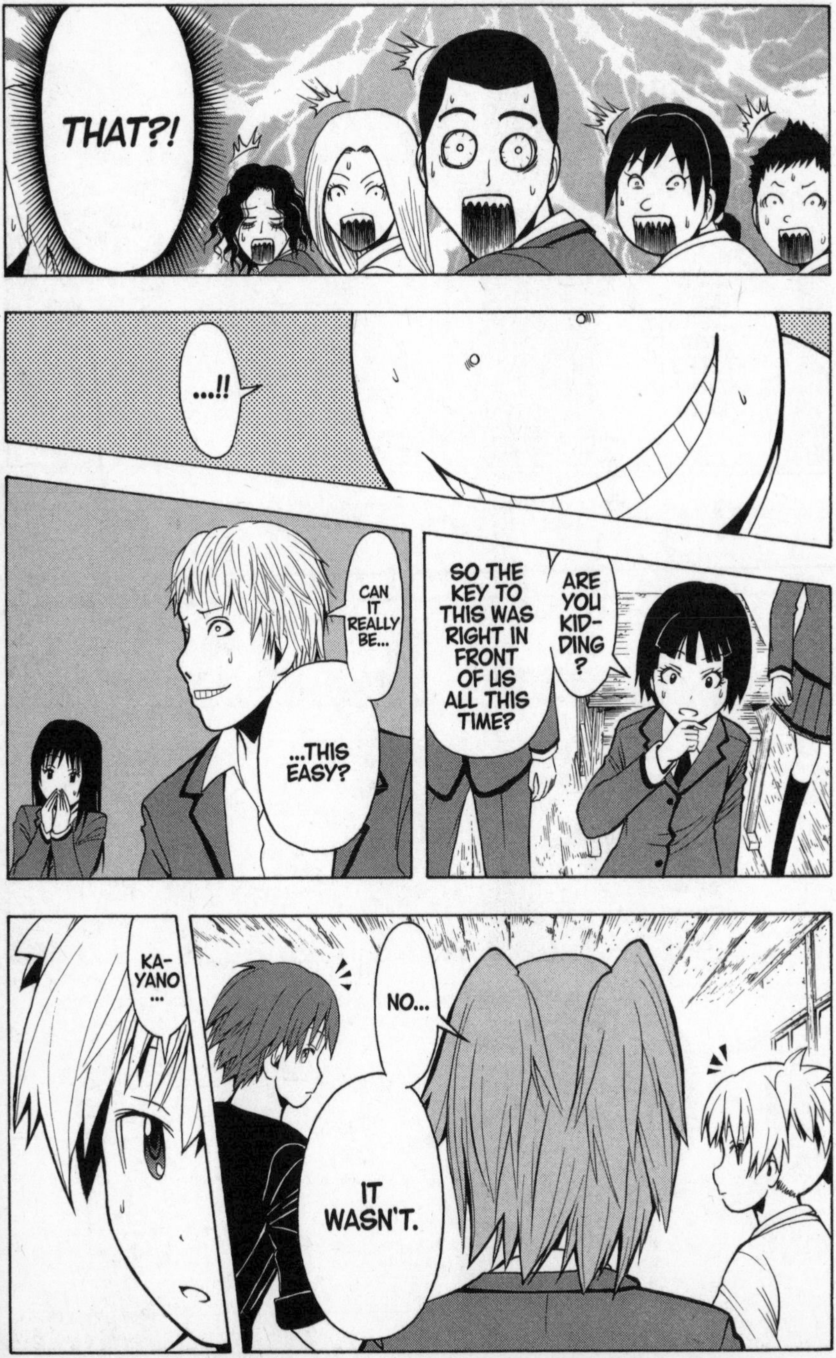
THAT?!
...!!
ARE YOU KID-DING?
SO THE KEY TO THIS WAS RIGHT IN FRONT OF US ALL THIS TIME?
CAN IT REALLY BE...
...THIS EASY?
NO...
IT WASN'T.
KA-YANO...

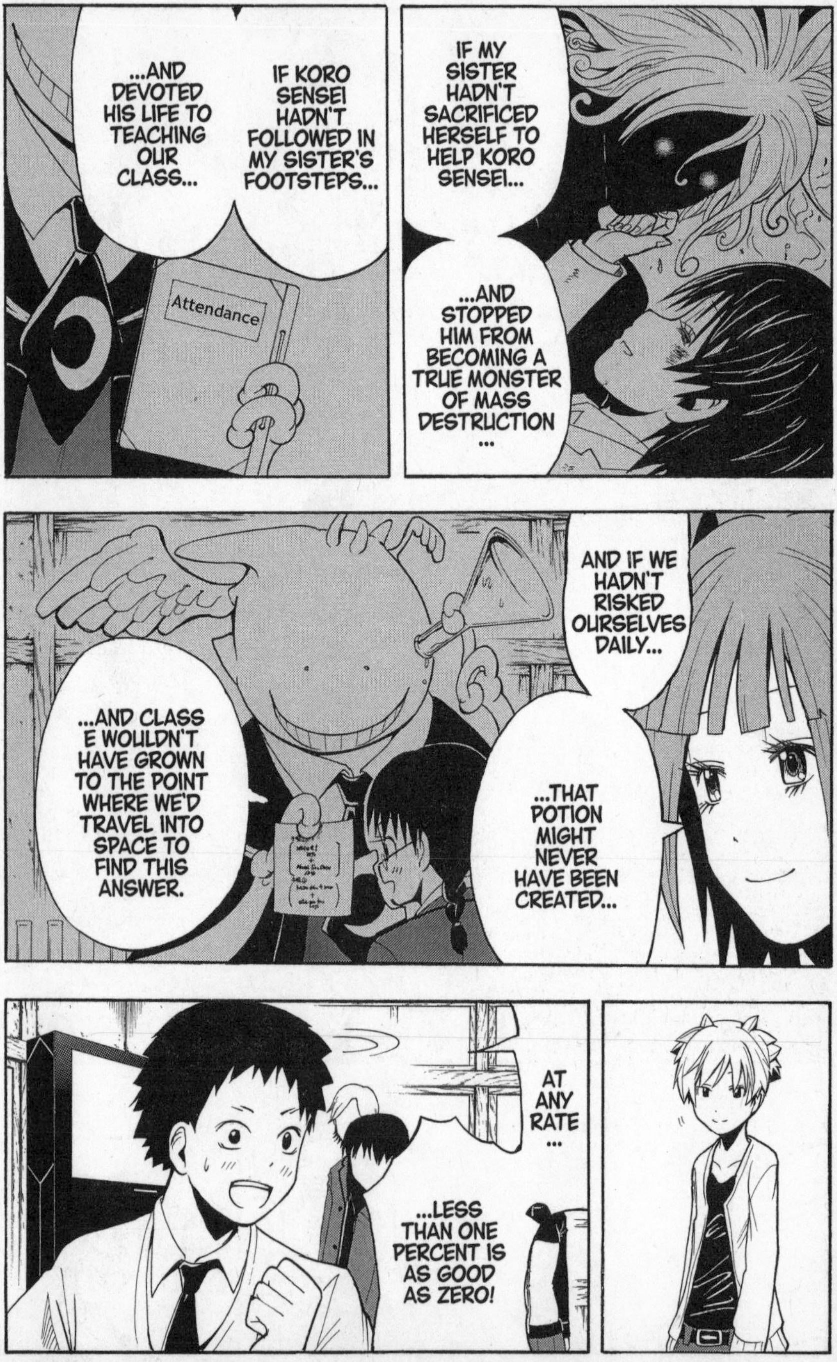
IF MY SISTER HADN'T SACRIFICED HERSELF TO HELP KORO SENSEI...
...AND STOPPED HIM FROM BECOMING A TRUE MONSTER OF MASS DESTRUCTION...
IF KORO SENSEI HADN'T FOLLOWED IN MY SISTER'S FOOTSTEPS...
...AND DEVOTED HIS LIFE TO TEACHING OUR CLASS...
Attendance
AND IF WE HADN'T RISKED OURSELVES DAILY...
...THAT POTION MIGHT NEVER HAVE BEEN CREATED...
...AND CLASS E WOULDN'T HAVE GROWN TO THE POINT WHERE WE'D TRAVEL INTO SPACE TO FIND THIS ANSWER.
AT ANY RATE...
...LESS THAN ONE PERCENT IS AS GOOD AS ZERO!

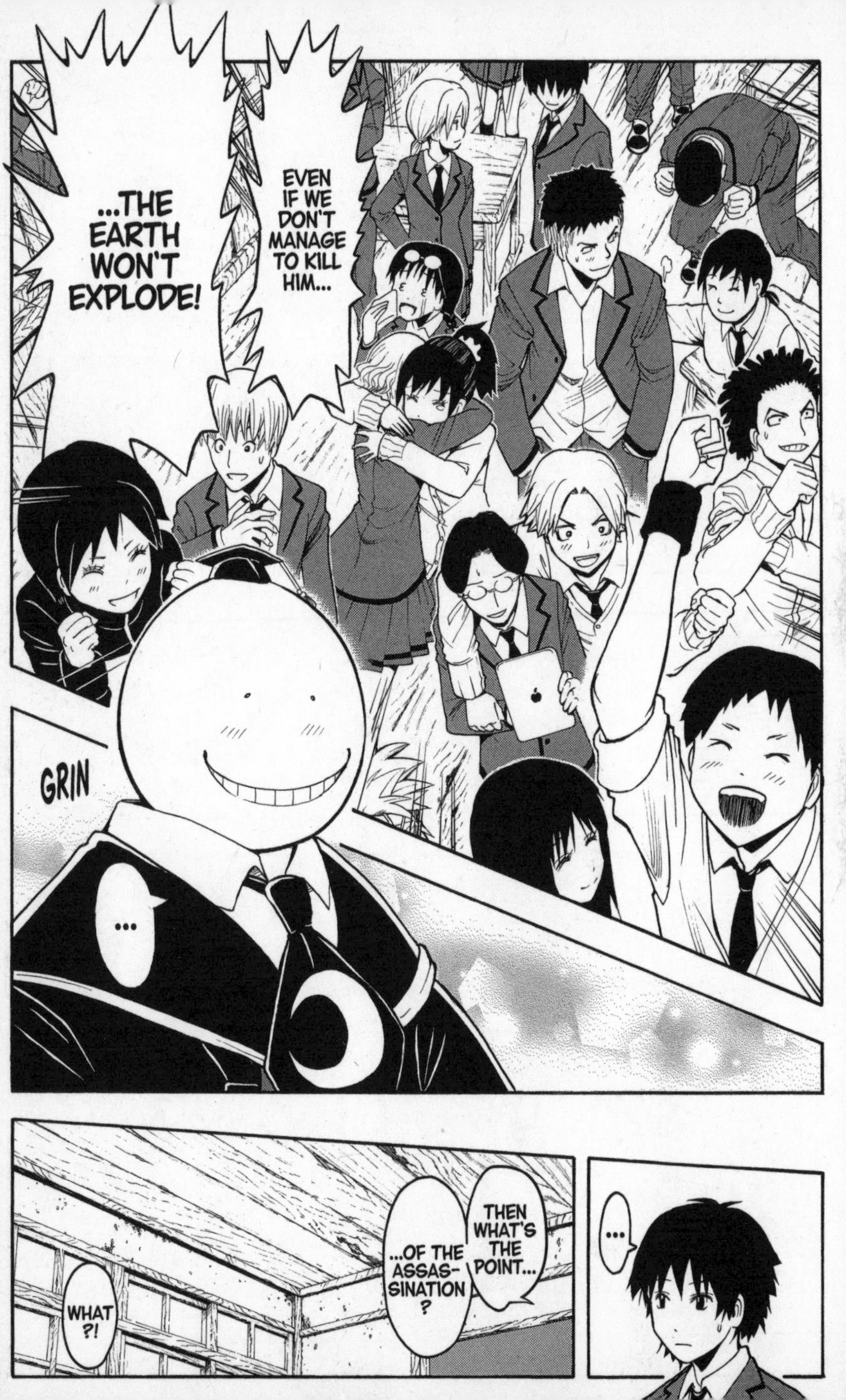
EVEN IF WE DON'T MANAGE TO KILL HIM...
...THE EARTH WON'T EXPLODE!
GRIN
...
...
THEN WHAT'S THE POINT...
...OF THE ASSAS-SINATION?
WHAT?!

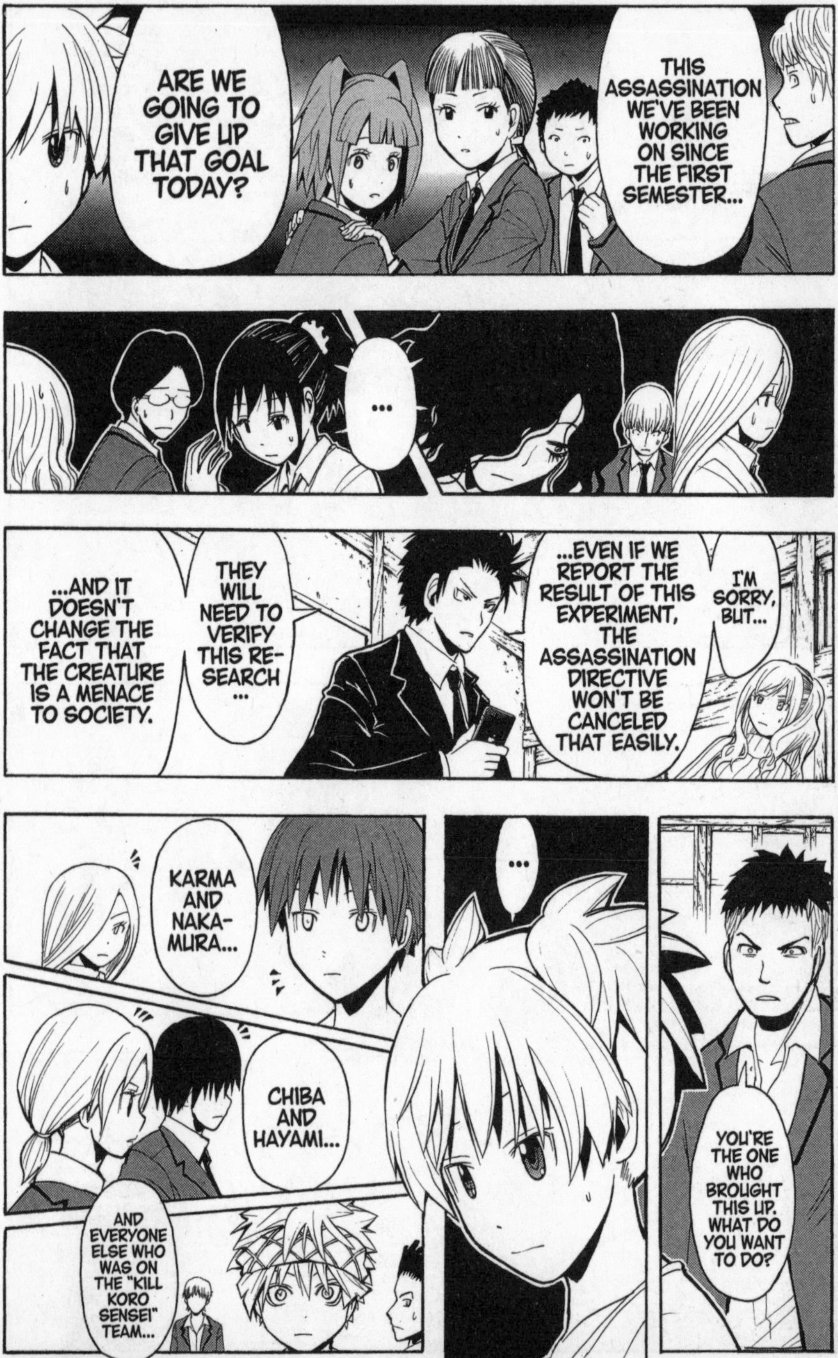
THIS ASSASSINATION WE'VE BEEN WORKING ON SINCE THE FIRST SEMESTER...
ARE WE GOING TO GIVE UP THAT GOAL TODAY?
...
I'M SORRY, BUT...
...EVEN IF WE REPORT THE RESULT OF THIS EXPERIMENT, THE ASSASSINATION DIRECTIVE WON'T BE CANCELED THAT EASILY.
THEY WILL NEED TO VERIFY THIS RE-SEARCH...
...AND IT DOESN'T CHANGE THE FACT THAT THE CREATURE IS A MENACE TO SOCIETY.
YOU'RE THE ONE WHO BROUGHT THIS UP. WHAT DO YOU WANT TO DO?
...
KARMA AND NAKA-MURA...
CHIBA AND HAYAMI...
AND EVERYONE ELSE WHO WAS ON THE "KILL KORO SENSEI" TEAM...

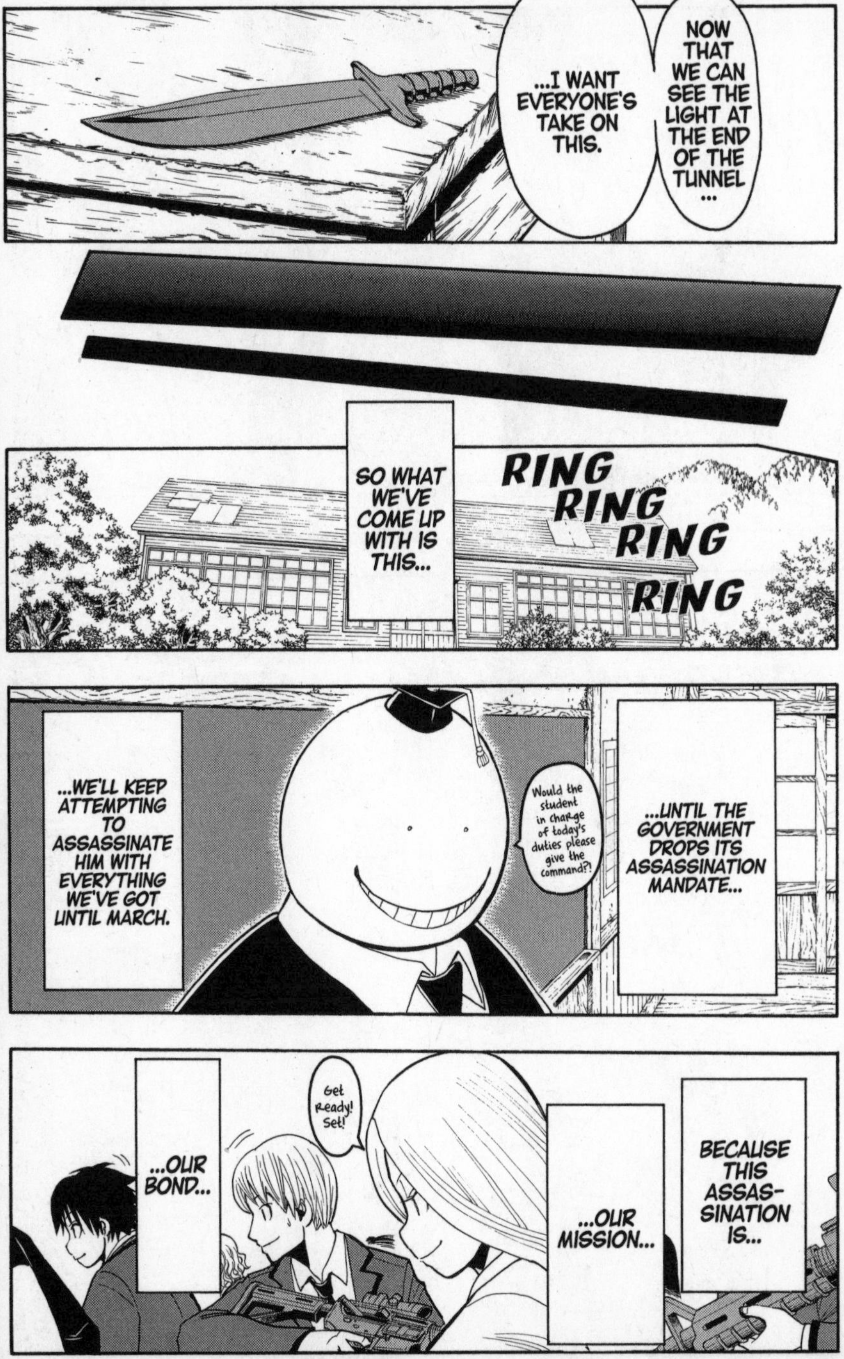
NOW THAT WE CAN SEE THE LIGHT AT THE END OF THE TUNNEL...
...I WANT EVERYONE'S TAKE ON THIS.
RING RING RING RING
SO WHAT WE'VE COME UP WITH IS THIS...
...UNTIL THE GOVERNMENT DROPS ITS ASSASSINATION MANDATE...
Would the student in charge of today's duties please give the command?!
...WE'LL KEEP ATTEMPTING TO ASSASSINATE HIM WITH EVERYTHING WE'VE GOT UNTIL MARCH.
BECAUSE THIS ASSAS-SINATION IS...
...OUR MISSION...
Get Ready! Set!
...OUR BOND...

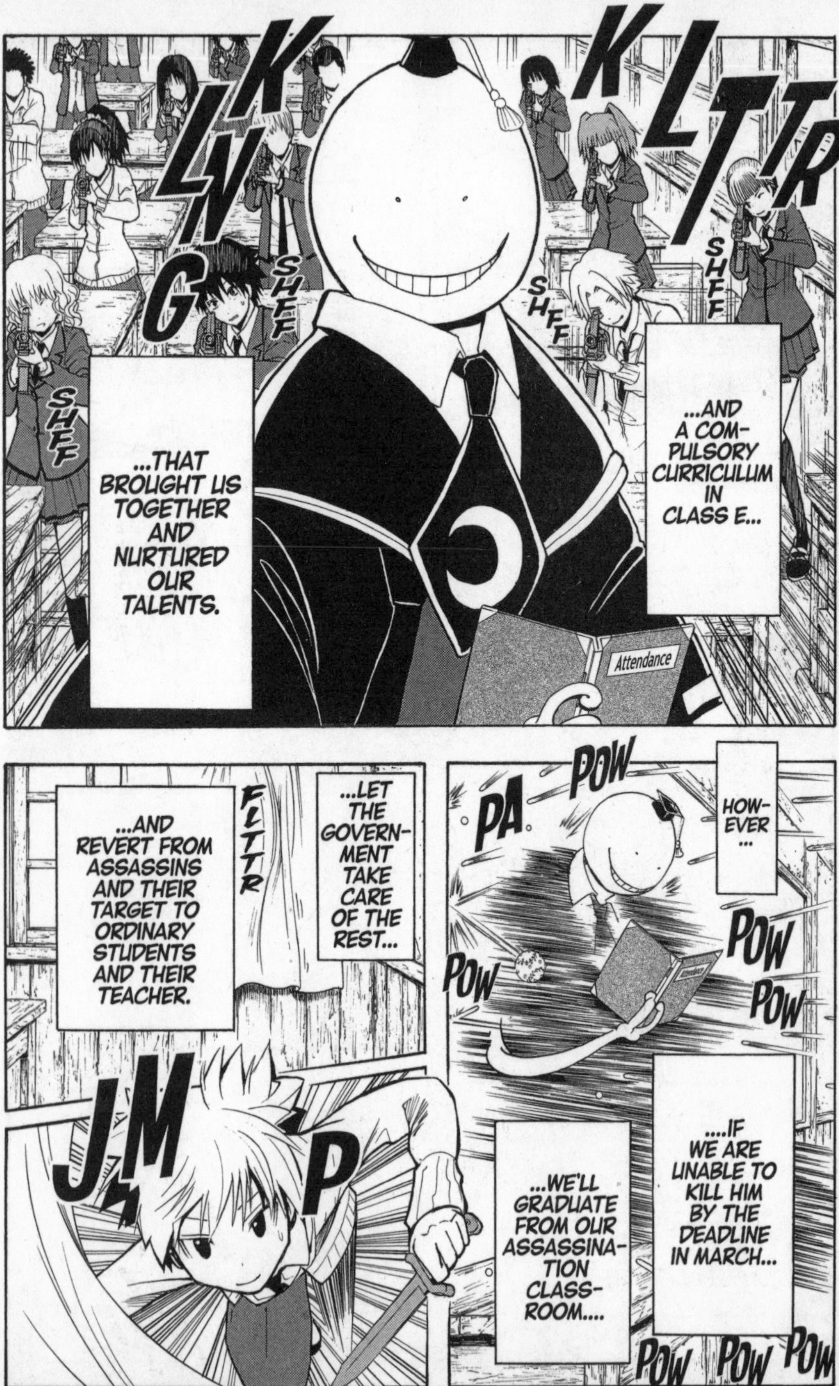
KLTTR
SHFF
SHFF
...AND A COMPULSORY CURRICULUM IN CLASS E...
KLNG
SHFF
SHFF
...THAT BROUGHT US TOGETHER AND NURTURED OUR TALENTS.
Attendance
POW
PA
HOW-EVER...
POW
POW
POW
....IF WE ARE UNABLE TO KILL HIM BY THE DEADLINE IN MARCH...
...WE'LL GRADUATE FROM OUR ASSASSINATION CLASSROOM....
POW POW POW
...LET THE GOVERNMENT TAKE CARE OF THE REST...
FLTTR
...AND REVERT FROM ASSASSINS AND THEIR TARGET TO ORDINARY STUDENTS AND THEIR TEACHER.
JMP

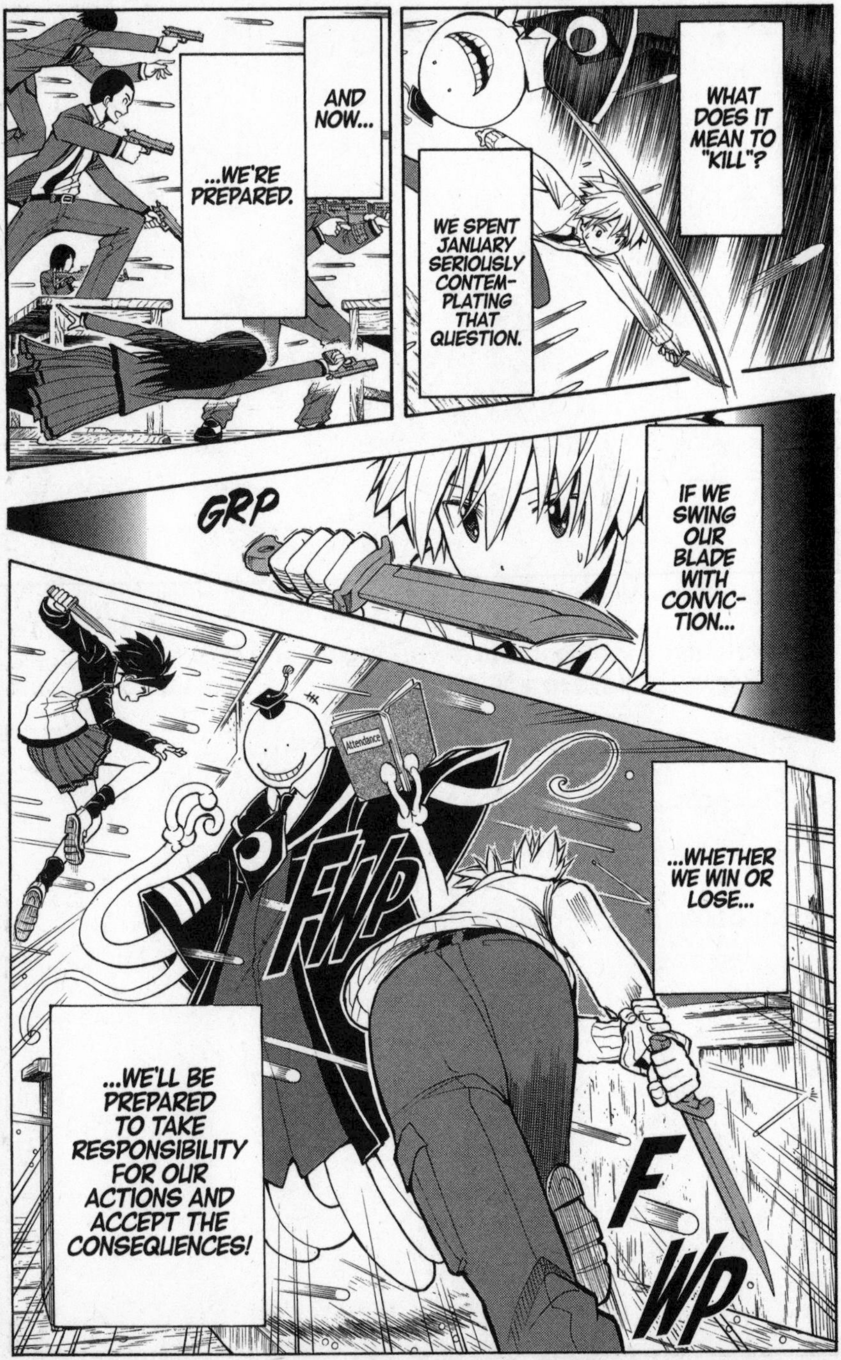
WHAT DOES IT MEAN TO "KILL"?
WE SPENT JANUARY SERIOUSLY CONTEM-PLATING THAT QUESTION.
AND NOW...
...WE'RE PREPARED.
IF WE SWING OUR BLADE WITH CONVIC-TION...
GRP
...WHETHER WE WIN OR LOSE...
Attendance
FWP
...WE'LL BE PREPARED TO TAKE RESPONSIBILITY FOR OUR ACTIONS AND ACCEPT THE CONSEQUENCES!
F WP

Class E Memoirs Chant

Akabane: We were up late on our futons...

Students: ...during our three nights and two days in low gravity.

Isogai: We plotted and succeeded...

Students: ...to hijack a space station.

Okajima: That's an adventure...

Students: ...we will never forget.

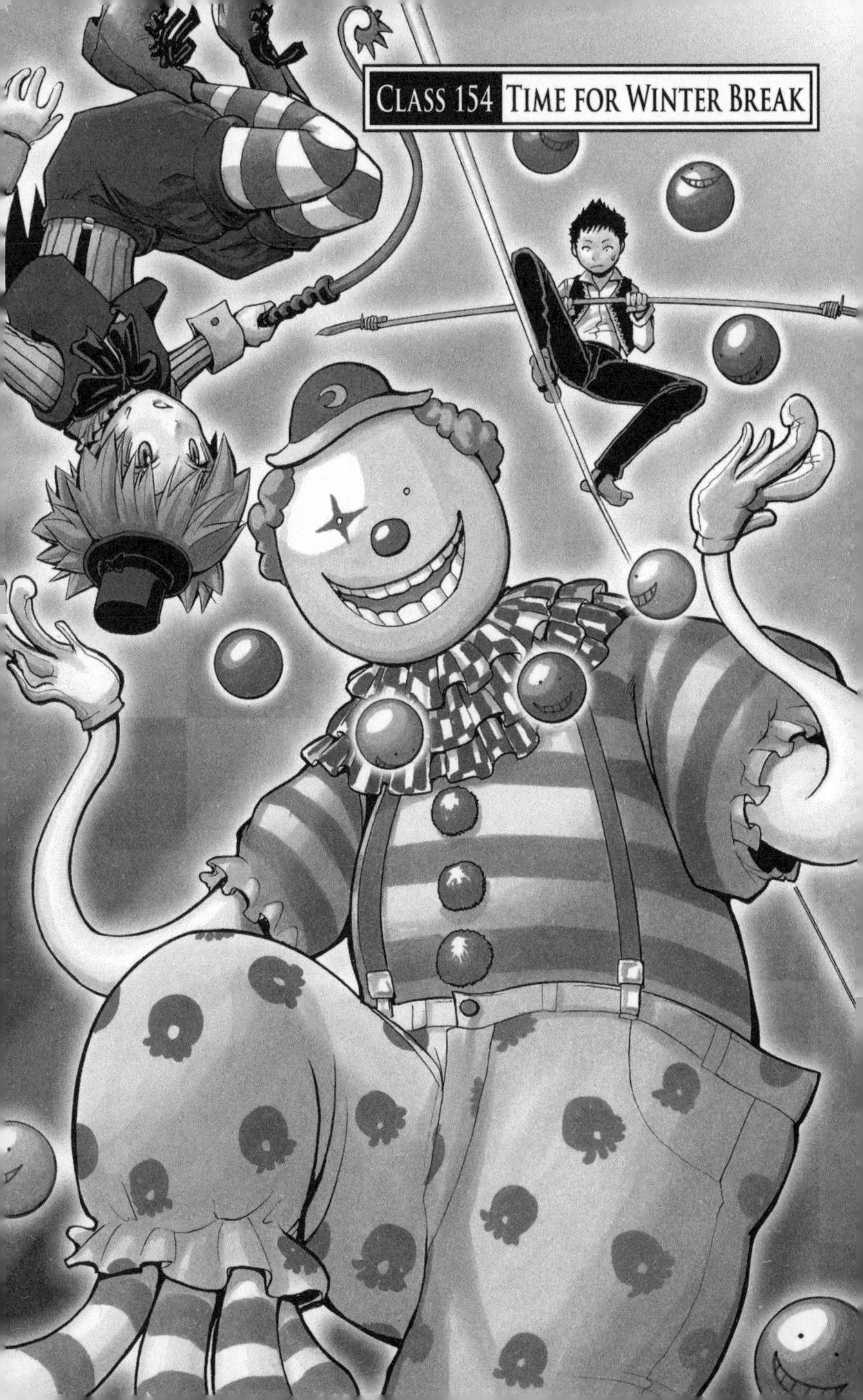
CLASS 154 TIME FOR WINTER BREAK

Koro Sensei's Secrets, Encyclopedia Entry ③ ~Food~

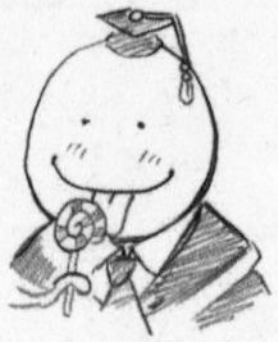

① Koro Sensei is always eating snacks and candy, but how does he sustain his extreme figure with just those foods?

$${}_{6}C + {}_{14}Si$$

② Allow me to explain! Koro Sensei's body is actually composed of a hybrid of carbon compounds—just like the rest of us humans—with the addition of silicon compounds that have high heat resistance.

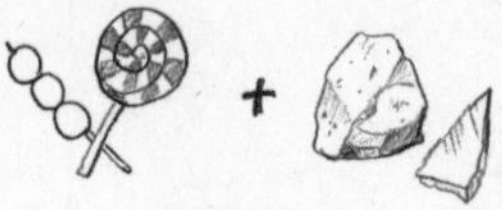

③ He needs to eat snacks and ordinary food to sustain the carbon compound components of his body. However, in order to sustain the silicon compound components, he must consume glass and rocks containing silicon.

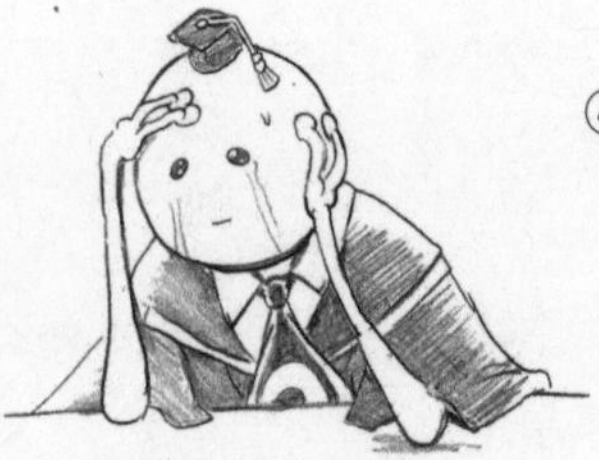

④ Sadly, Koro Sensei is convinced that it would destroy his cute image if the students observed him desperately munching on rocks!

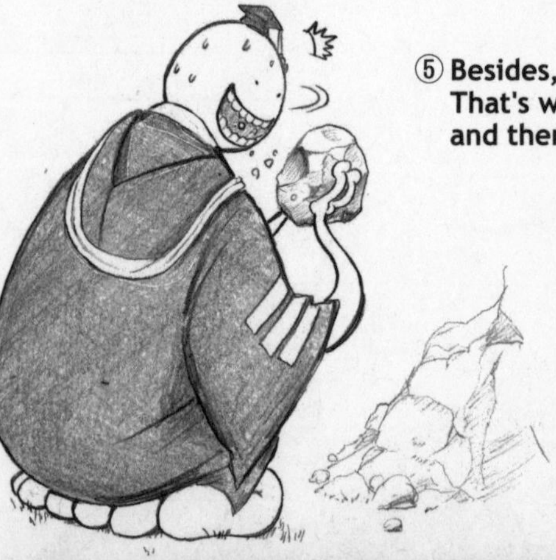

⑤ Besides, rocks don't taste good. That's why he nibbles on them here and there behind everyone's back.

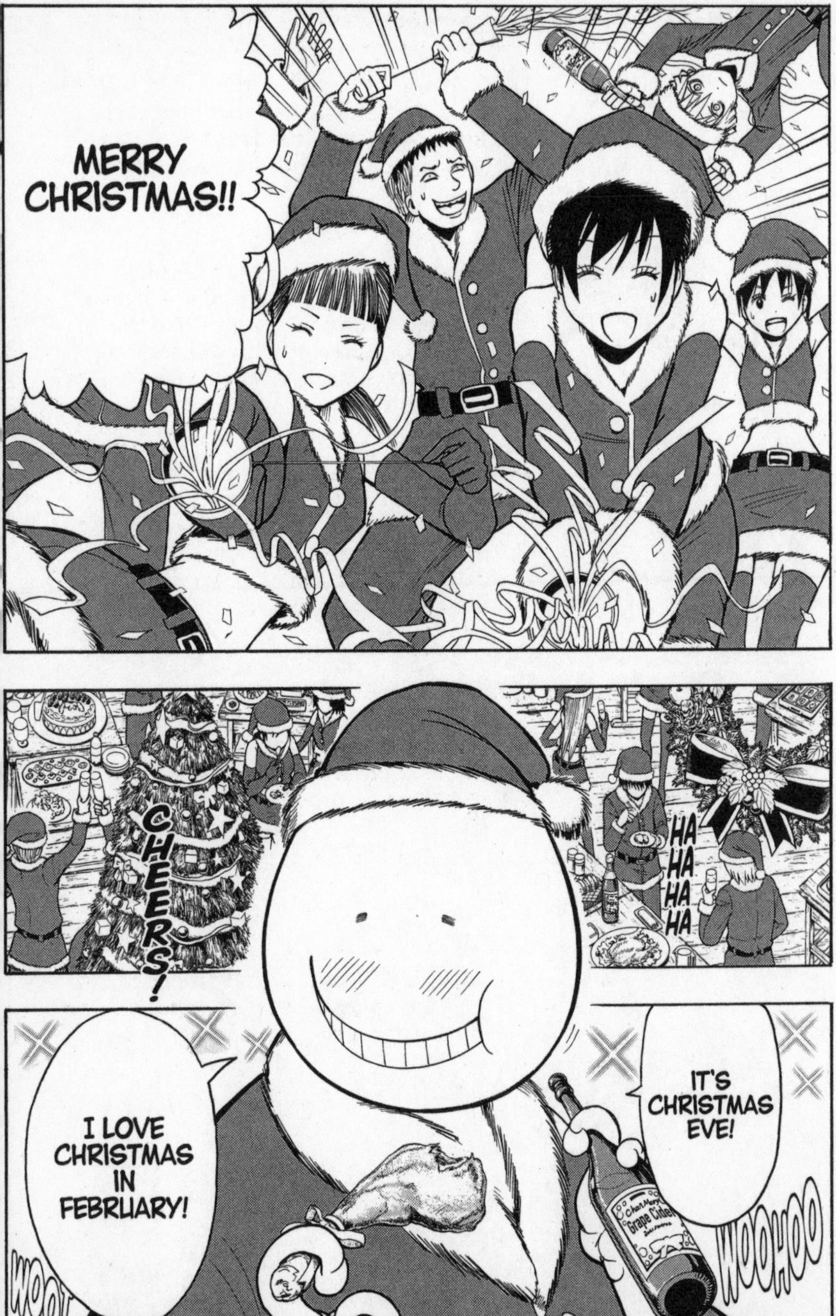
MERRY CHRISTMAS!!
HA HA HA HA HA
CHEERS!
IT'S CHRISTMAS EVE!
WOOHOO
I LOVE CHRISTMAS IN FEBRUARY!
WOOT

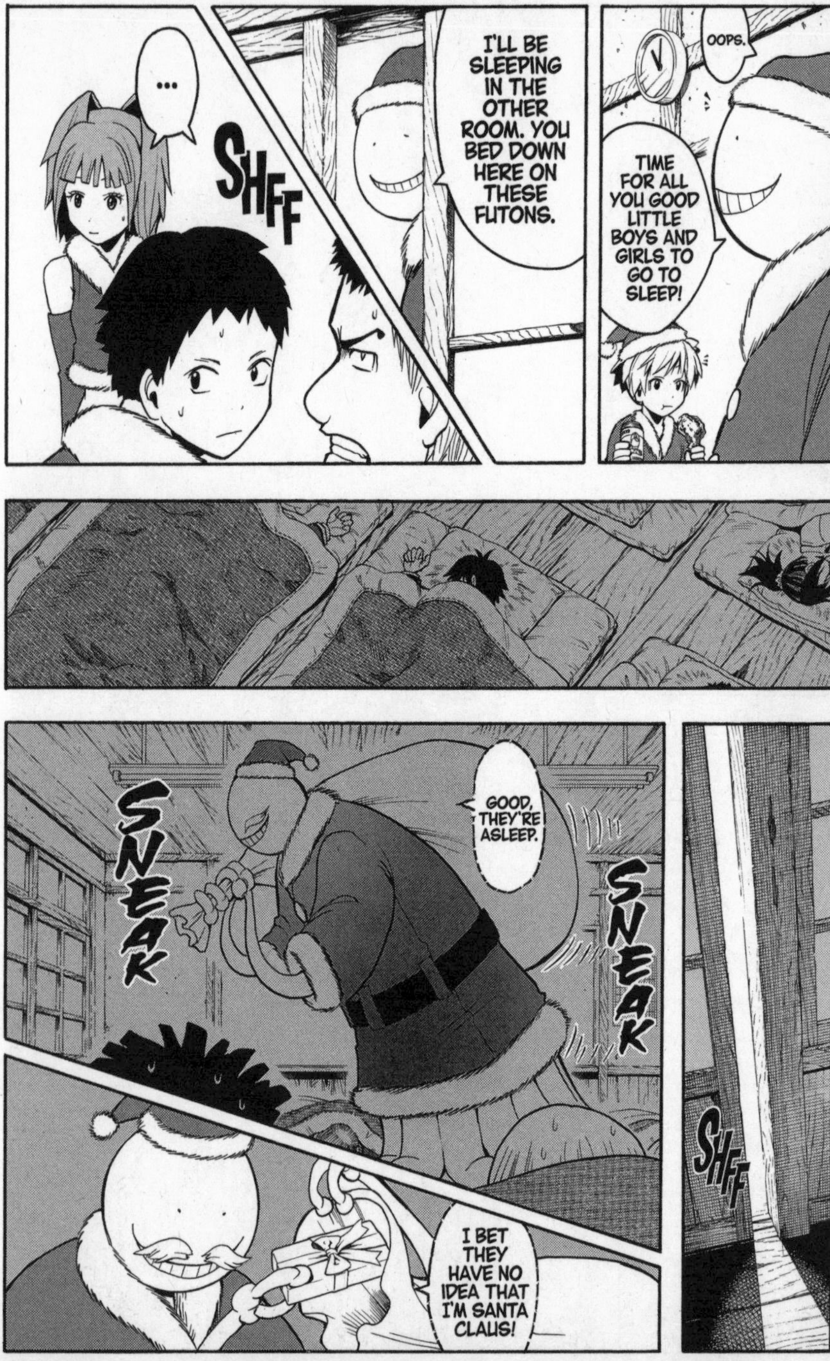
OOPS.
TIME FOR ALL YOU GOOD LITTLE BOYS AND GIRLS TO GO TO SLEEP!
I'LL BE SLEEPING IN THE OTHER ROOM. YOU BED DOWN HERE ON THESE FUTONS.
SHFF
...
SHFF
SNEAK
GOOD, THEY'RE ASLEEP.
SNEAK
I BET THEY HAVE NO IDEA THAT I'M SANTA CLAUS!

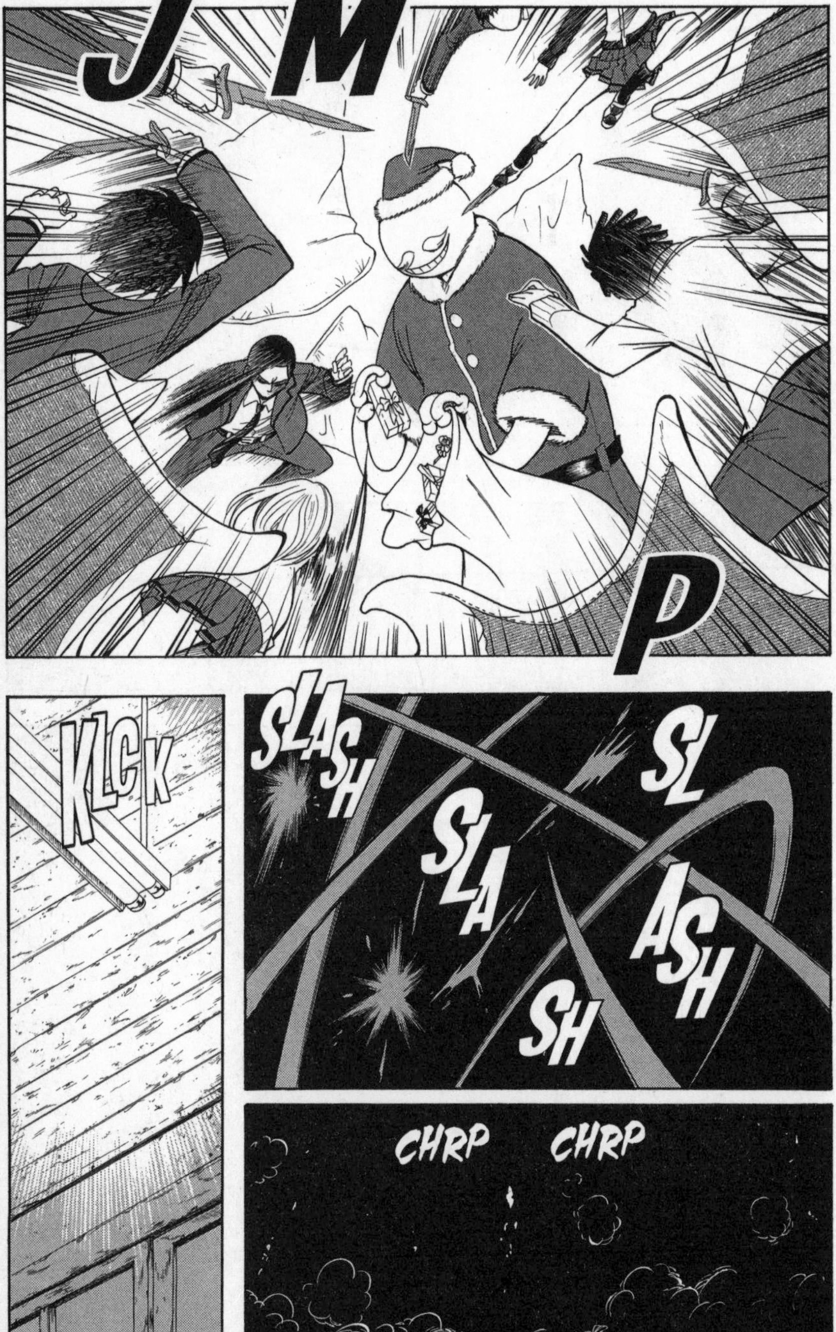
JMP
SLASH
SLASH
SLASH
CHRP CHRP
KLICK

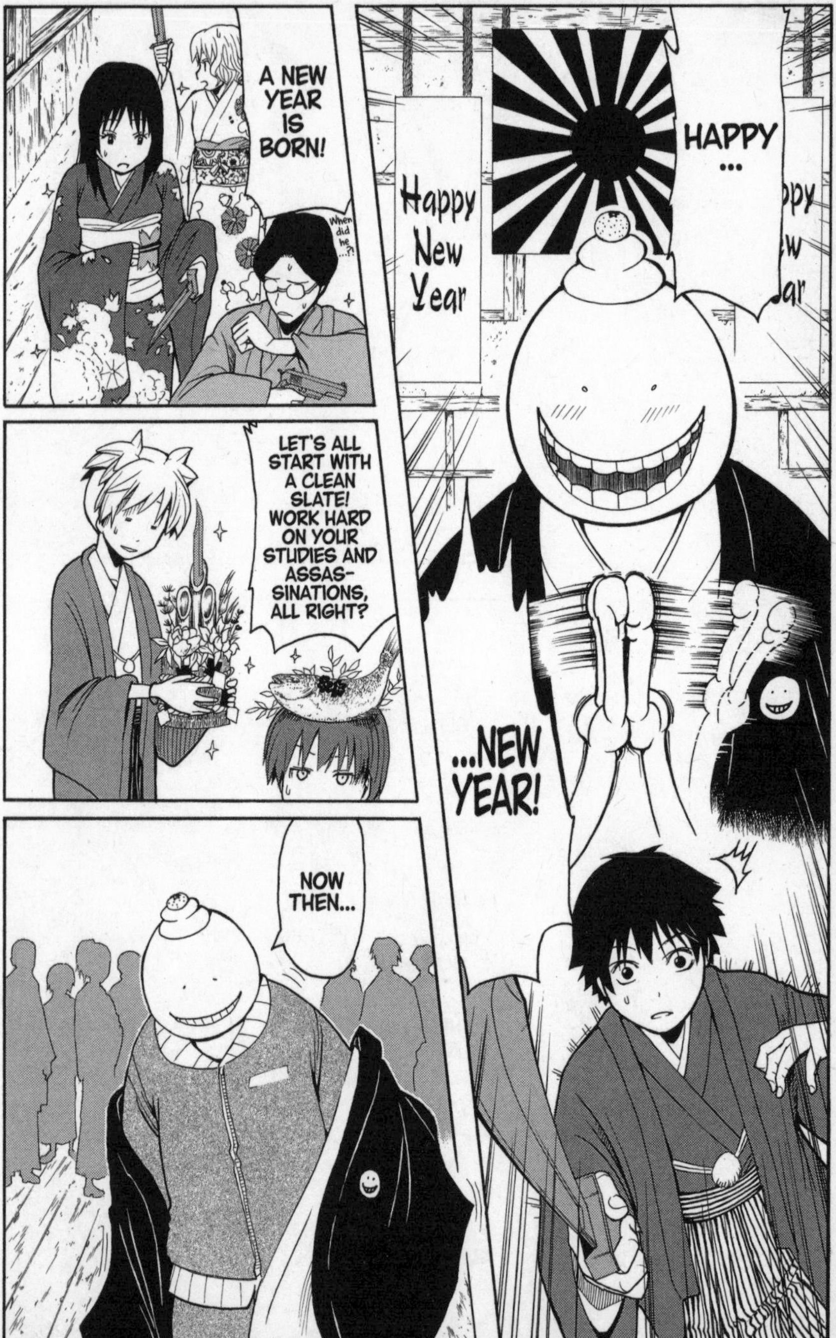
Happy New Year
HAPPY ...
...NEW YEAR!
A NEW YEAR IS BORN!
When did he ...?!
LET'S ALL START WITH A CLEAN SLATE! WORK HARD ON YOUR STUDIES AND ASSAS-SINATIONS, ALL RIGHT?
NOW THEN...

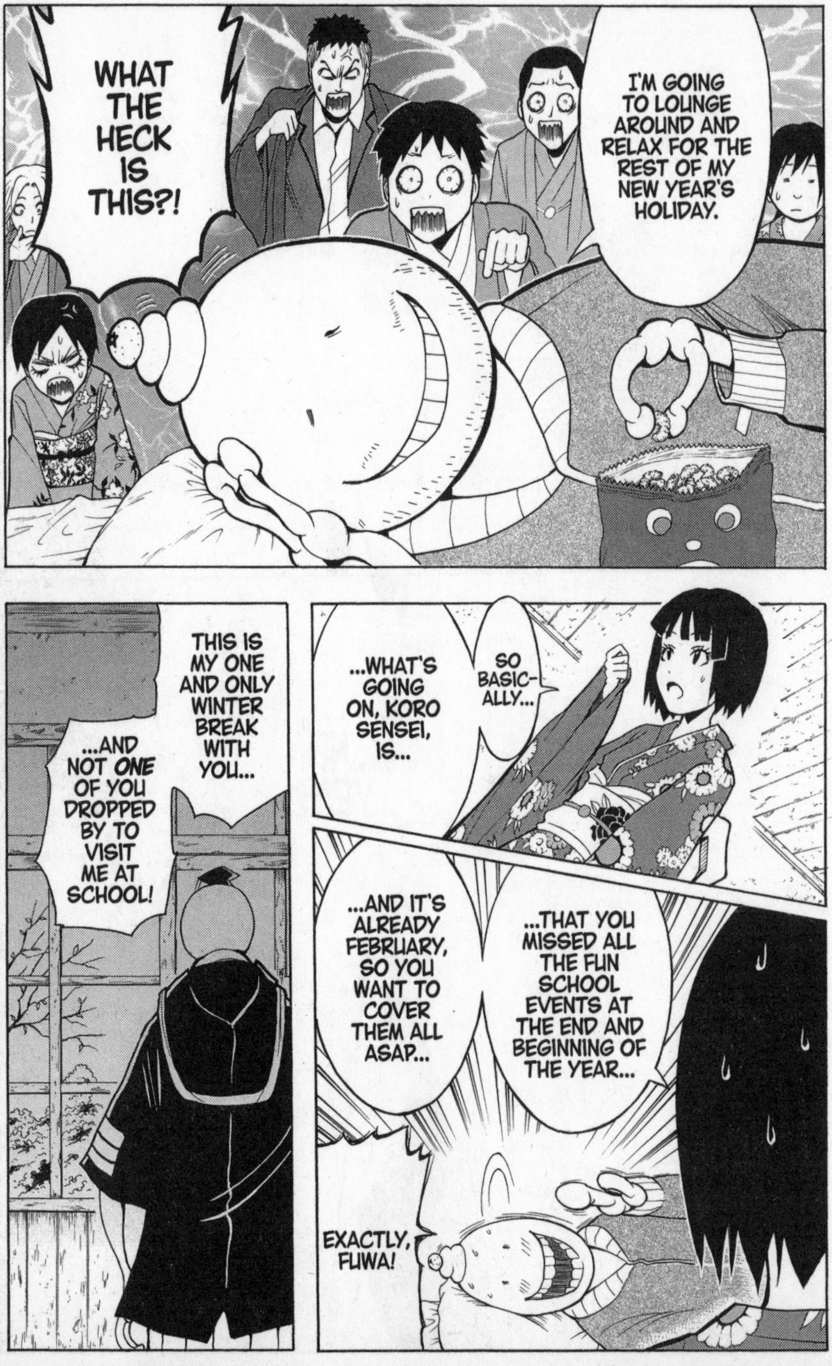
I'M GOING TO LOUNGE AROUND AND RELAX FOR THE REST OF MY NEW YEAR'S HOLIDAY.
WHAT THE HECK IS THIS?!
SO BASIC-ALLY...
...WHAT'S GOING ON, KORO SENSEI, IS...
...THAT YOU MISSED ALL THE FUN SCHOOL EVENTS AT THE END AND BEGINNING OF THE YEAR...
...AND IT'S ALREADY FEBRUARY, SO YOU WANT TO COVER THEM ALL ASAP...
EXACTLY, FUWA!
THIS IS MY ONE AND ONLY WINTER BREAK WITH YOU...
...AND NOT ONE OF YOU DROPPED BY TO VISIT ME AT SCHOOL!

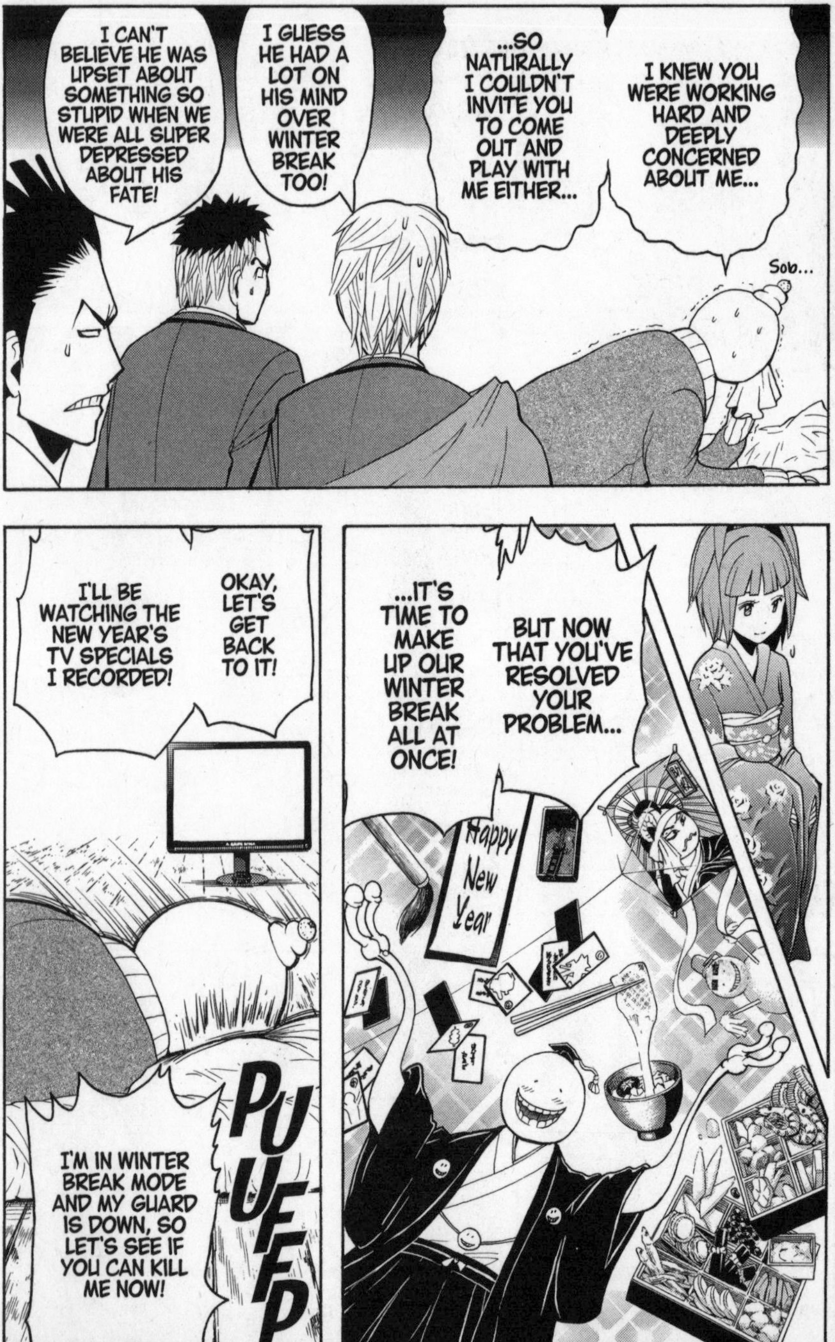
I KNEW YOU WERE WORKING HARD AND DEEPLY CONCERNED ABOUT ME...
...SO NATURALLY I COULDN'T INVITE YOU TO COME OUT AND PLAY WITH ME EITHER...
Sob...
I GUESS HE HAD A LOT ON HIS MIND OVER WINTER BREAK TOO!
I CAN'T BELIEVE HE WAS UPSET ABOUT SOMETHING SO STUPID WHEN WE WERE ALL SUPER DEPRESSED ABOUT HIS FATE!
BUT NOW THAT YOU'VE RESOLVED YOUR PROBLEM...
...IT'S TIME TO MAKE UP OUR WINTER BREAK ALL AT ONCE!
Happy New Year
OKAY, LET'S GET BACK TO IT!
I'LL BE WATCHING THE NEW YEAR'S TV SPECIALS I RECORDED!
PUFFP
I'M IN WINTER BREAK MODE AND MY GUARD IS DOWN, SO LET'S SEE IF YOU CAN KILL ME NOW!

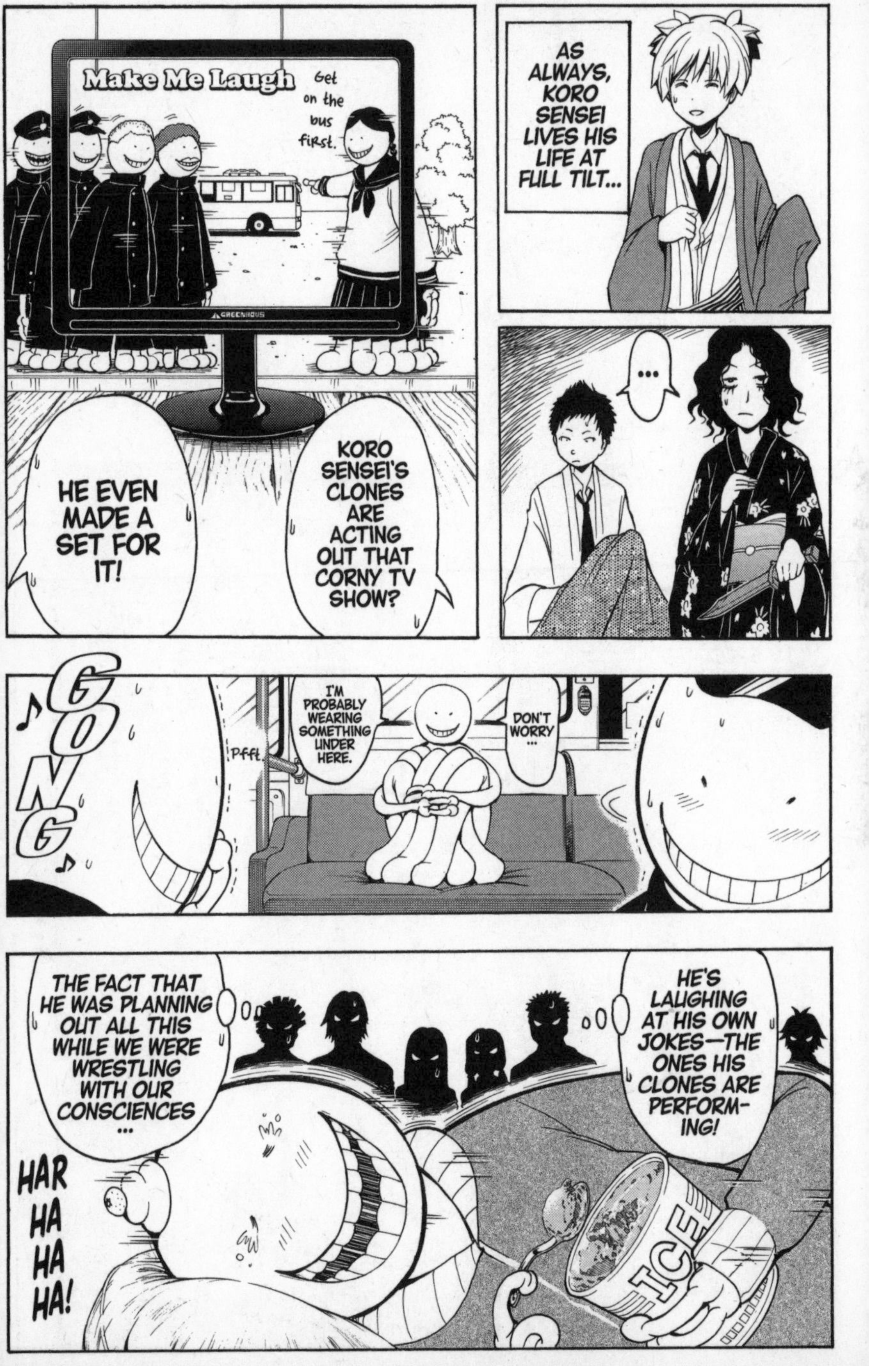
AS ALWAYS, KORO SENSEI LIVES HIS LIFE AT FULL TILT...
...
Make Me Laugh
Get on the bus first.
GREENHOUS
KORO SENSEI'S CLONES ARE ACTING OUT THAT CORNY TV SHOW?
HE EVEN MADE A SET FOR IT!
DON'T WORRY...
I'M PROBABLY WEARING SOMETHING UNDER HERE.
Pfft.
GONG
HE'S LAUGHING AT HIS OWN JOKES—THE ONES HIS CLONES ARE PERFORMING!
THE FACT THAT HE WAS PLANNING OUT ALL THIS WHILE WE WERE WRESTLING WITH OUR CONSCIENCES...
HAR HA HA HA!
ICE

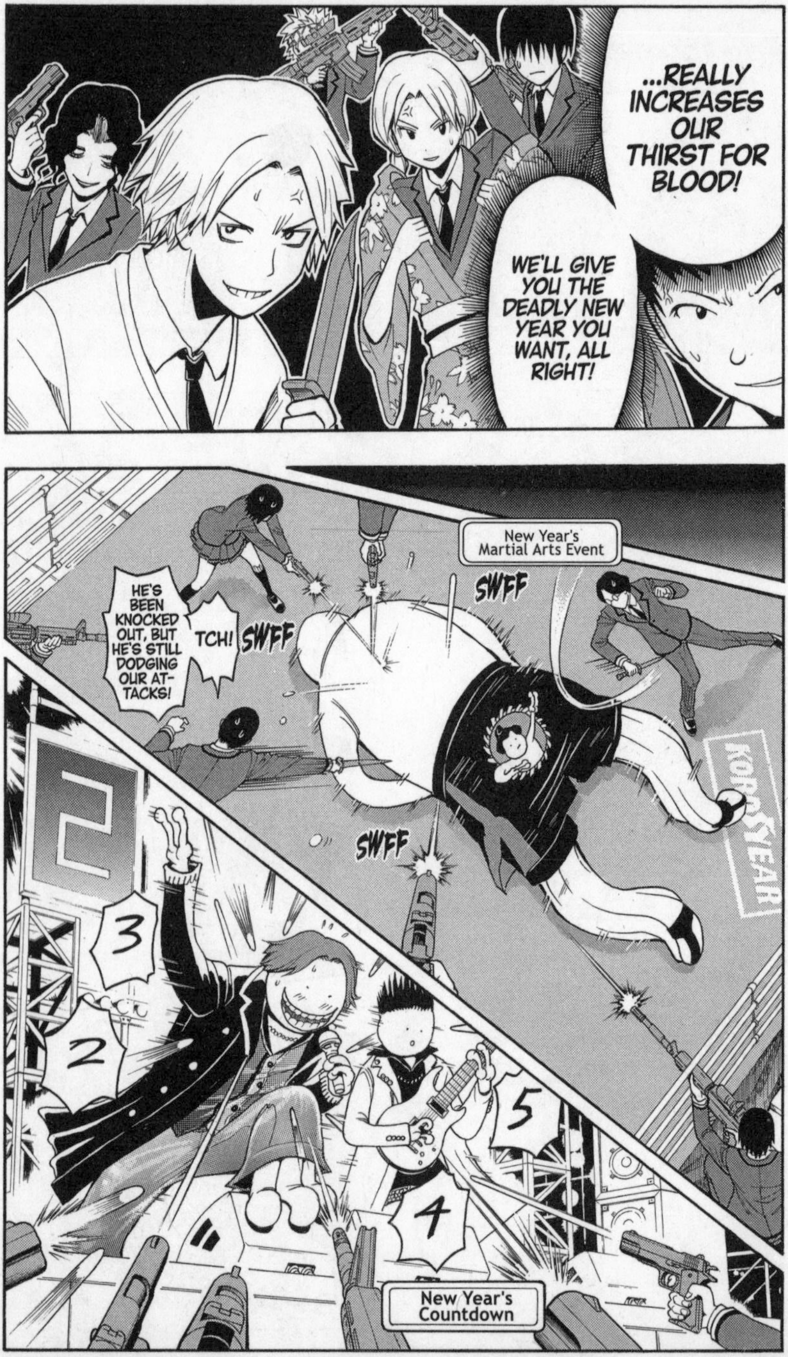
...REALLY INCREASES OUR THIRST FOR BLOOD!
WE'LL GIVE YOU THE DEADLY NEW YEAR YOU WANT, ALL RIGHT!
New Year's Martial Arts Event
SWFF
TCH!
HE'S BEEN KNOCKED OUT, BUT HE'S STILL DODGING OUR AT-TACKS!
SWFF
KORO YEAR
SWFF
5
3
4
2
New Year's Countdown

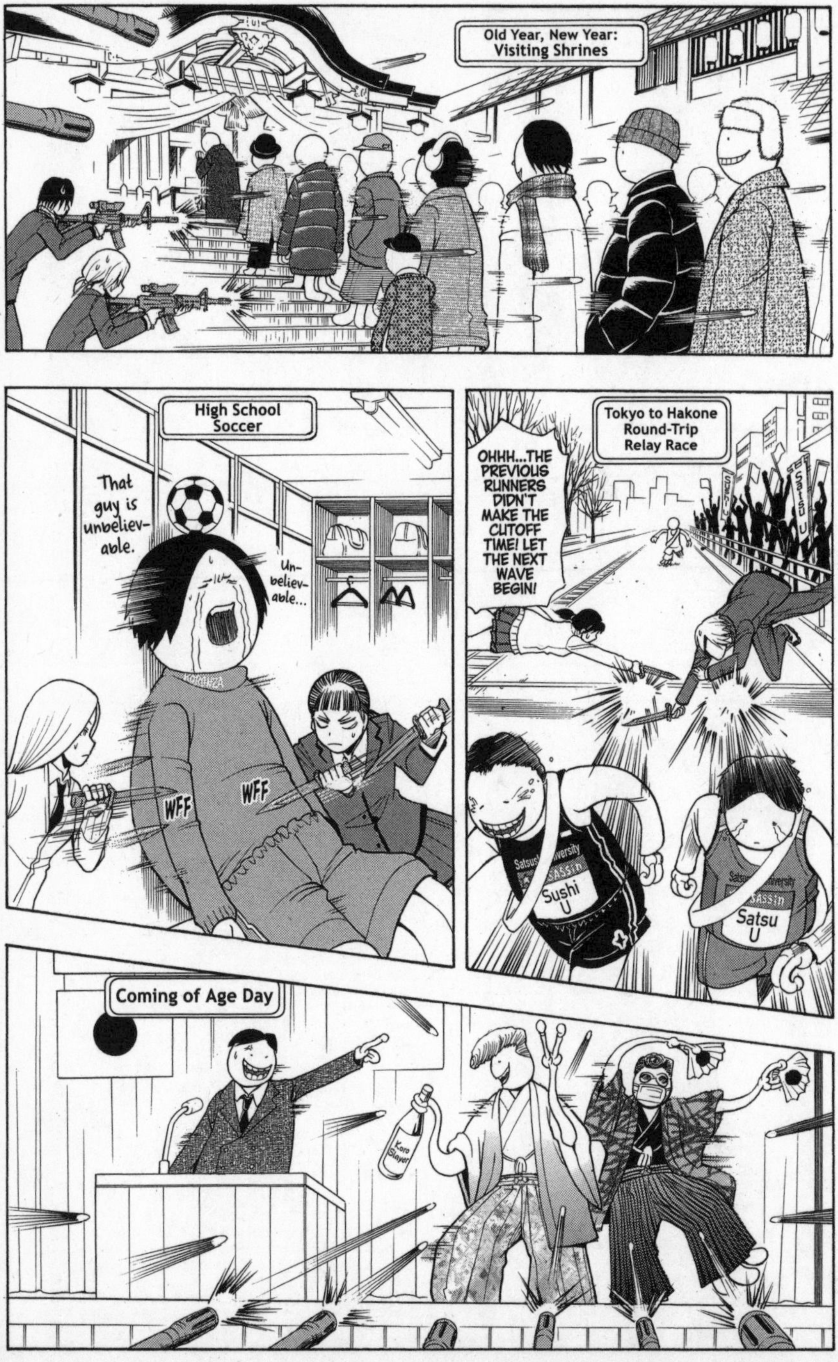
Old Year, New Year: Visiting Shrines
Tokyo to Hakone Round-Trip Relay Race
OHHH...THE PREVIOUS RUNNERS DIDN'T MAKE THE CUTOFF TIME! LET THE NEXT WAVE BEGIN!
Satsu U
Satsu U
Sushi U
Satsu U
High School Soccer
That guy is unbelievable.
Unbelievable...
WFF
WFF
Coming of Age Day
Koro Slayer

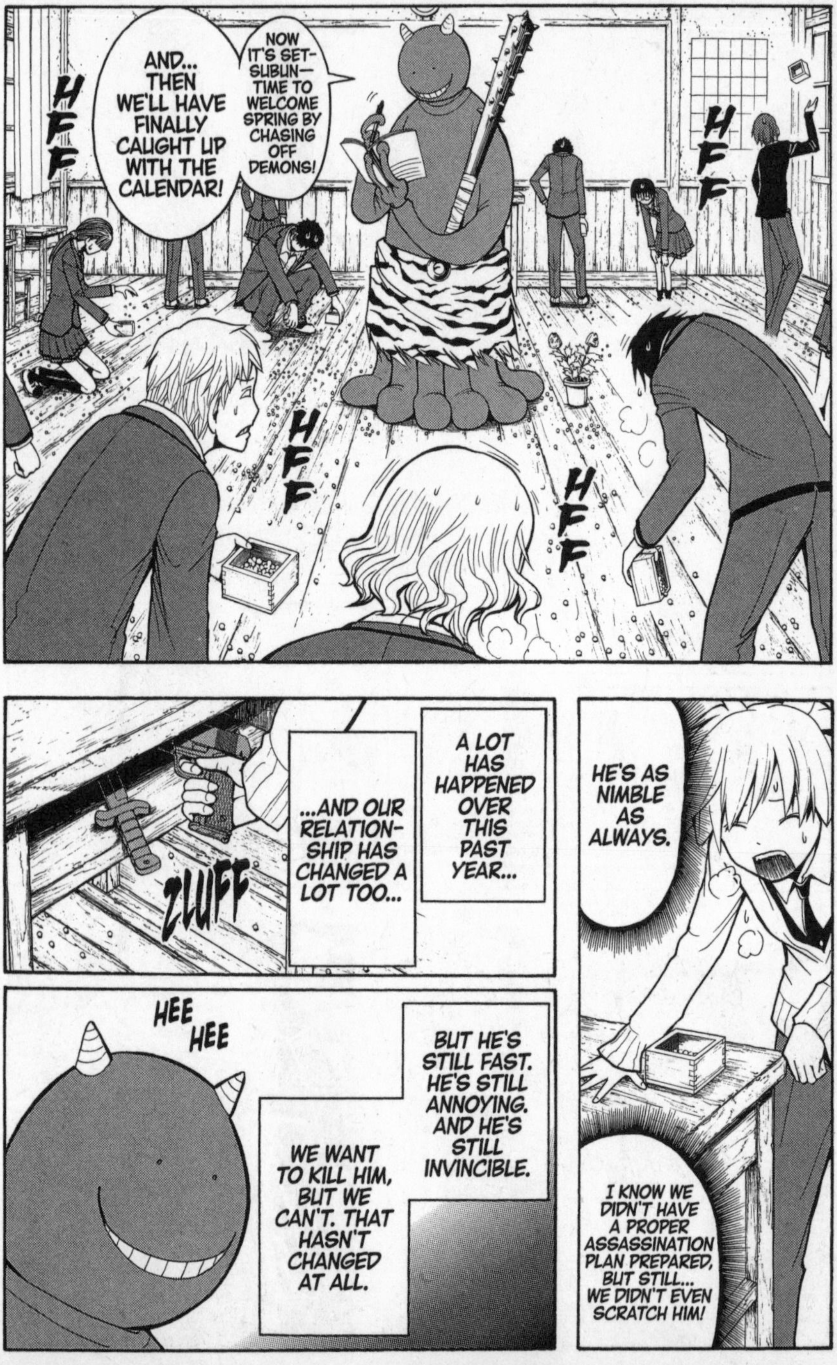
NOW IT'S SET-SUBUN—TIME TO WELCOME SPRING BY CHASING OFF DEMONS!
AND... THEN WE'LL HAVE FINALLY CAUGHT UP WITH THE CALENDAR!
HFF
HFF
HFF
HFF
HE'S AS NIMBLE AS ALWAYS.
I KNOW WE DIDN'T HAVE A PROPER ASSASSINATION PLAN PREPARED, BUT STILL... WE DIDN'T EVEN SCRATCH HIM!
A LOT HAS HAPPENED OVER THIS PAST YEAR...
...AND OUR RELATION-SHIP HAS CHANGED A LOT TOO...
ZLUFF
BUT HE'S STILL FAST. HE'S STILL ANNOYING. AND HE'S STILL INVINCIBLE.
WE WANT TO KILL HIM, BUT WE CAN'T. THAT HASN'T CHANGED AT ALL.
HEE HEE

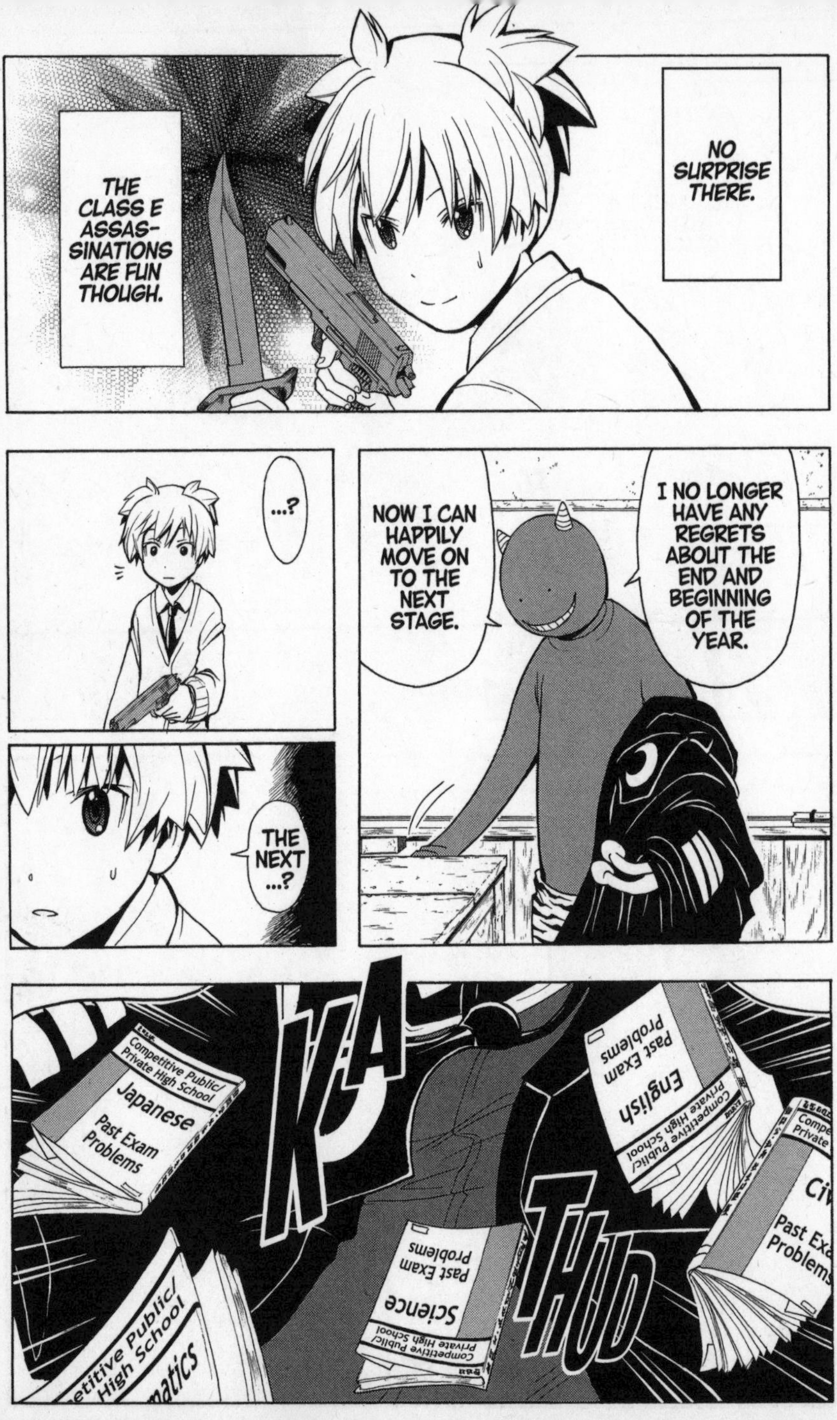
NO SURPRISE THERE.
THE CLASS E ASSAS-SINATIONS ARE FUN THOUGH.
I NO LONGER HAVE ANY REGRETS ABOUT THE END AND BEGINNING OF THE YEAR.
NOW I CAN HAPPILY MOVE ON TO THE NEXT STAGE.
...?
THE NEXT ...?
KA-THUD
Competitive Public/ Private High School English Past Exam Problems
Competitive Public/ Private High School Japanese Past Exam Problems
Past Exam Problems
Competitive Public/ Private High School Science Past Exam Problems
High School

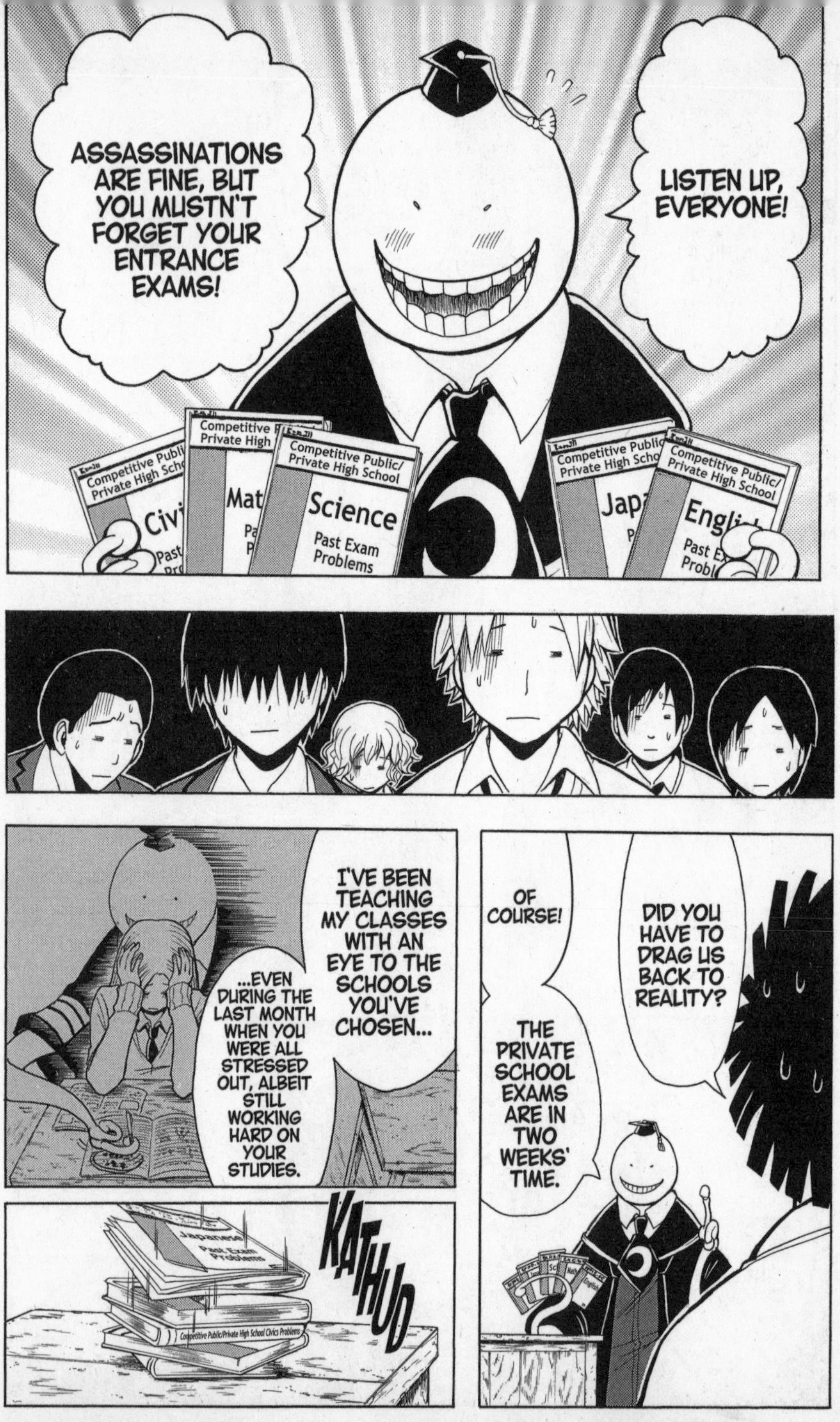

LISTEN UP, EVERYONE!
ASSASSINATIONS ARE FINE, BUT YOU MUSTN'T FORGET YOUR ENTRANCE EXAMS!
Competitive Public/ Private High School
Science
Past Exam Problems
Competitive Public/ Private High School
DID YOU HAVE TO DRAG US BACK TO REALITY?
OF COURSE!
THE PRIVATE SCHOOL EXAMS ARE IN TWO WEEKS' TIME.
I'VE BEEN TEACHING MY CLASSES WITH AN EYE TO THE SCHOOLS YOU'VE CHOSEN...
...EVEN DURING THE LAST MONTH WHEN YOU WERE ALL STRESSED OUT, ALBEIT STILL WORKING HARD ON YOUR STUDIES.
KATHUD
Japanese
Past Exam Problems
Competitive Public/Private High School Civics Problems

AND THEN, AFTER THE EXAM RESULTS ARE OUT... ...YOU'LL HAVE ANOTHER CAREER COUNSELING SESSION WITH ME.

Name	
School of Choice	
Career (First Choice)	
Career (Second Choice)	

WHAT FUTURE...

...WILL EACH OF YOU CHOOSE AFTER MOVING ON FROM CLASS E?

Attendance

Name	
School of Choice	
Career	
Career	

...!!

AND YOU HAVE ALSO...

...DECIDED TO QUIT YOUR ASSASSINA-TIONS AFTER GRADUATION.

YOU HAVE IN-FORMED ME...

...THAT MY CHANCES OF EXPLODING ARE NOT VERY HIGH.

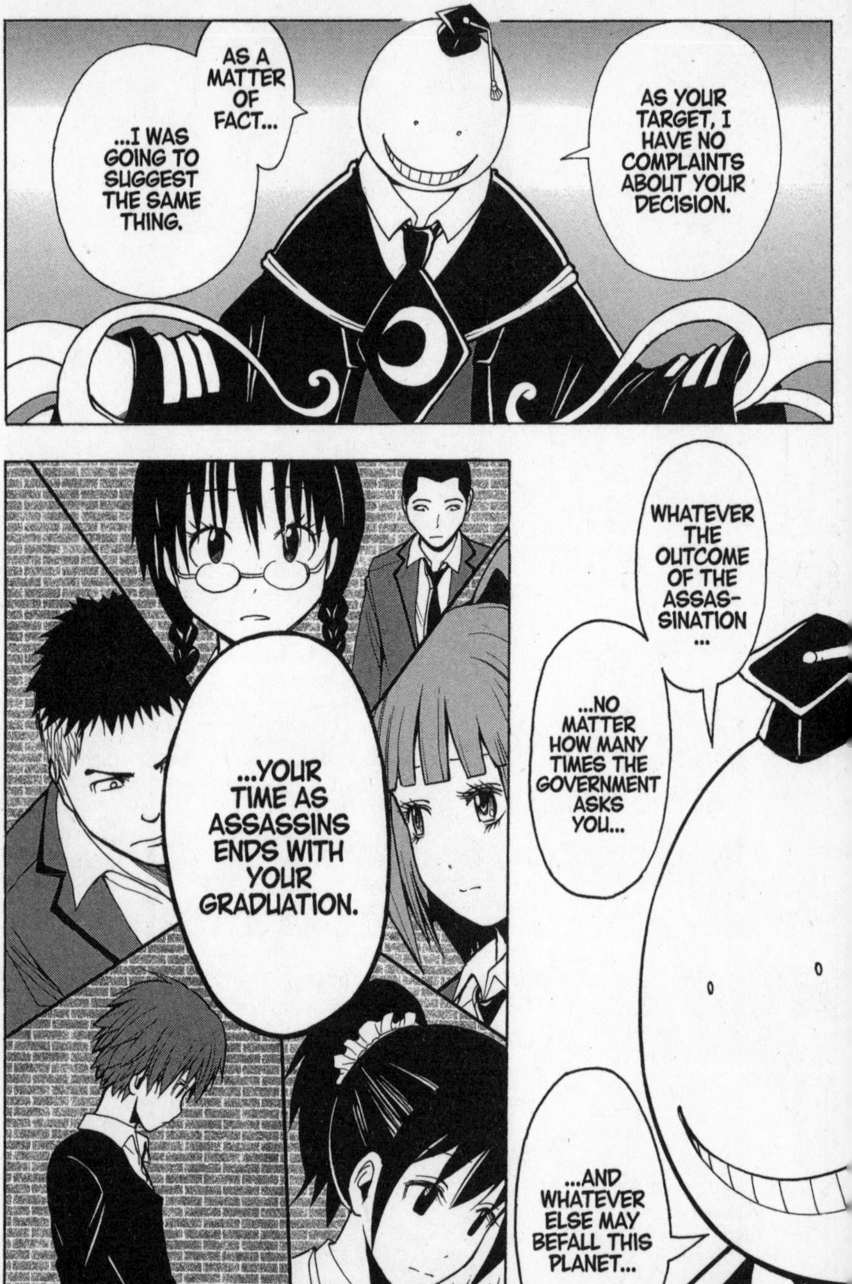
AS YOUR TARGET, I HAVE NO COMPLAINTS ABOUT YOUR DECISION.
AS A MATTER OF FACT...
...I WAS GOING TO SUGGEST THE SAME THING.
WHATEVER THE OUTCOME OF THE ASSAS-SINATION...
...NO MATTER HOW MANY TIMES THE GOVERNMENT ASKS YOU...
...AND WHATEVER ELSE MAY BEFALL THIS PLANET...
...YOUR TIME AS ASSASSINS ENDS WITH YOUR GRADUATION.

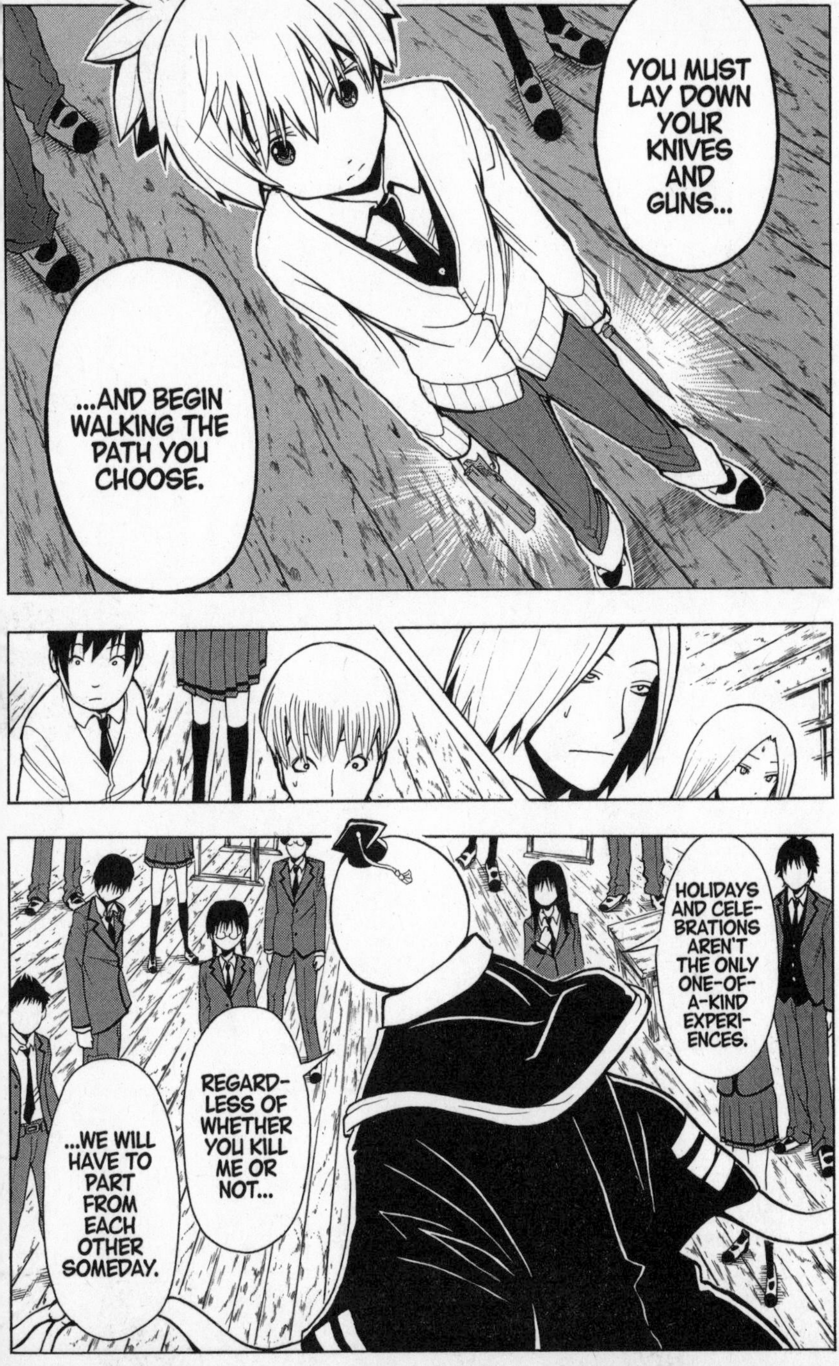
YOU MUST LAY DOWN YOUR KNIVES AND GUNS...
...AND BEGIN WALKING THE PATH YOU CHOOSE.
HOLIDAYS AND CELEBRATIONS AREN'T THE ONLY ONE-OF-A-KIND EXPERIENCES.
REGARDLESS OF WHETHER YOU KILL ME OR NOT...
...WE WILL HAVE TO PART FROM EACH OTHER SOMEDAY.

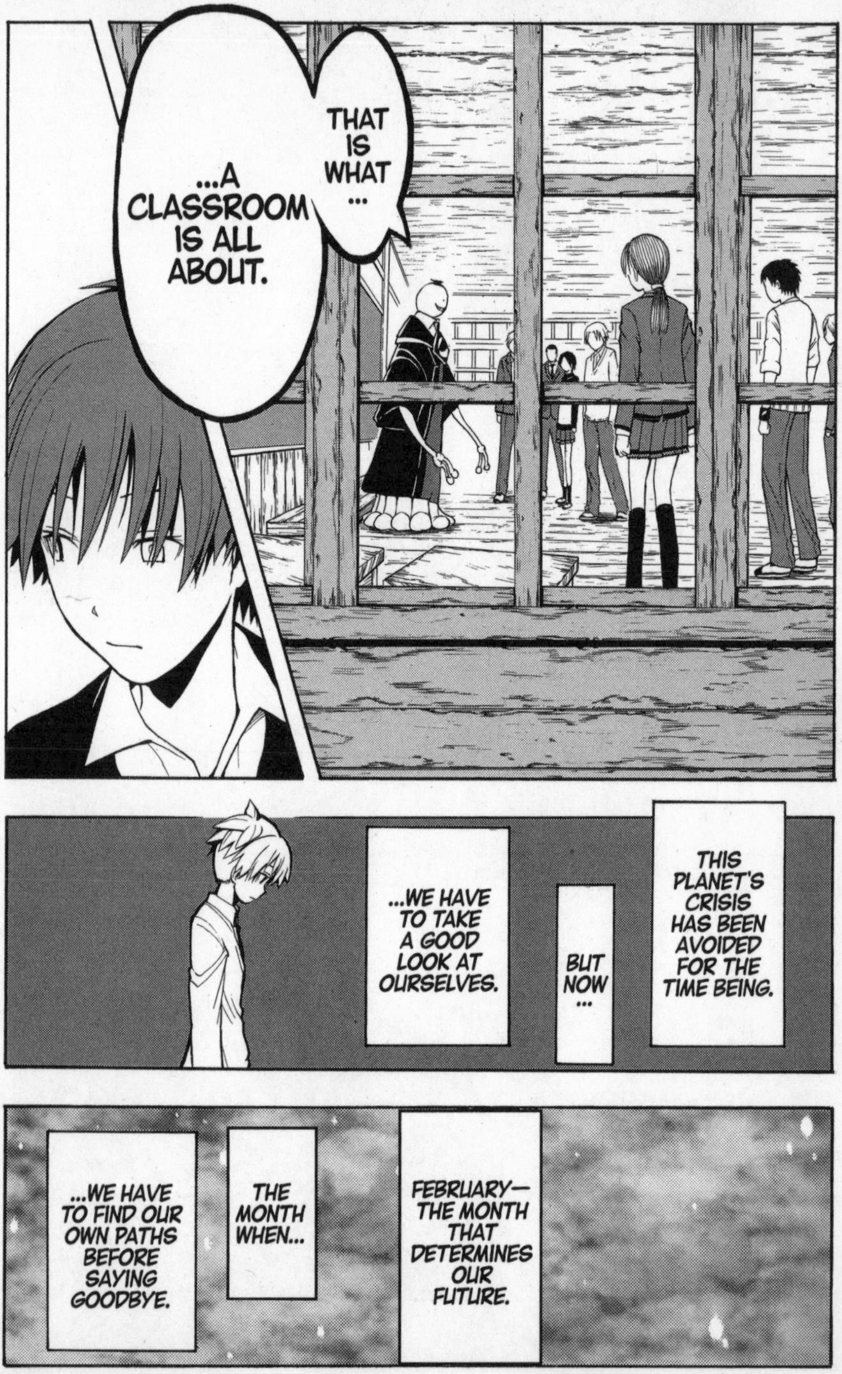
THAT IS WHAT...
...A CLASSROOM IS ALL ABOUT.
THIS PLANET'S CRISIS HAS BEEN AVOIDED FOR THE TIME BEING.
BUT NOW...
...WE HAVE TO TAKE A GOOD LOOK AT OURSELVES.
FEBRUARY—THE MONTH THAT DETERMINES OUR FUTURE.
THE MONTH WHEN...
...WE HAVE TO FIND OUR OWN PATHS BEFORE SAYING GOODBYE.

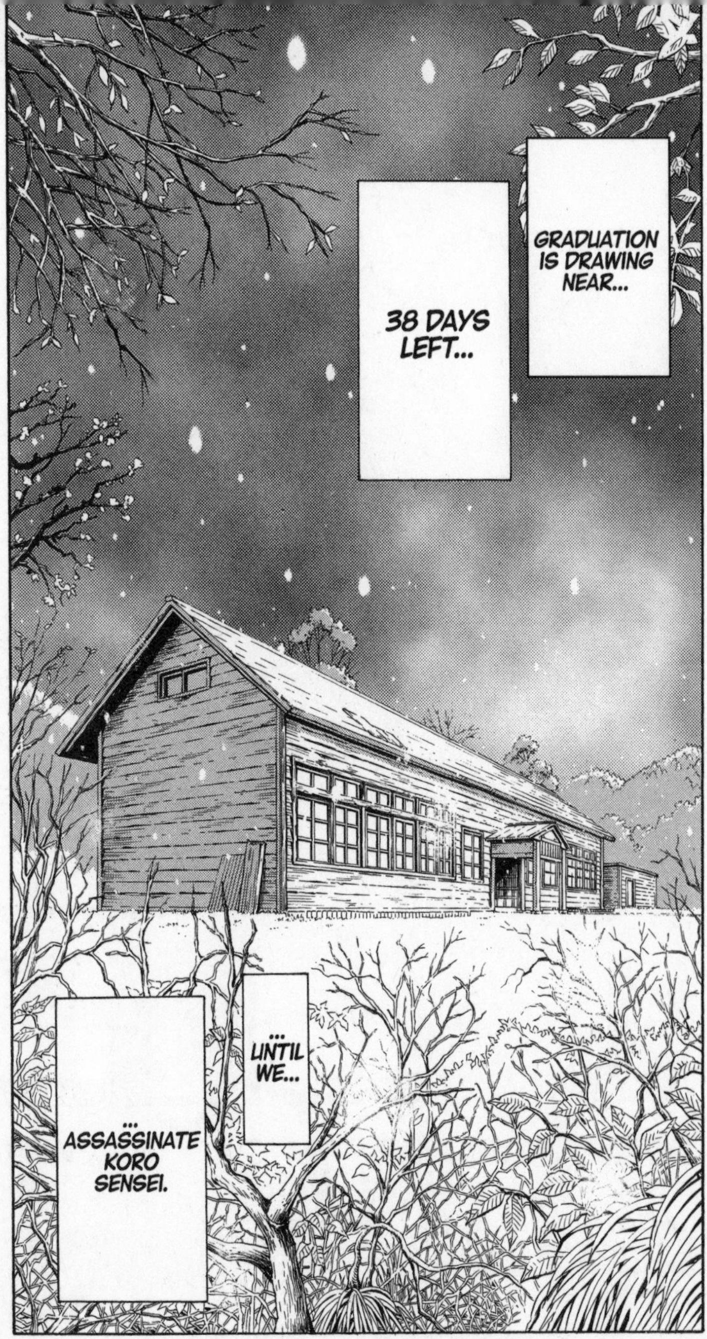
GRADUATION IS DRAWING NEAR...
38 DAYS LEFT...
...UNTIL WE...
...ASSASSINATE KORO SENSEI.

Far more events occurred in the real world than the manga...

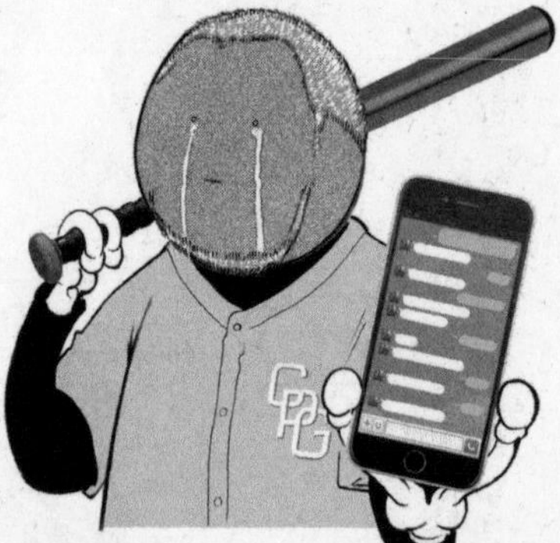
CPG

...at the beginning of 2016.

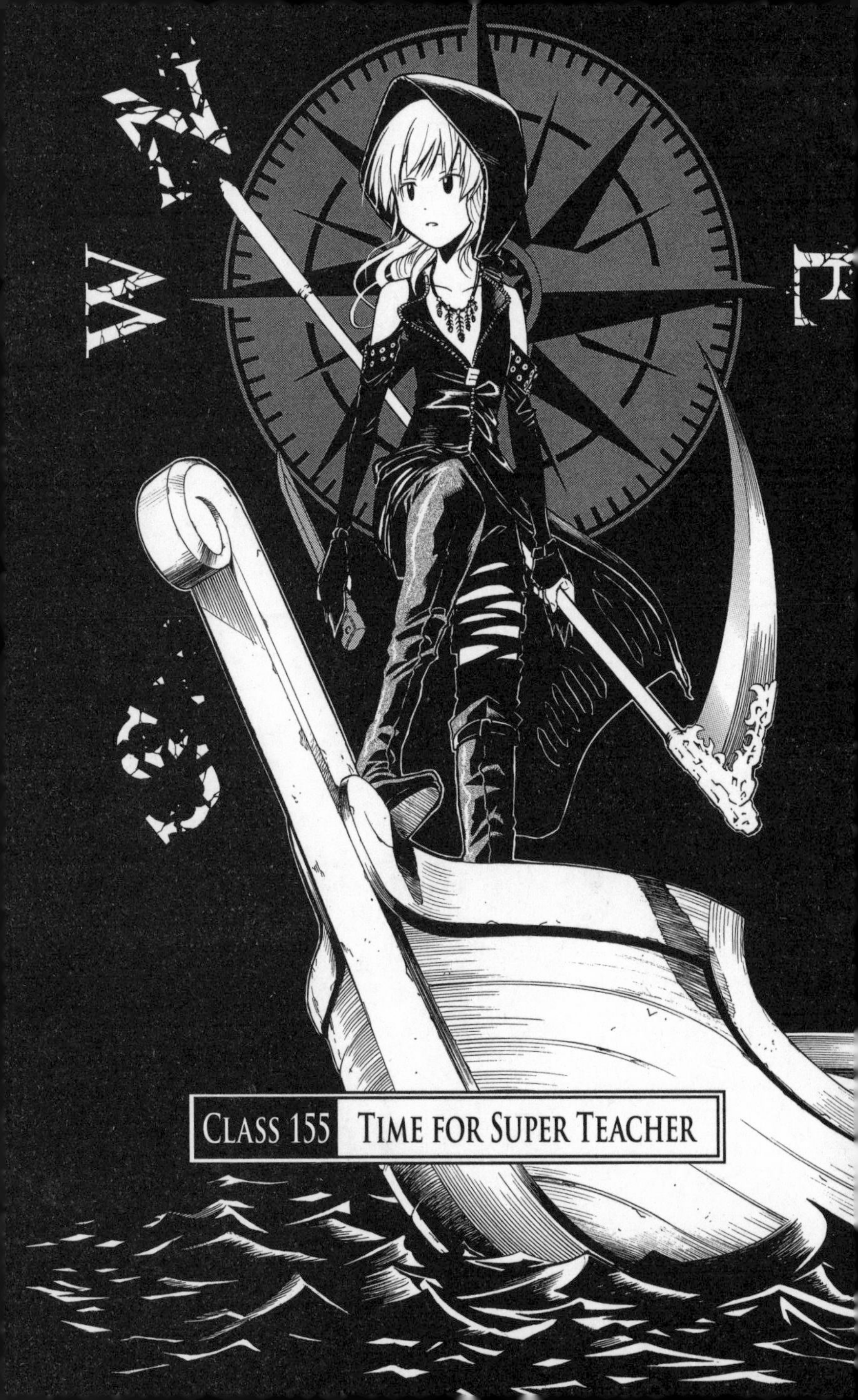

Class 155 Time for Super Teacher

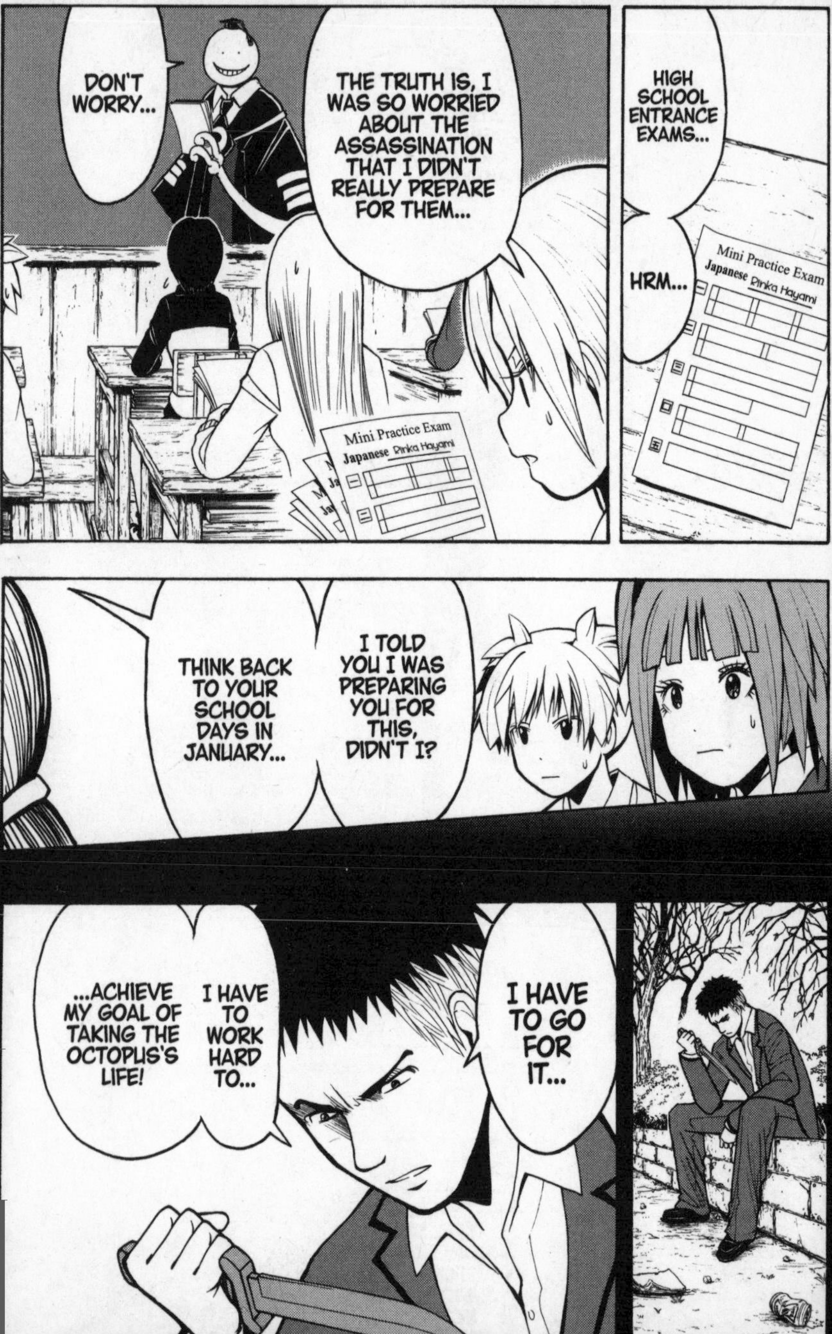
HIGH SCHOOL ENTRANCE EXAMS...
HRM...
Mini Practice Exam
Japanese Rinka Hayami
THE TRUTH IS, I WAS SO WORRIED ABOUT THE ASSASSINATION THAT I DIDN'T REALLY PREPARE FOR THEM...
DON'T WORRY...
Mini Practice Exam
Japanese Rinka Hayami
I TOLD YOU I WAS PREPARING YOU FOR THIS, DIDN'T I?
THINK BACK TO YOUR SCHOOL DAYS IN JANUARY...
I HAVE TO GO FOR IT...
I HAVE TO WORK HARD TO...
...ACHIEVE MY GOAL OF TAKING THE OCTOPUS'S LIFE!

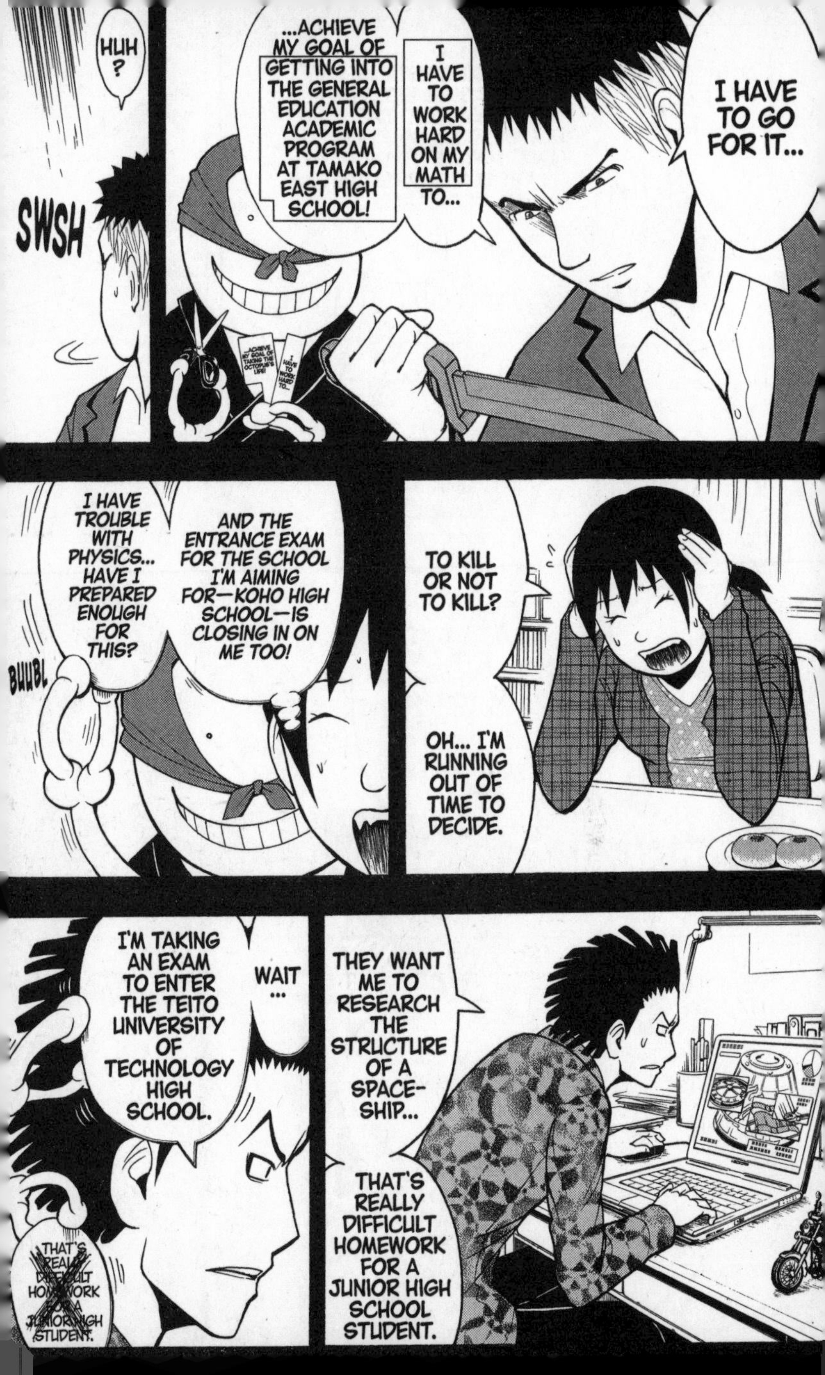
I HAVE TO GO FOR IT...
I HAVE TO WORK HARD ON MY MATH TO...
...ACHIEVE MY GOAL OF GETTING INTO THE GENERAL EDUCATION ACADEMIC PROGRAM AT TAMAKO EAST HIGH SCHOOL!
I HAVE TO WORK HARD TO...
...ACHIEVE MY GOAL OF TAKING THE OCTOPUS'S LIFE!
SWSH
HUH?
TO KILL OR NOT TO KILL?
OH... I'M RUNNING OUT OF TIME TO DECIDE.
AND THE ENTRANCE EXAM FOR THE SCHOOL I'M AIMING FOR—KOHO HIGH SCHOOL—IS CLOSING IN ON ME TOO!
I HAVE TROUBLE WITH PHYSICS... HAVE I PREPARED ENOUGH FOR THIS?
BUUBL
THEY WANT ME TO RESEARCH THE STRUCTURE OF A SPACE-SHIP...
THAT'S REALLY DIFFICULT HOMEWORK FOR A JUNIOR HIGH SCHOOL STUDENT.
WAIT...
I'M TAKING AN EXAM TO ENTER THE TEITO UNIVERSITY OF TECHNOLOGY HIGH SCHOOL.
THAT'S REALLY DIFFICULT HOMEWORK FOR A JUNIOR HIGH STUDENT.

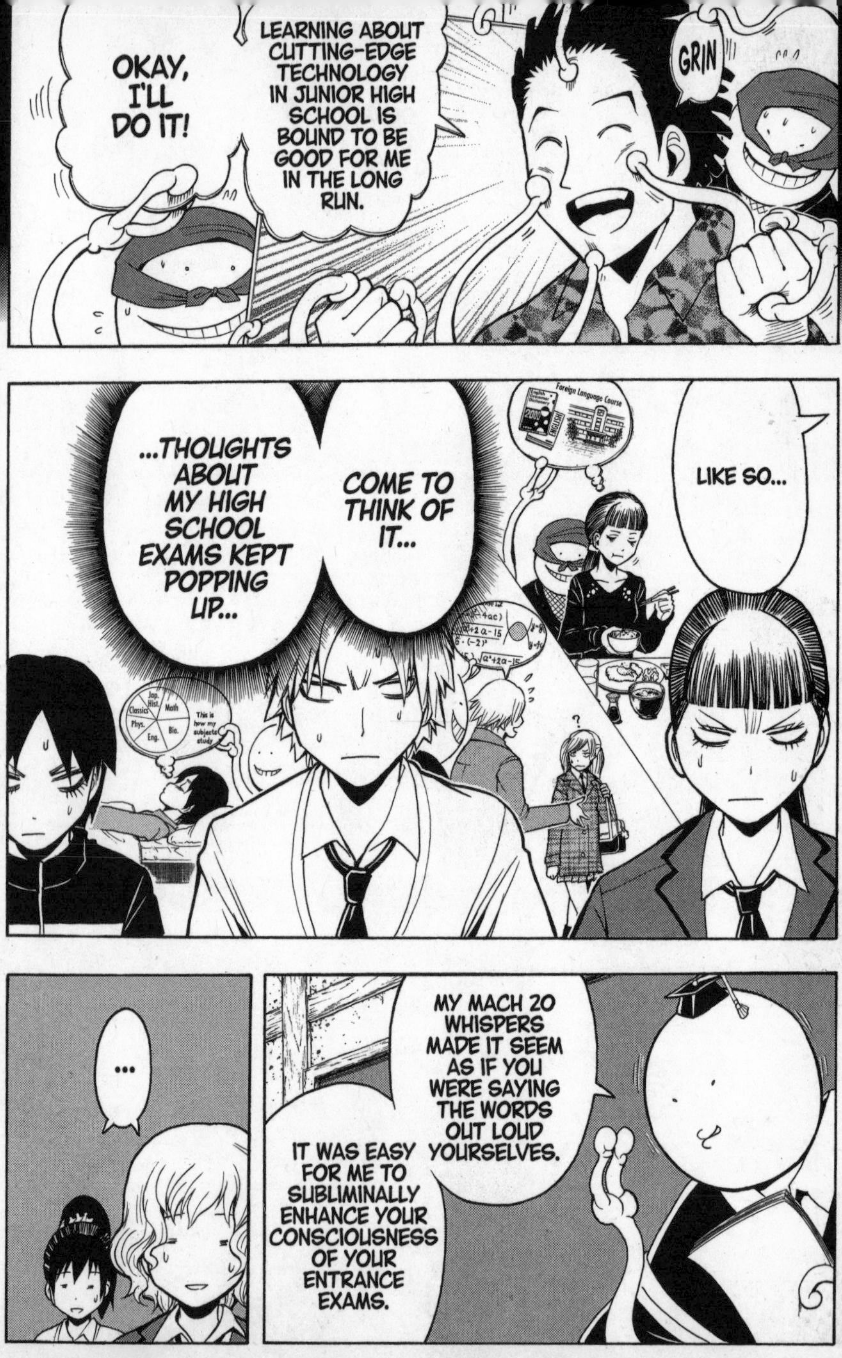
GRIN
LEARNING ABOUT CUTTING-EDGE TECHNOLOGY IN JUNIOR HIGH SCHOOL IS BOUND TO BE GOOD FOR ME IN THE LONG RUN.
OKAY, I'LL DO IT!
LIKE SO...
Foreign Language Course
ENGLISH
COME TO THINK OF IT...
...THOUGHTS ABOUT MY HIGH SCHOOL EXAMS KEPT POPPING UP...
Jap. Hist.
Math
Classics
Phys.
Eng.
Bio.
This is how my subjects study
MY MACH 20 WHISPERS MADE IT SEEM AS IF YOU WERE SAYING THE WORDS OUT LOUD YOURSELVES.
IT WAS EASY FOR ME TO SUBLIMINALLY ENHANCE YOUR CONSCIOUSNESS OF YOUR ENTRANCE EXAMS.
...

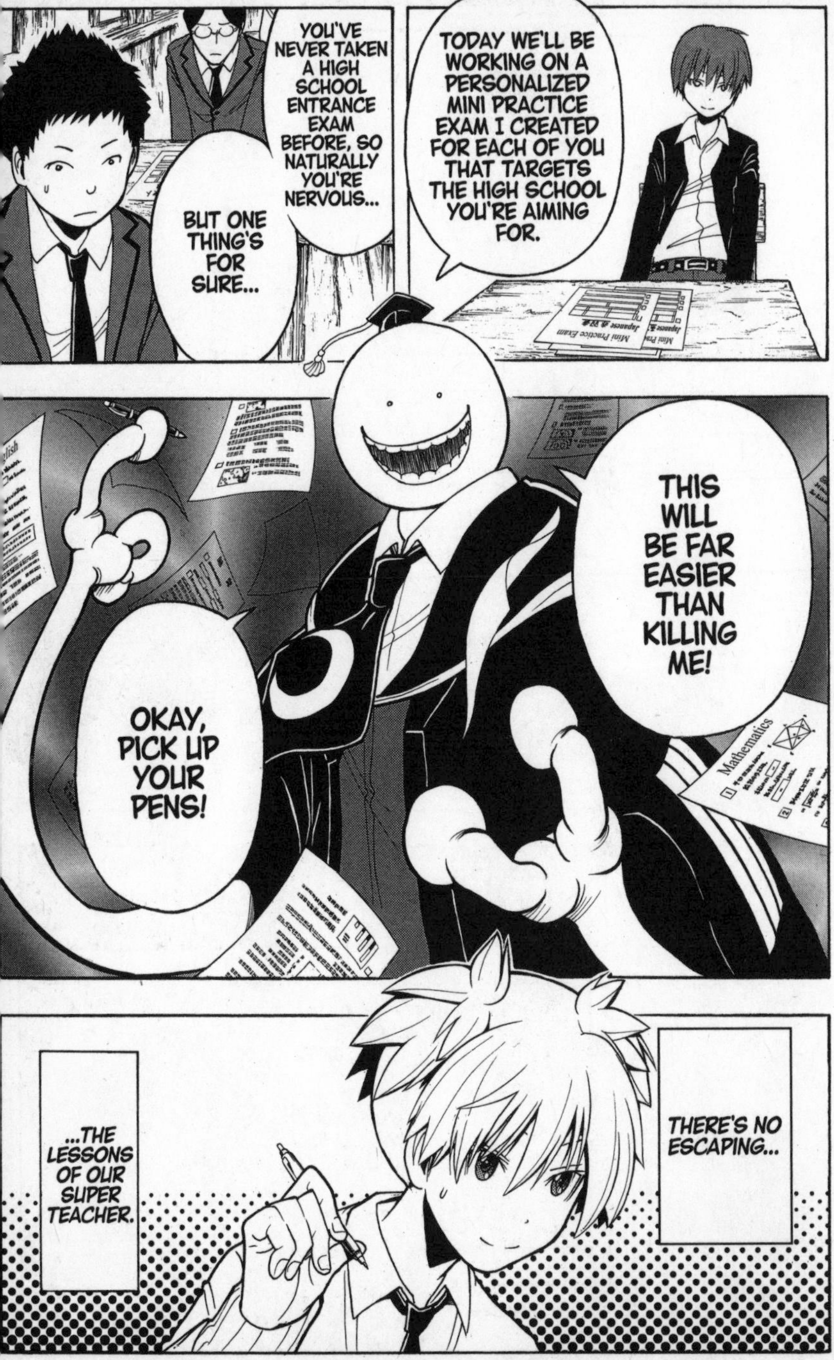
TODAY WE'LL BE WORKING ON A PERSONALIZED MINI PRACTICE EXAM I CREATED FOR EACH OF YOU THAT TARGETS THE HIGH SCHOOL YOU'RE AIMING FOR.
YOU'VE NEVER TAKEN A HIGH SCHOOL ENTRANCE EXAM BEFORE, SO NATURALLY YOU'RE NERVOUS...
BUT ONE THING'S FOR SURE...
THIS WILL BE FAR EASIER THAN KILLING ME!
OKAY, PICK UP YOUR PENS!
Mathematics
THERE'S NO ESCAPING...
...THE LESSONS OF OUR SUPER TEACHER.

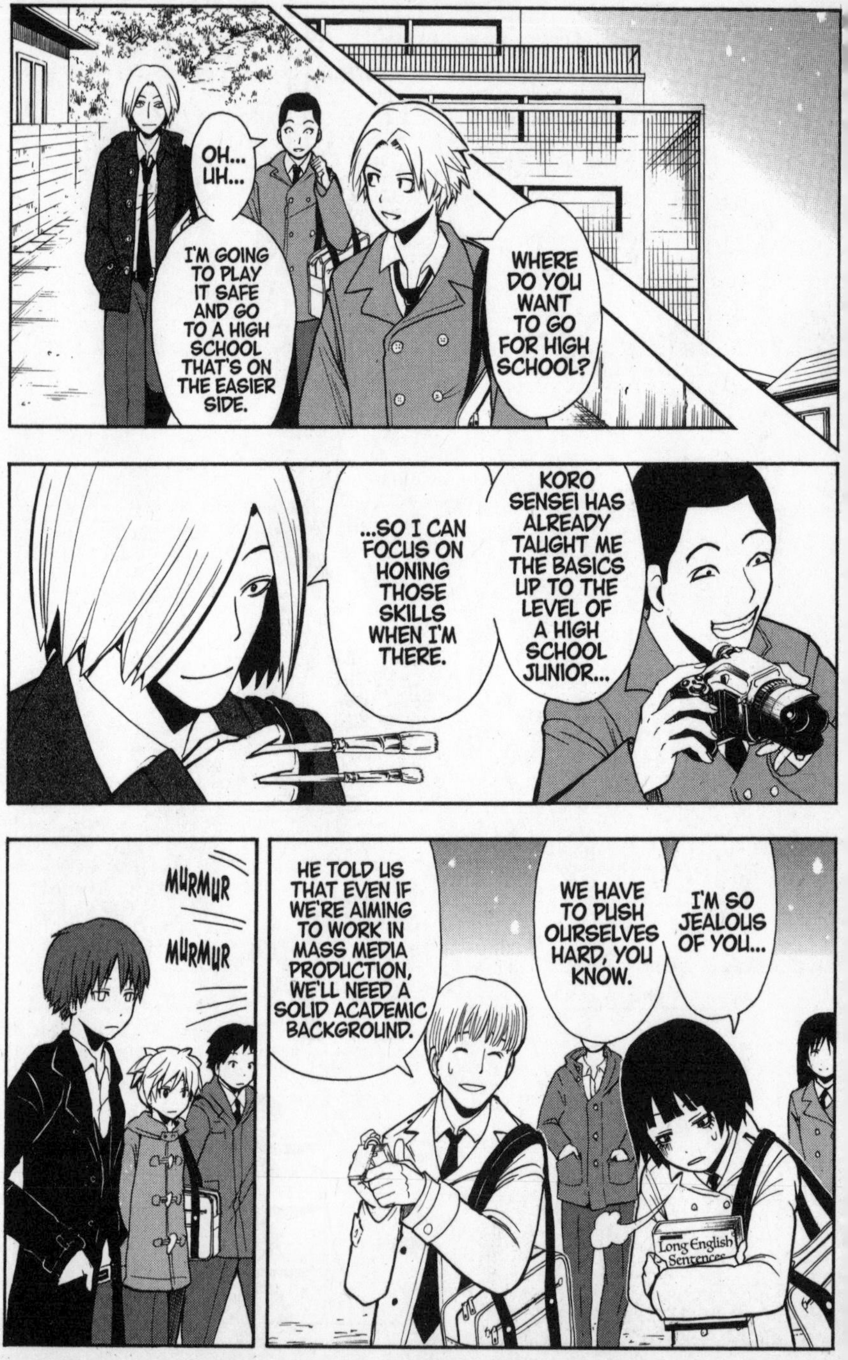
WHERE DO YOU WANT TO GO FOR HIGH SCHOOL?
OH... UH...
I'M GOING TO PLAY IT SAFE AND GO TO A HIGH SCHOOL THAT'S ON THE EASIER SIDE.
KORO SENSEI HAS ALREADY TAUGHT ME THE BASICS UP TO THE LEVEL OF A HIGH SCHOOL JUNIOR...
...SO I CAN FOCUS ON HONING THOSE SKILLS WHEN I'M THERE.
I'M SO JEALOUS OF YOU...
WE HAVE TO PUSH OURSELVES HARD, YOU KNOW.
HE TOLD US THAT EVEN IF WE'RE AIMING TO WORK IN MASS MEDIA PRODUCTION, WE'LL NEED A SOLID ACADEMIC BACKGROUND.
Long English Sentences
MURMUR
MURMUR

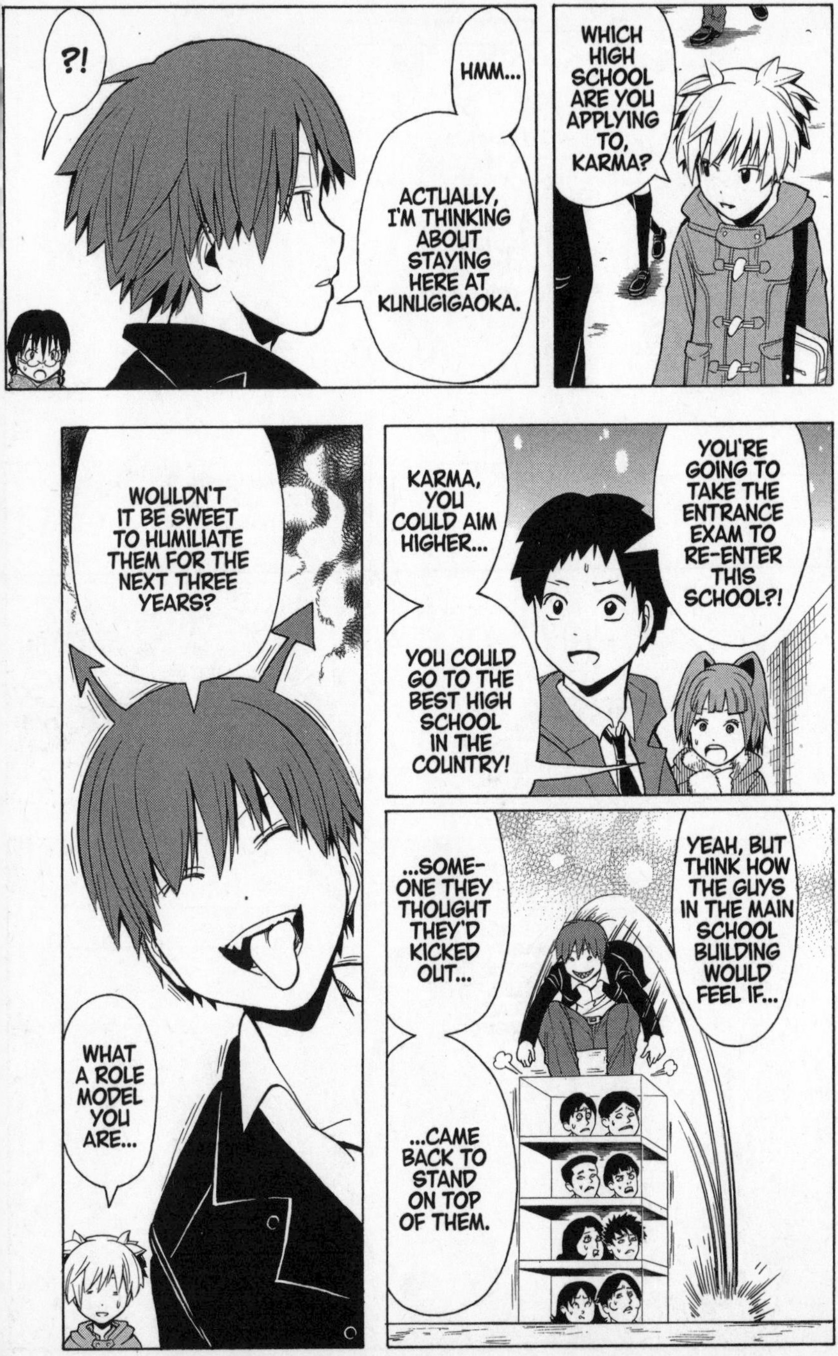
WHICH HIGH SCHOOL ARE YOU APPLYING TO, KARMA?
HMM...
ACTUALLY, I'M THINKING ABOUT STAYING HERE AT KUNUGIGAOKA.
?!
YOU'RE GOING TO TAKE THE ENTRANCE EXAM TO RE-ENTER THIS SCHOOL?!
KARMA, YOU COULD AIM HIGHER...
YOU COULD GO TO THE BEST HIGH SCHOOL IN THE COUNTRY!
YEAH, BUT THINK HOW THE GUYS IN THE MAIN SCHOOL BUILDING WOULD FEEL IF...
...SOME-ONE THEY THOUGHT THEY'D KICKED OUT...
...CAME BACK TO STAND ON TOP OF THEM.
WOULDN'T IT BE SWEET TO HUMILIATE THEM FOR THE NEXT THREE YEARS?
WHAT A ROLE MODEL YOU ARE...

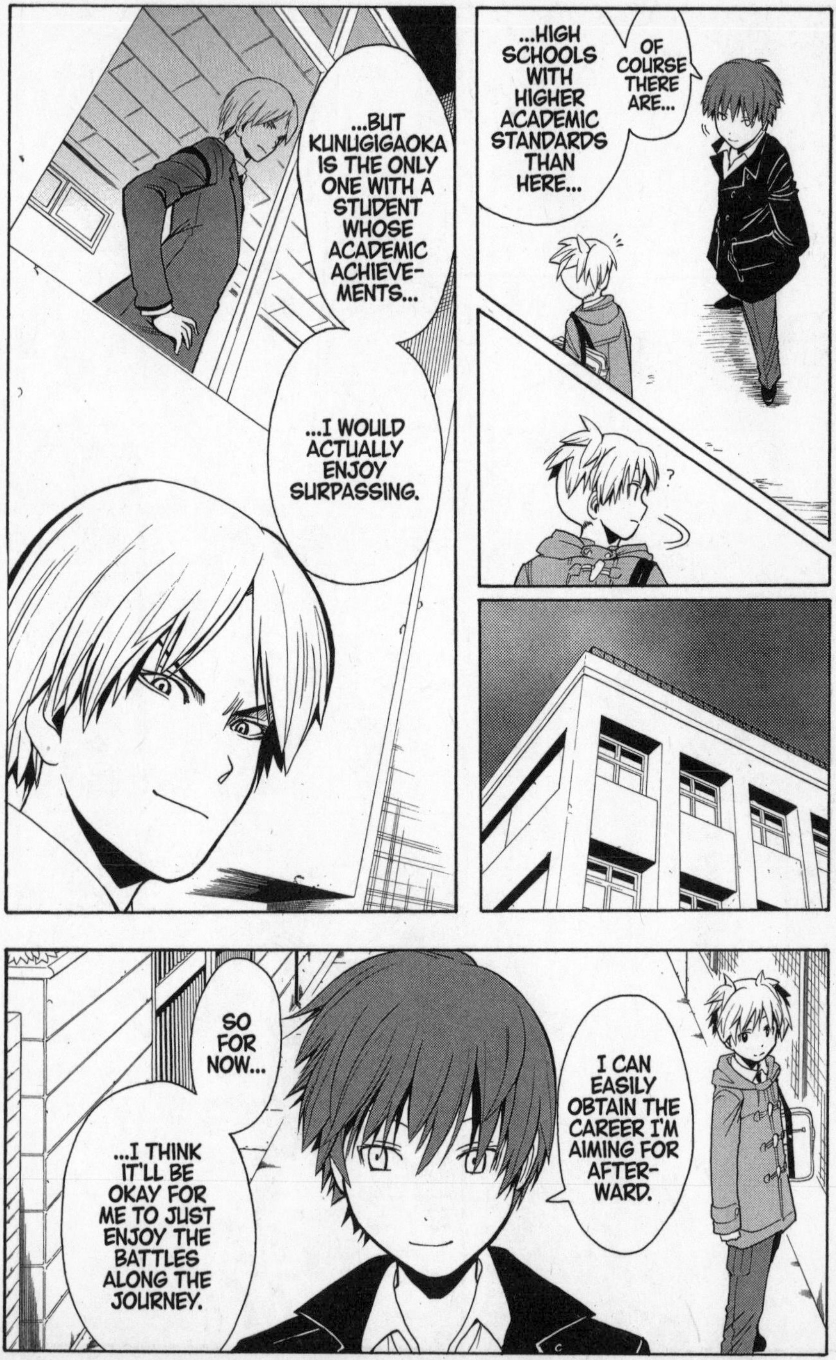
OF COURSE THERE ARE...
...HIGH SCHOOLS WITH HIGHER ACADEMIC STANDARDS THAN HERE...
...BUT KUNUGIGAOKA IS THE ONLY ONE WITH A STUDENT WHOSE ACADEMIC ACHIEVEMENTS...
...I WOULD ACTUALLY ENJOY SURPASSING.
I CAN EASILY OBTAIN THE CAREER I'M AIMING FOR AFTERWARD.
SO FOR NOW...
...I THINK IT'LL BE OKAY FOR ME TO JUST ENJOY THE BATTLES ALONG THE JOURNEY.

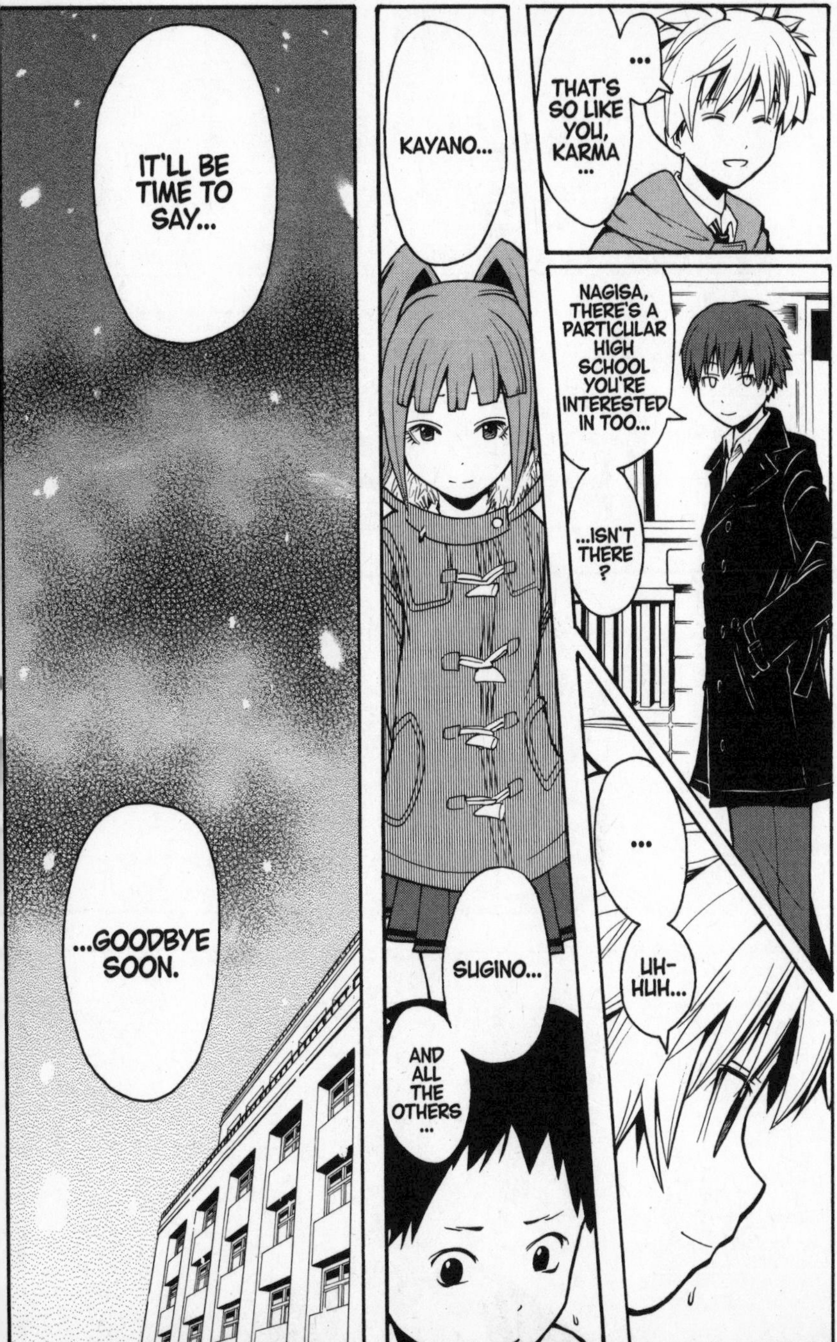
... THAT'S SO LIKE YOU, KARMA ...
NAGISA, THERE'S A PARTICULAR HIGH SCHOOL YOU'RE INTERESTED IN TOO...
...ISN'T THERE?
...
UH-HUH...
KAYANO...
SUGINO...
AND ALL THE OTHERS ...
IT'LL BE TIME TO SAY...
...GOODBYE SOON.

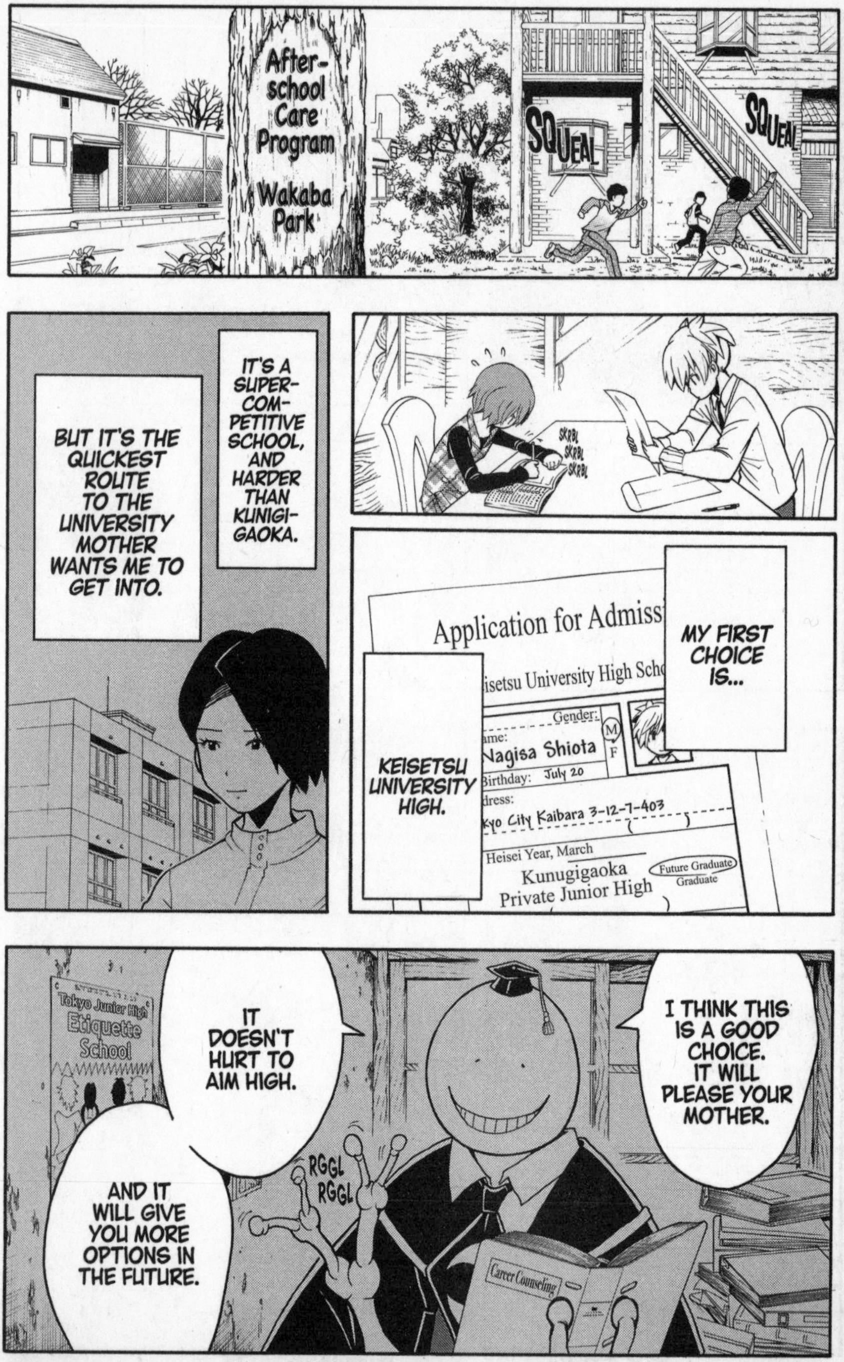
SQUEAL
SQUEAL
After-school Care Program
Wakaba Park
SKRBL SKRBL SKRBL
MY FIRST CHOICE IS...
KEISETSU UNIVERSITY HIGH.
Application for Admissi
eisetsu University High Scho
Gender:
ame:
Nagisa Shiota
M
F
Birthday: July 20
dress:
kyo City Kaibara 3-12-7-403
Heisei Year, March
Kunugigaoka Private Junior High
Future Graduate
Graduate
IT'S A SUPER-COMPETITIVE SCHOOL, AND HARDER THAN KUNIGIGAOKA.
BUT IT'S THE QUICKEST ROUTE TO THE UNIVERSITY MOTHER WANTS ME TO GET INTO.
I THINK THIS IS A GOOD CHOICE. IT WILL PLEASE YOUR MOTHER.
IT DOESN'T HURT TO AIM HIGH.
AND IT WILL GIVE YOU MORE OPTIONS IN THE FUTURE.
RGGL RGGL
Career Counseling
Tokyo Junior High
Etiquette School

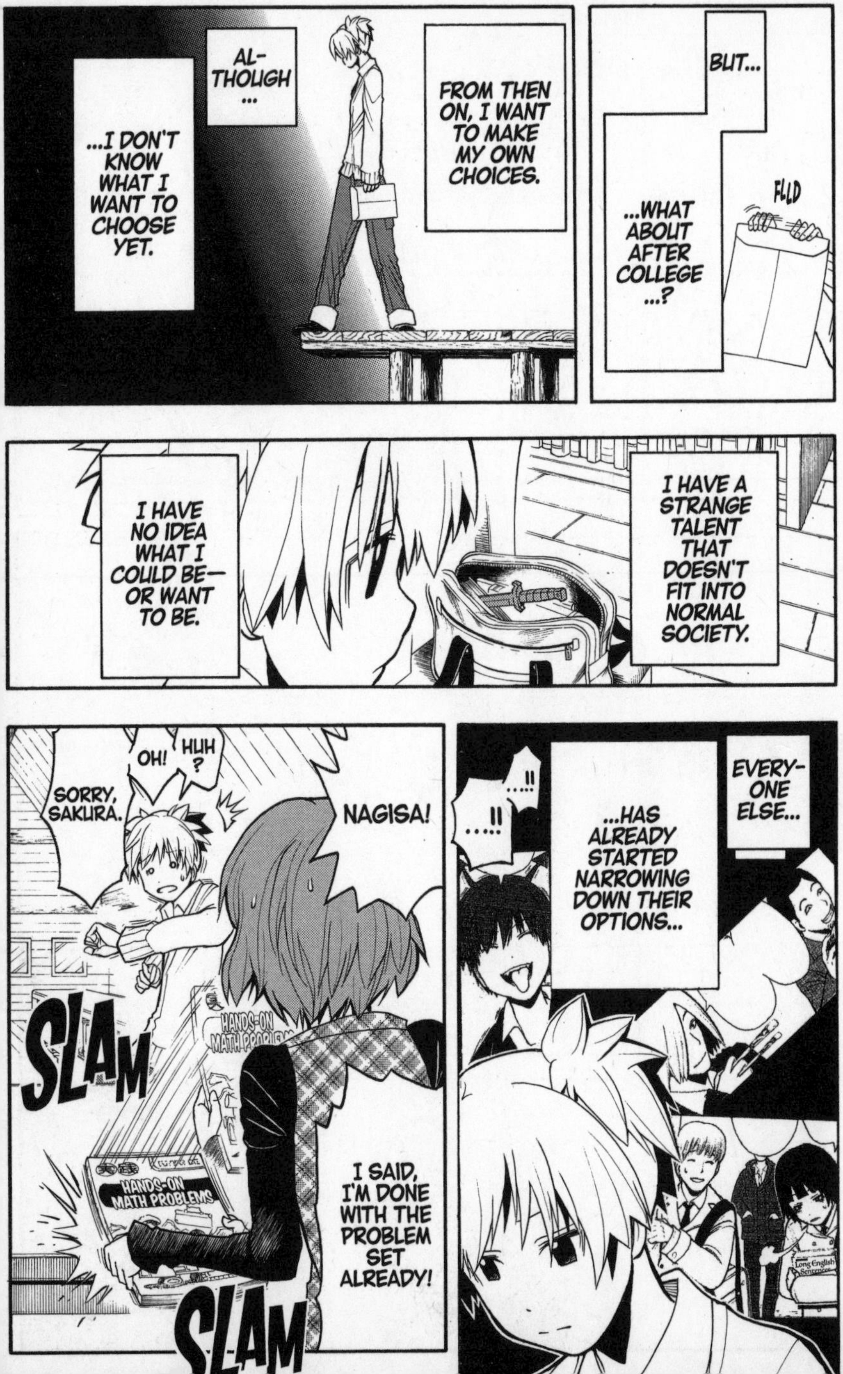
BUT...
...WHAT ABOUT AFTER COLLEGE ...?
FLLD
FROM THEN ON, I WANT TO MAKE MY OWN CHOICES.
ALTHOUGH...
...I DON'T KNOW WHAT I WANT TO CHOOSE YET.
I HAVE A STRANGE TALENT THAT DOESN'T FIT INTO NORMAL SOCIETY.
I HAVE NO IDEA WHAT I COULD BE—OR WANT TO BE.
EVERYONE ELSE...
...HAS ALREADY STARTED NARROWING DOWN THEIR OPTIONS...
....!!
....!!
Long English Sentences
NAGISA!
HUH?
OH!
SORRY, SAKURA.
HANDS-ON MATH PROBLEMS
SLAM
I SAID, I'M DONE WITH THE PROBLEM SET ALREADY!
HANDS-ON MATH PROBLEMS
SLAM

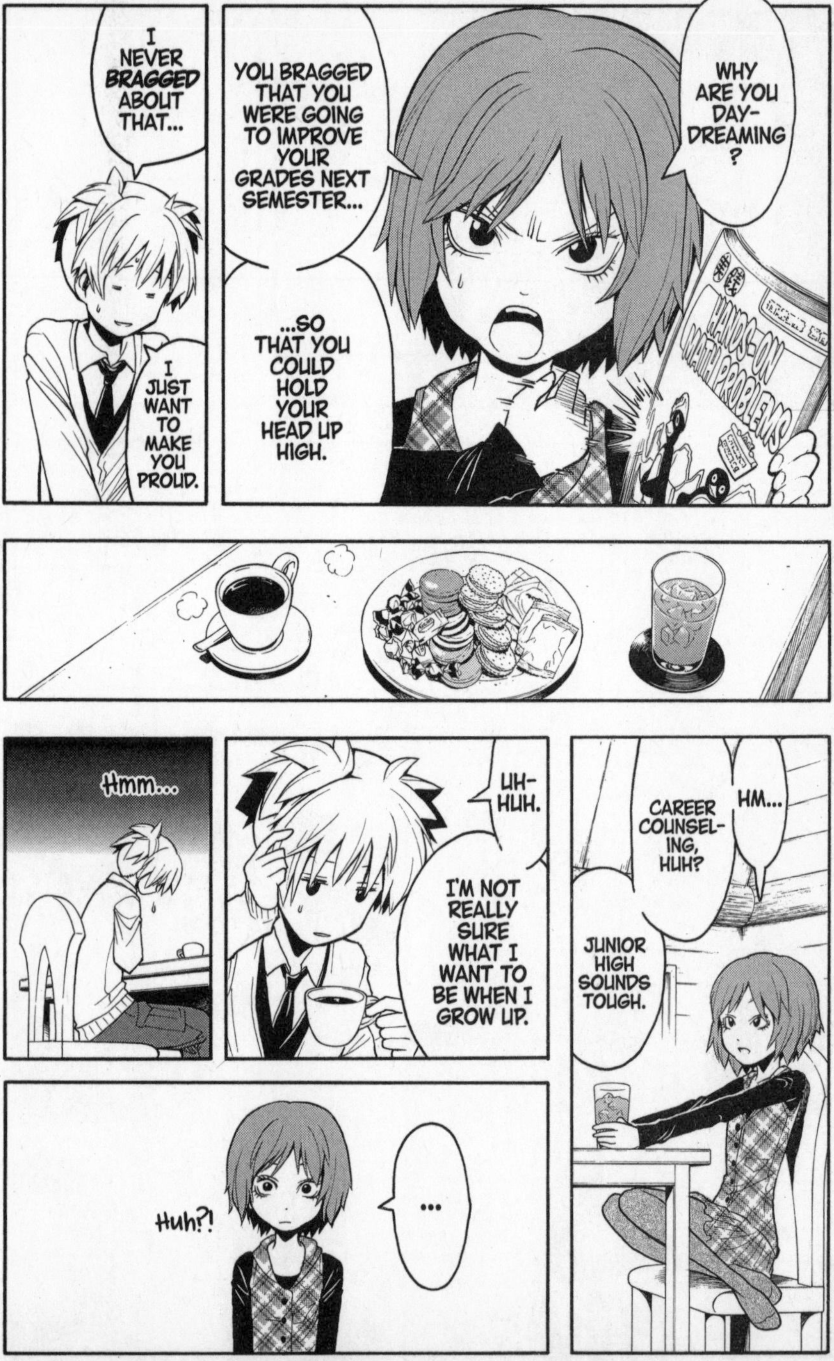
WHY ARE YOU DAY-DREAMING?
YOU BRAGGED THAT YOU WERE GOING TO IMPROVE YOUR GRADES NEXT SEMESTER...
...SO THAT YOU COULD HOLD YOUR HEAD UP HIGH.
HANDS-ON MATH PROBLEMS
I NEVER BRAGGED ABOUT THAT...
I JUST WANT TO MAKE YOU PROUD.
HM...
CAREER COUNSEL-ING, HUH?
JUNIOR HIGH SOUNDS TOUGH.
UH-HUH.
I'M NOT REALLY SURE WHAT I WANT TO BE WHEN I GROW UP.
Hmm...
...
Huh?!

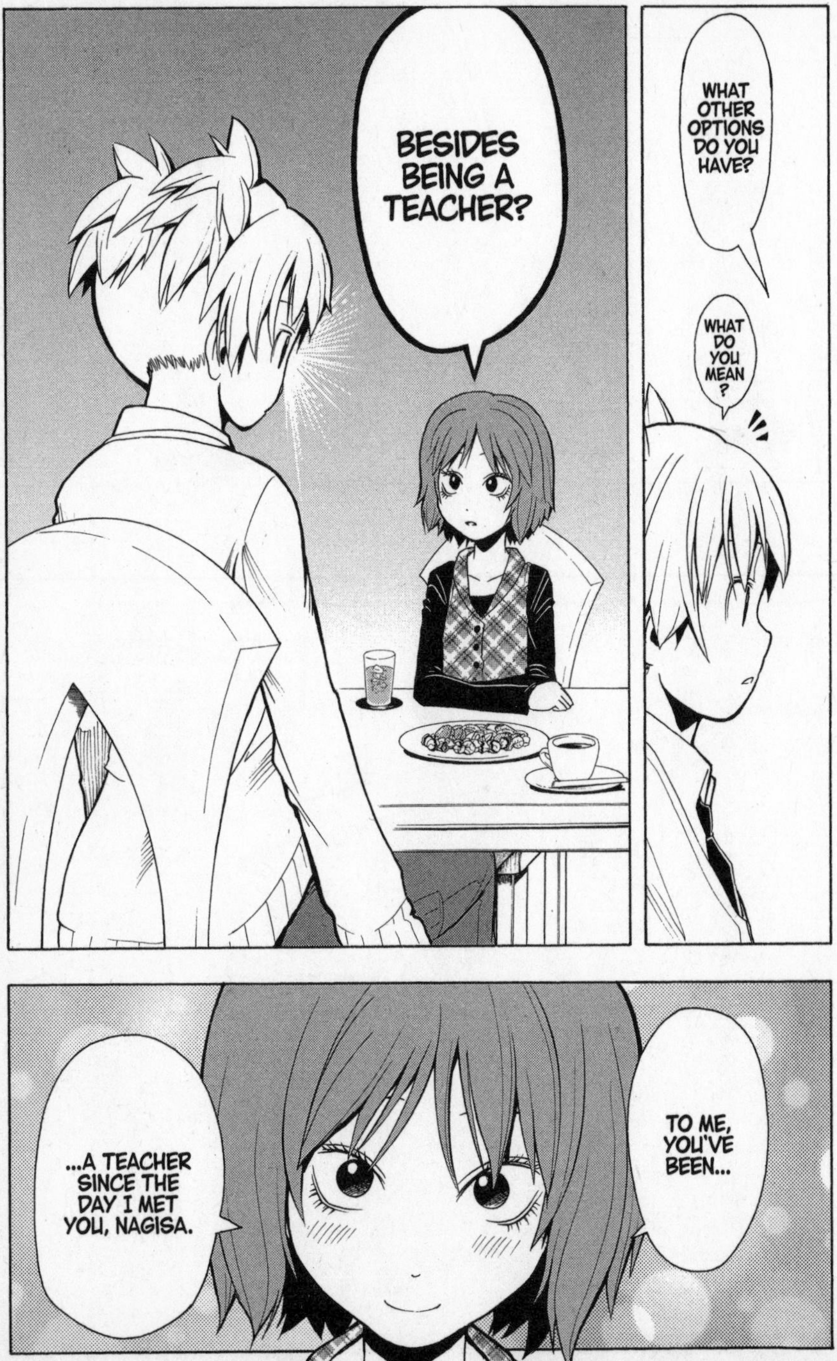
WHAT OTHER OPTIONS DO YOU HAVE?
WHAT DO YOU MEAN?
BESIDES BEING A TEACHER?
TO ME, YOU'VE BEEN...
...A TEACHER SINCE THE DAY I MET YOU, NAGISA.

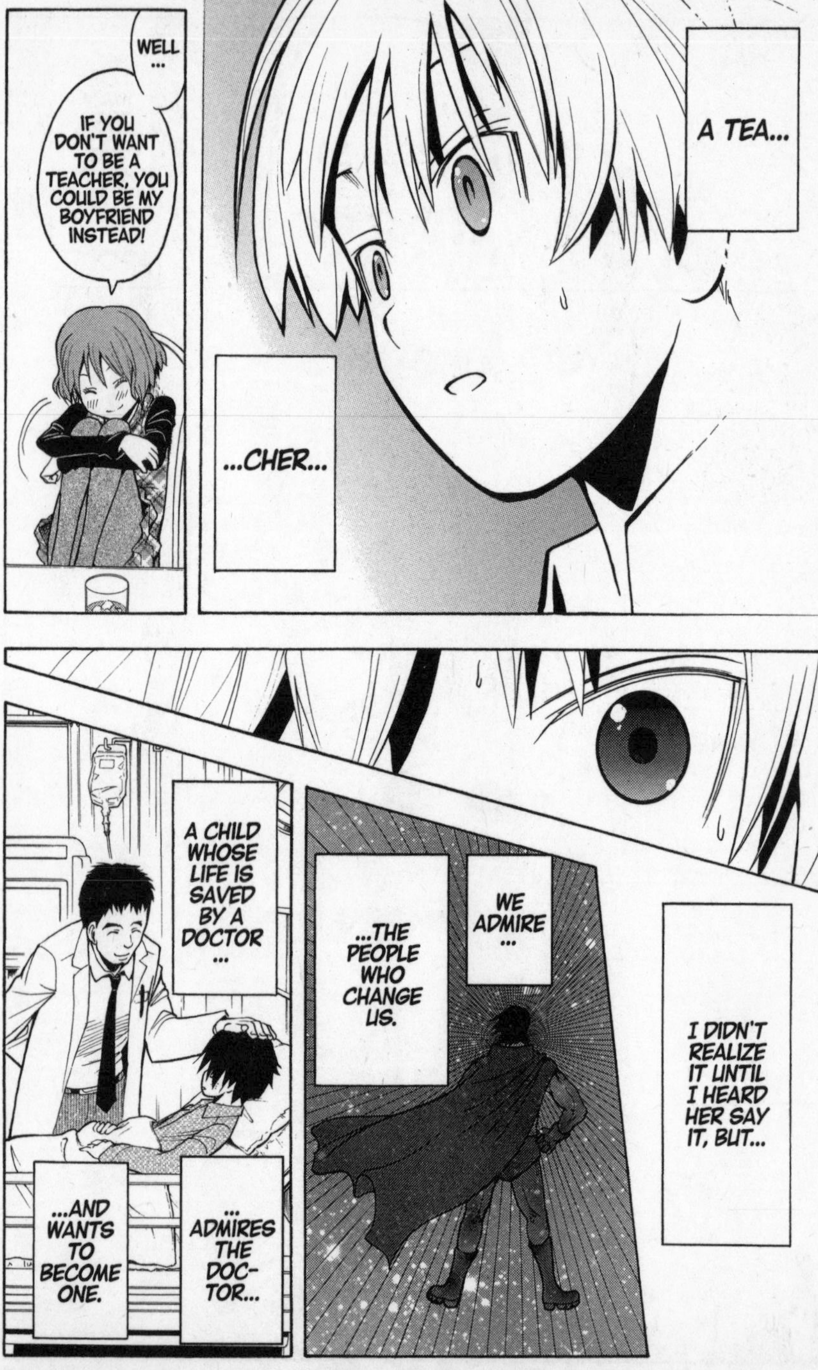
A TEA...
...CHER...
WELL ...
IF YOU DON'T WANT TO BE A TEACHER, YOU COULD BE MY BOYFRIEND INSTEAD!
I DIDN'T REALIZE IT UNTIL I HEARD HER SAY IT, BUT...
WE ADMIRE ...
...THE PEOPLE WHO CHANGE US.
A CHILD WHOSE LIFE IS SAVED BY A DOCTOR ...
... ADMIRES THE DOC-TOR...
...AND WANTS TO BECOME ONE.

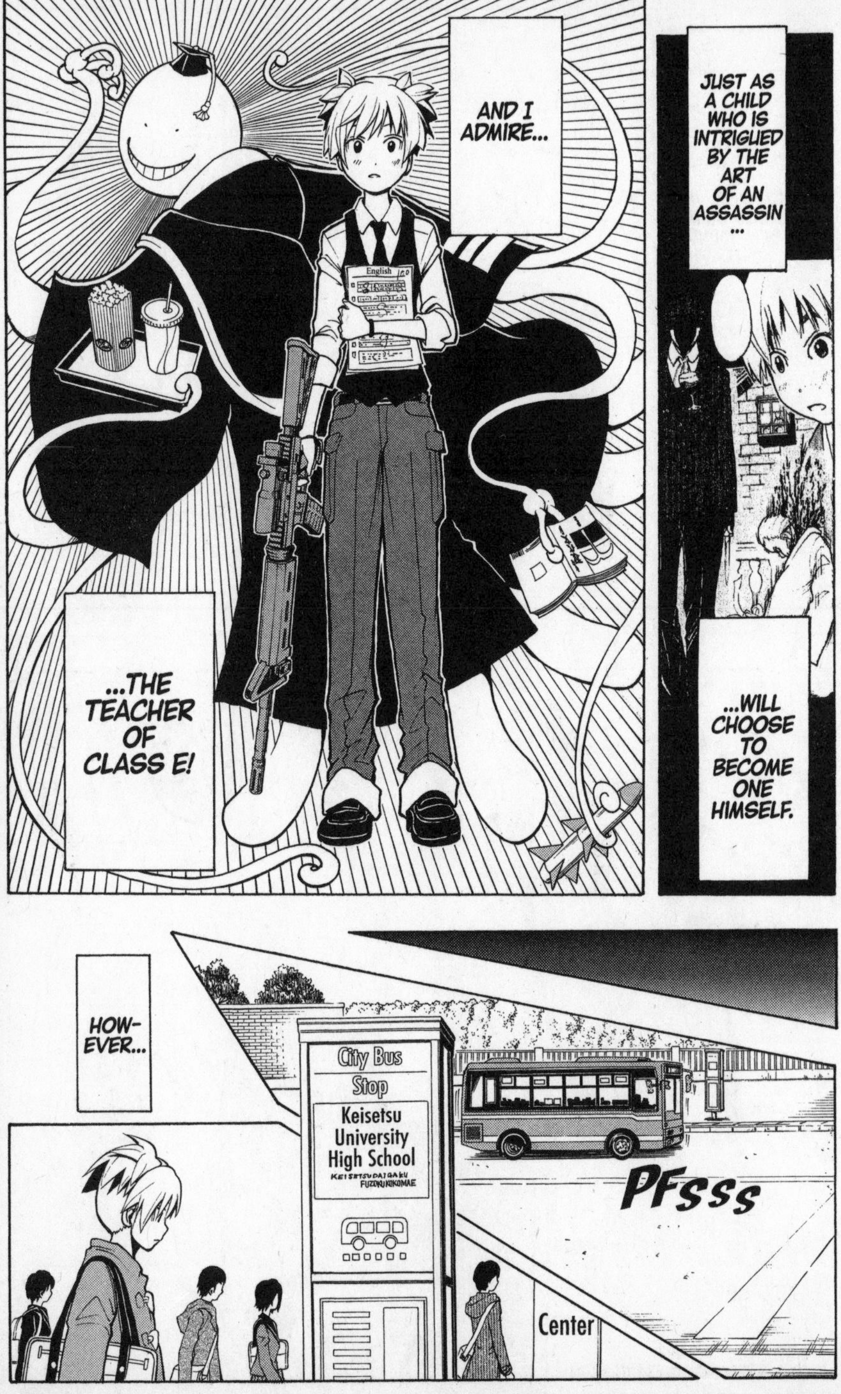
JUST AS A CHILD WHO IS INTRIGUED BY THE ART OF AN ASSASSIN ...
...WILL CHOOSE TO BECOME ONE HIMSELF.
AND I ADMIRE...
English
...THE TEACHER OF CLASS E!
HOW-EVER...
City Bus Stop
Keisetsu University High School
KEISETSUDAIGAKU FUZOKUKOKOMAE
PFSSS
Center

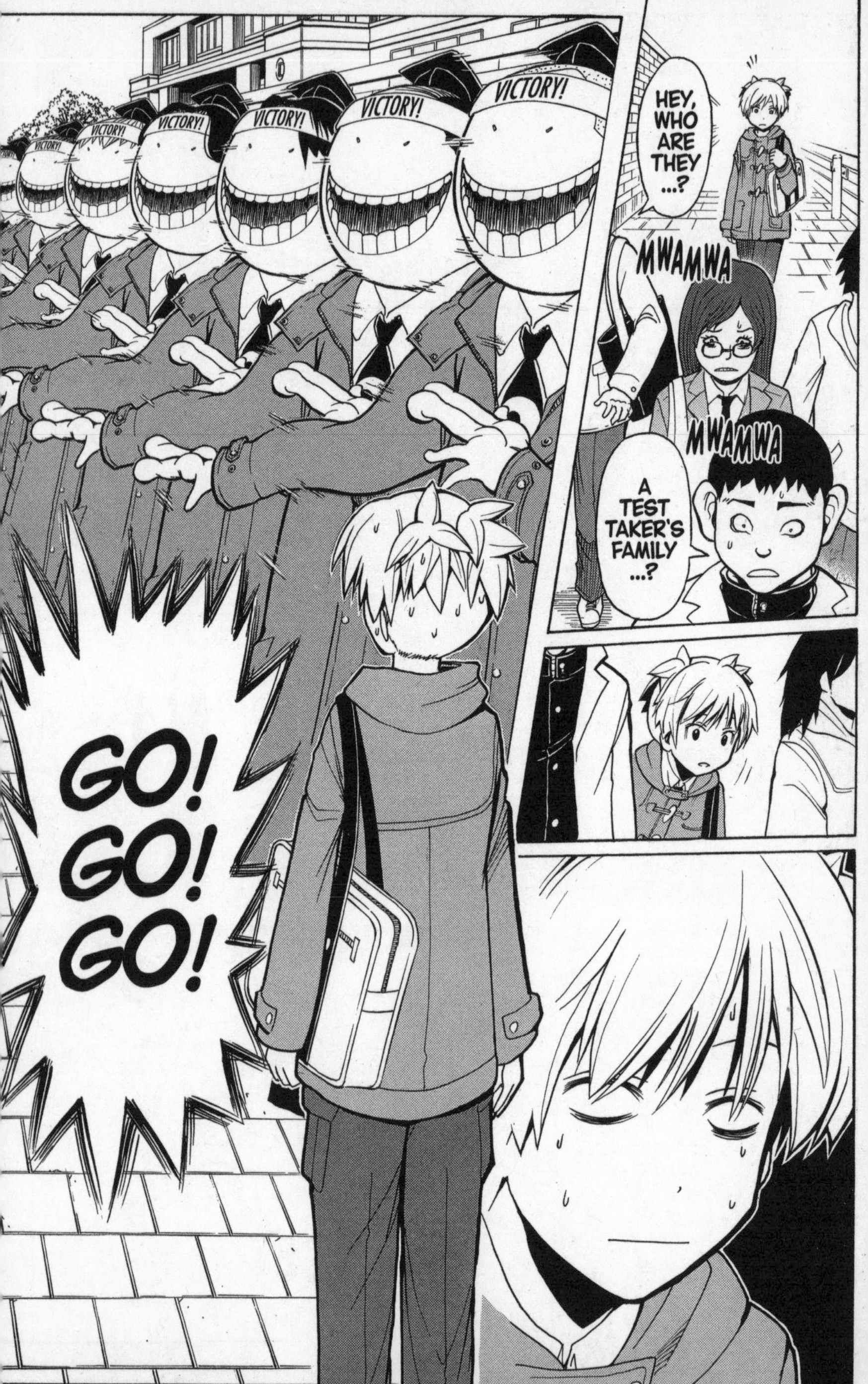

HEY, WHO ARE THEY ...?
MWAMWA
MWAMWA
A TEST TAKER'S FAMILY ...?
VICTORY!
VICTORY!
VICTORY!
VICTORY!
VICTORY!
VICTORY!
GO! GO! GO!

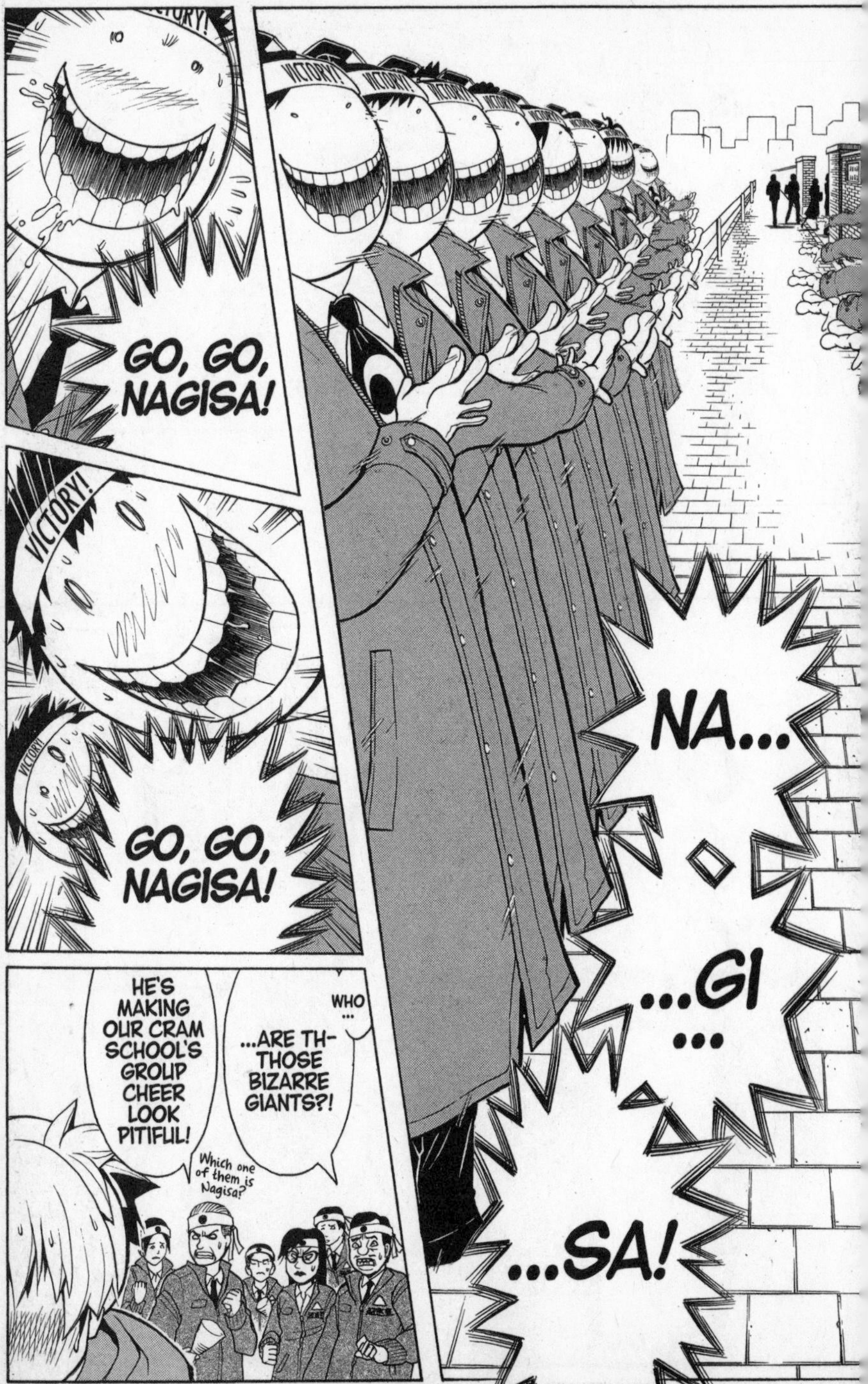

VICTORY!
NA...
...GI...
...SA!
VICTORY!
GO, GO, NAGISA!
VICTORY!
VICTORY!
GO, GO, NAGISA!
WHO...
...ARE TH-THOSE BIZARRE GIANTS?!
HE'S MAKING OUR CRAM SCHOOL'S GROUP CHEER LOOK PITIFUL!
Which one of them is Nagisa?

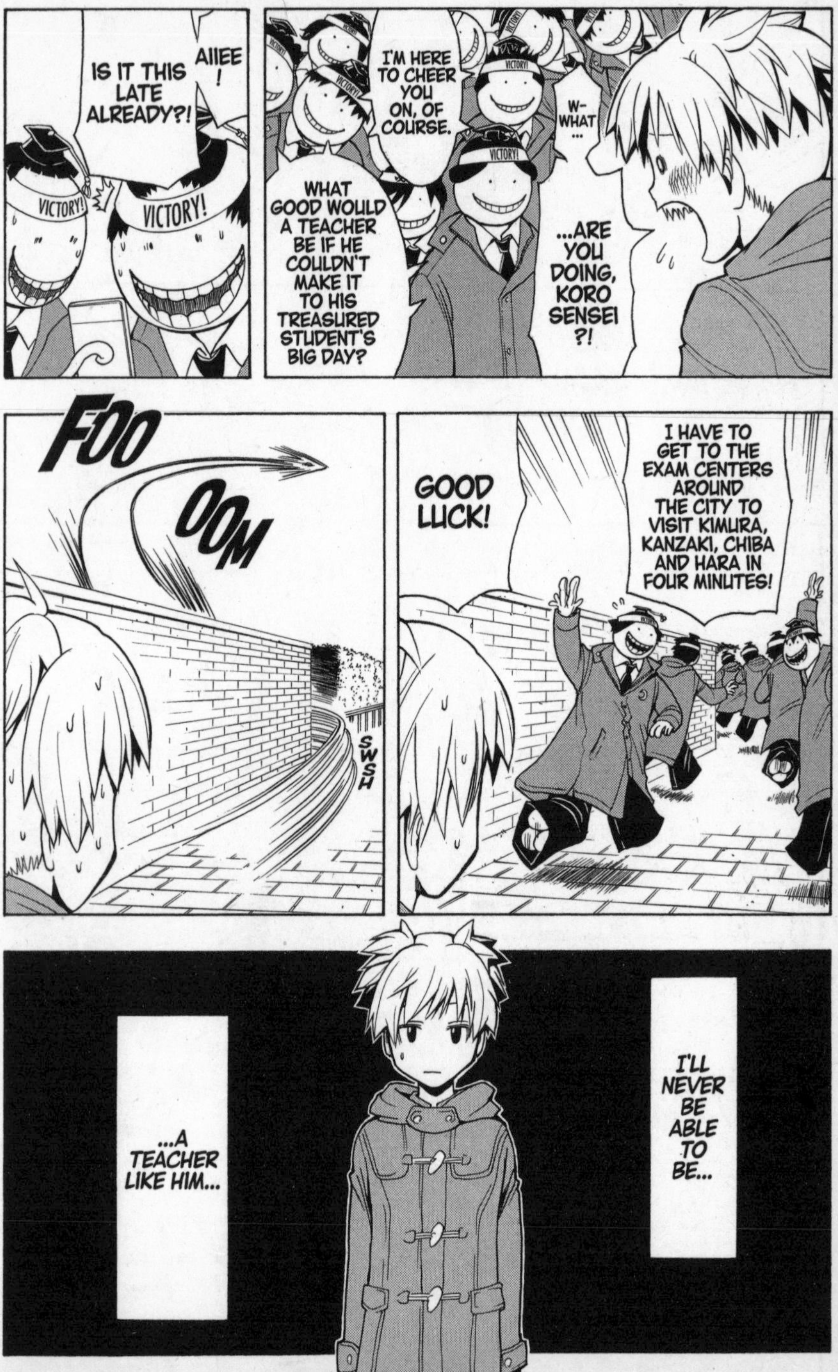
W-WHAT ...
...ARE YOU DOING, KORO SENSEI?!
I'M HERE TO CHEER YOU ON, OF COURSE.
WHAT GOOD WOULD A TEACHER BE IF HE COULDN'T MAKE IT TO HIS TREASURED STUDENT'S BIG DAY?
AIIEE!
IS IT THIS LATE ALREADY?!
VICTORY!
VICTORY!
I HAVE TO GET TO THE EXAM CENTERS AROUND THE CITY TO VISIT KIMURA, KANZAKI, CHIBA AND HARA IN FOUR MINUTES!
GOOD LUCK!
FOO
OOM
SWSH
I'LL NEVER BE ABLE TO BE...
...A TEACHER LIKE HIM...

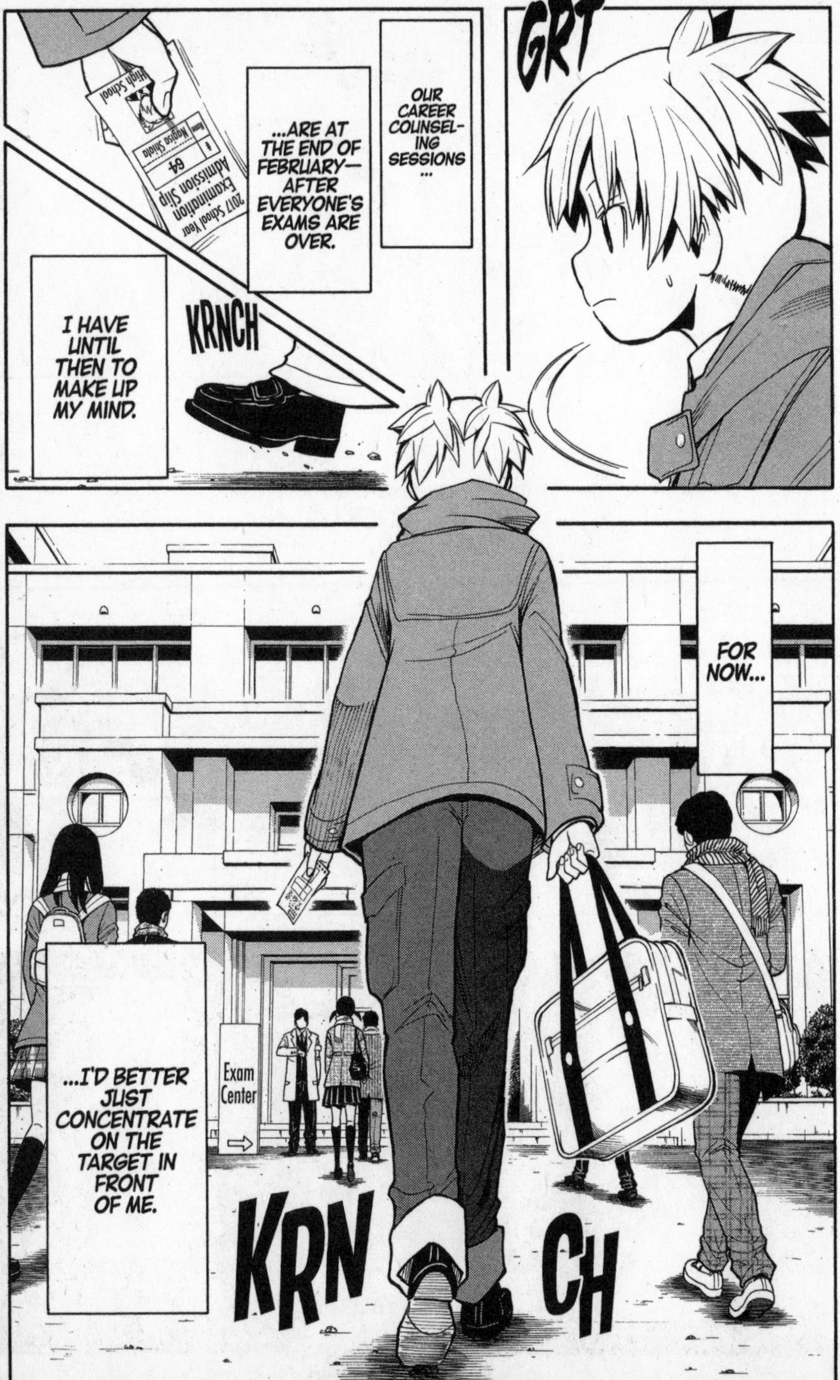
GRT
OUR CAREER COUNSELING SESSIONS...
...ARE AT THE END OF FEBRUARY—AFTER EVERYONE'S EXAMS ARE OVER.
2017 School Year Examination Admission Slip
64
Nagisa Shiota
High School
KRNCH
I HAVE UNTIL THEN TO MAKE UP MY MIND.
FOR NOW...
Exam Center
...I'D BETTER JUST CONCENTRATE ON THE TARGET IN FRONT OF ME.
KRNCH

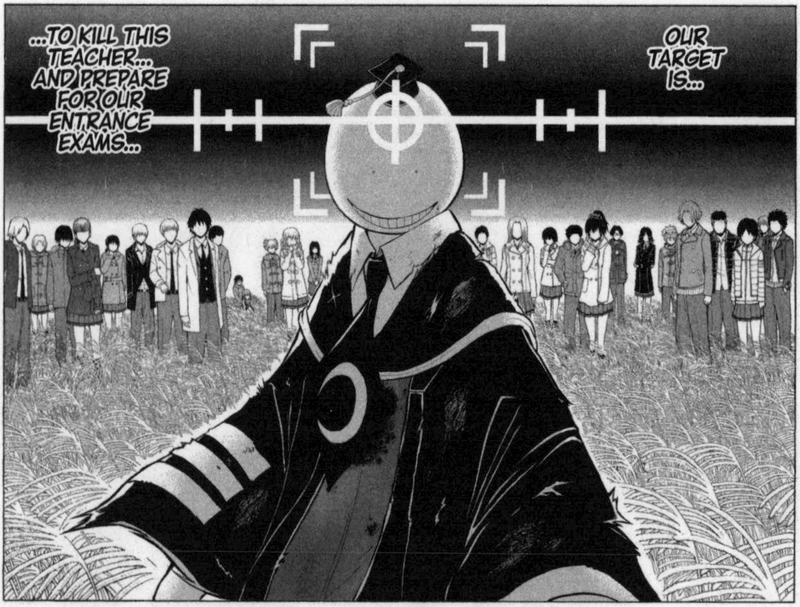
OUR TARGET IS...
...TO KILL THIS TEACHER... AND PREPARE FOR OUR ENTRANCE EXAMS...

It all started on that day...

Class 156 Time for a Side Part

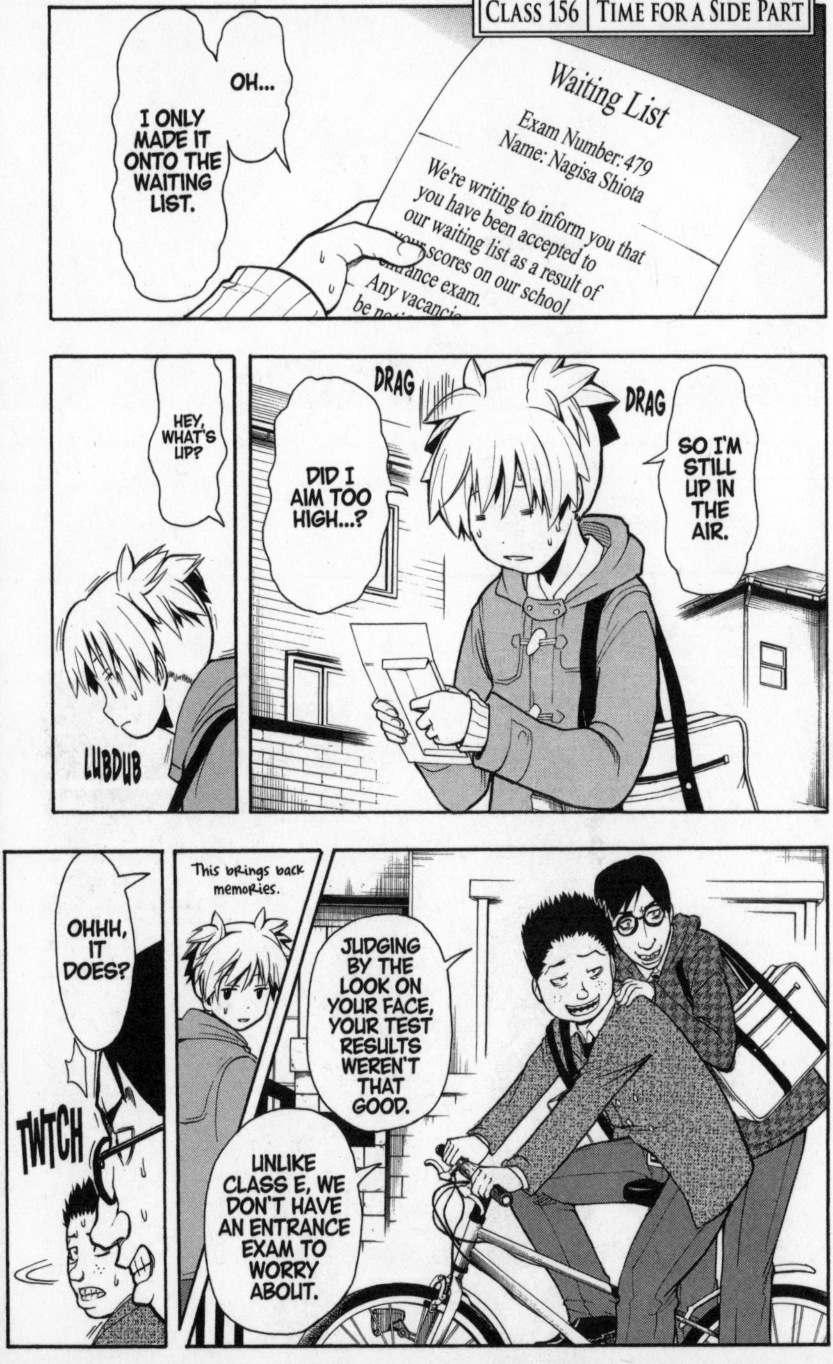

Waiting List
Exam Number: 479
Name: Nagisa Shiota
We're writing to inform you that you have been accepted to our waiting list as a result of your scores on our school entrance exam.
Any vacancies
OH...
I ONLY MADE IT ONTO THE WAITING LIST.
DRAG
SO I'M STILL UP IN THE AIR.
DRAG
DID I AIM TOO HIGH...?
HEY, WHAT'S UP?
LUBDUB
JUDGING BY THE LOOK ON YOUR FACE, YOUR TEST RESULTS WEREN'T THAT GOOD.
This brings back memories.
UNLIKE CLASS E, WE DON'T HAVE AN ENTRANCE EXAM TO WORRY ABOUT.
OHHH, IT DOES?
TWTCH

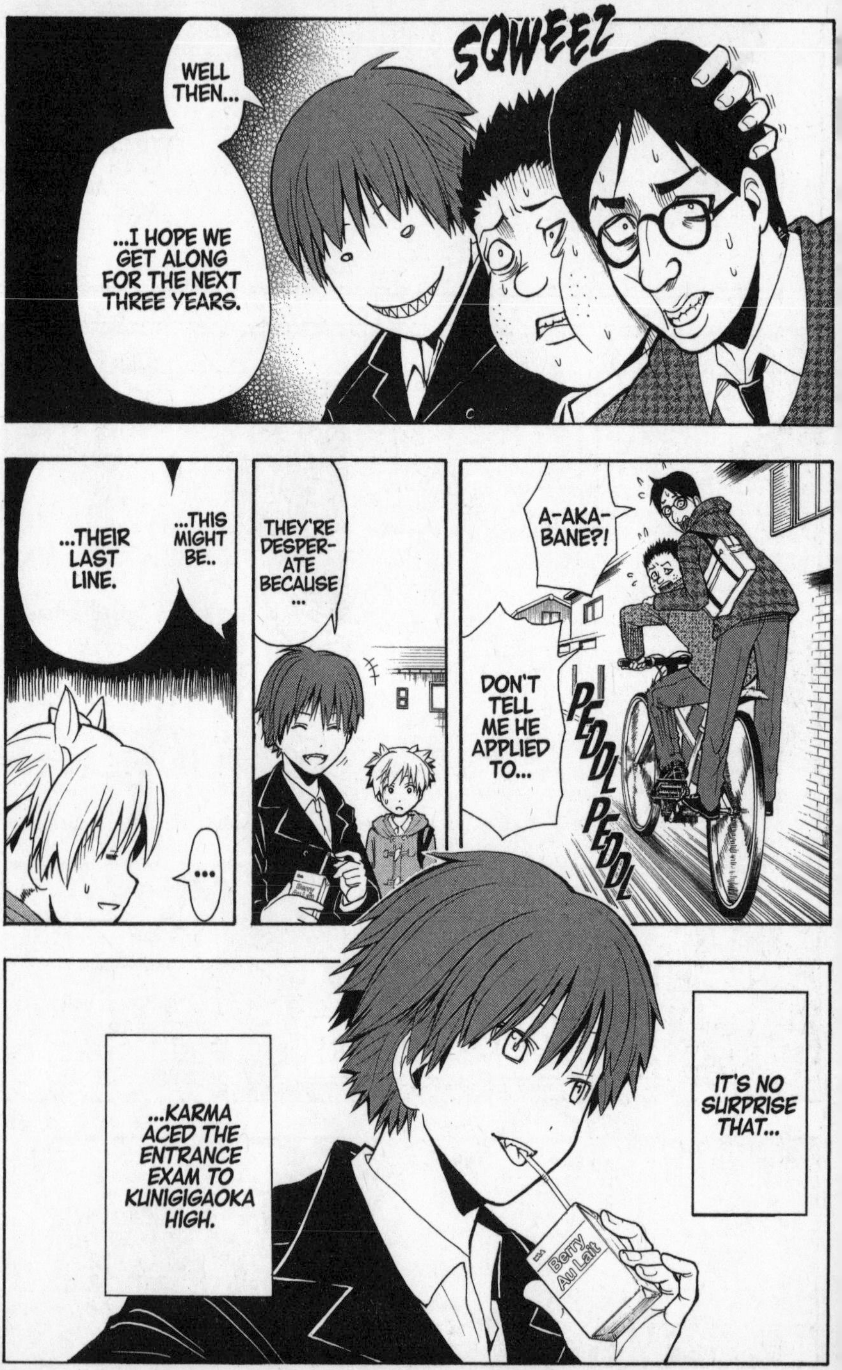
SQWEEZ
WELL THEN...
...I HOPE WE GET ALONG FOR THE NEXT THREE YEARS.
A-AKA-BANE?!
DON'T TELL ME HE APPLIED TO...
PEDDL PEDDL
THEY'RE DESPER-ATE BECAUSE ...
...THIS MIGHT BE..
...THEIR LAST LINE.
...
IT'S NO SURPRISE THAT...
...KARMA ACED THE ENTRANCE EXAM TO KUNIGIGAOKA HIGH.
Berry Au Lait

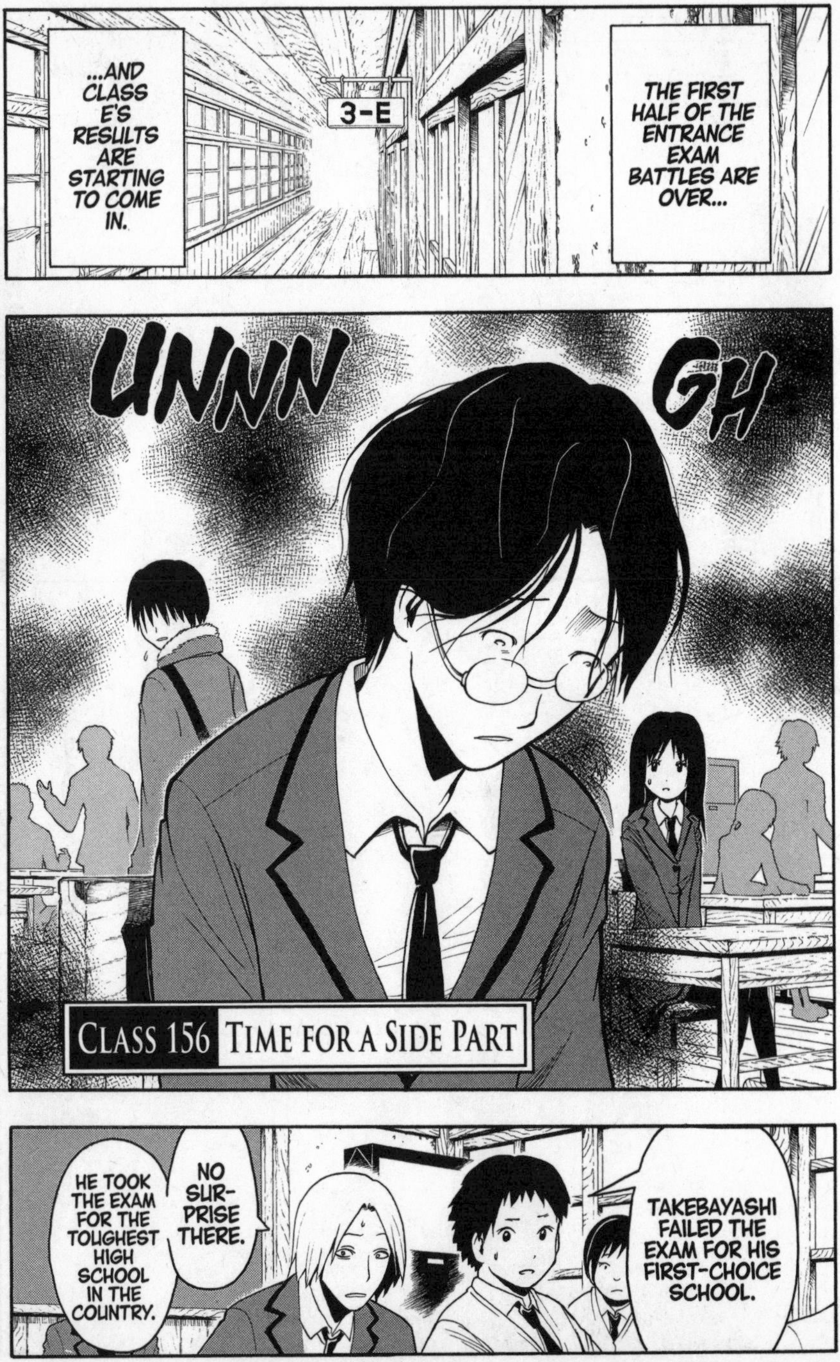
THE FIRST HALF OF THE ENTRANCE EXAM BATTLES ARE OVER...
3-E
...AND CLASS E'S RESULTS ARE STARTING TO COME IN.
UNNN GH
CLASS 156 TIME FOR A SIDE PART
TAKEBAYASHI FAILED THE EXAM FOR HIS FIRST-CHOICE SCHOOL.
NO SUR-PRISE THERE.
HE TOOK THE EXAM FOR THE TOUGHEST HIGH SCHOOL IN THE COUNTRY.

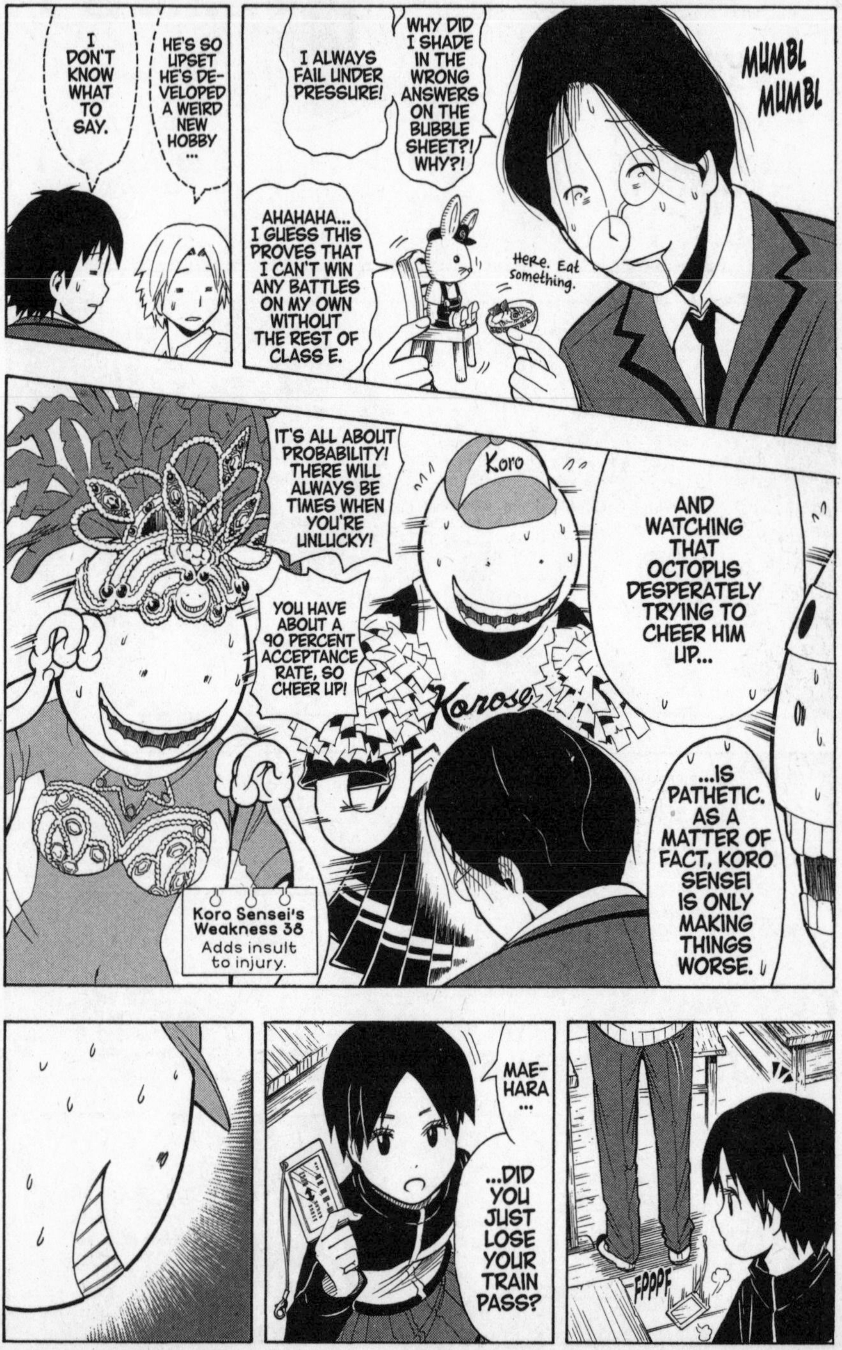
MUMBL MUMBL
WHY DID I SHADE IN THE WRONG ANSWERS ON THE BUBBLE SHEET?! WHY?!
I ALWAYS FAIL UNDER PRESSURE!
Here. Eat something.
AHAHAHA... I GUESS THIS PROVES THAT I CAN'T WIN ANY BATTLES ON MY OWN WITHOUT THE REST OF CLASS E.
HE'S SO UPSET HE'S DEVELOPED A WEIRD NEW HOBBY...
I DON'T KNOW WHAT TO SAY.
AND WATCHING THAT OCTOPUS DESPERATELY TRYING TO CHEER HIM UP...
...IS PATHETIC. AS A MATTER OF FACT, KORO SENSEI IS ONLY MAKING THINGS WORSE.
Koro
IT'S ALL ABOUT PROBABILITY! THERE WILL ALWAYS BE TIMES WHEN YOU'RE UNLUCKY!
YOU HAVE ABOUT A 90 PERCENT ACCEPTANCE RATE, SO CHEER UP!
Koro Sensei's Weakness 38
Adds insult to injury.
FPPPF
MAE-HARA...
...DID YOU JUST LOSE YOUR TRAIN PASS?

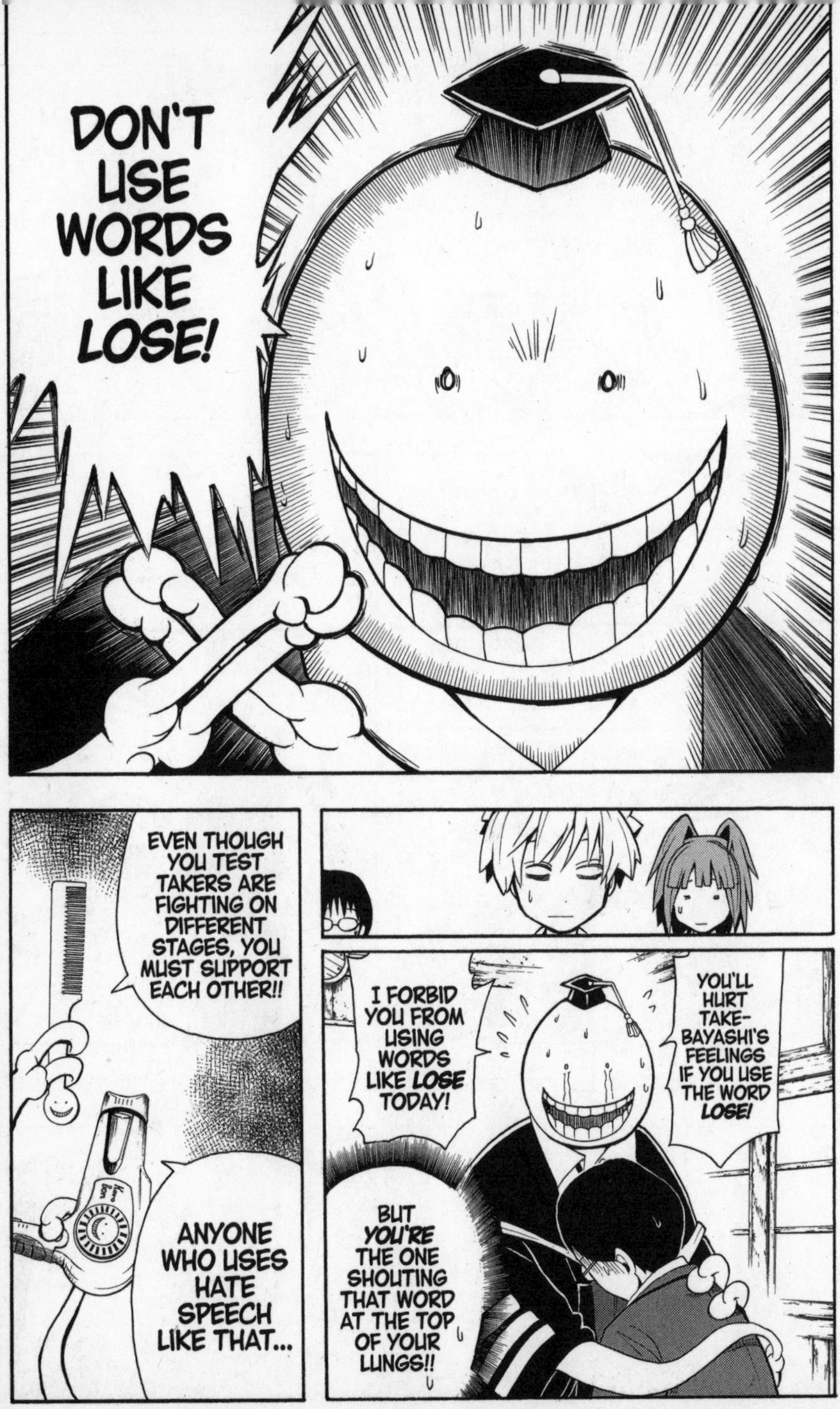
DON'T USE WORDS LIKE LOSE!
YOU'LL HURT TAKE-BAYASHI'S FEELINGS IF YOU USE THE WORD LOSE!
I FORBID YOU FROM USING WORDS LIKE LOSE TODAY!
BUT YOU'RE THE ONE SHOUTING THAT WORD AT THE TOP OF YOUR LUNGS!!
EVEN THOUGH YOU TEST TAKERS ARE FIGHTING ON DIFFERENT STAGES, YOU MUST SUPPORT EACH OTHER!!
ANYONE WHO USES HATE SPEECH LIKE THAT...

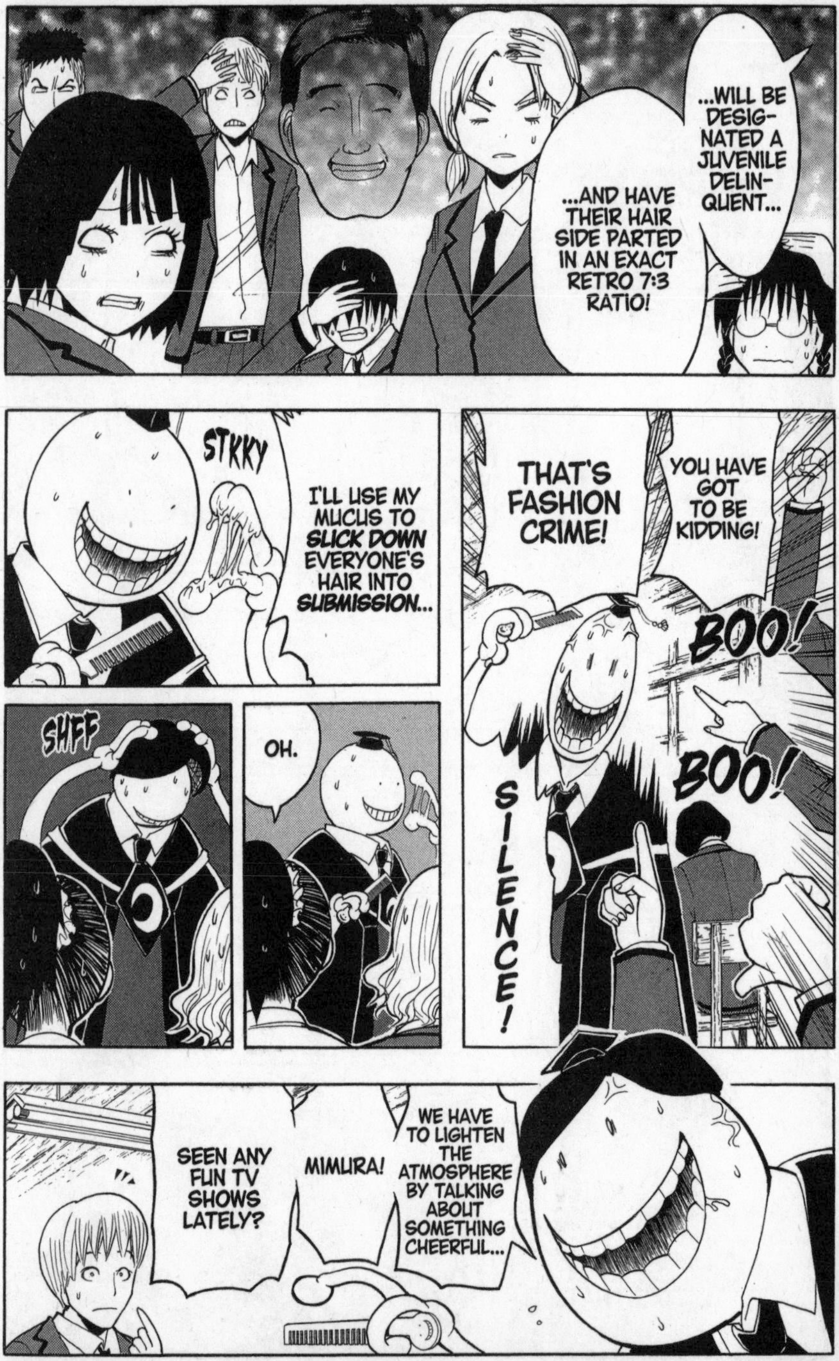

...WILL BE DESIGNATED A JUVENILE DELINQUENT...
...AND HAVE THEIR HAIR SIDE PARTED IN AN EXACT RETRO 7:3 RATIO!
YOU HAVE GOT TO BE KIDDING!
THAT'S FASHION CRIME!
BOO!
BOO!
SILENCE!
STKKY
I'LL USE MY MUCUS TO SLICK DOWN EVERYONE'S HAIR INTO SUBMISSION...
OH.
SHFF
WE HAVE TO LIGHTEN THE ATMOSPHERE BY TALKING ABOUT SOMETHING CHEERFUL...
MIMURA!
SEEN ANY FUN TV SHOWS LATELY?

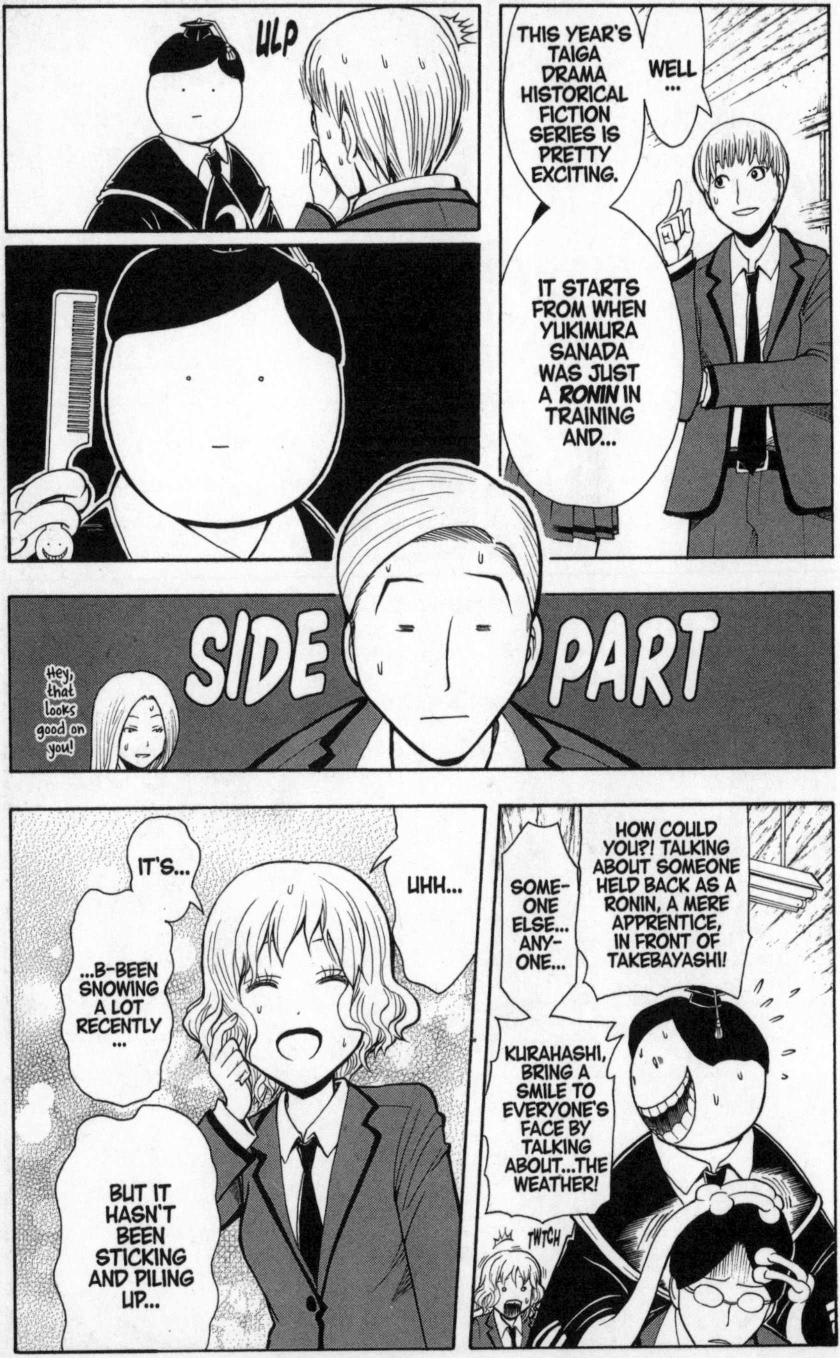
WELL...
THIS YEAR'S TAIGA DRAMA HISTORICAL FICTION SERIES IS PRETTY EXCITING.
IT STARTS FROM WHEN YUKIMURA SANADA WAS JUST A RONIN IN TRAINING AND...
ULP
SIDE PART
Hey, that looks good on you!
HOW COULD YOU?! TALKING ABOUT SOMEONE HELD BACK AS A RONIN, A MERE APPRENTICE, IN FRONT OF TAKEBAYASHI!
SOME-ONE ELSE... ANY-ONE...
KURAHASHI, BRING A SMILE TO EVERYONE'S FACE BY TALKING ABOUT...THE WEATHER!
TWITCH
UHH...
IT'S...
...B-BEEN SNOWING A LOT RECENTLY...
BUT IT HASN'T BEEN STICKING AND PILING UP...

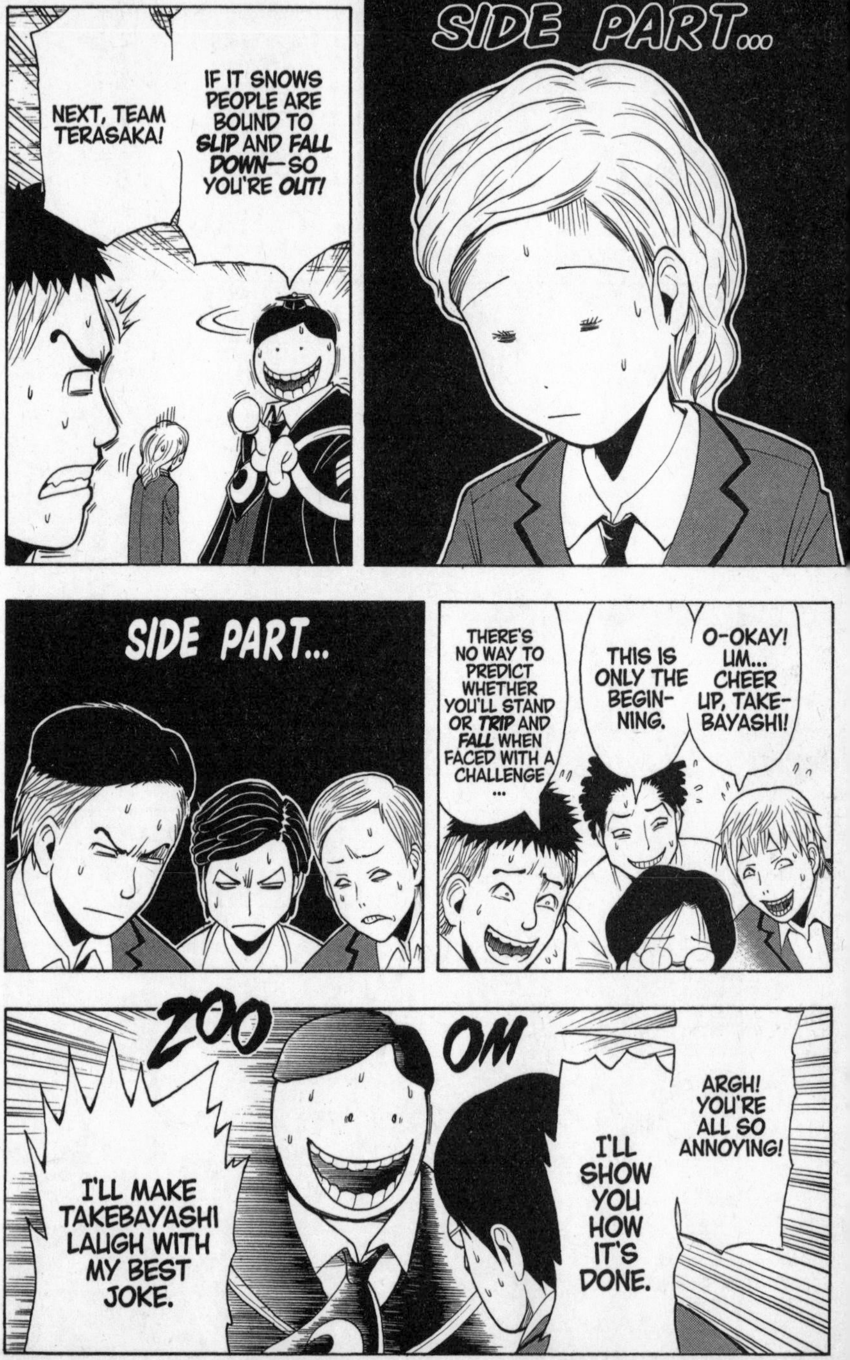
SIDE PART...
IF IT SNOWS PEOPLE ARE BOUND TO SLIP AND FALL DOWN—SO YOU'RE OUT!
NEXT, TEAM TERASAKA!
O-OKAY! UM... CHEER UP, TAKE-BAYASHI!
THIS IS ONLY THE BEGIN-NING.
THERE'S NO WAY TO PREDICT WHETHER YOU'LL STAND OR TRIP AND FALL WHEN FACED WITH A CHALLENGE...
SIDE PART...
ARGH! YOU'RE ALL SO ANNOYING!
I'LL SHOW YOU HOW IT'S DONE.
ZOOOM
I'LL MAKE TAKEBAYASHI LAUGH WITH MY BEST JOKE.

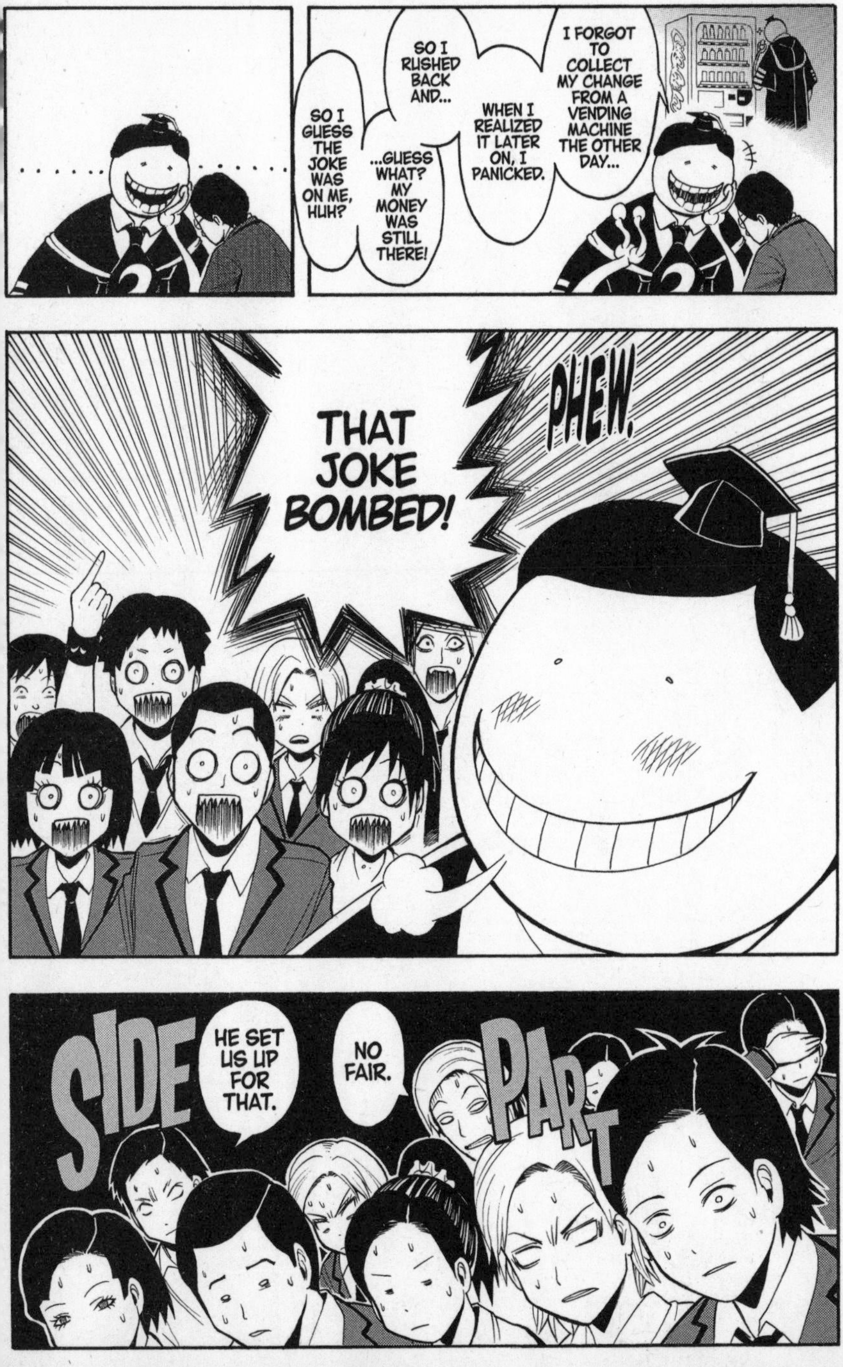
I FORGOT TO COLLECT MY CHANGE FROM A VENDING MACHINE THE OTHER DAY...
WHEN I REALIZED IT LATER ON, I PANICKED.
SO I RUSHED BACK AND...
...GUESS WHAT? MY MONEY WAS STILL THERE!
SO I GUESS THE JOKE WAS ON ME, HUH?
......
PHEW.
THAT JOKE BOMBED!
NO FAIR.
HE SET US UP FOR THAT.
SIDE PART

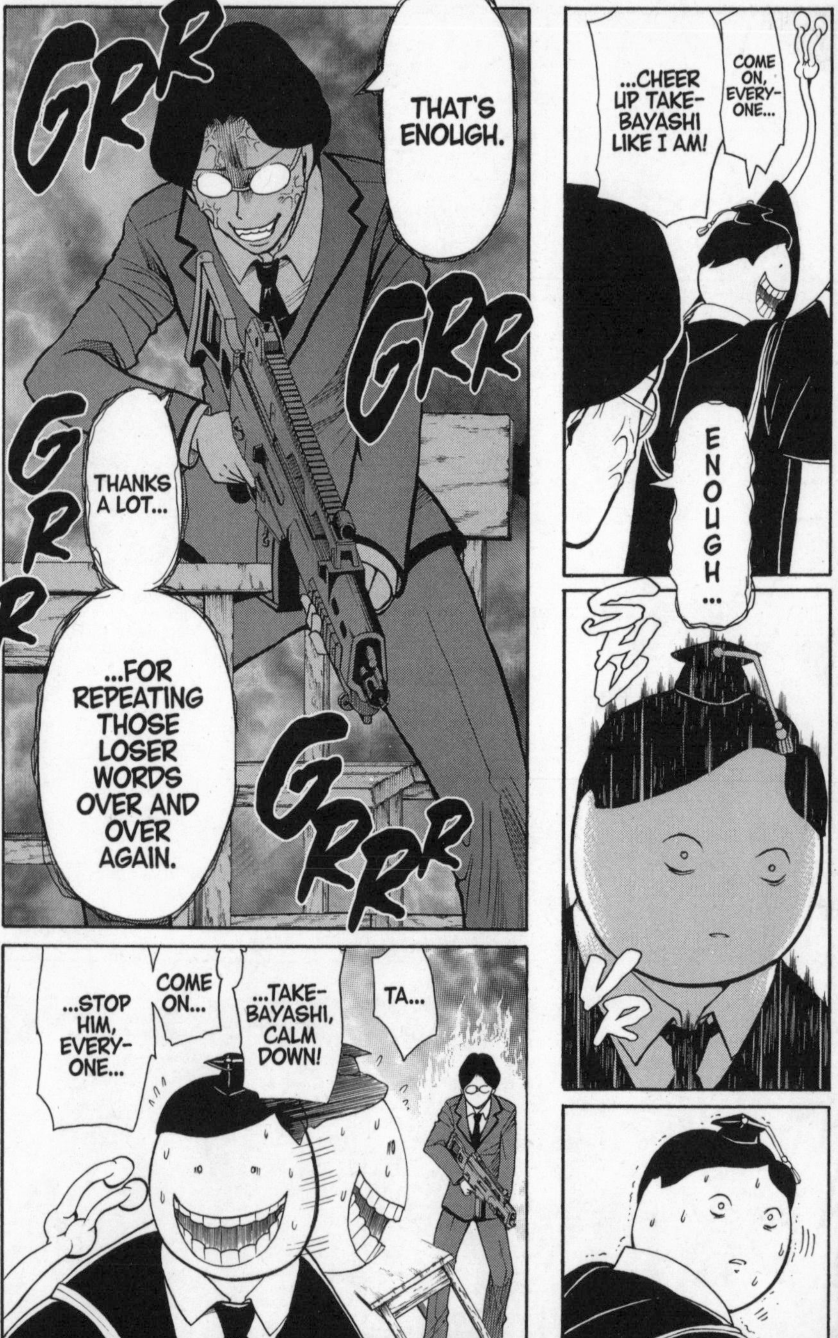
COME ON, EVERY-ONE...
...CHEER UP TAKE-BAYASHI LIKE I AM!
ENOUGH...
SH
VR
THAT'S ENOUGH.
GRR
GRR
GRR
THANKS A LOT...
...FOR REPEATING THOSE LOSER WORDS OVER AND OVER AGAIN.
GRRR
TA...
...TAKE-BAYASHI, CALM DOWN!
COME ON...
...STOP HIM, EVERY-ONE...

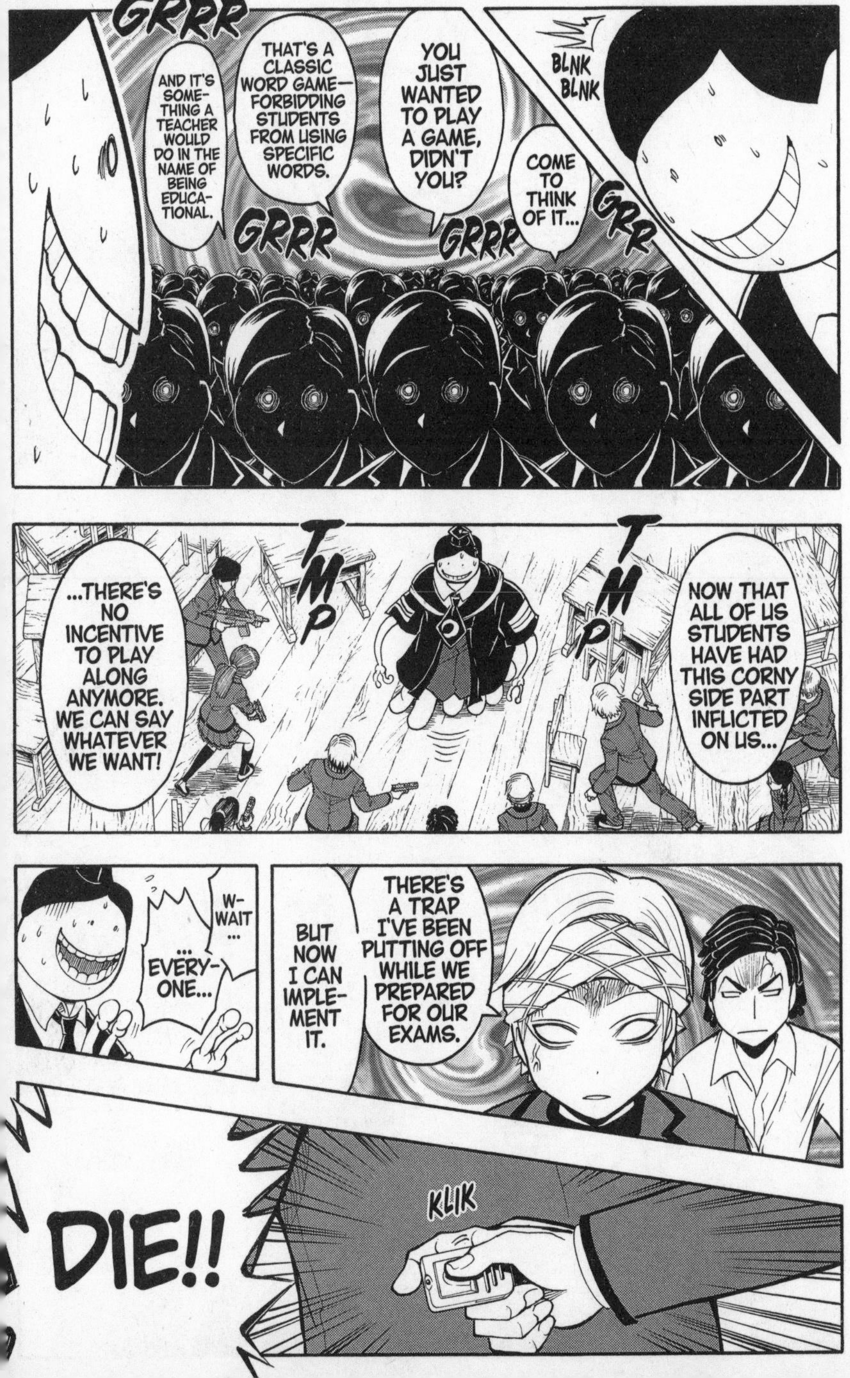
BLNK BLNK
GRR
COME TO THINK OF IT...
GRRR
YOU JUST WANTED TO PLAY A GAME, DIDN'T YOU?
GRRR
THAT'S A CLASSIC WORD GAME—FORBIDDING STUDENTS FROM USING SPECIFIC WORDS.
GRRR
AND IT'S SOMETHING A TEACHER WOULD DO IN THE NAME OF BEING EDUCATIONAL.
TMP
NOW THAT ALL OF US STUDENTS HAVE HAD THIS CORNY SIDE PART INFLICTED ON US...
TMP
...THERE'S NO INCENTIVE TO PLAY ALONG ANYMORE. WE CAN SAY WHATEVER WE WANT!
THERE'S A TRAP I'VE BEEN PUTTING OFF WHILE WE PREPARED FOR OUR EXAMS.
BUT NOW I CAN IMPLEMENT IT.
W-WAIT... ...EVERYONE...
KLIK
DIE!!

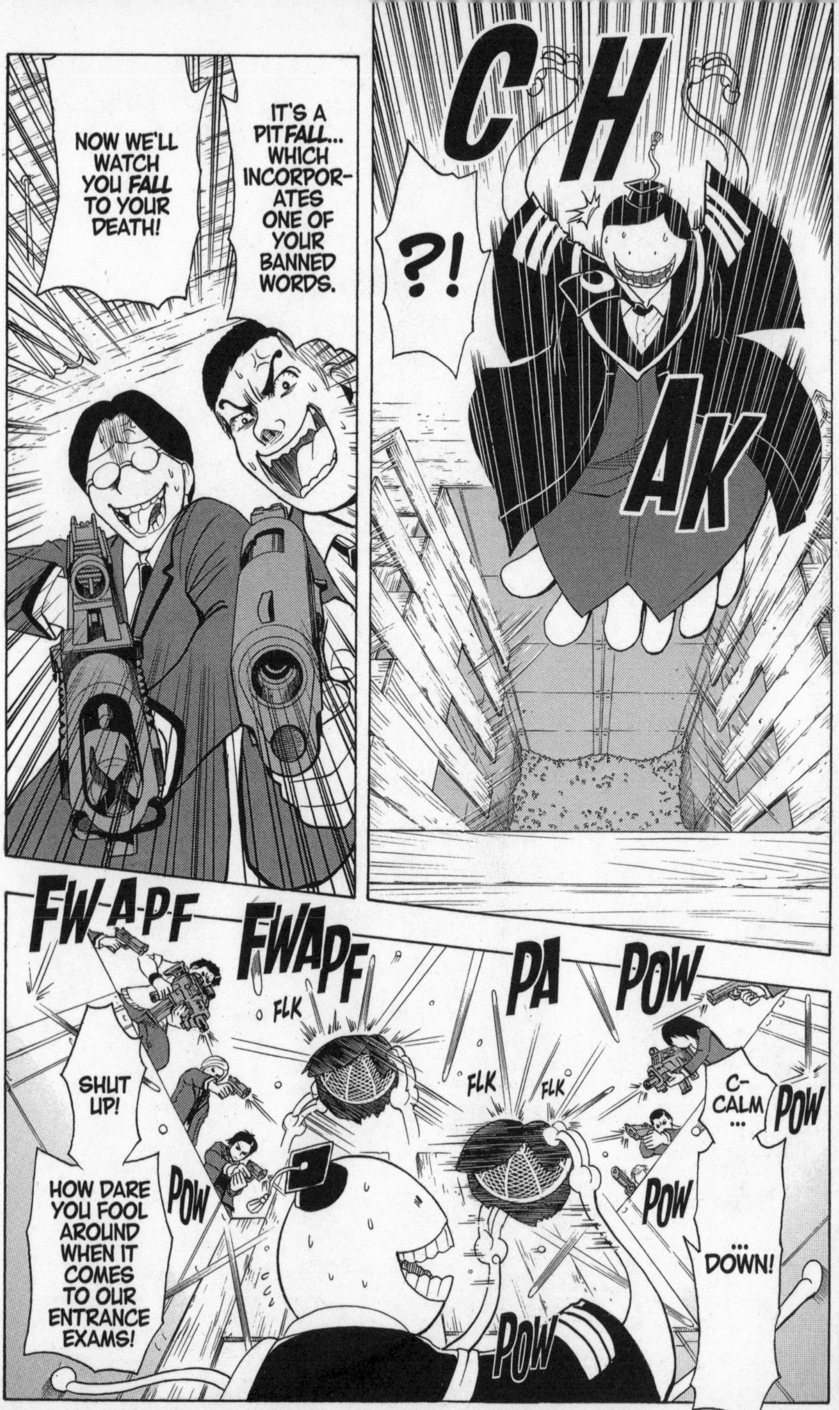
CH
AK
?!
IT'S A PITFALL... WHICH INCORPORATES ONE OF YOUR BANNED WORDS.
NOW WE'LL WATCH YOU FALL TO YOUR DEATH!
PA POW
POW
C-CALM...
FLK
FLK
POW
...DOWN!
FWAPF
FLK
FW-A-P-F
SHUT UP!
HOW DARE YOU FOOL AROUND WHEN IT COMES TO OUR ENTRANCE EXAMS!
POW
POW

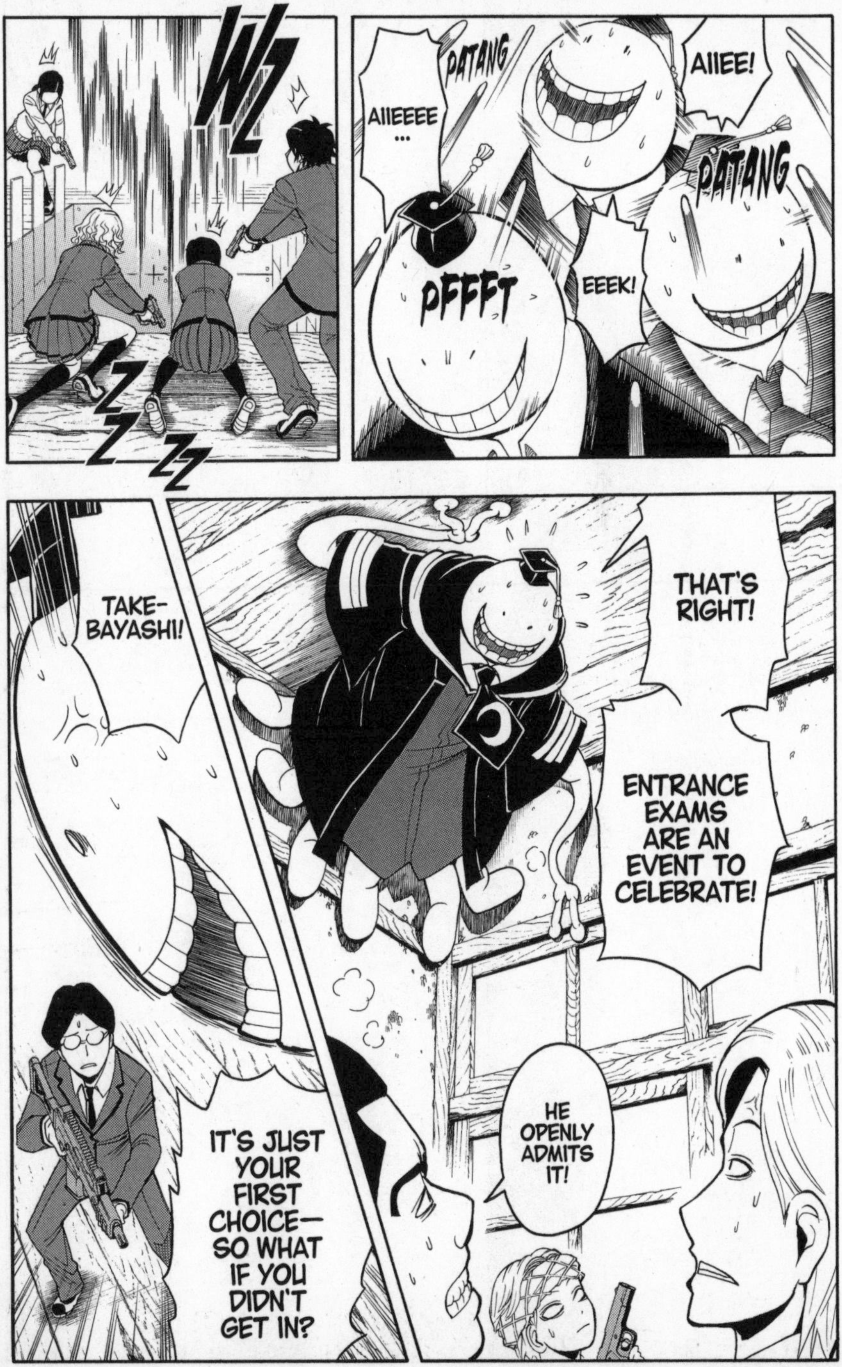
AIIEE!
PATANG
PATANG
AIIEEEE ...
EEEK!
PFFFT
THAT'S RIGHT!
ENTRANCE EXAMS ARE AN EVENT TO CELEBRATE!
HE OPENLY ADMITS IT!
TAKE-BAYASHI!
IT'S JUST YOUR FIRST CHOICE— SO WHAT IF YOU DIDN'T GET IN?

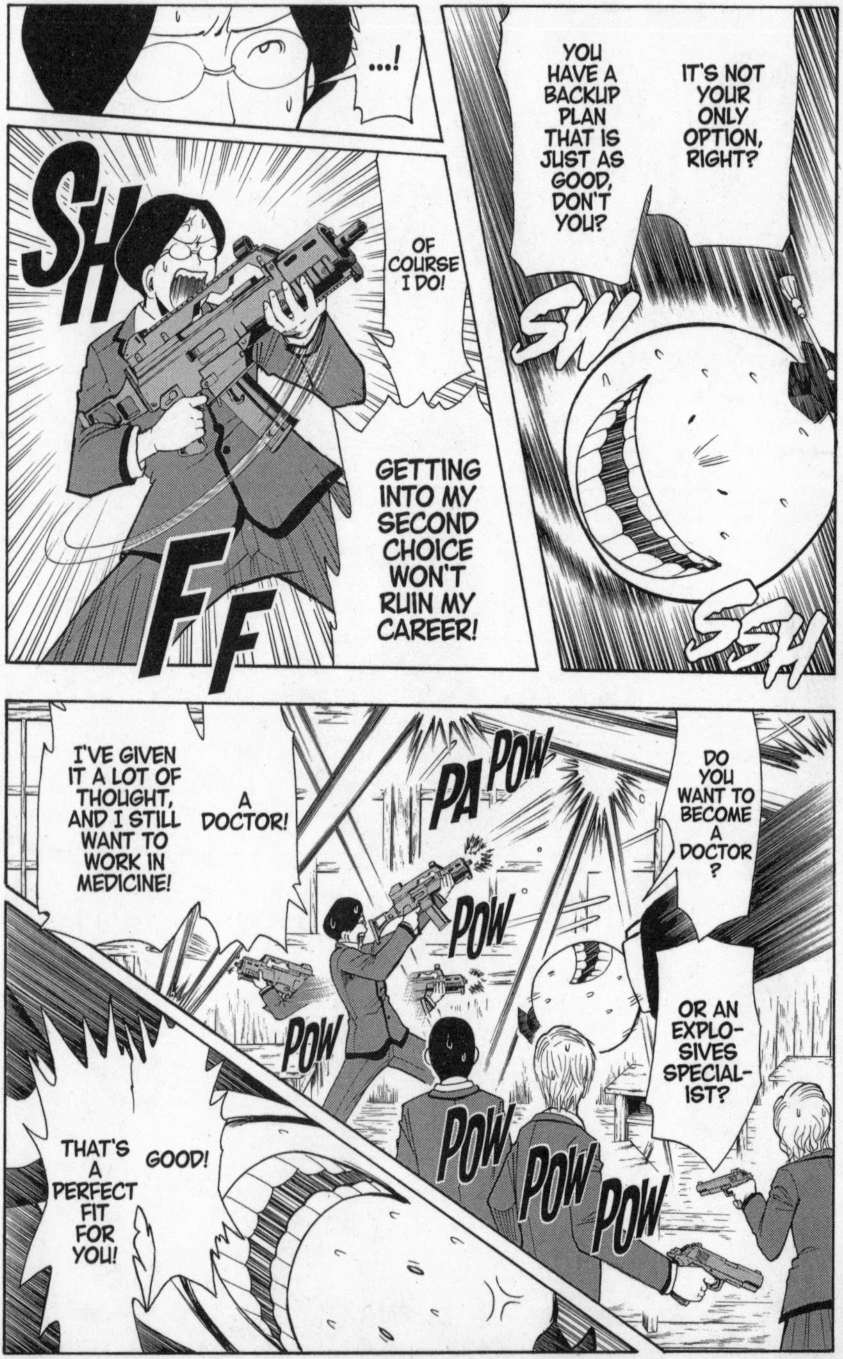
IT'S NOT YOUR ONLY OPTION, RIGHT?
YOU HAVE A BACKUP PLAN THAT IS JUST AS GOOD, DON'T YOU?
SW
SSH
...!
SH
OF COURSE I DO!
GETTING INTO MY SECOND CHOICE WON'T RUIN MY CAREER!
FF
DO YOU WANT TO BECOME A DOCTOR?
OR AN EXPLOSIVES SPECIALIST?
A DOCTOR!
I'VE GIVEN IT A LOT OF THOUGHT, AND I STILL WANT TO WORK IN MEDICINE!
PA POW
POW
POW
POW
POW
POW
GOOD!
THAT'S A PERFECT FIT FOR YOU!

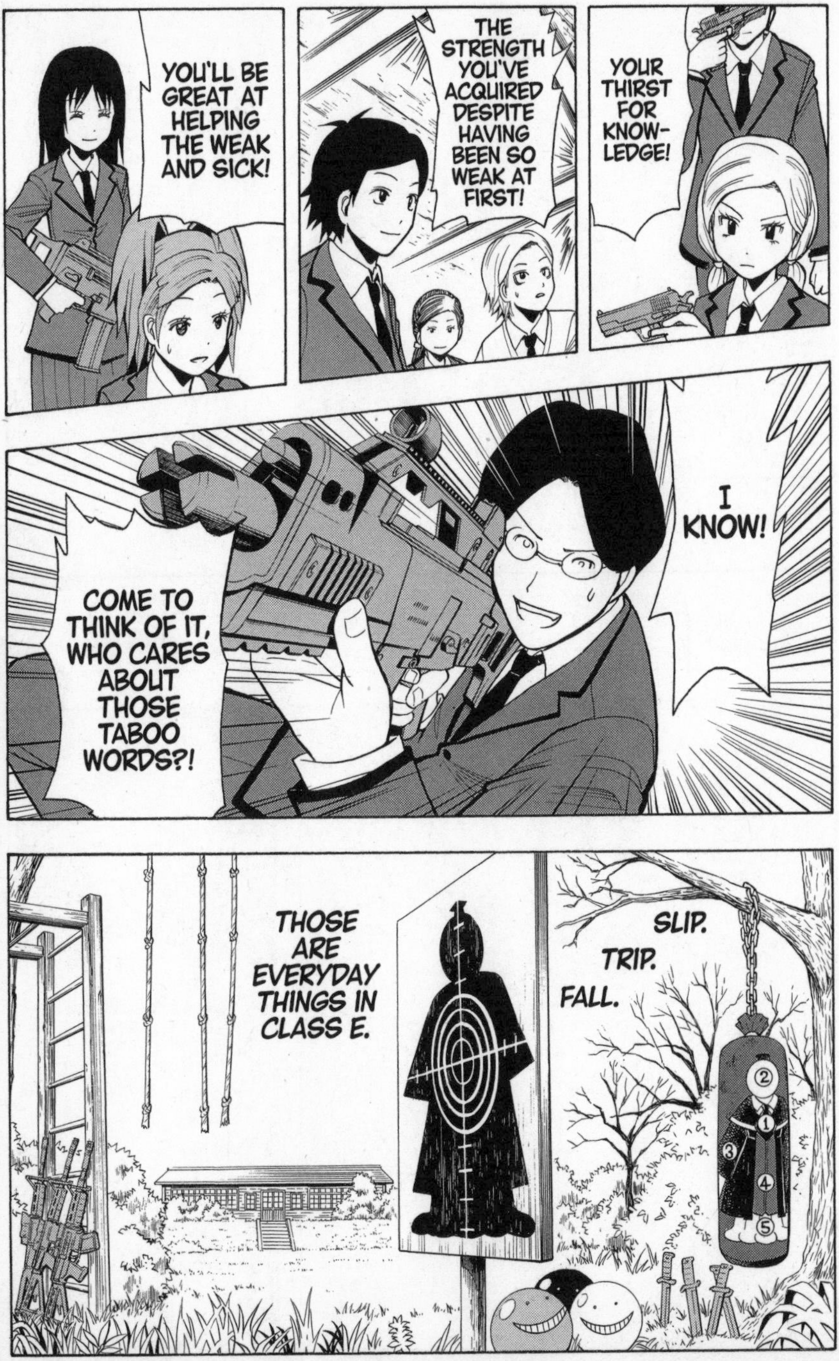
YOUR THIRST FOR KNOW-LEDGE!
THE STRENGTH YOU'VE ACQUIRED DESPITE HAVING BEEN SO WEAK AT FIRST!
YOU'LL BE GREAT AT HELPING THE WEAK AND SICK!
I KNOW!
COME TO THINK OF IT, WHO CARES ABOUT THOSE TABOO WORDS?!
SLIP.
TRIP.
FALL.
THOSE ARE EVERYDAY THINGS IN CLASS E.

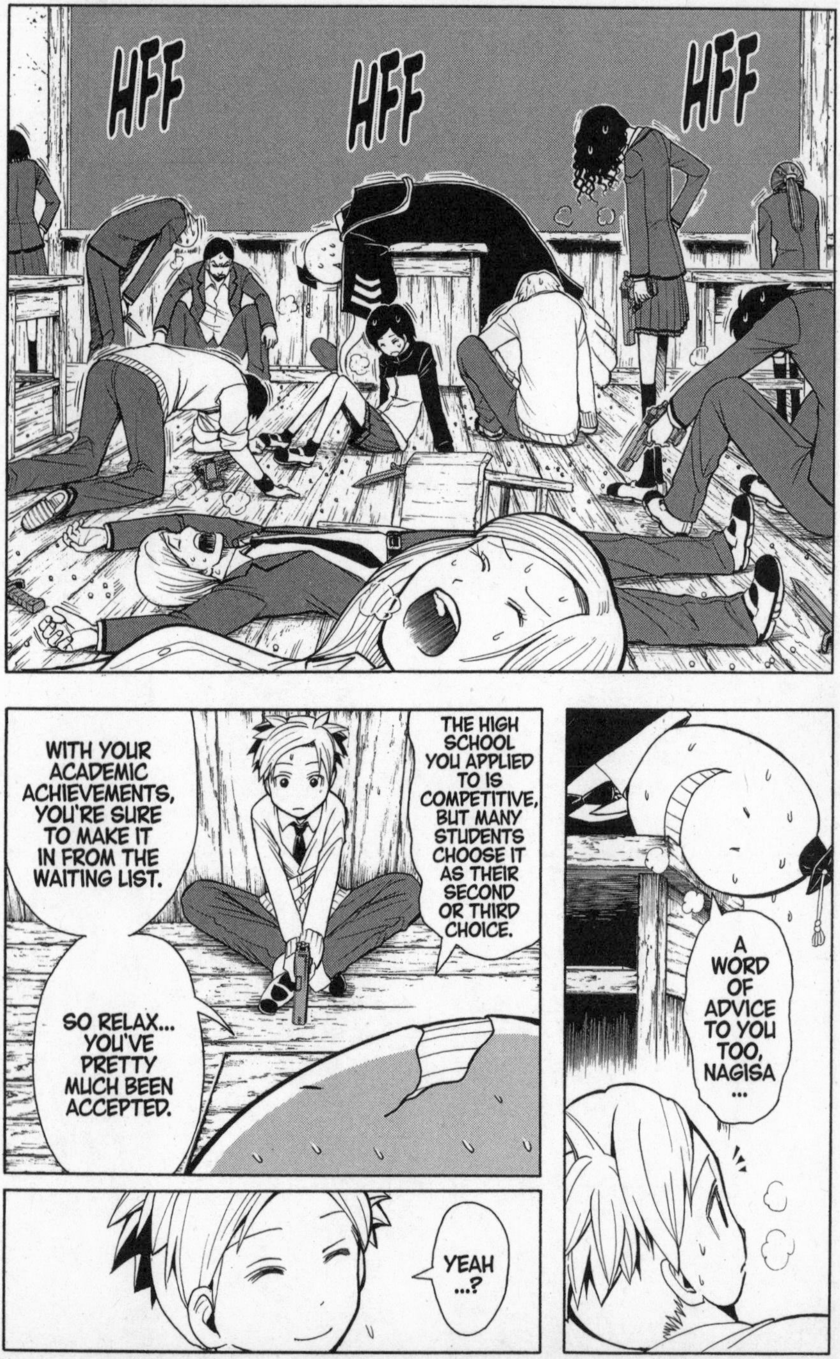
HFF
HFF
HFF
A WORD OF ADVICE TO YOU TOO, NAGISA...
THE HIGH SCHOOL YOU APPLIED TO IS COMPETITIVE, BUT MANY STUDENTS CHOOSE IT AS THEIR SECOND OR THIRD CHOICE.
WITH YOUR ACADEMIC ACHIEVEMENTS, YOU'RE SURE TO MAKE IT IN FROM THE WAITING LIST.
SO RELAX... YOU'VE PRETTY MUCH BEEN ACCEPTED.
YEAH ...?

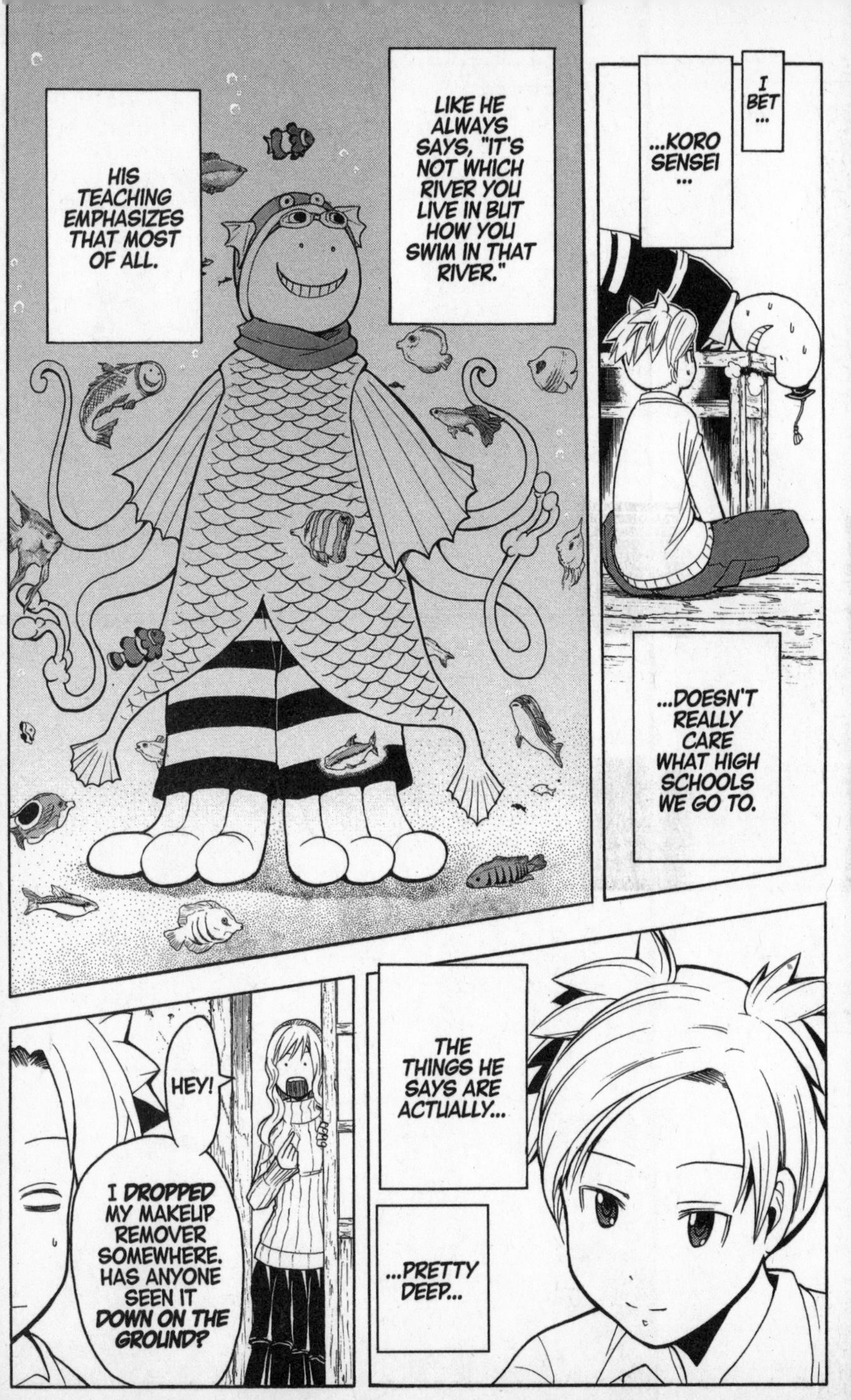
I BET...
...KORO SENSEI...
...DOESN'T REALLY CARE WHAT HIGH SCHOOLS WE GO TO.
LIKE HE ALWAYS SAYS, "IT'S NOT WHICH RIVER YOU LIVE IN BUT HOW YOU SWIM IN THAT RIVER."
HIS TEACHING EMPHASIZES THAT MOST OF ALL.
THE THINGS HE SAYS ARE ACTUALLY...
...PRETTY DEEP...
HEY!
I DROPPED MY MAKEUP REMOVER SOMEWHERE. HAS ANYONE SEEN IT DOWN ON THE GROUND?

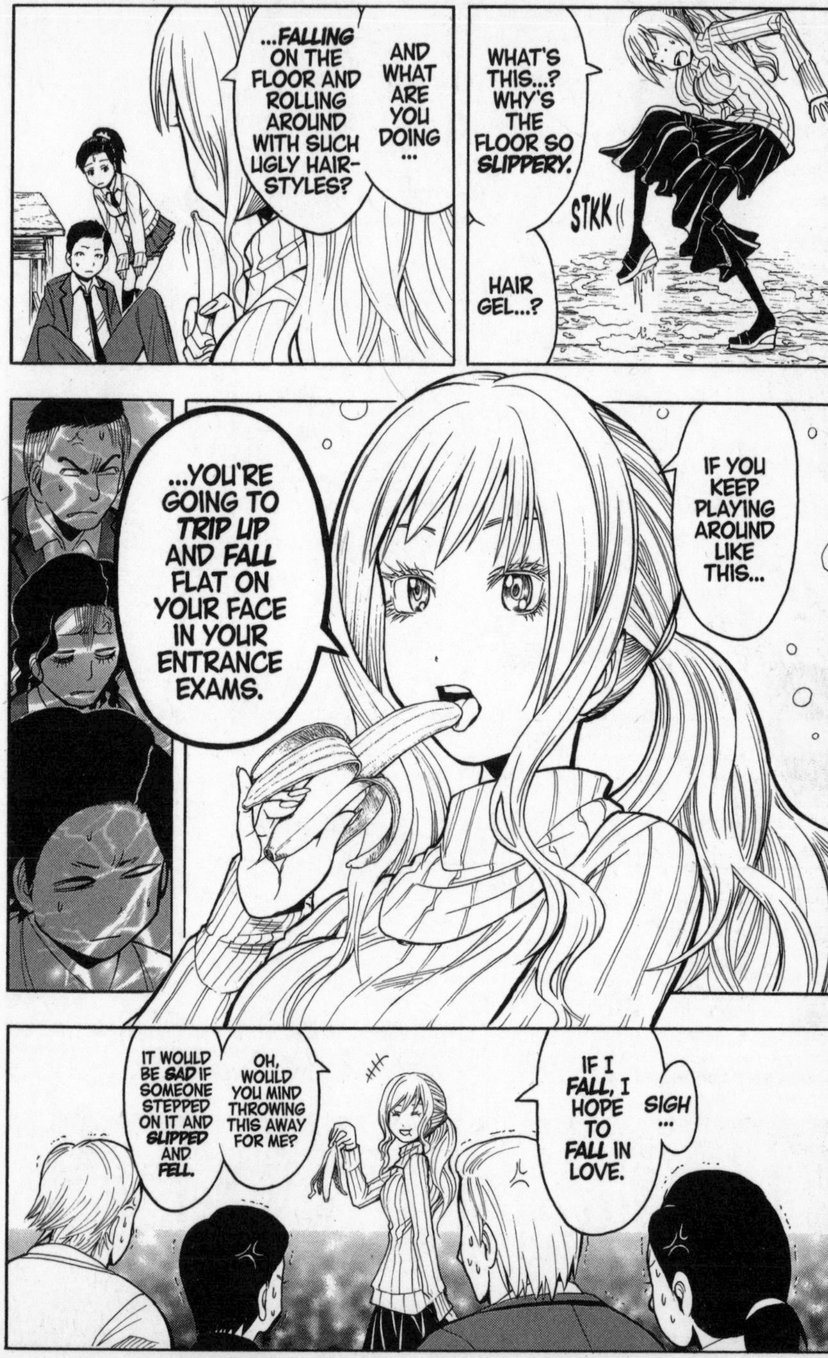
WHAT'S THIS...? WHY'S THE FLOOR SO SLIPPERY.
STKK
HAIR GEL...?
AND WHAT ARE YOU DOING...
...FALLING ON THE FLOOR AND ROLLING AROUND WITH SUCH UGLY HAIR-STYLES?
IF YOU KEEP PLAYING AROUND LIKE THIS...
...YOU'RE GOING TO TRIP UP AND FALL FLAT ON YOUR FACE IN YOUR ENTRANCE EXAMS.
SIGH...
IF I FALL, I HOPE TO FALL IN LOVE.
OH, WOULD YOU MIND THROWING THIS AWAY FOR ME?
IT WOULD BE SAD IF SOMEONE STEPPED ON IT AND SLIPPED AND FELL.

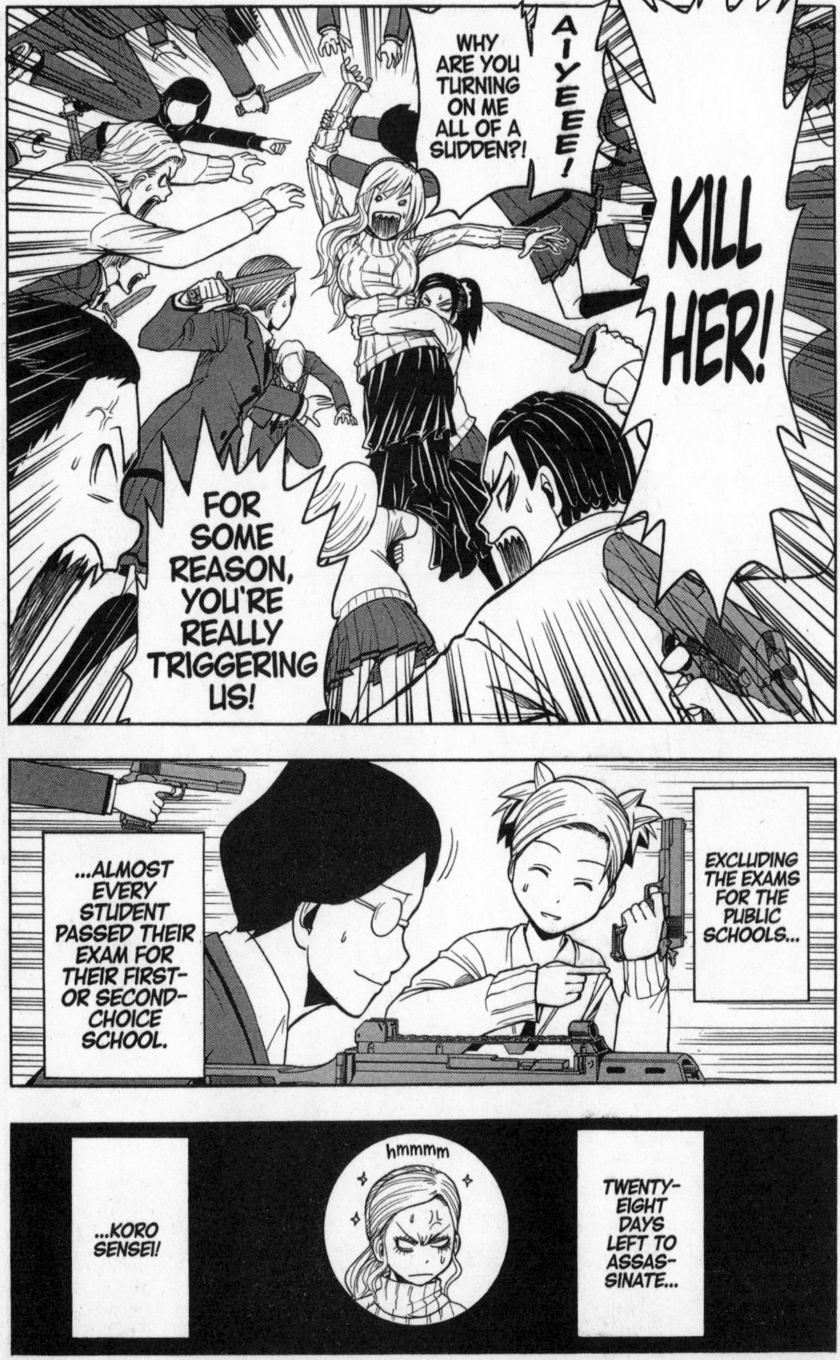
KILL HER!
AIYEEE!
WHY ARE YOU TURNING ON ME ALL OF A SUDDEN?!
FOR SOME REASON, YOU'RE REALLY TRIGGERING US!
EXCLUDING THE EXAMS FOR THE PUBLIC SCHOOLS...
...ALMOST EVERY STUDENT PASSED THEIR EXAM FOR THEIR FIRST- OR SECOND-CHOICE SCHOOL.
TWENTY-EIGHT DAYS LEFT TO ASSAS-SINATE...
hmmmm
...KORO SENSEI!

Master Gamer

She didn't make a single mistake in
the word game. And when she played
Ghost in the Graveyard with the
entire class, she managed to kill
25 out of the 28 students.

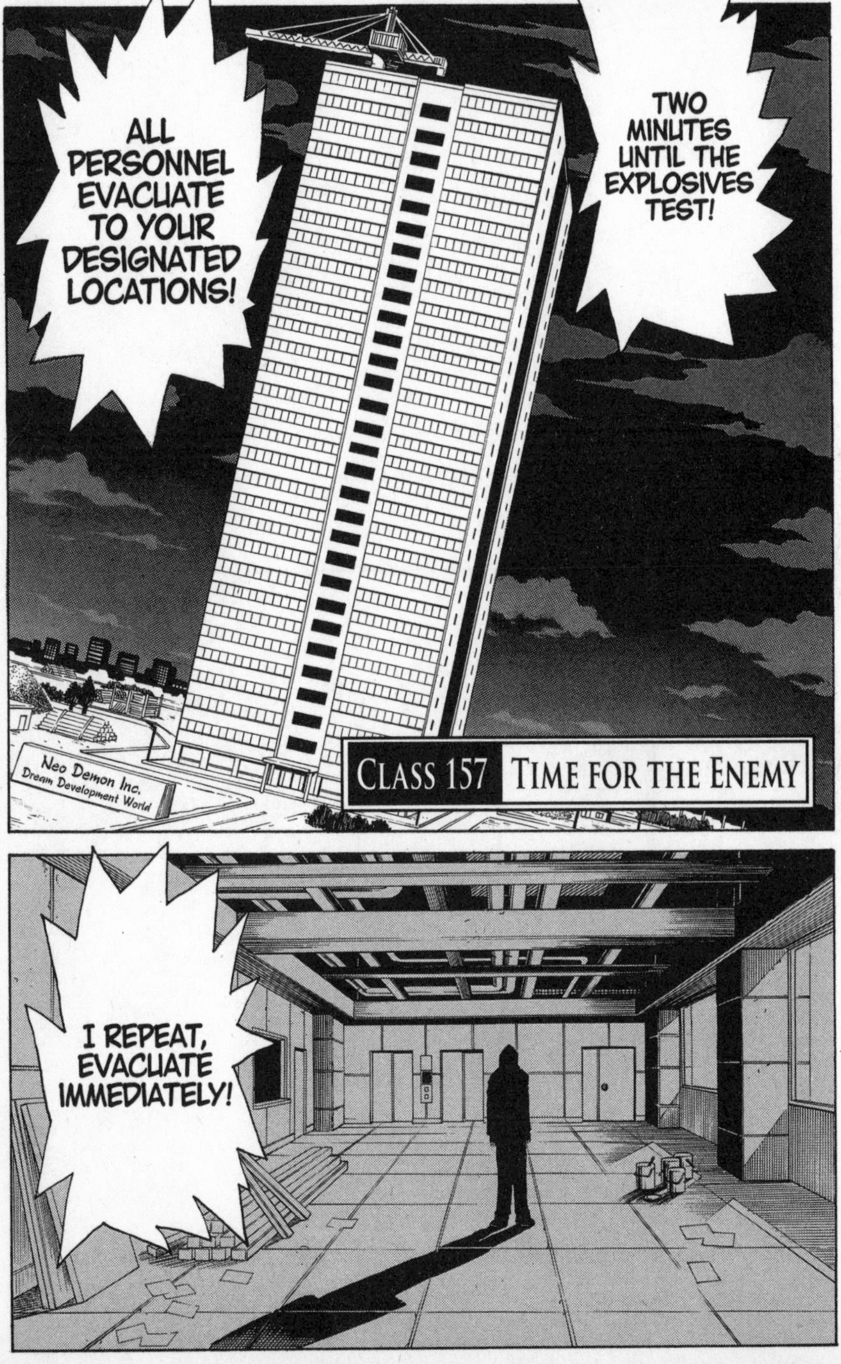
TWO MINUTES UNTIL THE EXPLOSIVES TEST!
ALL PERSONNEL EVACUATE TO YOUR DESIGNATED LOCATIONS!
CLASS 157 TIME FOR THE ENEMY
Neo Demon Inc. Dream Development World
I REPEAT, EVACUATE IMMEDIATELY!

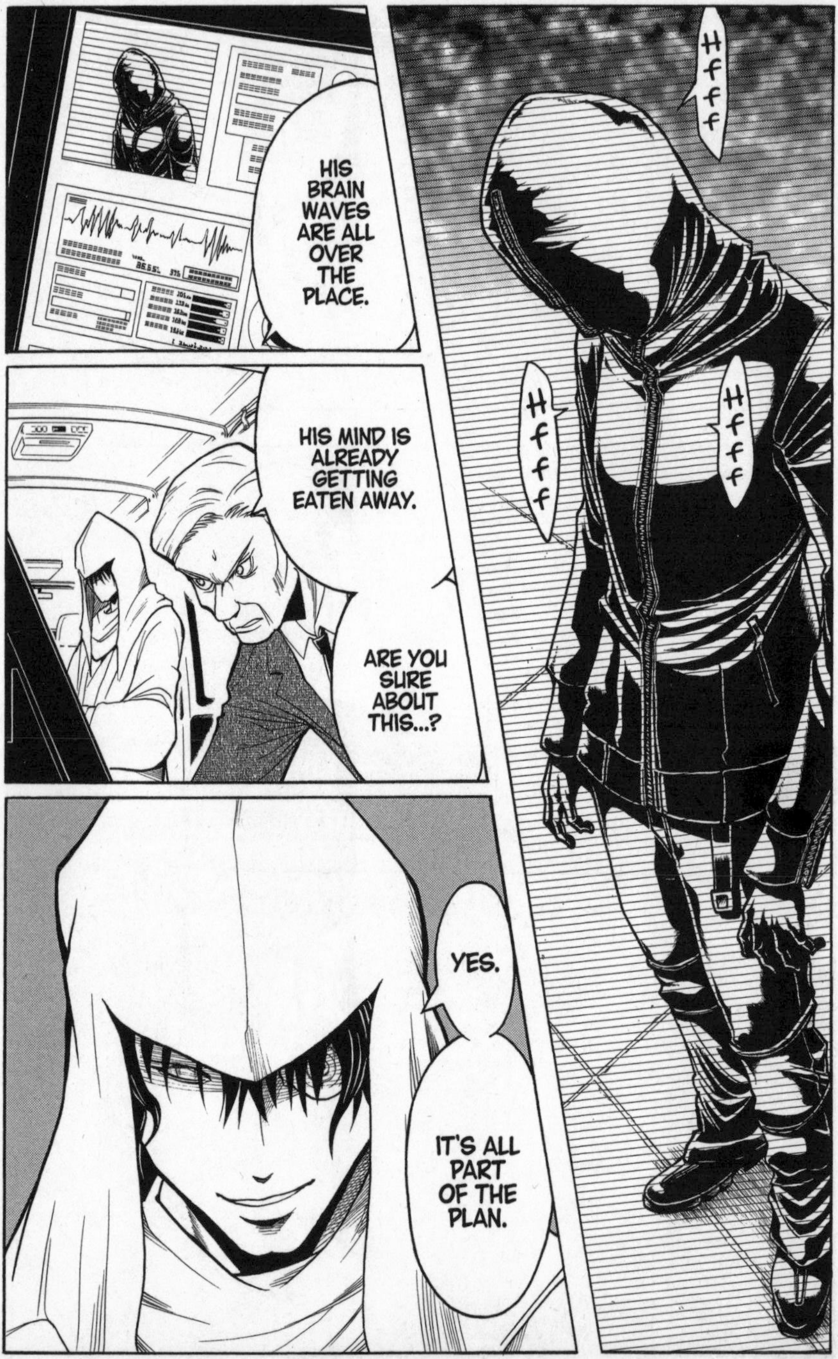
Hfff
Hfff
Hfff
HIS BRAIN WAVES ARE ALL OVER THE PLACE.
HIS MIND IS ALREADY GETTING EATEN AWAY.
ARE YOU SURE ABOUT THIS...?
YES.
IT'S ALL PART OF THE PLAN.

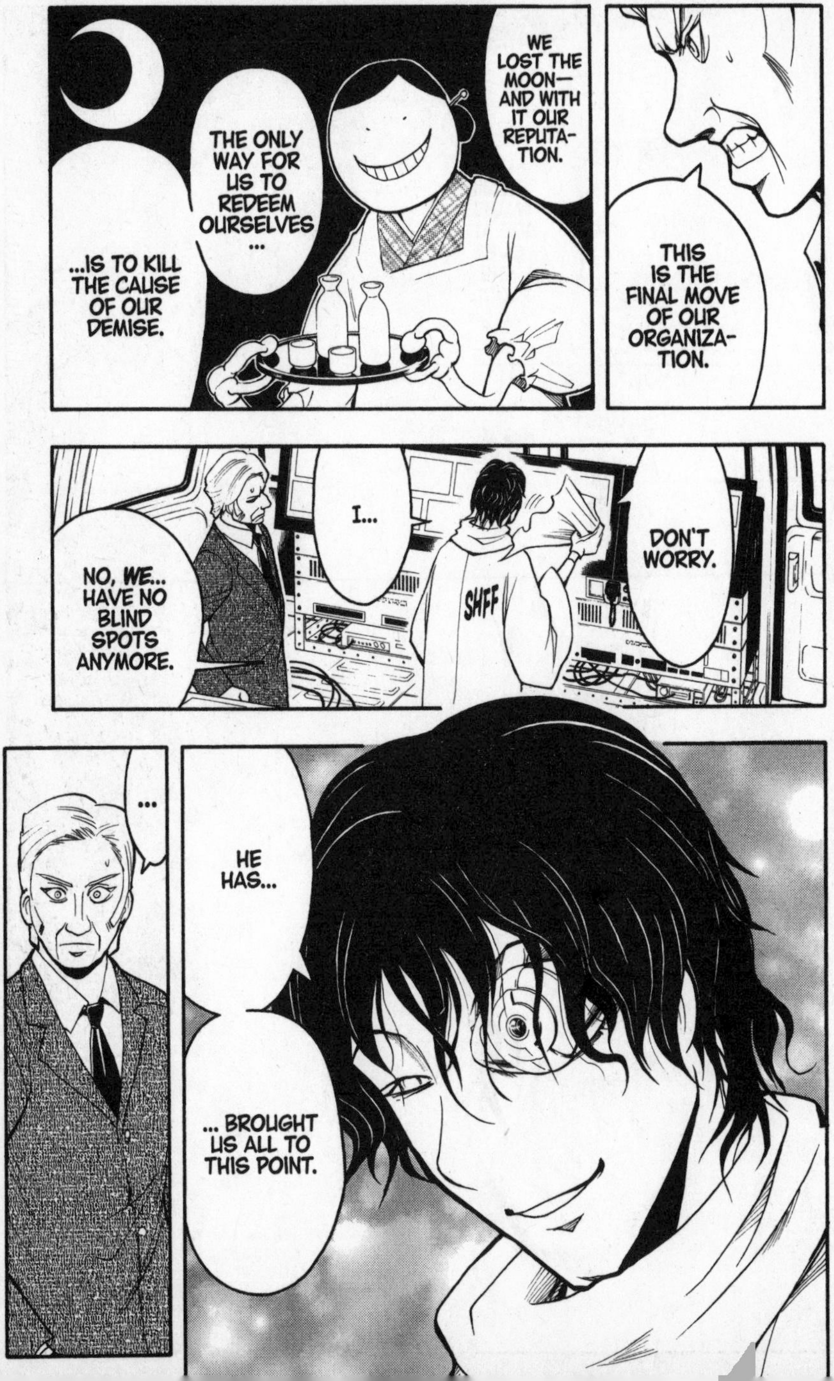
THIS IS THE FINAL MOVE OF OUR ORGANIZATION.
WE LOST THE MOON—AND WITH IT OUR REPUTATION.
THE ONLY WAY FOR US TO REDEEM OURSELVES...
...IS TO KILL THE CAUSE OF OUR DEMISE.
DON'T WORRY.
I...
NO, WE... HAVE NO BLIND SPOTS ANYMORE.
HE HAS...
... BROUGHT US ALL TO THIS POINT.
...

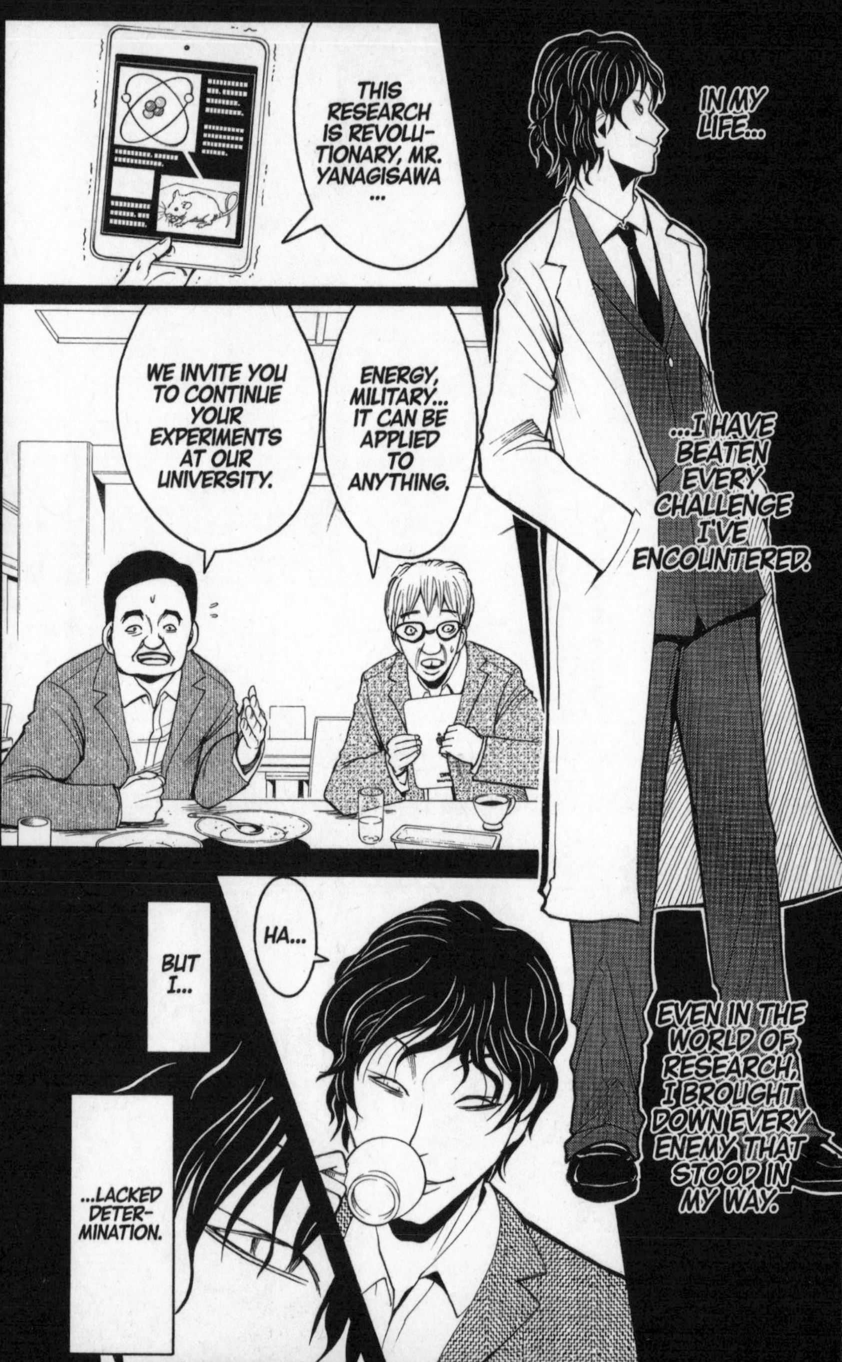
IN MY LIFE...
...I HAVE BEATEN EVERY CHALLENGE I'VE ENCOUNTERED.
EVEN IN THE WORLD OF RESEARCH, I BROUGHT DOWN EVERY ENEMY THAT STOOD IN MY WAY.
THIS RESEARCH IS REVOLUTIONARY, MR. YANAGISAWA...
ENERGY, MILITARY... IT CAN BE APPLIED TO ANYTHING.
WE INVITE YOU TO CONTINUE YOUR EXPERIMENTS AT OUR UNIVERSITY.
HA...
BUT I...
...LACKED DETERMINATION.

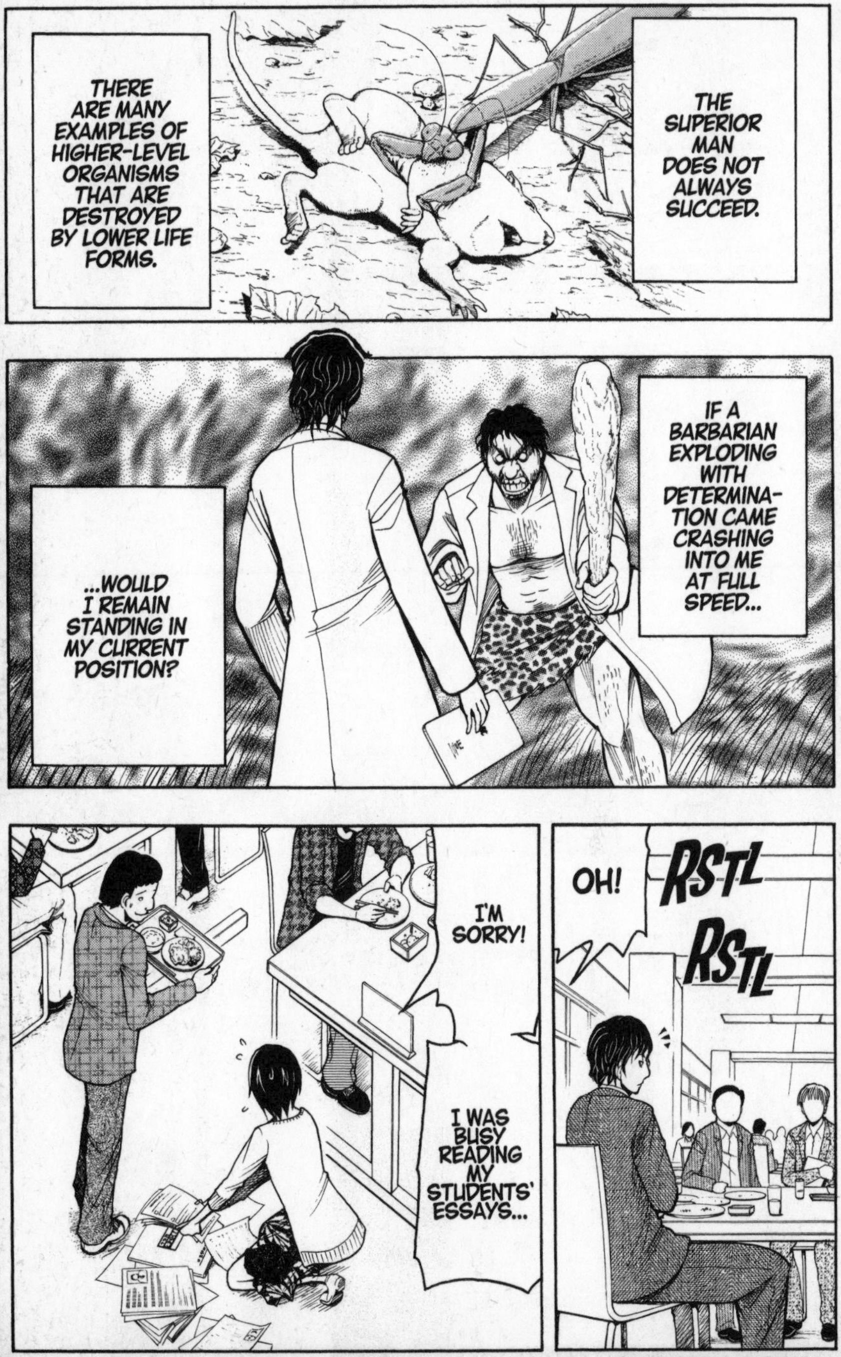
THE SUPERIOR MAN DOES NOT ALWAYS SUCCEED.
THERE ARE MANY EXAMPLES OF HIGHER-LEVEL ORGANISMS THAT ARE DESTROYED BY LOWER LIFE FORMS.
IF A BARBARIAN EXPLODING WITH DETERMINATION CAME CRASHING INTO ME AT FULL SPEED...
...WOULD I REMAIN STANDING IN MY CURRENT POSITION?
RSTL
RSTL
OH!
I'M SORRY!
I WAS BUSY READING MY STUDENTS' ESSAYS...

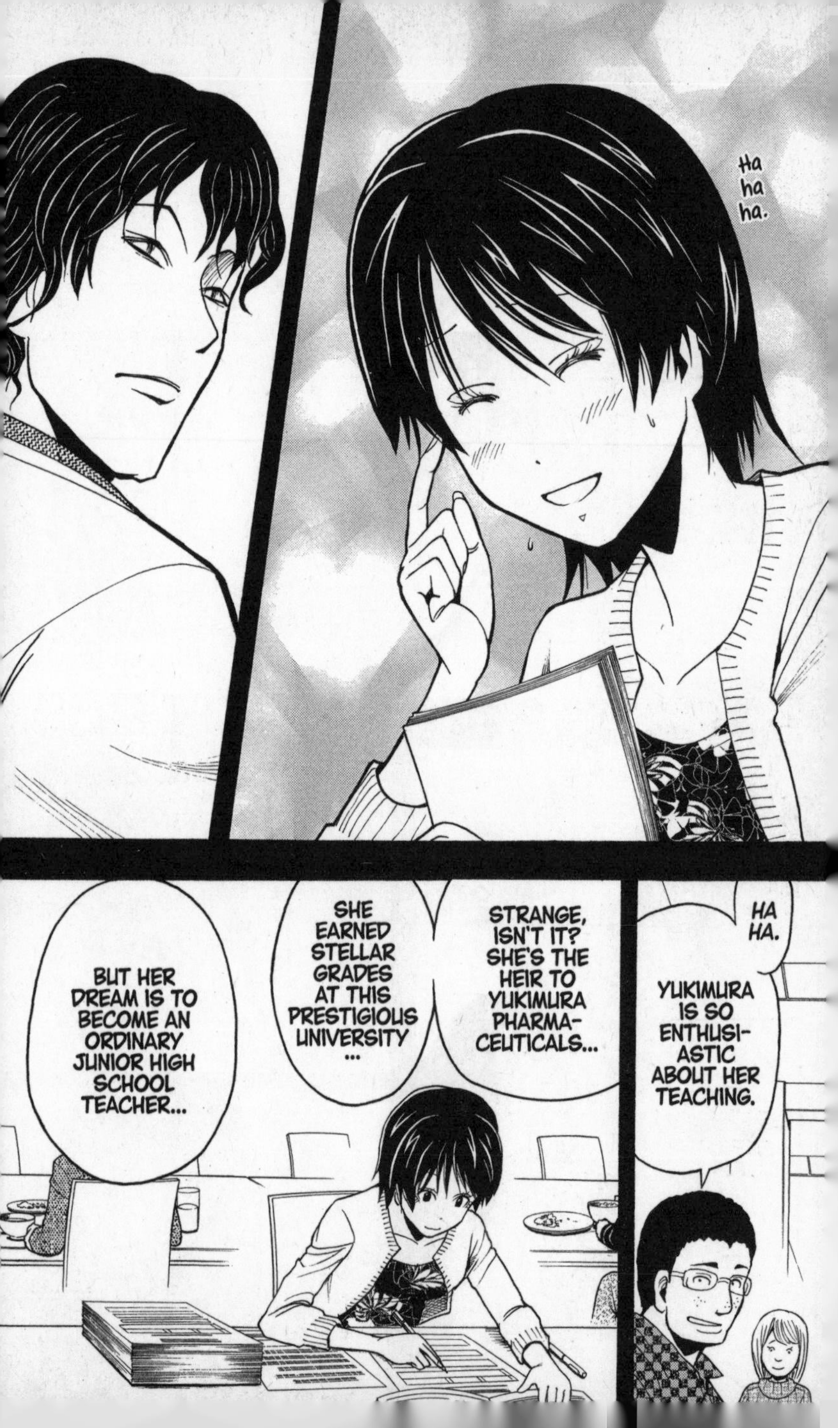
Ha ha ha.
HA HA.
YUKIMURA IS SO ENTHUSI-ASTIC ABOUT HER TEACHING.
STRANGE, ISN'T IT? SHE'S THE HEIR TO YUKIMURA PHARMA-CEUTICALS...
SHE EARNED STELLAR GRADES AT THIS PRESTIGIOUS UNIVERSITY ...
BUT HER DREAM IS TO BECOME AN ORDINARY JUNIOR HIGH SCHOOL TEACHER...

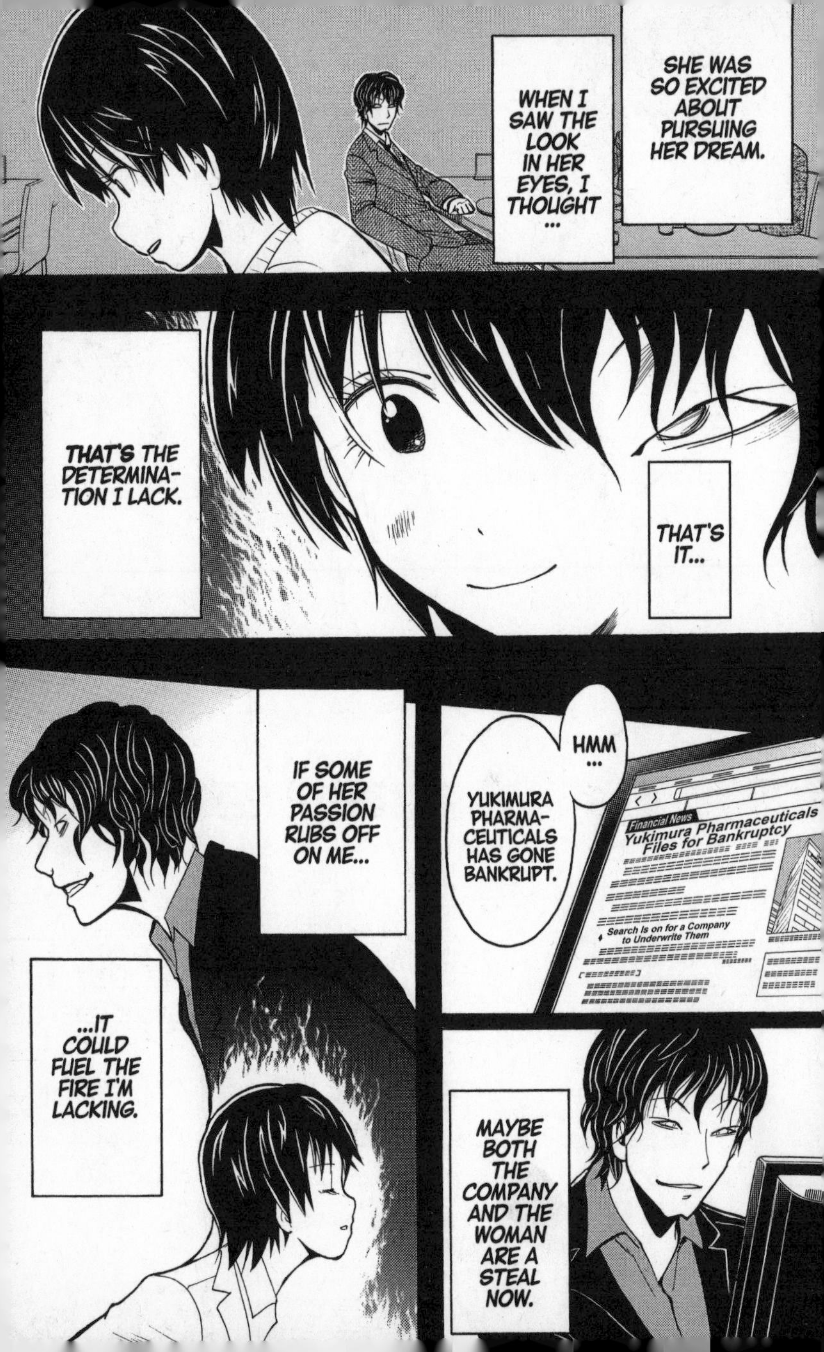
SHE WAS SO EXCITED ABOUT PURSUING HER DREAM.
WHEN I SAW THE LOOK IN HER EYES, I THOUGHT ...
THAT'S IT...
THAT'S THE DETERMINATION I LACK.
HMM ...
YUKIMURA PHARMACEUTICALS HAS GONE BANKRUPT.
Financial News
Yukimura Pharmaceuticals Files for Bankruptcy
Search Is on for a Company to Underwrite Them
MAYBE BOTH THE COMPANY AND THE WOMAN ARE A STEAL NOW.
IF SOME OF HER PASSION RUBS OFF ON ME...
...IT COULD FUEL THE FIRE I'M LACKING.

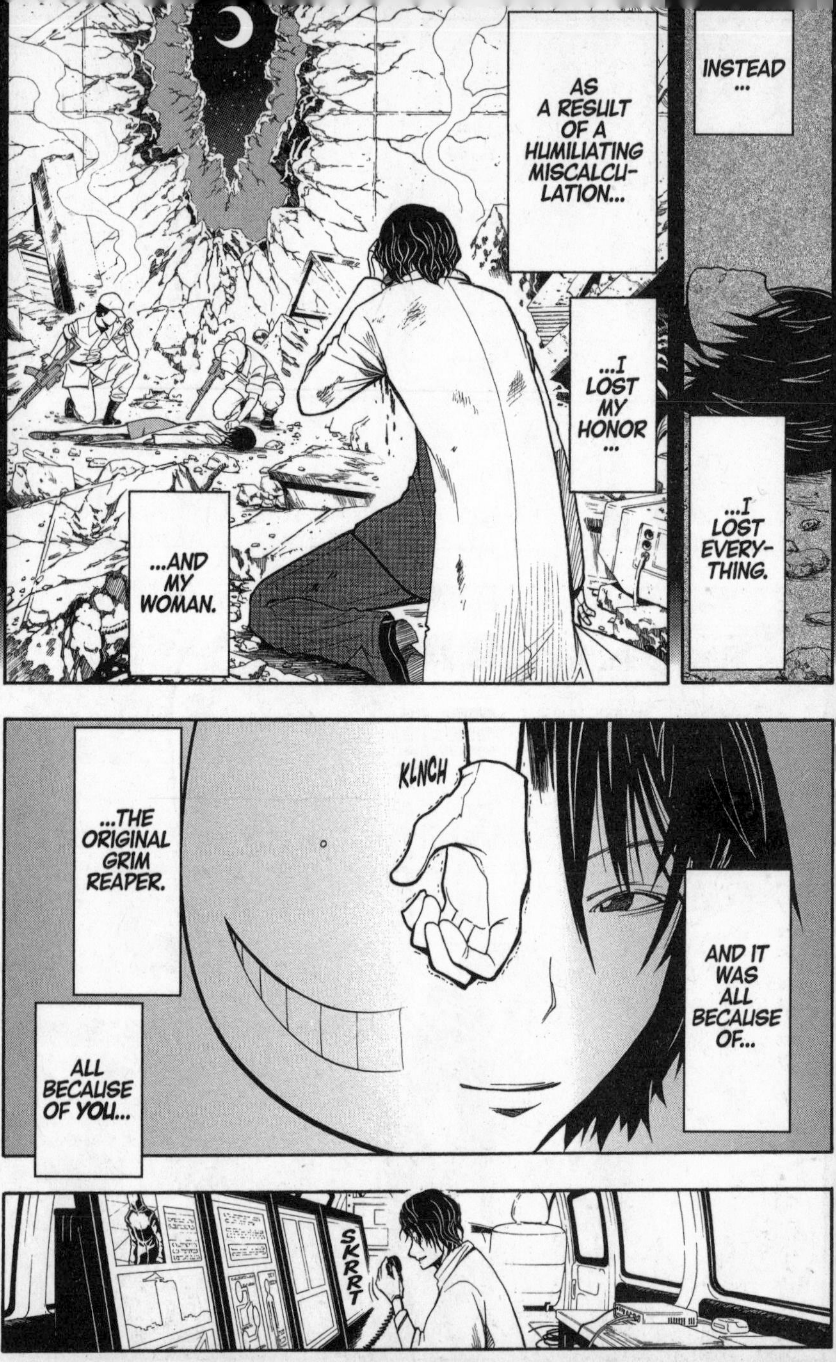
INSTEAD...
...I LOST EVERYTHING.
AS A RESULT OF A HUMILIATING MISCALCULATION...
...I LOST MY HONOR...
...AND MY WOMAN.
KLNCH
AND IT WAS ALL BECAUSE OF...
...THE ORIGINAL GRIM REAPER.
ALL BECAUSE OF YOU...
SKRRT

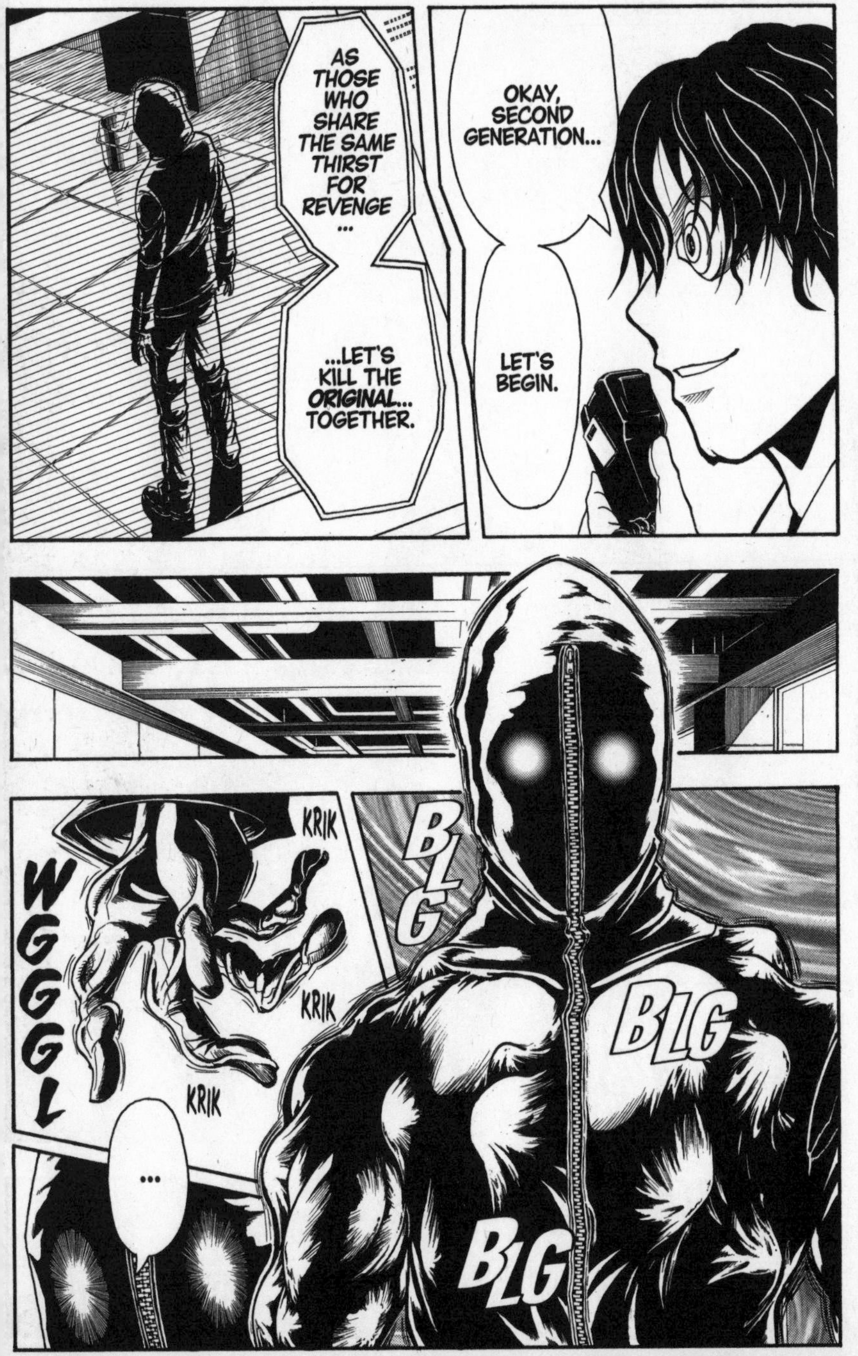
OKAY, SECOND GENERATION...
LET'S BEGIN.
AS THOSE WHO SHARE THE SAME THIRST FOR REVENGE...
...LET'S KILL THE ORIGINAL... TOGETHER.
BLG
BLG
BLG
KRIK
KRIK
KRIK
WGGGL
...

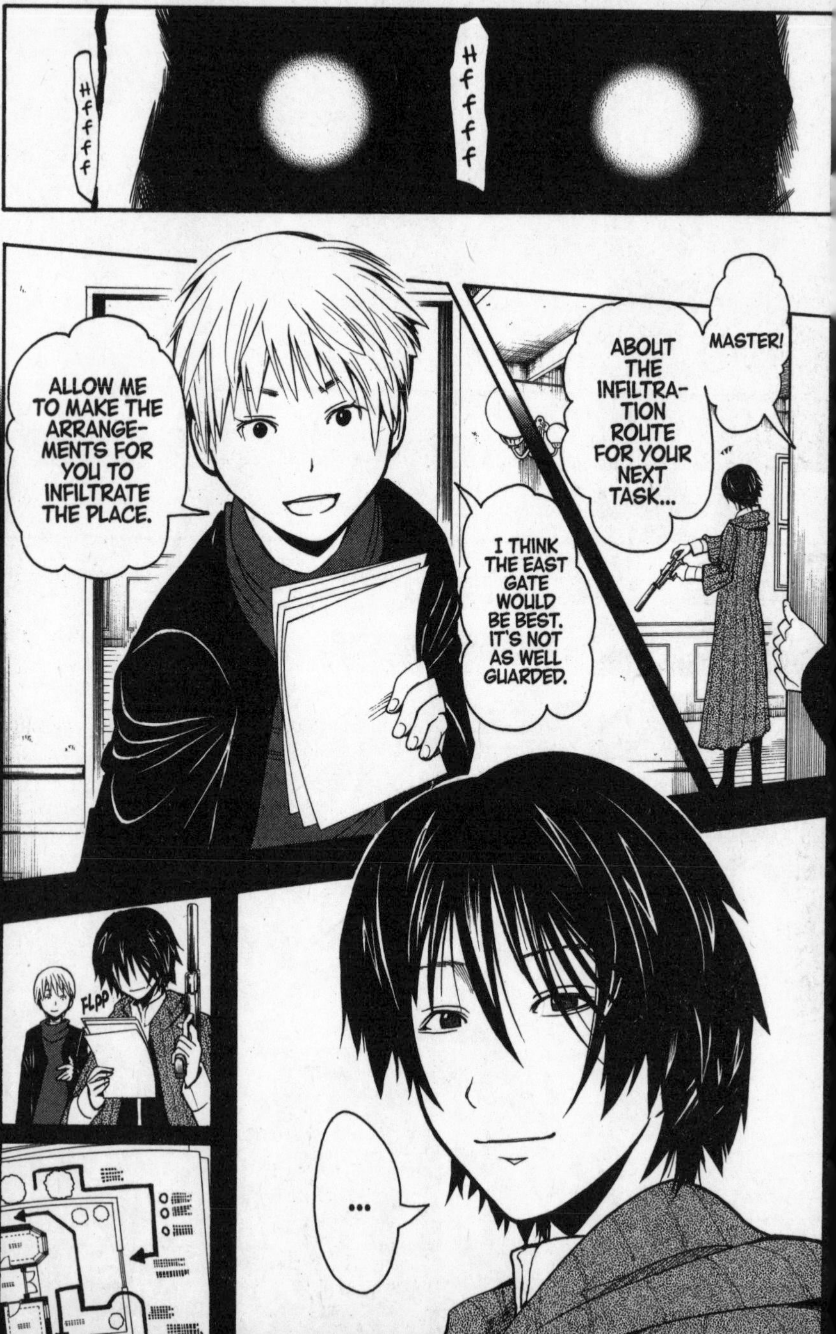
Hffff
Hffff
MASTER!
ABOUT THE INFILTRATION ROUTE FOR YOUR NEXT TASK...
I THINK THE EAST GATE WOULD BE BEST. IT'S NOT AS WELL GUARDED.
ALLOW ME TO MAKE THE ARRANGEMENTS FOR YOU TO INFILTRATE THE PLACE.
...
FLPP

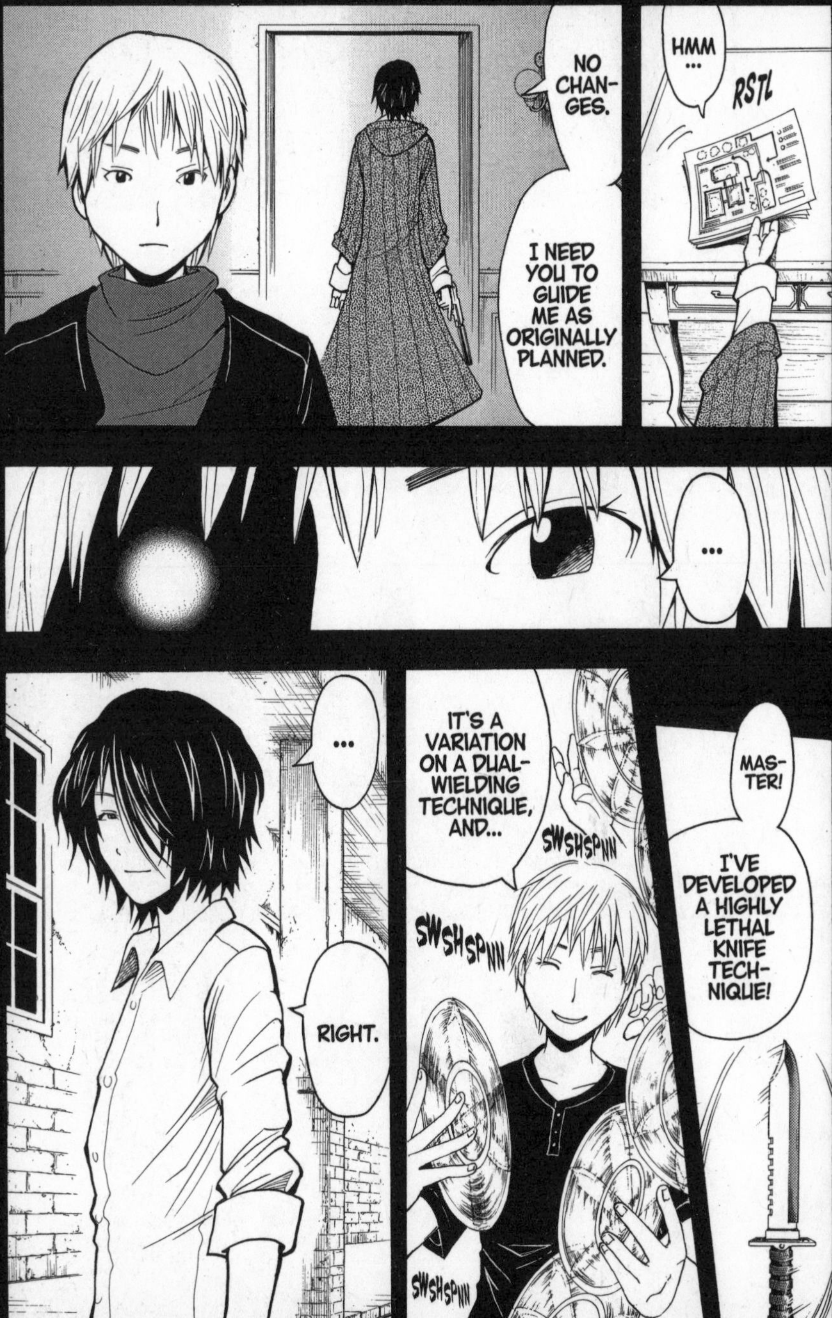
HMM...
RSTL
NO CHANGES.
I NEED YOU TO GUIDE ME AS ORIGINALLY PLANNED.
...
MASTER!
I'VE DEVELOPED A HIGHLY LETHAL KNIFE TECHNIQUE!
IT'S A VARIATION ON A DUAL-WIELDING TECHNIQUE, AND...
SWSHSPNN
SWSHSPNN
SWSHSPNN
...
RIGHT.

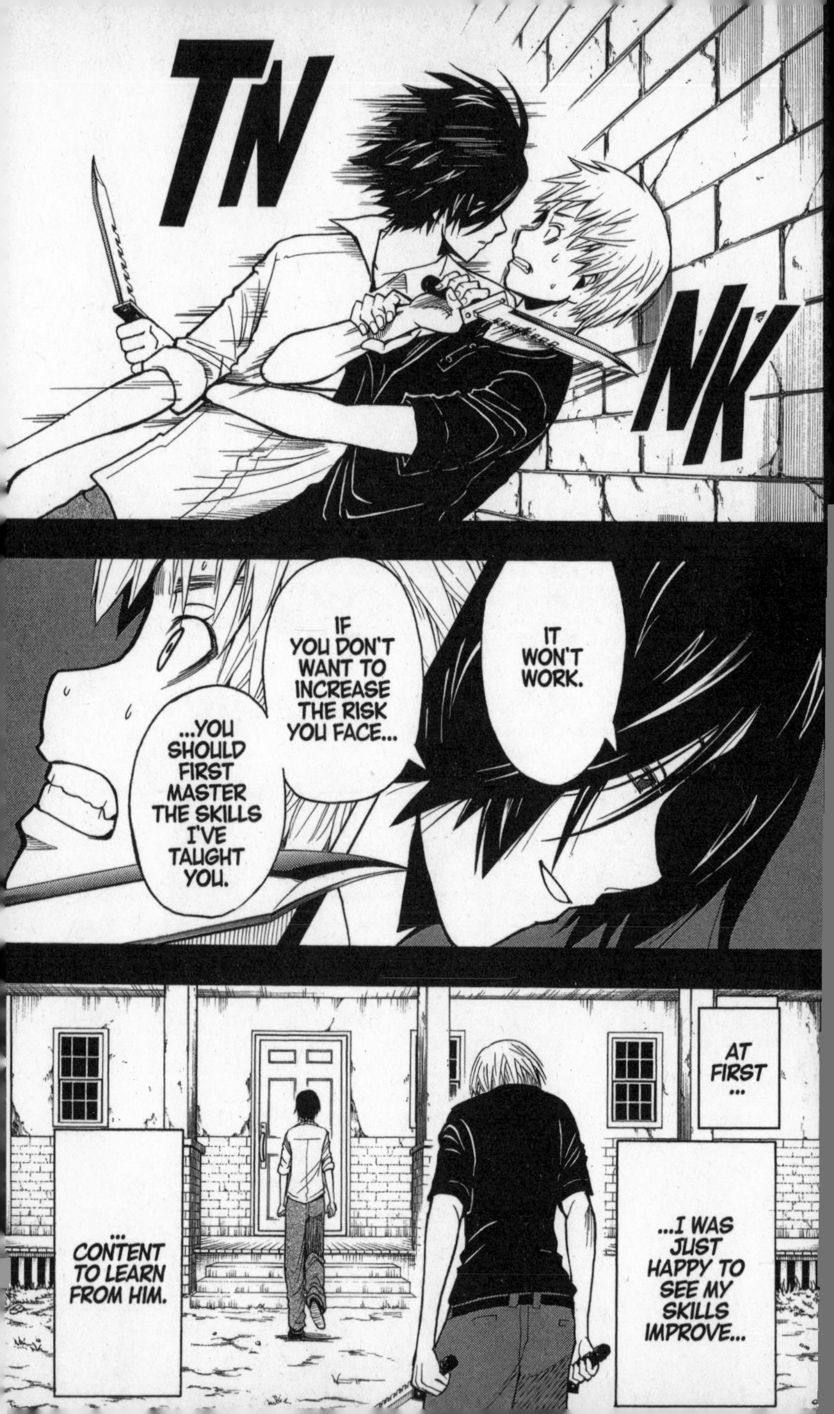
TN
NK
IT WON'T WORK.
IF YOU DON'T WANT TO INCREASE THE RISK YOU FACE...
...YOU SHOULD FIRST MASTER THE SKILLS I'VE TAUGHT YOU.
AT FIRST...
...I WAS JUST HAPPY TO SEE MY SKILLS IMPROVE...
...CONTENT TO LEARN FROM HIM.

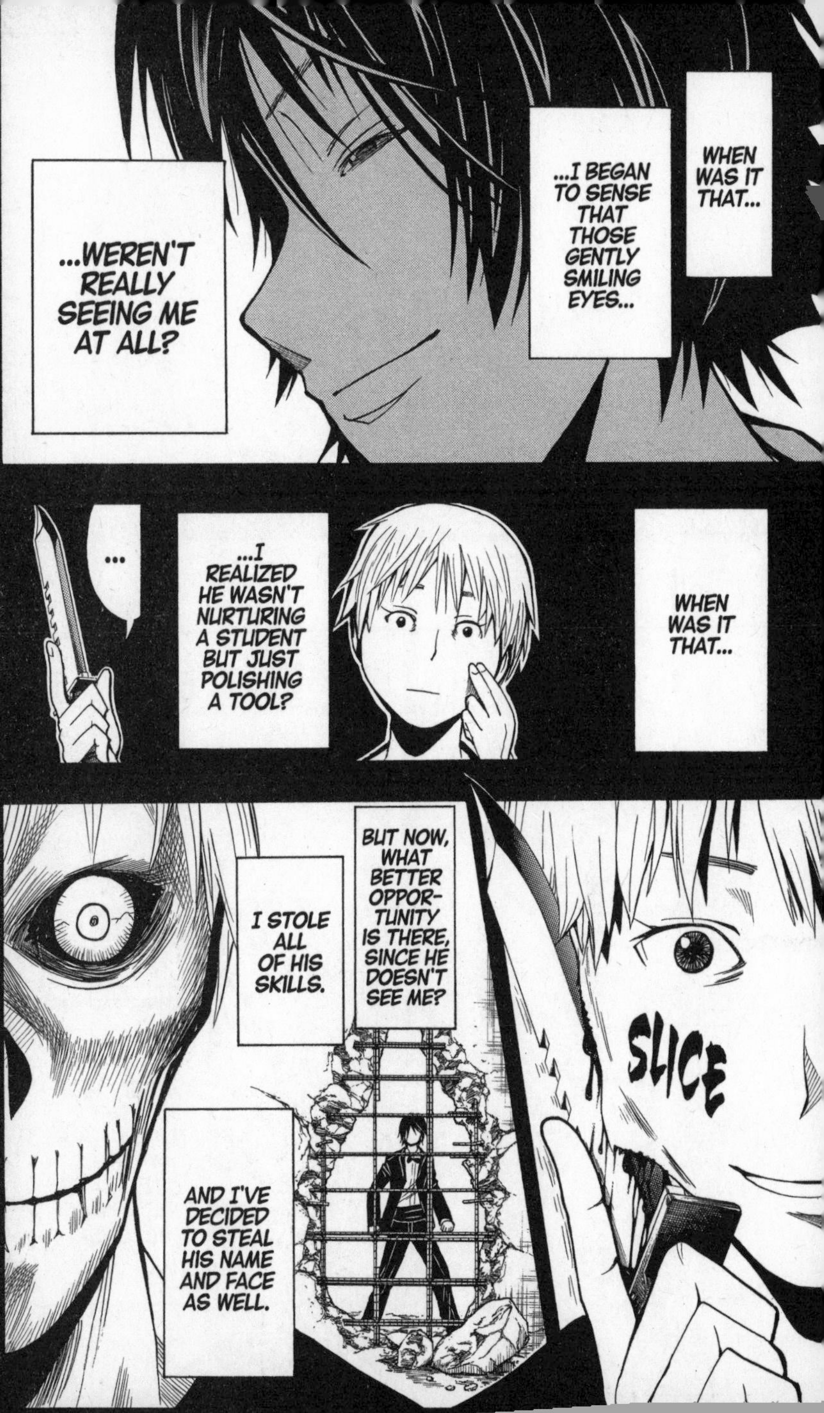
WHEN WAS IT THAT...
...I BEGAN TO SENSE THAT THOSE GENTLY SMILING EYES...
...WEREN'T REALLY SEEING ME AT ALL?
WHEN WAS IT THAT...
...I REALIZED HE WASN'T NURTURING A STUDENT BUT JUST POLISHING A TOOL?
...
SLICE
BUT NOW, WHAT BETTER OPPOR-TUNITY IS THERE, SINCE HE DOESN'T SEE ME?
I STOLE ALL OF HIS SKILLS.
AND I'VE DECIDED TO STEAL HIS NAME AND FACE AS WELL.

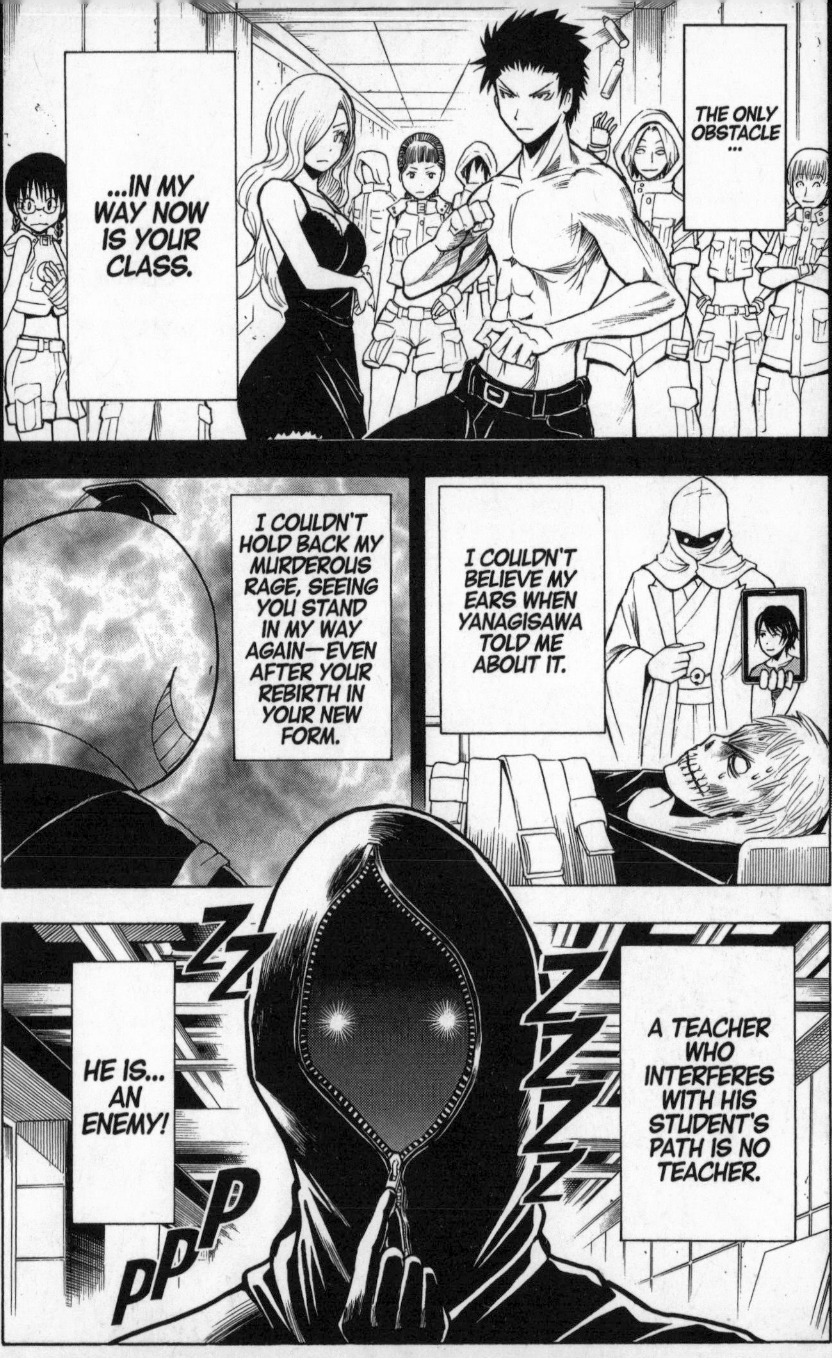
THE ONLY OBSTACLE ...
...IN MY WAY NOW IS YOUR CLASS.
I COULDN'T BELIEVE MY EARS WHEN YANAGISAWA TOLD ME ABOUT IT.
I COULDN'T HOLD BACK MY MURDEROUS RAGE, SEEING YOU STAND IN MY WAY AGAIN—EVEN AFTER YOUR REBIRTH IN YOUR NEW FORM.
A TEACHER WHO INTERFERES WITH HIS STUDENT'S PATH IS NO TEACHER.
HE IS... AN ENEMY!

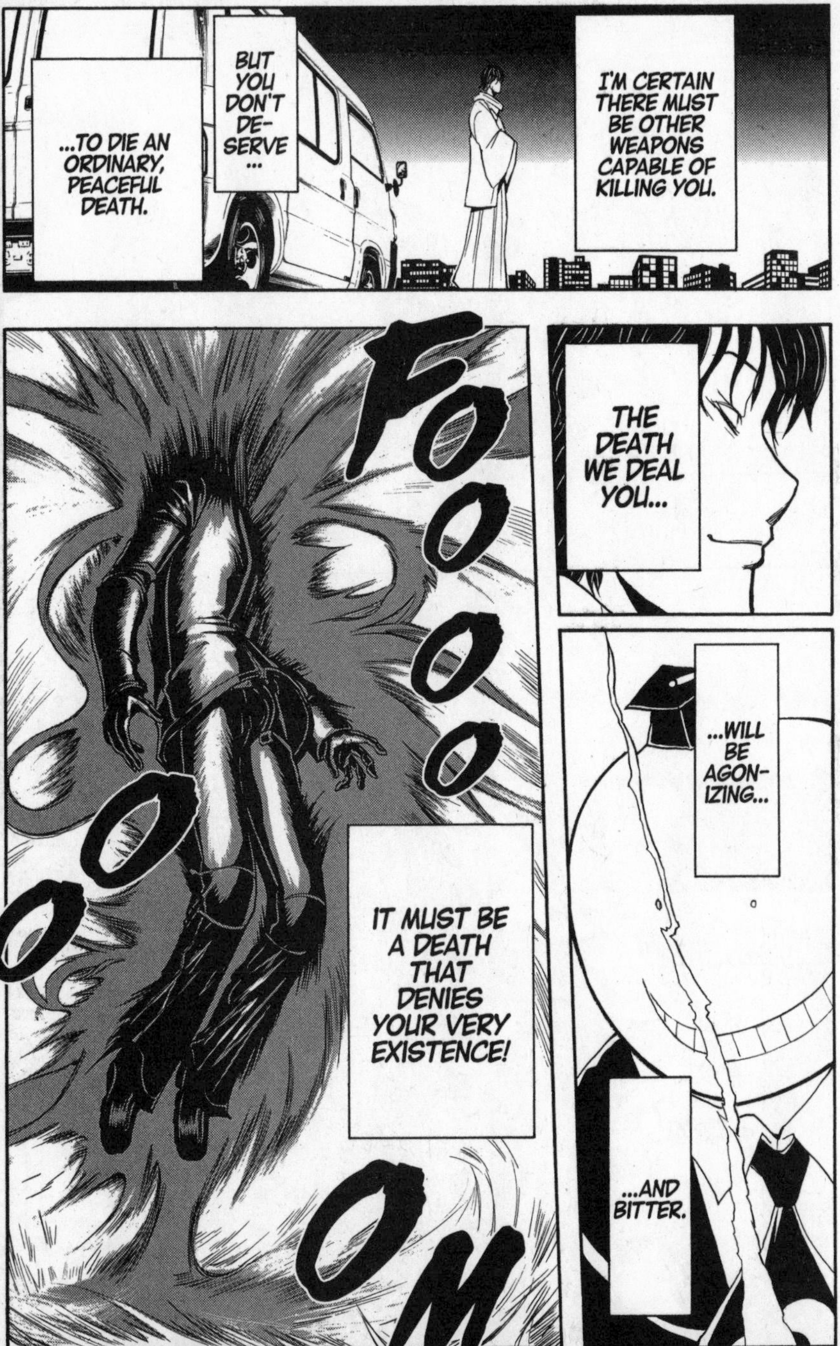
I'M CERTAIN THERE MUST BE OTHER WEAPONS CAPABLE OF KILLING YOU.
BUT YOU DON'T DE-SERVE...
...TO DIE AN ORDINARY, PEACEFUL DEATH.
THE DEATH WE DEAL YOU...
...WILL BE AGON-IZING...
...AND BITTER.
FOOOOOOOOM
IT MUST BE A DEATH THAT DENIES YOUR VERY EXISTENCE!

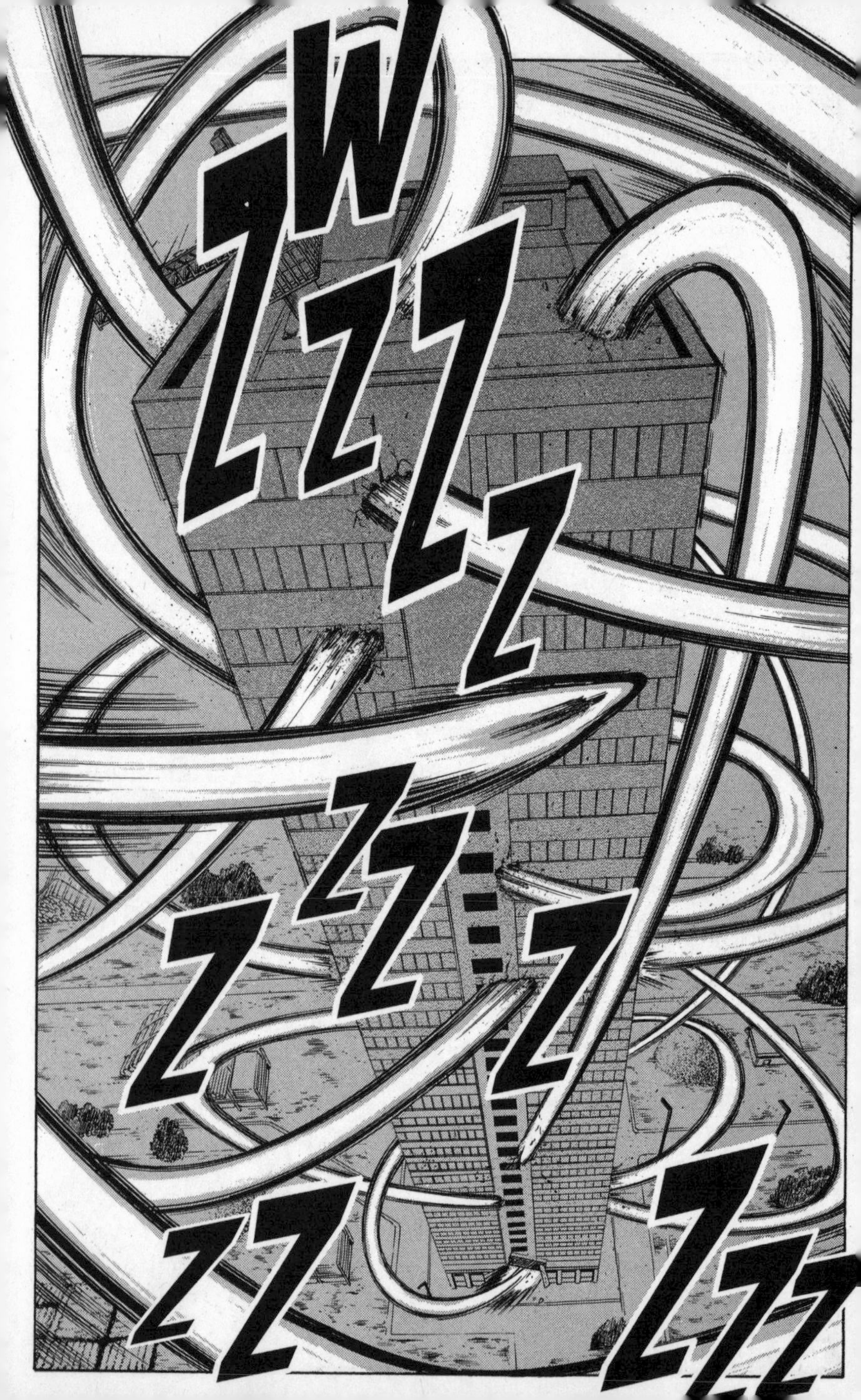
ZWZZZ
ZZZZ
ZZZ
ZZ

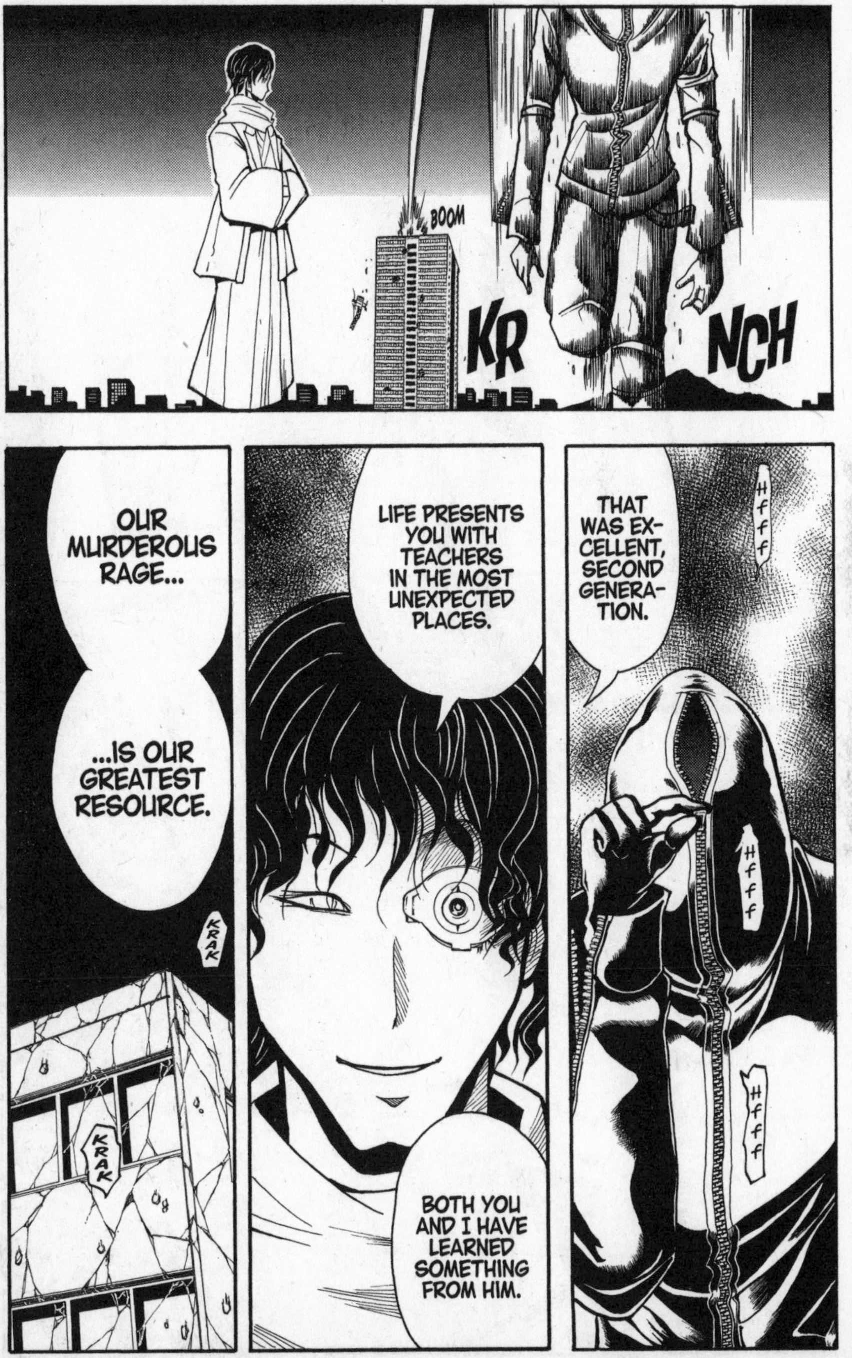
BOOM
KR NCH
Hfff
THAT WAS EX- CELLENT, SECOND GENERA- TION.
Hfff
Hfff
LIFE PRESENTS YOU WITH TEACHERS IN THE MOST UNEXPECTED PLACES.
BOTH YOU AND I HAVE LEARNED SOMETHING FROM HIM.
OUR MURDEROUS RAGE...
...IS OUR GREATEST RESOURCE.
KRAK
KRAK

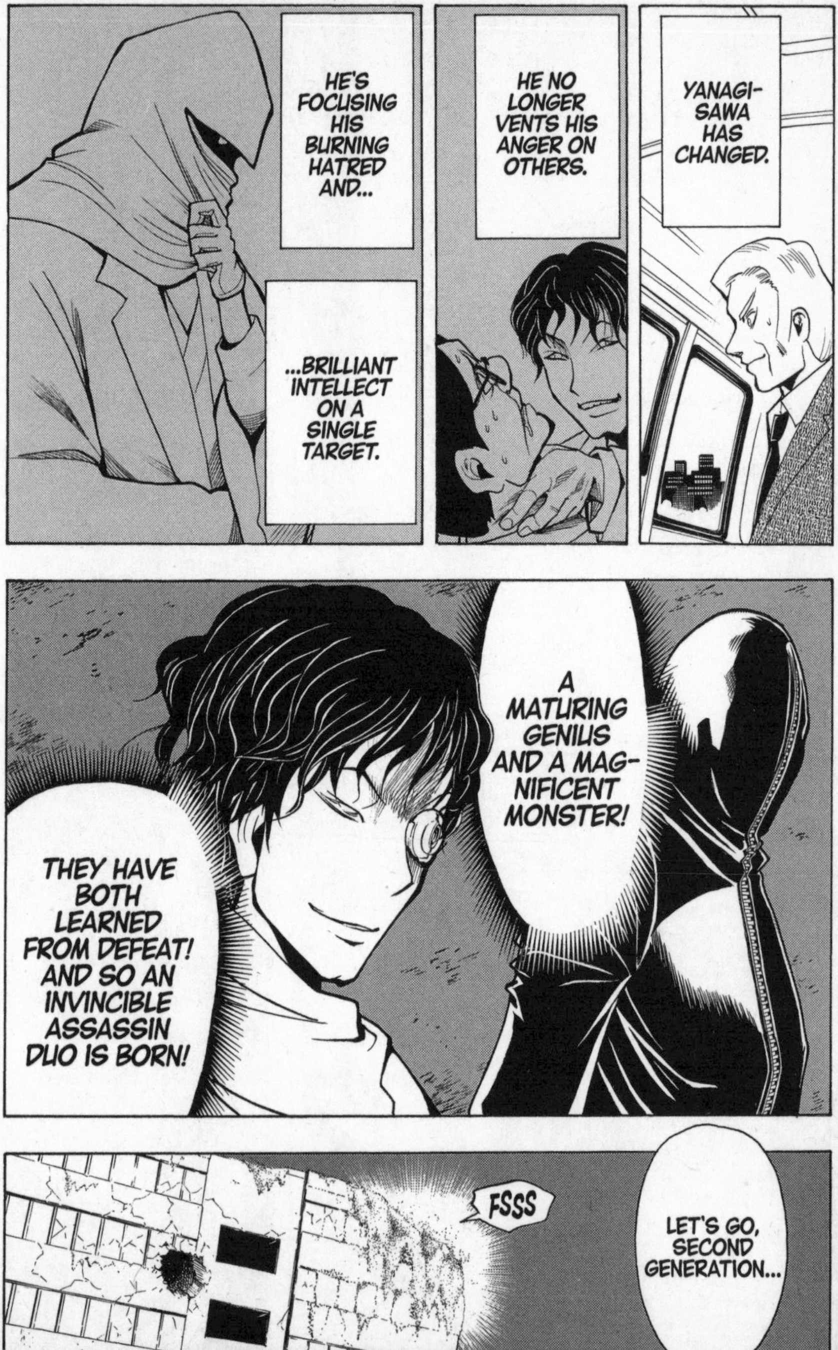
YANAGI-SAWA HAS CHANGED.
HE NO LONGER VENTS HIS ANGER ON OTHERS.
HE'S FOCUSING HIS BURNING HATRED AND...
...BRILLIANT INTELLECT ON A SINGLE TARGET.
A MATURING GENIUS AND A MAG-NIFICENT MONSTER!
THEY HAVE BOTH LEARNED FROM DEFEAT! AND SO AN INVINCIBLE ASSASSIN DUO IS BORN!
LET'S GO, SECOND GENERATION...
FSSS

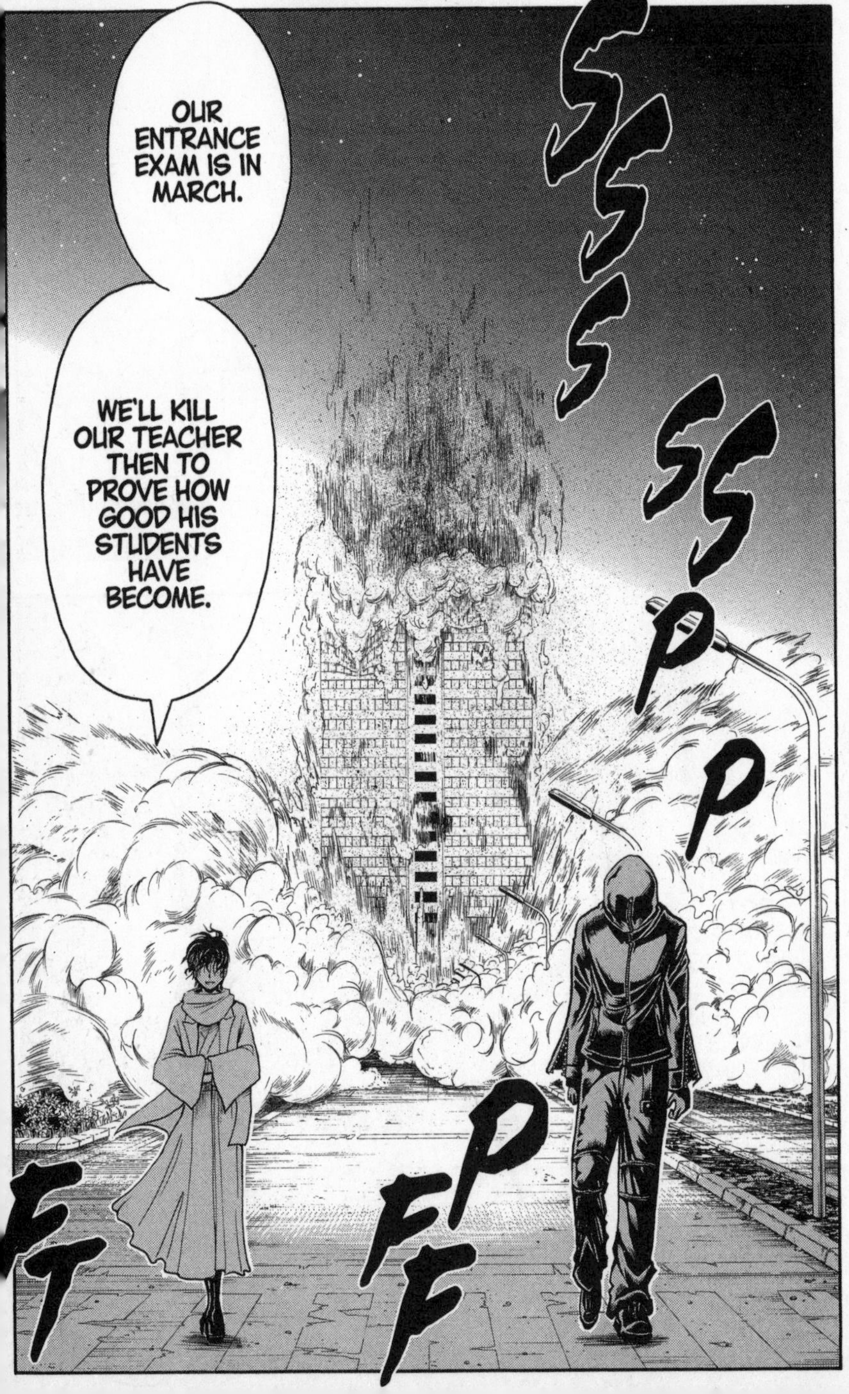
OUR ENTRANCE EXAM IS IN MARCH.
WE'LL KILL OUR TEACHER THEN TO PROVE HOW GOOD HIS STUDENTS HAVE BECOME.

GRIM REAPER II

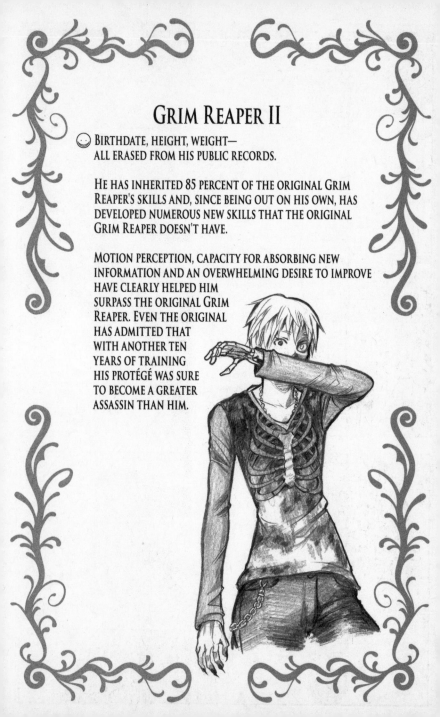

BIRTHDATE, HEIGHT, WEIGHT—
ALL ERASED FROM HIS PUBLIC RECORDS.

HE HAS INHERITED 85 PERCENT OF THE ORIGINAL GRIM
REAPER'S SKILLS AND, SINCE BEING OUT ON HIS OWN, HAS
DEVELOPED NUMEROUS NEW SKILLS THAT THE ORIGINAL
GRIM REAPER DOESN'T HAVE.

MOTION PERCEPTION, CAPACITY FOR ABSORBING NEW
INFORMATION AND AN OVERWHELMING DESIRE TO IMPROVE
HAVE CLEARLY HELPED HIM
SURPASS THE ORIGINAL GRIM
REAPER. EVEN THE ORIGINAL
HAS ADMITTED THAT
WITH ANOTHER TEN
YEARS OF TRAINING
HIS PROTÉGÉ WAS SURE
TO BECOME A GREATER
ASSASSIN THAN HIM.

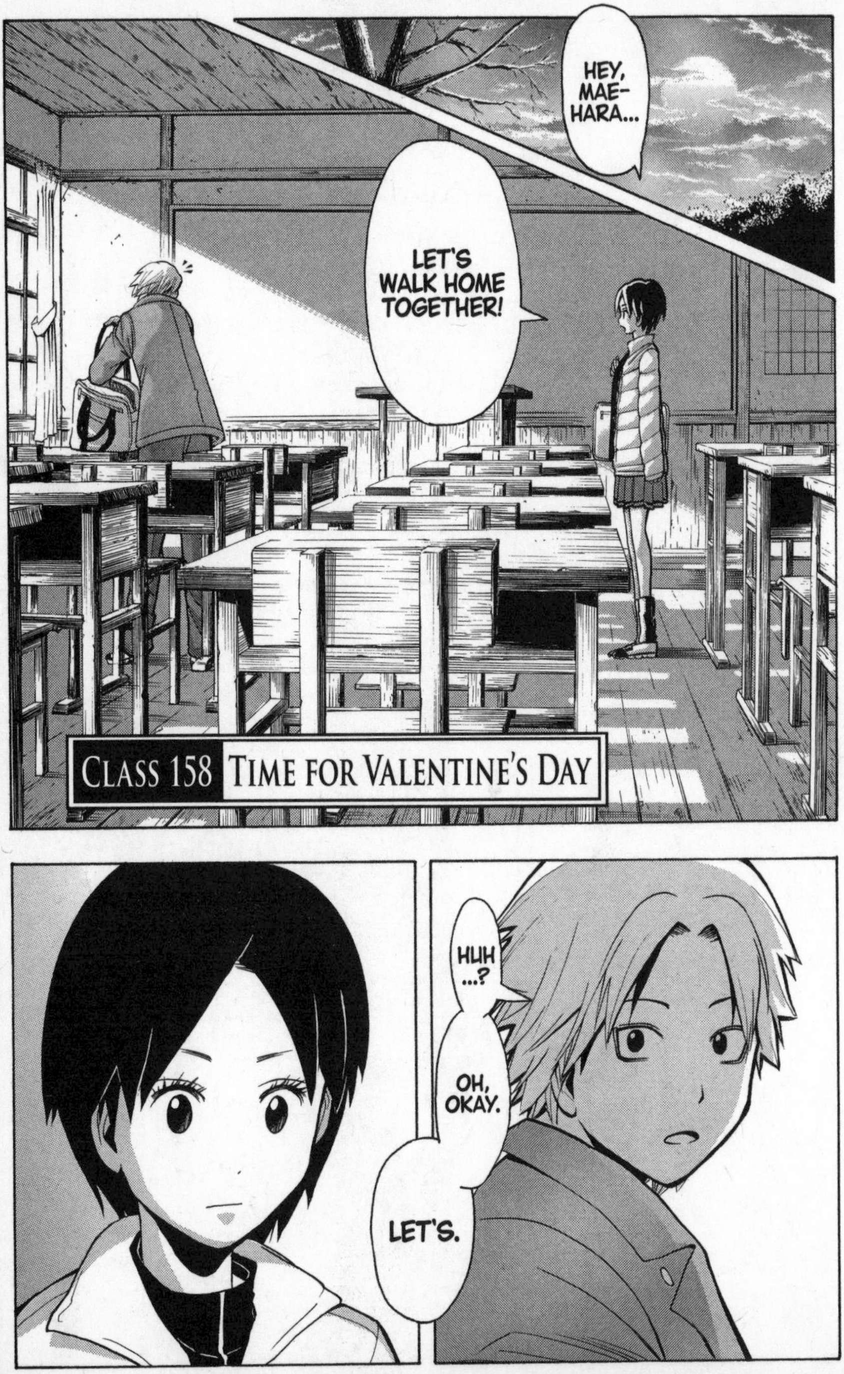
HEY, MAE-HARA...
LET'S WALK HOME TOGETHER!
CLASS 158 TIME FOR VALENTINE'S DAY
HUH ...?
OH, OKAY.
LET'S.

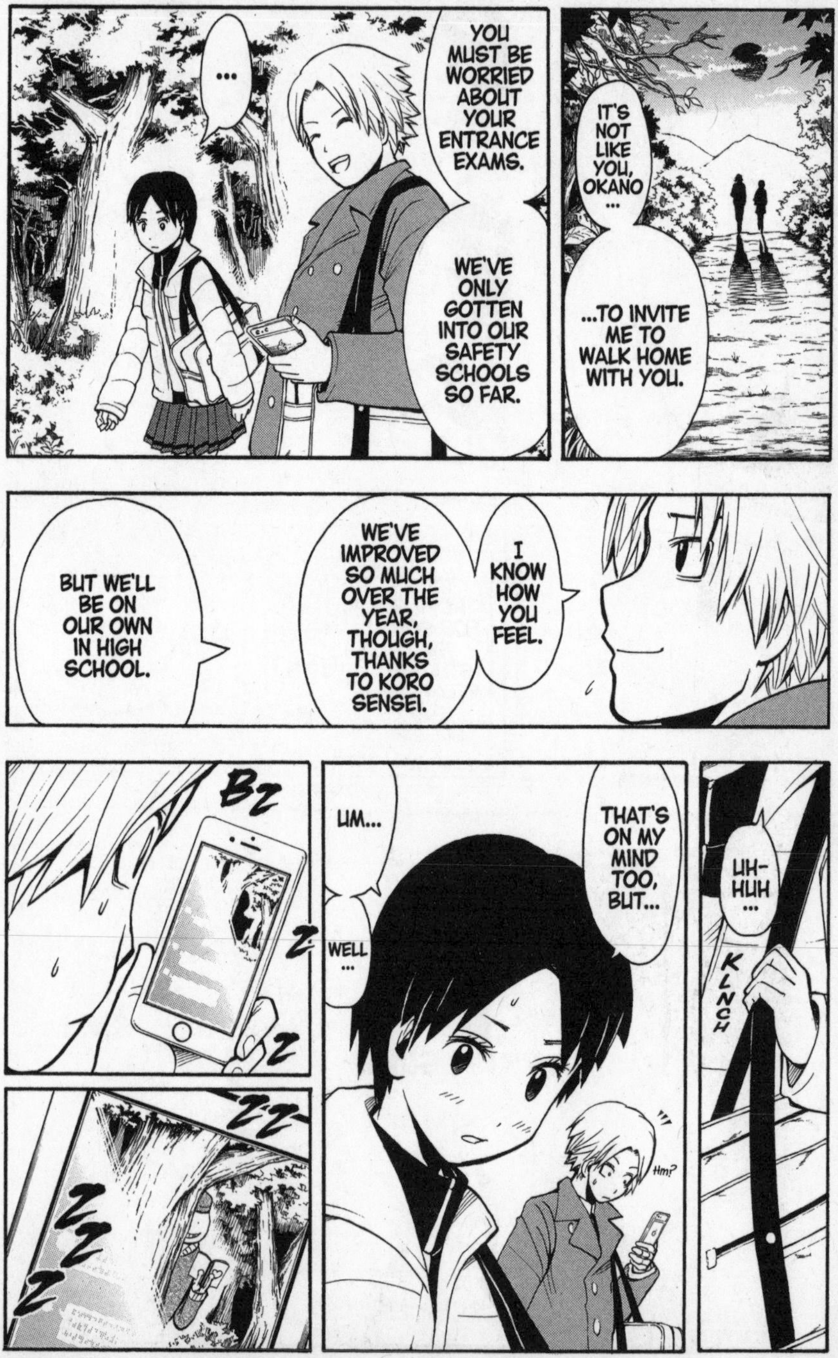
IT'S NOT LIKE YOU, OKANO...
...TO INVITE ME TO WALK HOME WITH YOU.
YOU MUST BE WORRIED ABOUT YOUR ENTRANCE EXAMS.
WE'VE ONLY GOTTEN INTO OUR SAFETY SCHOOLS SO FAR.
...
I KNOW HOW YOU FEEL.
WE'VE IMPROVED SO MUCH OVER THE YEAR, THOUGH, THANKS TO KORO SENSEI.
BUT WE'LL BE ON OUR OWN IN HIGH SCHOOL.
UH-HUH...
KLNCH
THAT'S ON MY MIND TOO, BUT...
UM...
WELL...
Hm?
BZ
Z
Z
ZZ
ZZZ

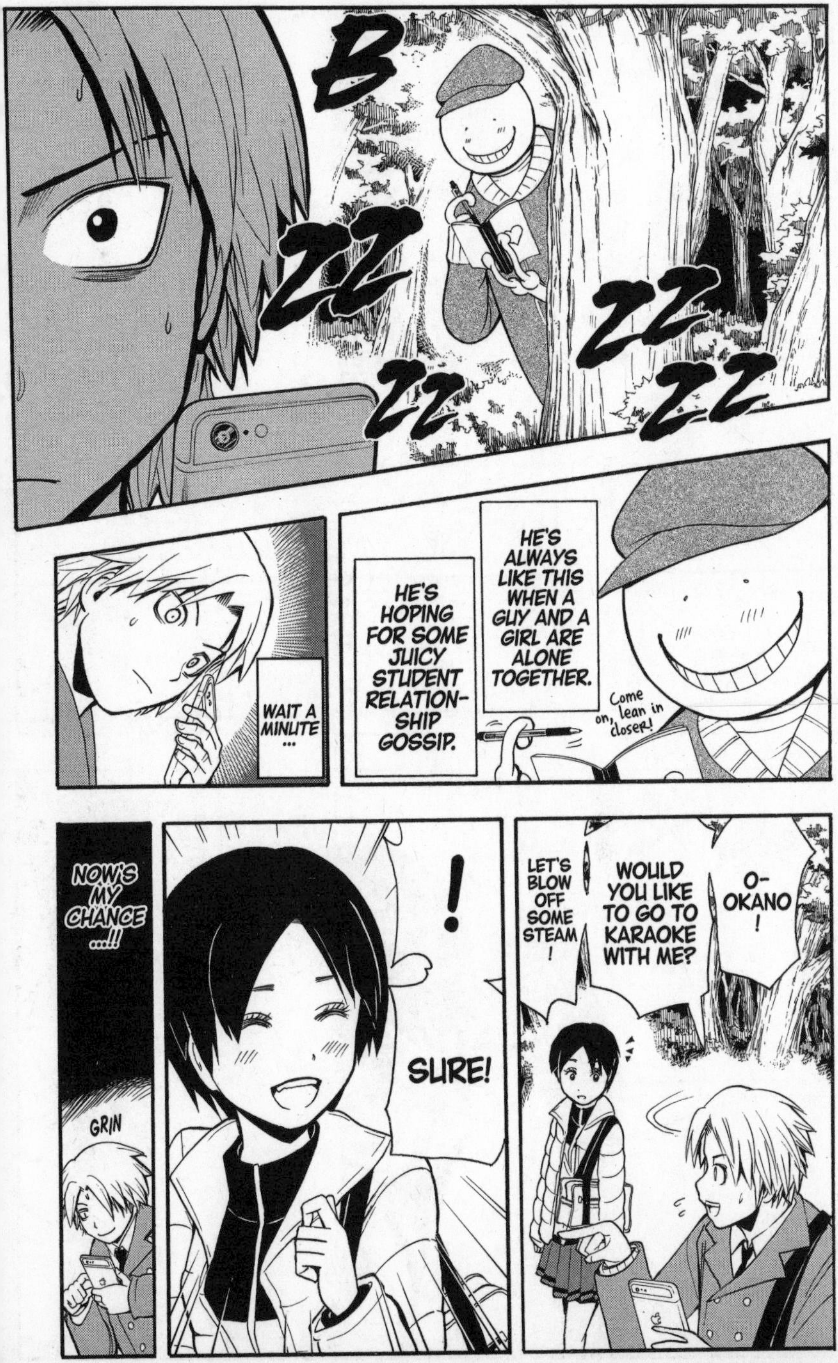

BZZZZZZZZ
HE'S ALWAYS LIKE THIS WHEN A GUY AND A GIRL ARE ALONE TOGETHER.
Come on, lean in closer!
HE'S HOPING FOR SOME JUICY STUDENT RELATIONSHIP GOSSIP.
WAIT A MINUTE ...
O-OKANO!
WOULD YOU LIKE TO GO TO KARAOKE WITH ME?
LET'S BLOW OFF SOME STEAM!
!
SURE!
NOW'S MY CHANCE ...!!
GRIN

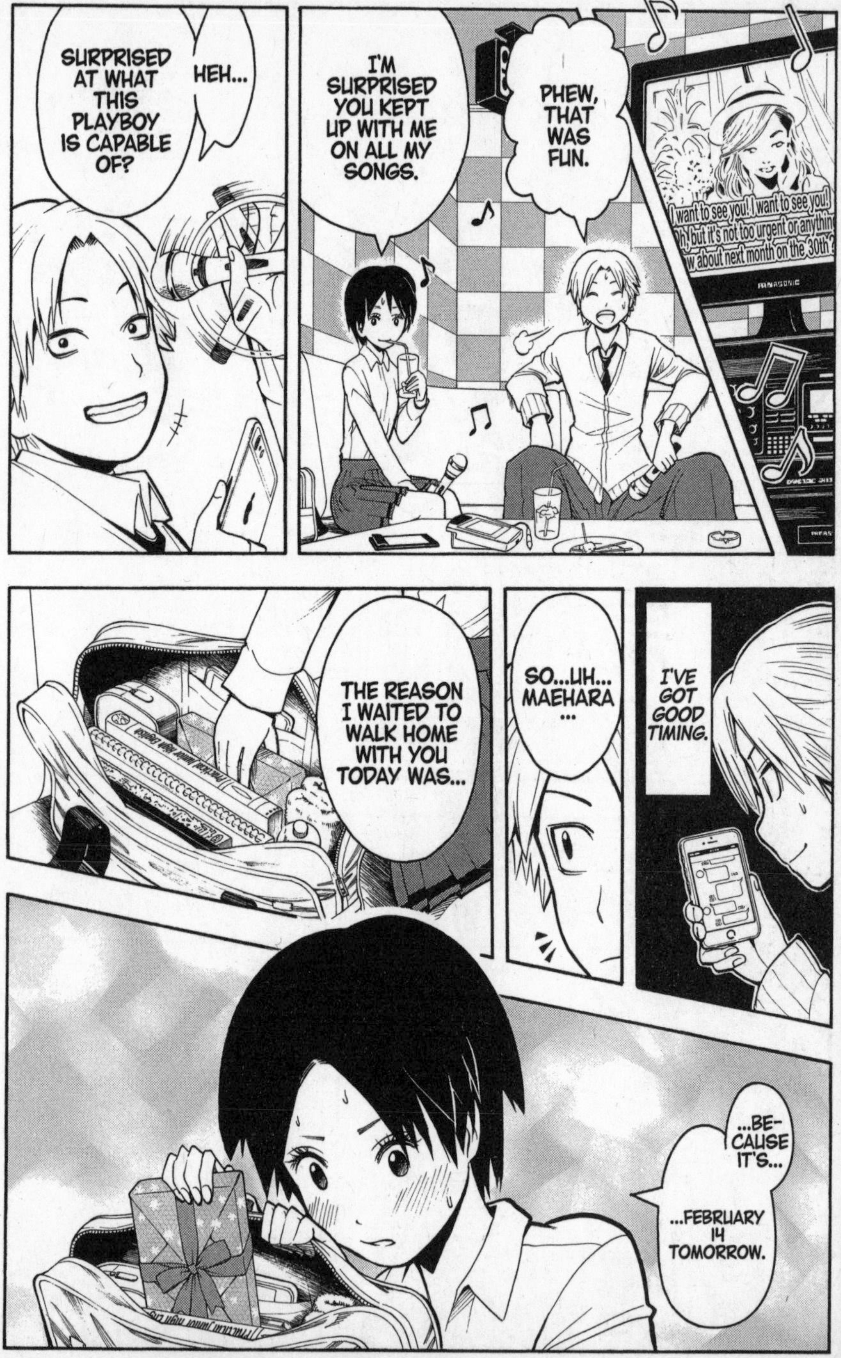
I want to see you! I want to see you!
h, but it's not too urgent or anythin
w about next month on the 30th?
PHEW, THAT WAS FUN.
I'M SURPRISED YOU KEPT UP WITH ME ON ALL MY SONGS.
HEH...
SURPRISED AT WHAT THIS PLAYBOY IS CAPABLE OF?
I'VE GOT GOOD TIMING.
SO...UH... MAEHARA ...
THE REASON I WAITED TO WALK HOME WITH YOU TODAY WAS...
...BE-CAUSE IT'S...
...FEBRUARY 14 TOMORROW.

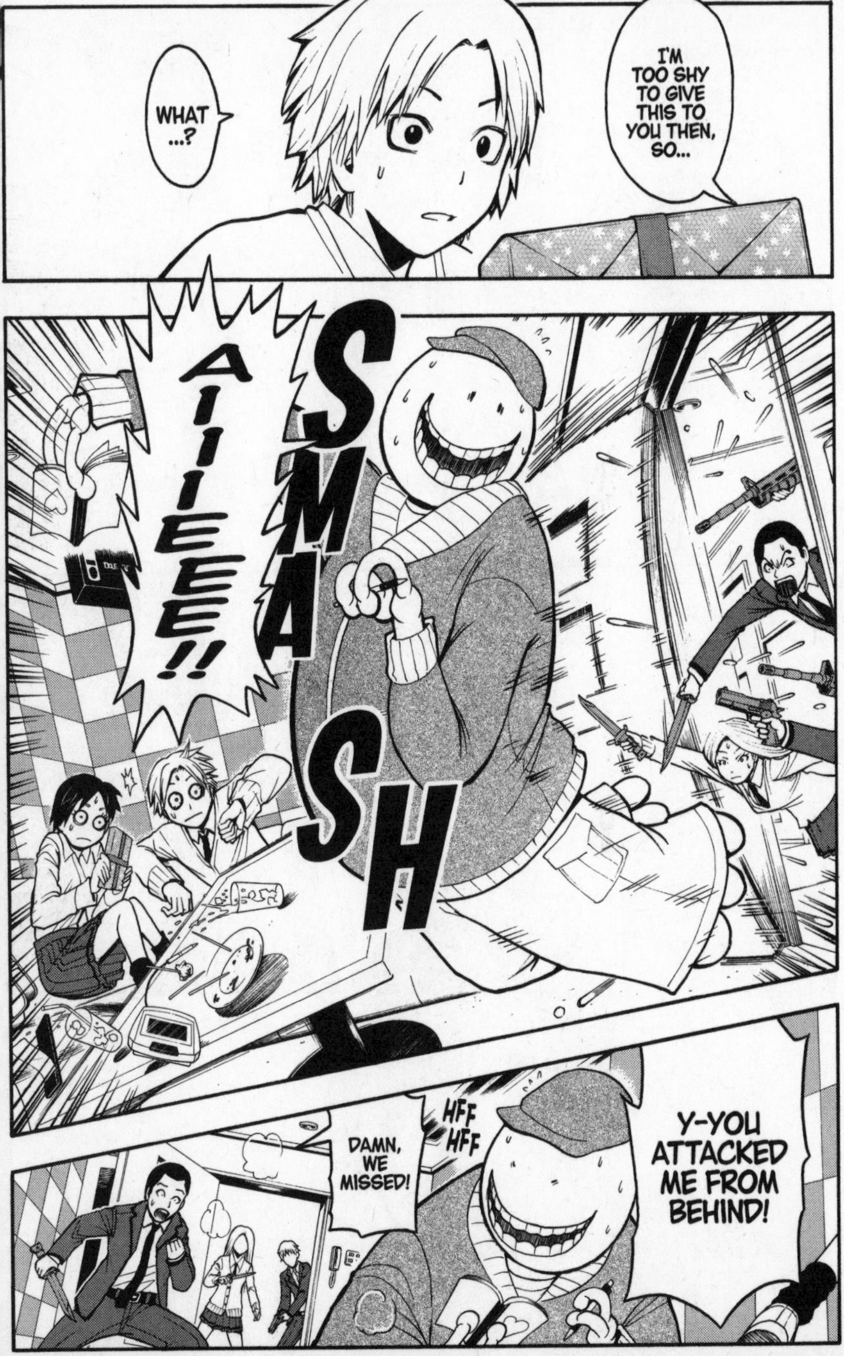
I'M TOO SHY TO GIVE THIS TO YOU THEN, SO...
WHAT ...?
SMASH
AIIIEEEE!!
Y-YOU ATTACKED ME FROM BEHIND!
HFF HFF
DAMN, WE MISSED!

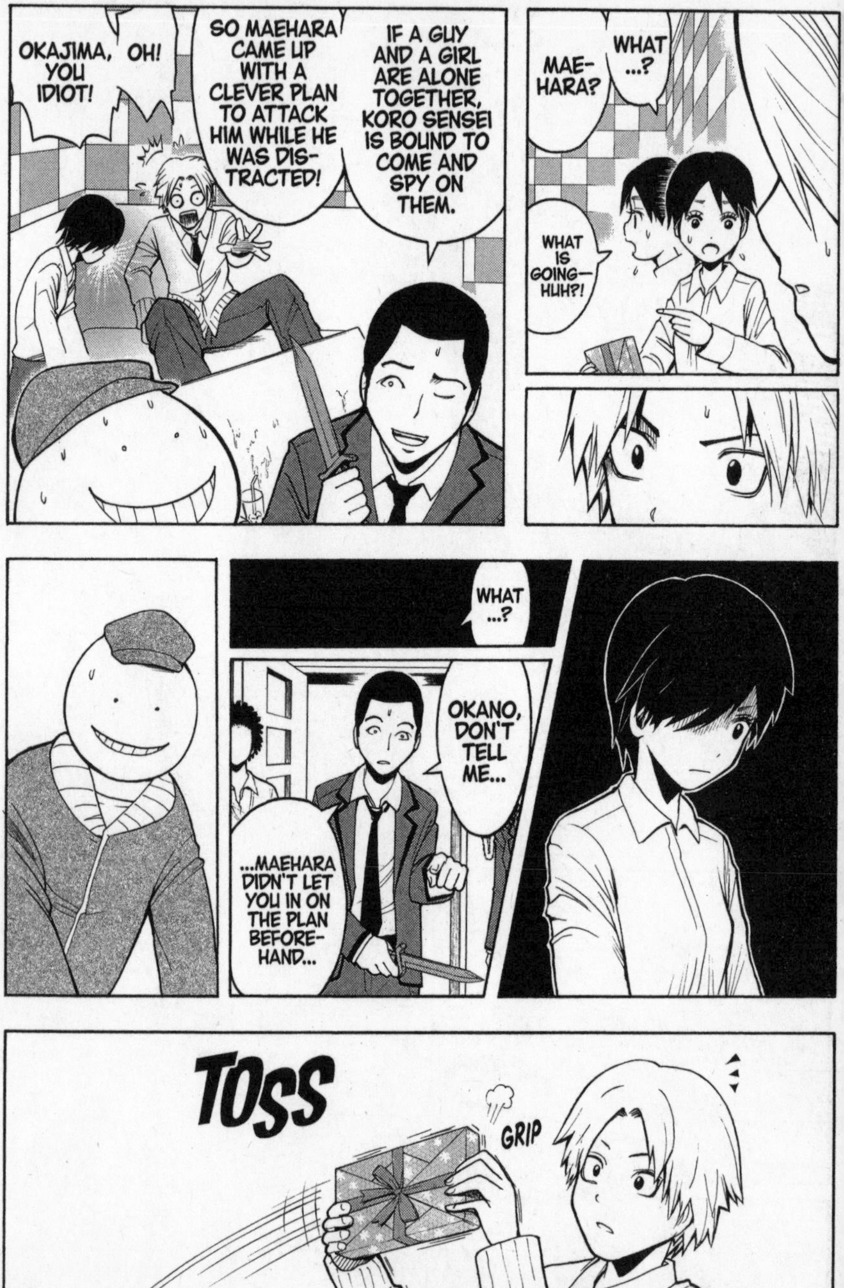
WHAT ...?
MAE-HARA?
WHAT IS GOING-HUH?!
IF A GUY AND A GIRL ARE ALONE TOGETHER, KORO SENSEI IS BOUND TO COME AND SPY ON THEM.
SO MAEHARA CAME UP WITH A CLEVER PLAN TO ATTACK HIM WHILE HE WAS DIS-TRACTED!
OH!
OKAJIMA, YOU IDIOT!
WHAT ...?
OKANO, DON'T TELL ME...
...MAEHARA DIDN'T LET YOU IN ON THE PLAN BEFORE-HAND...
TOSS
GRIP

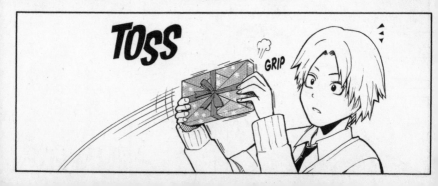

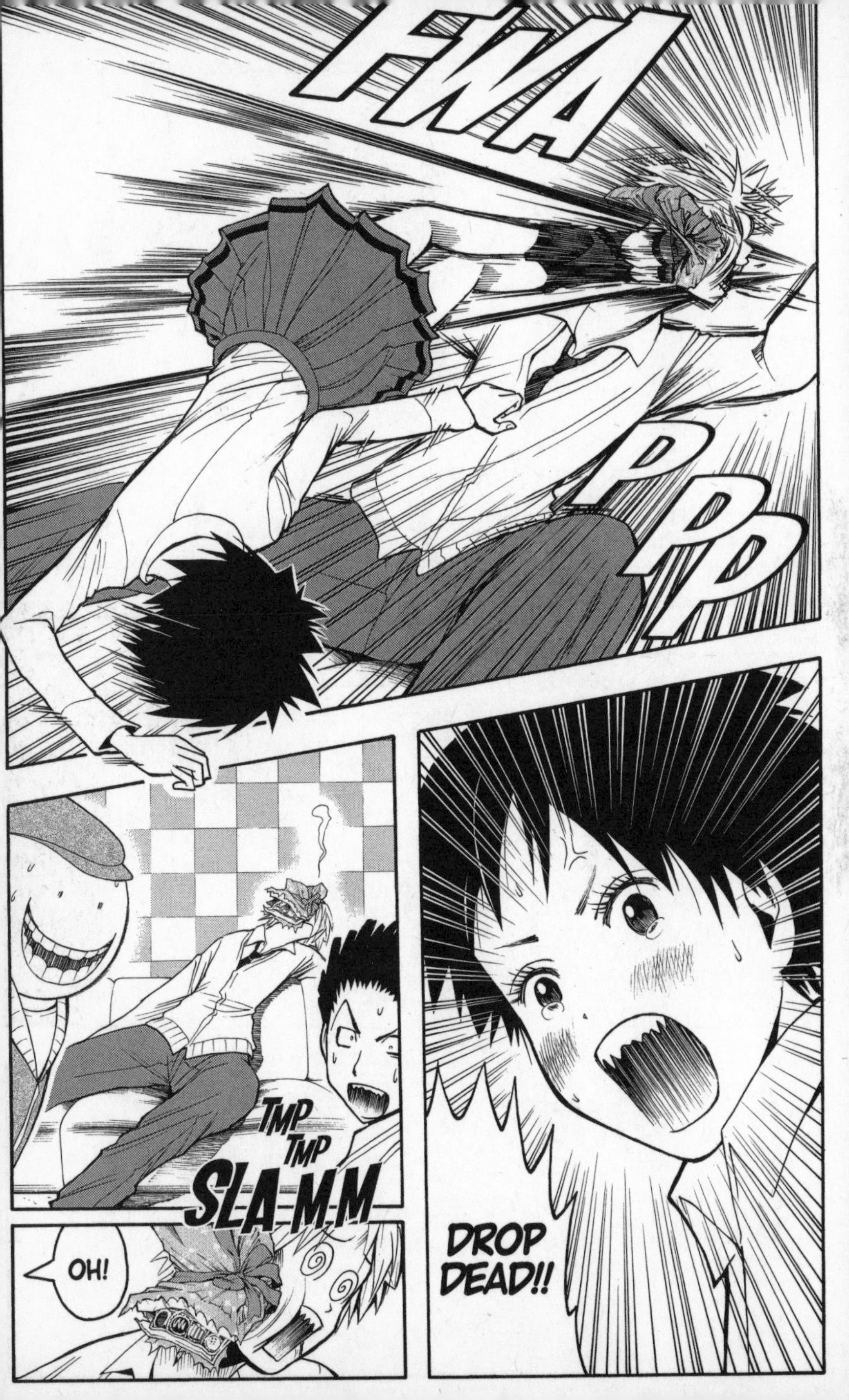
FWA
PPP
DROP DEAD!!
TMP TMP
SLAMM
OH!

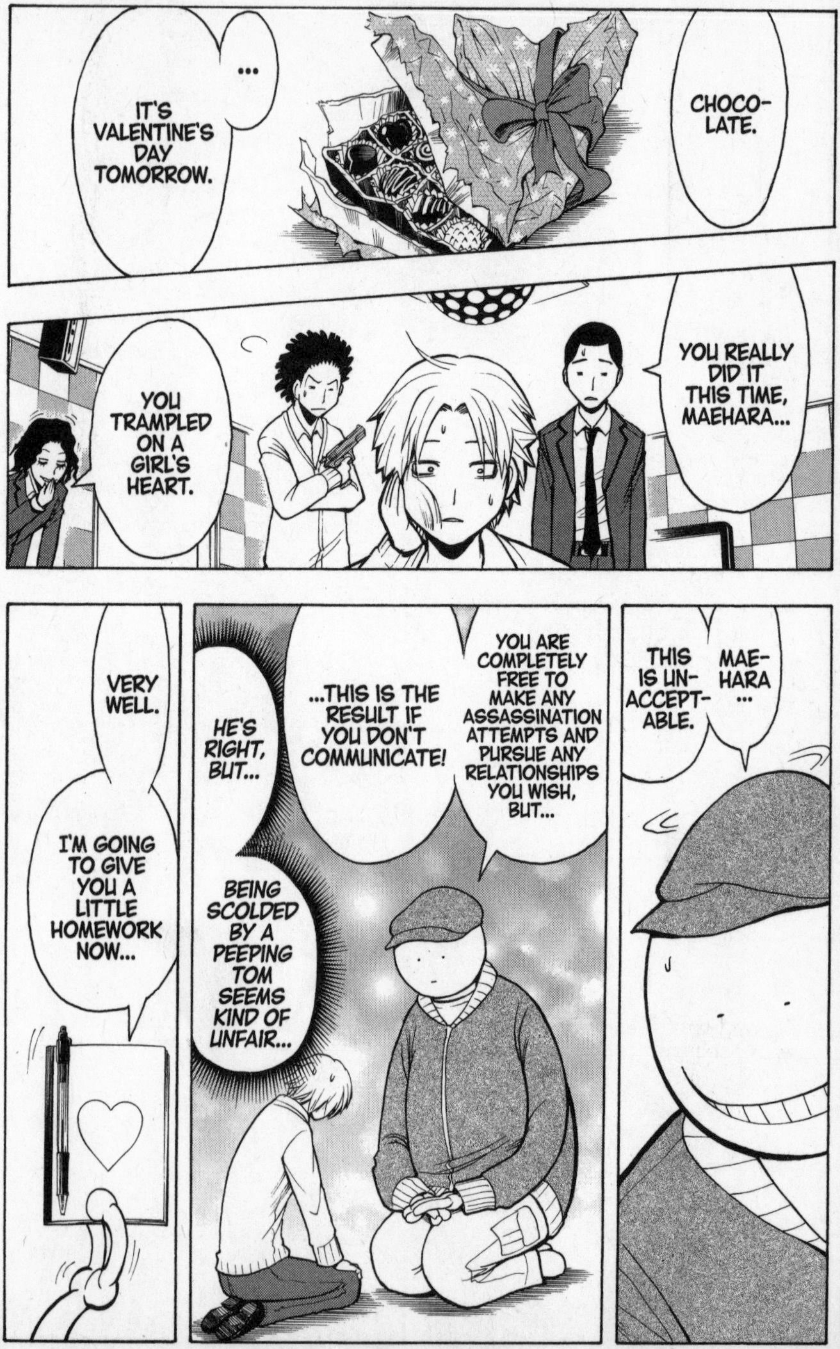
CHOCO-LATE.
...
IT'S VALENTINE'S DAY TOMORROW.
YOU REALLY DID IT THIS TIME, MAEHARA...
YOU TRAMPLED ON A GIRL'S HEART.
MAE-HARA...
THIS IS UN-ACCEPT-ABLE.
YOU ARE COMPLETELY FREE TO MAKE ANY ASSASSINATION ATTEMPTS AND PURSUE ANY RELATIONSHIPS YOU WISH, BUT...
...THIS IS THE RESULT IF YOU DON'T COMMUNICATE!
HE'S RIGHT, BUT...
BEING SCOLDED BY A PEEPING TOM SEEMS KIND OF UNFAIR...
VERY WELL.
I'M GOING TO GIVE YOU A LITTLE HOMEWORK NOW...

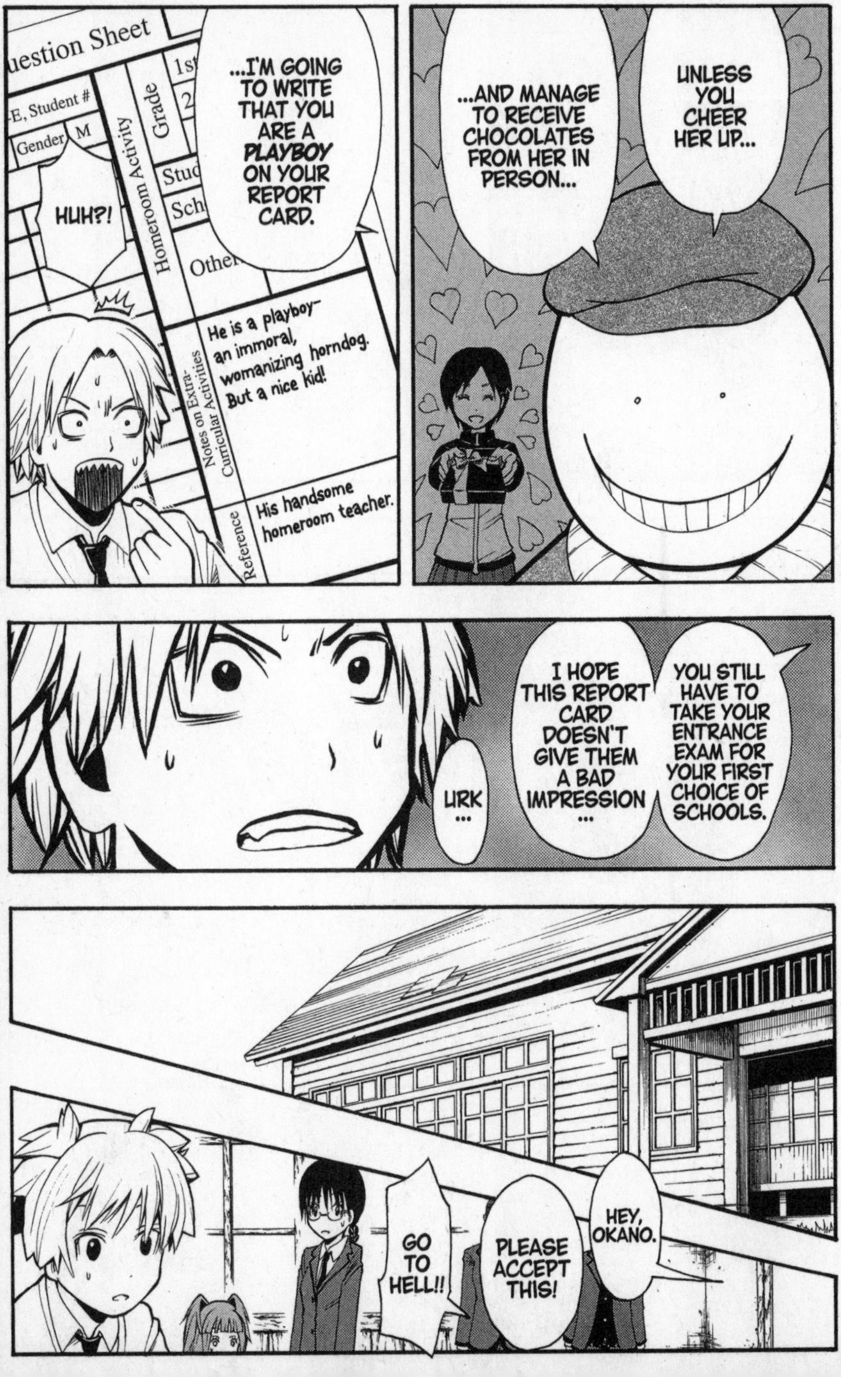
UNLESS YOU CHEER HER UP...
...AND MANAGE TO RECEIVE CHOCOLATES FROM HER IN PERSON...
...I'M GOING TO WRITE THAT YOU ARE A *PLAYBOY* ON YOUR REPORT CARD.
HUH?!
uestion Sheet
-E, Student #
Gender
M
Grade
1st
Homeroom Activity
Notes on Extra-Curricular Activities
He is a playboy–an immoral, womanizing horndog. But a nice kid!
Reference
His handsome homeroom teacher.
YOU STILL HAVE TO TAKE YOUR ENTRANCE EXAM FOR YOUR FIRST CHOICE OF SCHOOLS.
I HOPE THIS REPORT CARD DOESN'T GIVE THEM A BAD IMPRESSION...
URK...
HEY, OKANO.
PLEASE ACCEPT THIS!
GO TO HELL!!

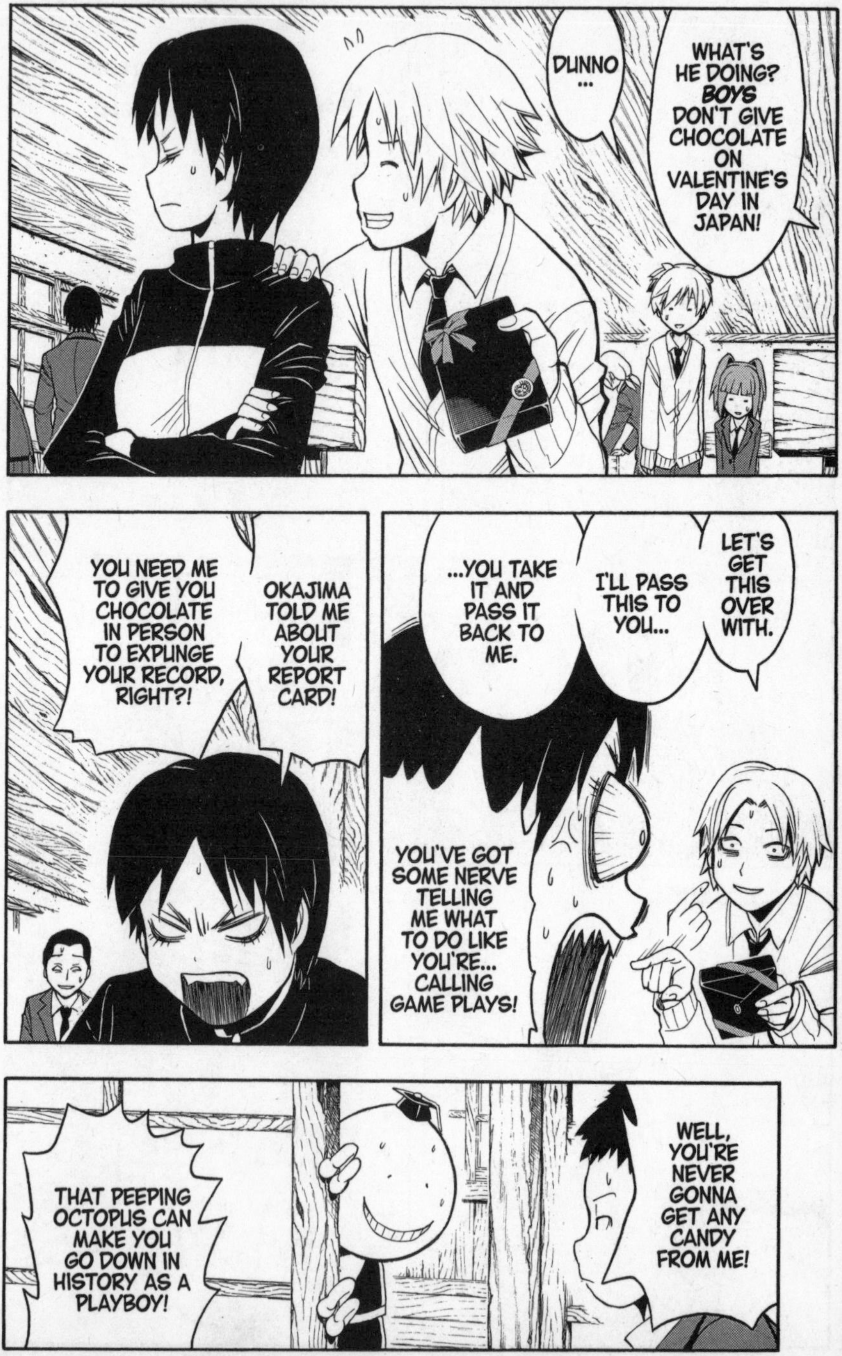
WHAT'S HE DOING? BOYS DON'T GIVE CHOCOLATE ON VALENTINE'S DAY IN JAPAN!
DUNNO...
LET'S GET THIS OVER WITH.
I'LL PASS THIS TO YOU...
...YOU TAKE IT AND PASS IT BACK TO ME.
YOU'VE GOT SOME NERVE TELLING ME WHAT TO DO LIKE YOU'RE... CALLING GAME PLAYS!
OKAJIMA TOLD ME ABOUT YOUR REPORT CARD!
YOU NEED ME TO GIVE YOU CHOCOLATE IN PERSON TO EXPUNGE YOUR RECORD, RIGHT?!
WELL, YOU'RE NEVER GONNA GET ANY CANDY FROM ME!
THAT PEEPING OCTOPUS CAN MAKE YOU GO DOWN IN HISTORY AS A PLAYBOY!

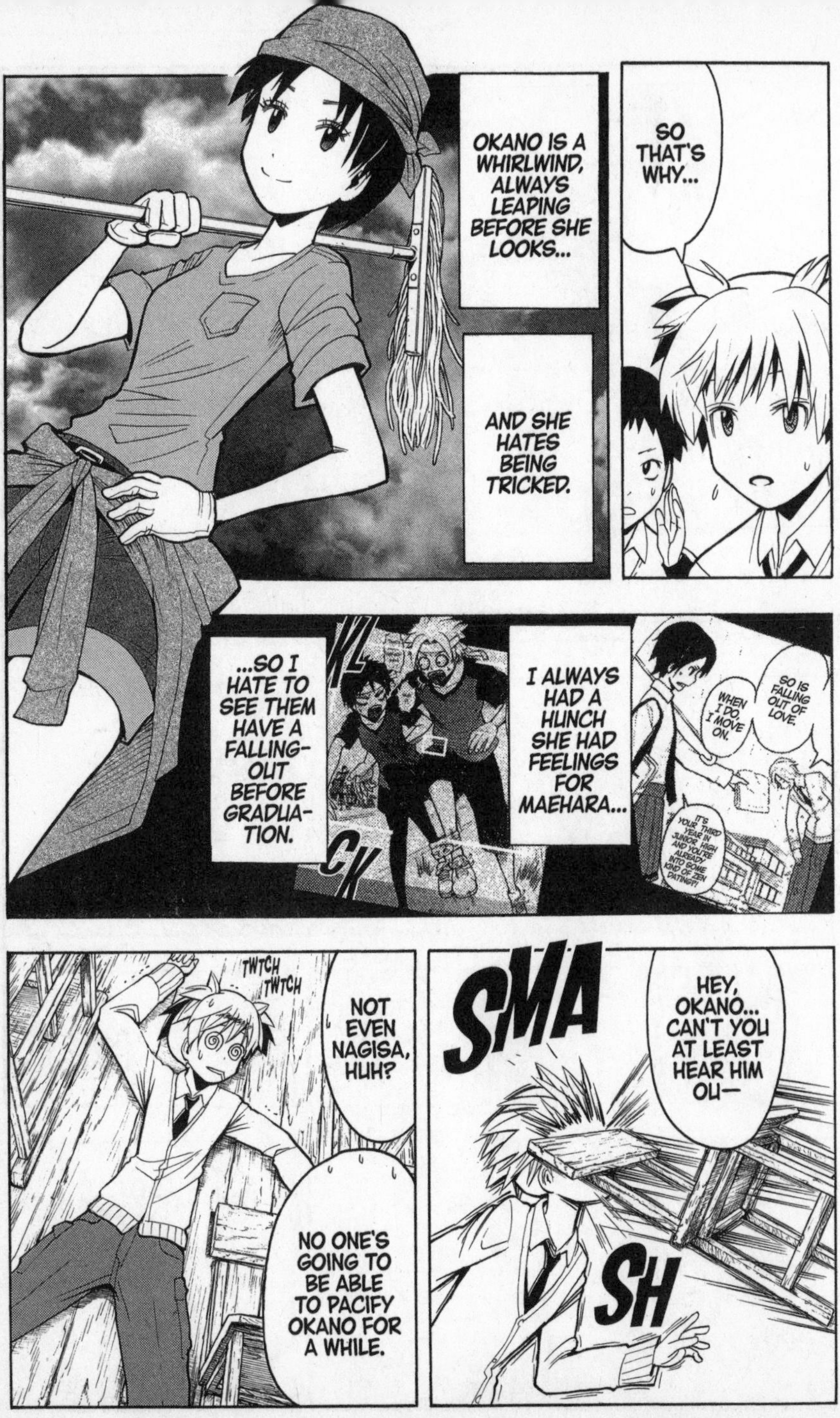
SO THAT'S WHY...
OKANO IS A WHIRLWIND, ALWAYS LEAPING BEFORE SHE LOOKS...
AND SHE HATES BEING TRICKED.
SO IS FALLING OUT OF LOVE.
WHEN I DO, I MOVE ON.
IT'S YOUR THIRD YEAR IN JUNIOR HIGH AND YOU'RE ALREADY INTO SOME KIND OF ZEN DATING?!
I ALWAYS HAD A HUNCH SHE HAD FEELINGS FOR MAEHARA...
...SO I HATE TO SEE THEM HAVE A FALLING-OUT BEFORE GRADUATION.
CK
HEY, OKANO... CAN'T YOU AT LEAST HEAR HIM OU—
SMA
SH
TWTCH TWTCH
NOT EVEN NAGISA, HUH?
NO ONE'S GOING TO BE ABLE TO PACIFY OKANO FOR A WHILE.

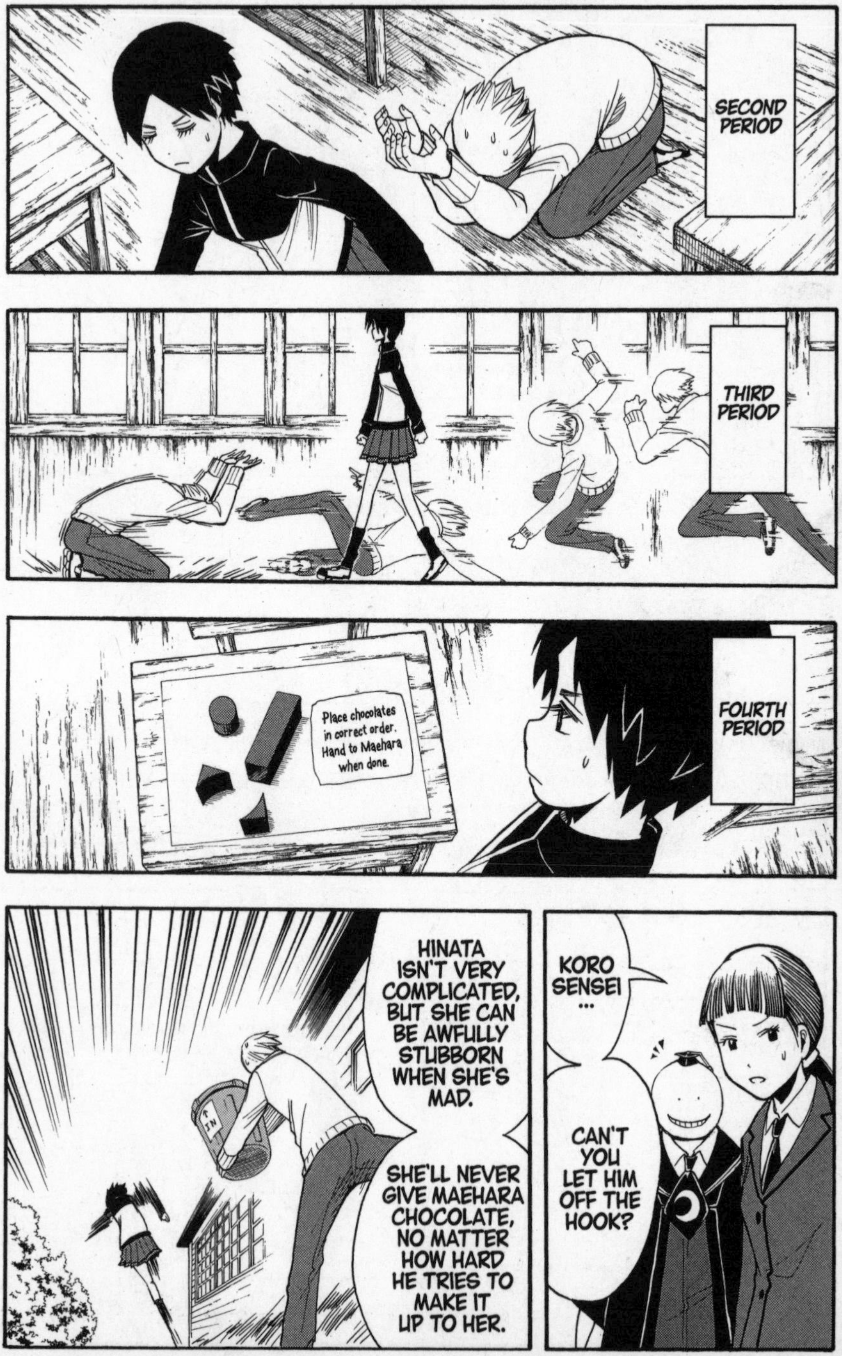
SECOND PERIOD
THIRD PERIOD
FOURTH PERIOD
Place chocolates in correct order. Hand to Maehara when done.
KORO SENSEI...
CAN'T YOU LET HIM OFF THE HOOK?
HINATA ISN'T VERY COMPLICATED, BUT SHE CAN BE AWFULLY STUBBORN WHEN SHE'S MAD.
SHE'LL NEVER GIVE MAEHARA CHOCOLATE, NO MATTER HOW HARD HE TRIES TO MAKE IT UP TO HER.

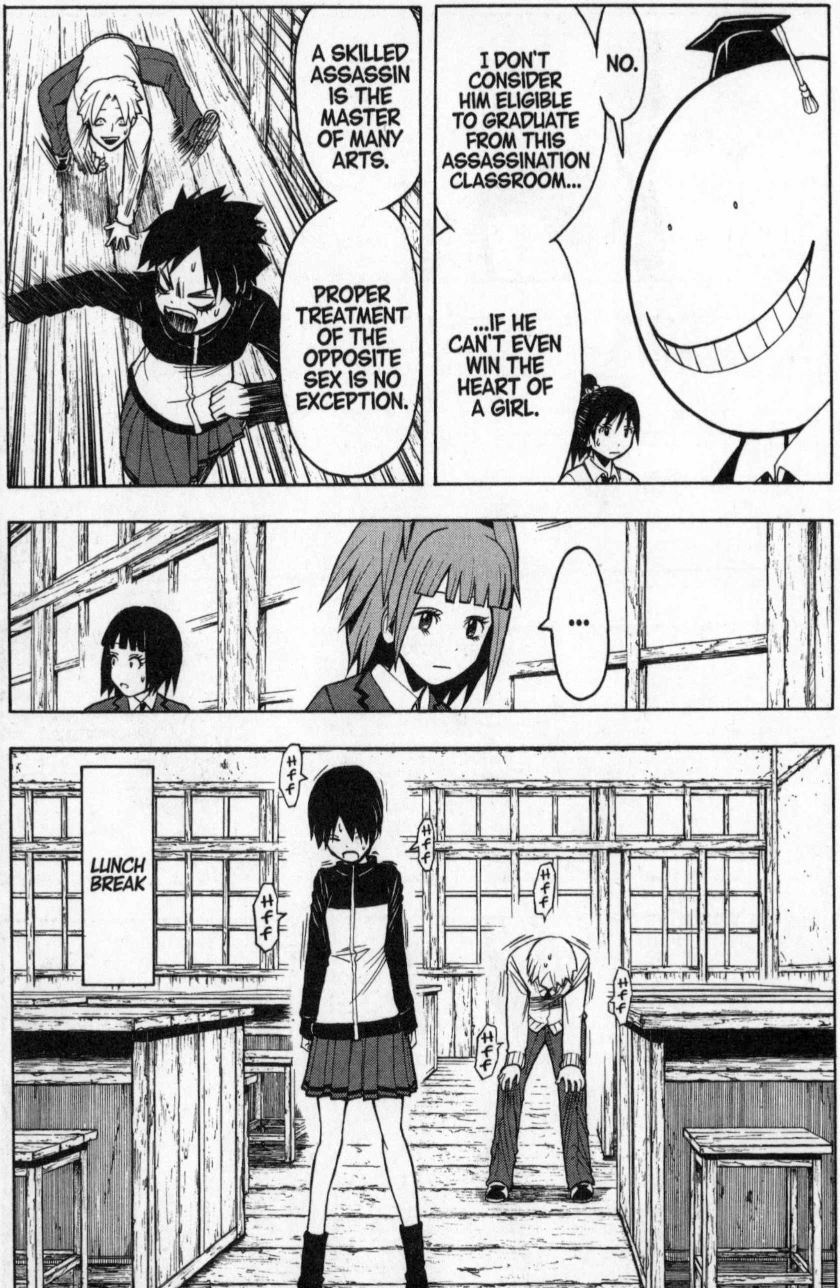
NO.
I DON'T CONSIDER HIM ELIGIBLE TO GRADUATE FROM THIS ASSASSINATION CLASSROOM...
...IF HE CAN'T EVEN WIN THE HEART OF A GIRL.
A SKILLED ASSASSIN IS THE MASTER OF MANY ARTS.
PROPER TREATMENT OF THE OPPOSITE SEX IS NO EXCEPTION.
...
HFF
HFF
HFF
HFF
HFF
HFF
LUNCH BREAK

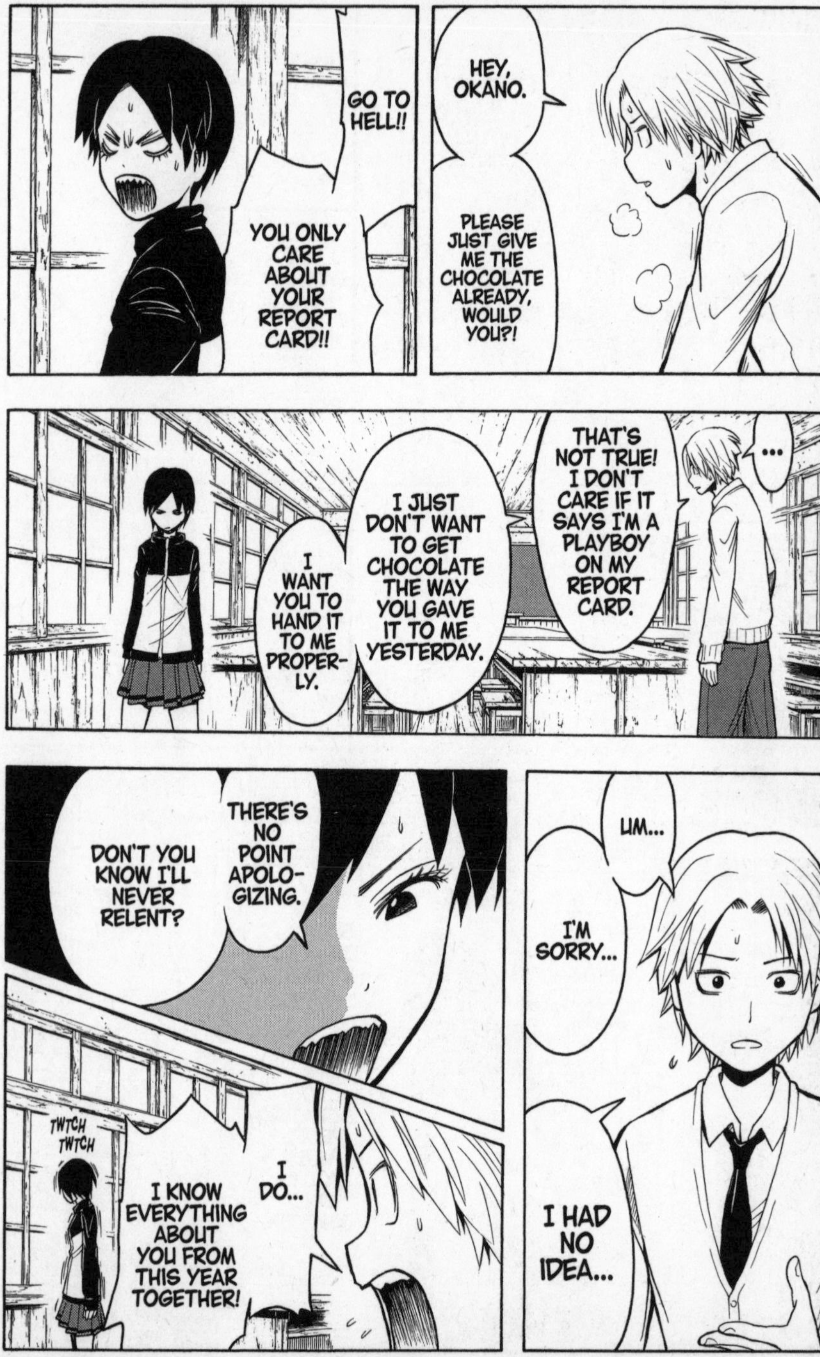
HEY, OKANO.
PLEASE JUST GIVE ME THE CHOCOLATE ALREADY, WOULD YOU?!
GO TO HELL!!
YOU ONLY CARE ABOUT YOUR REPORT CARD!!
...
THAT'S NOT TRUE! I DON'T CARE IF IT SAYS I'M A PLAYBOY ON MY REPORT CARD.
I JUST DON'T WANT TO GET CHOCOLATE THE WAY YOU GAVE IT TO ME YESTERDAY.
I WANT YOU TO HAND IT TO ME PROPER-LY.
UM...
I'M SORRY...
I HAD NO IDEA...
THERE'S NO POINT APOLO-GIZING.
DON'T YOU KNOW I'LL NEVER RELENT?
I DO...
I KNOW EVERYTHING ABOUT YOU FROM THIS YEAR TOGETHER!
TWTCH TWTCH

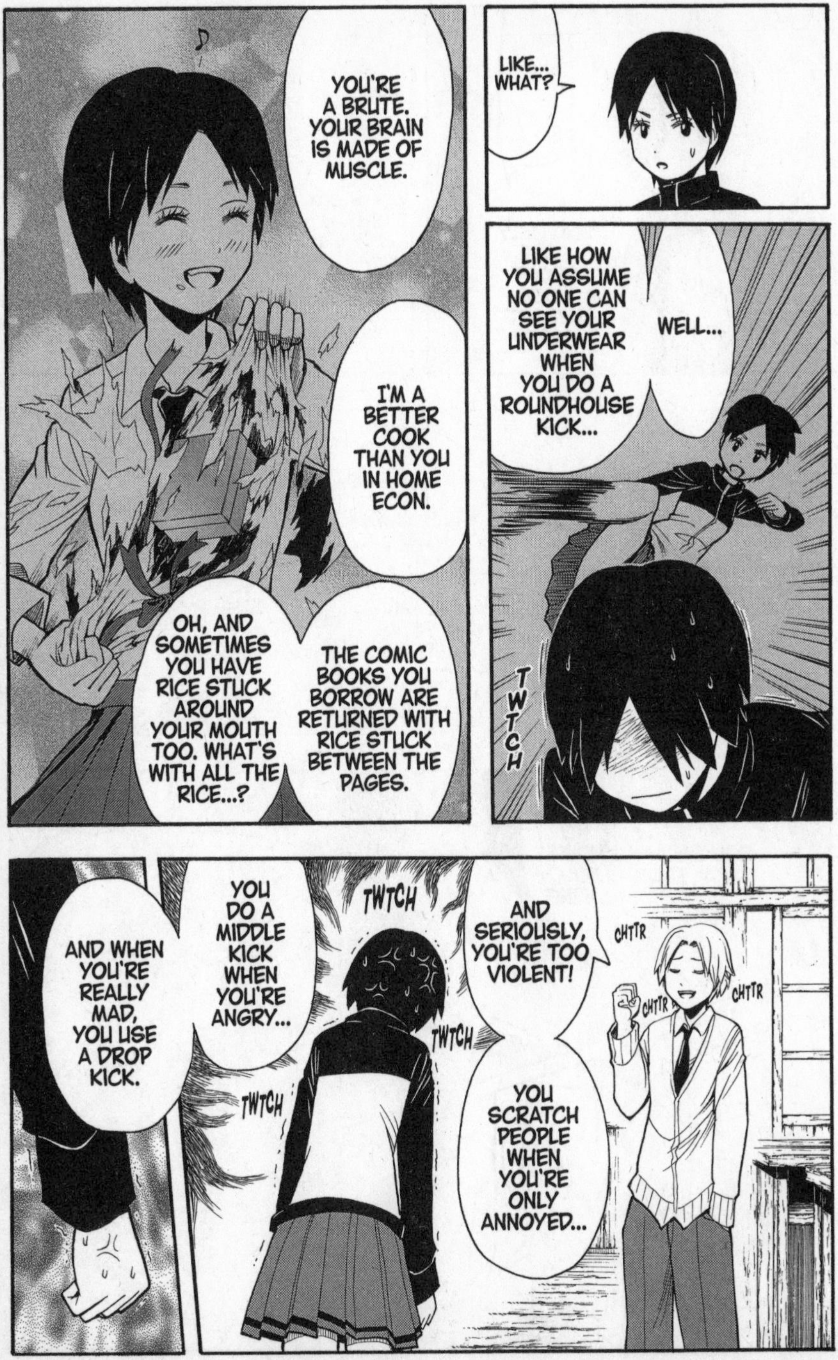
LIKE... WHAT?
WELL...
LIKE HOW YOU ASSUME NO ONE CAN SEE YOUR UNDERWEAR WHEN YOU DO A ROUNDHOUSE KICK...
TWTCH
YOU'RE A BRUTE. YOUR BRAIN IS MADE OF MUSCLE.
I'M A BETTER COOK THAN YOU IN HOME ECON.
THE COMIC BOOKS YOU BORROW ARE RETURNED WITH RICE STUCK BETWEEN THE PAGES.
OH, AND SOMETIMES YOU HAVE RICE STUCK AROUND YOUR MOUTH TOO. WHAT'S WITH ALL THE RICE...?
AND SERIOUSLY, YOU'RE TOO VIOLENT!
CHTTR
CHTTR
CHTTR
YOU SCRATCH PEOPLE WHEN YOU'RE ONLY ANNOYED...
TWTCH
YOU DO A MIDDLE KICK WHEN YOU'RE ANGRY...
TWTCH
TWTCH
AND WHEN YOU'RE REALLY MAD, YOU USE A DROP KICK.

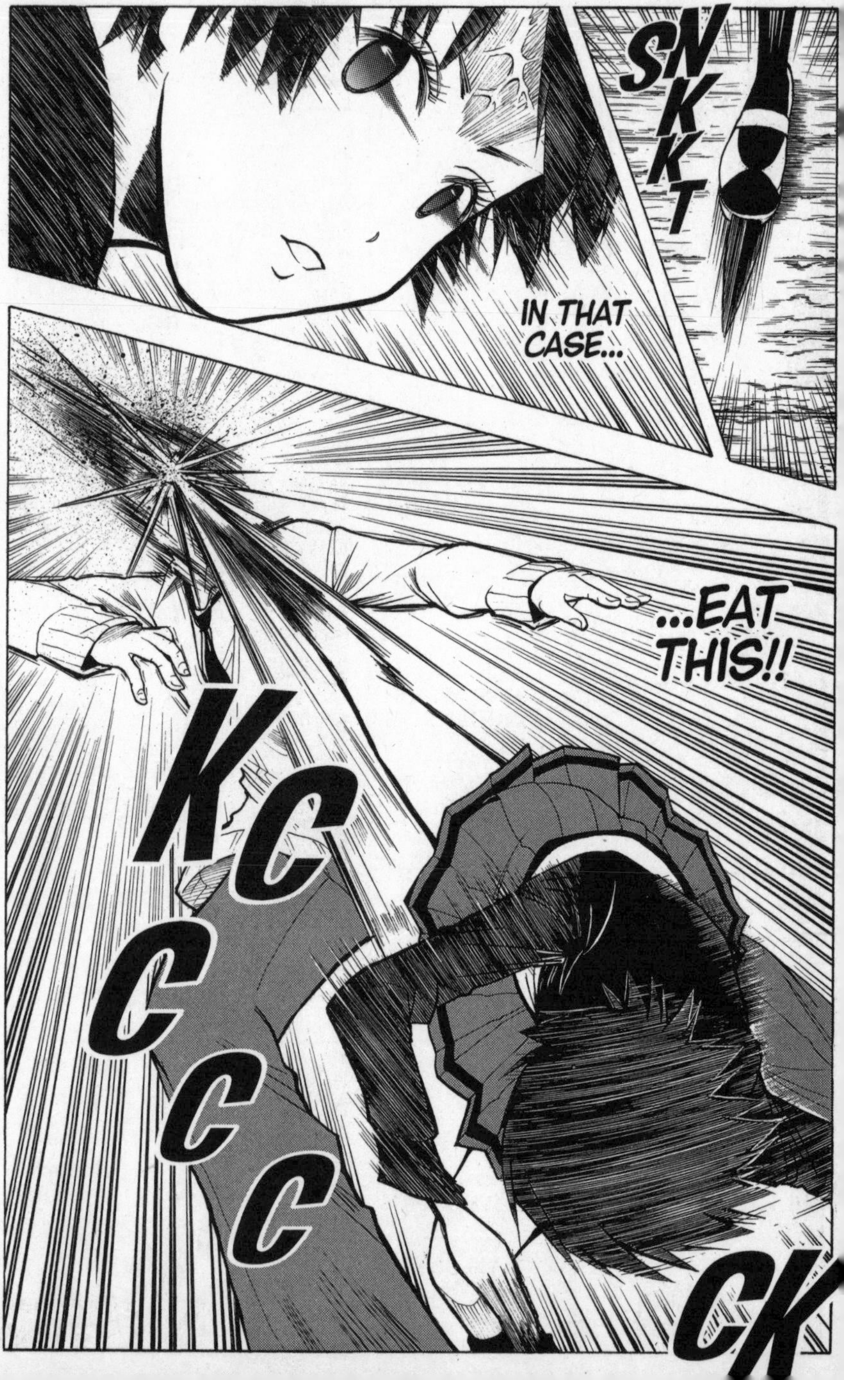
SNKKT
IN THAT CASE...
...EAT THIS!!
KCCCC
CK

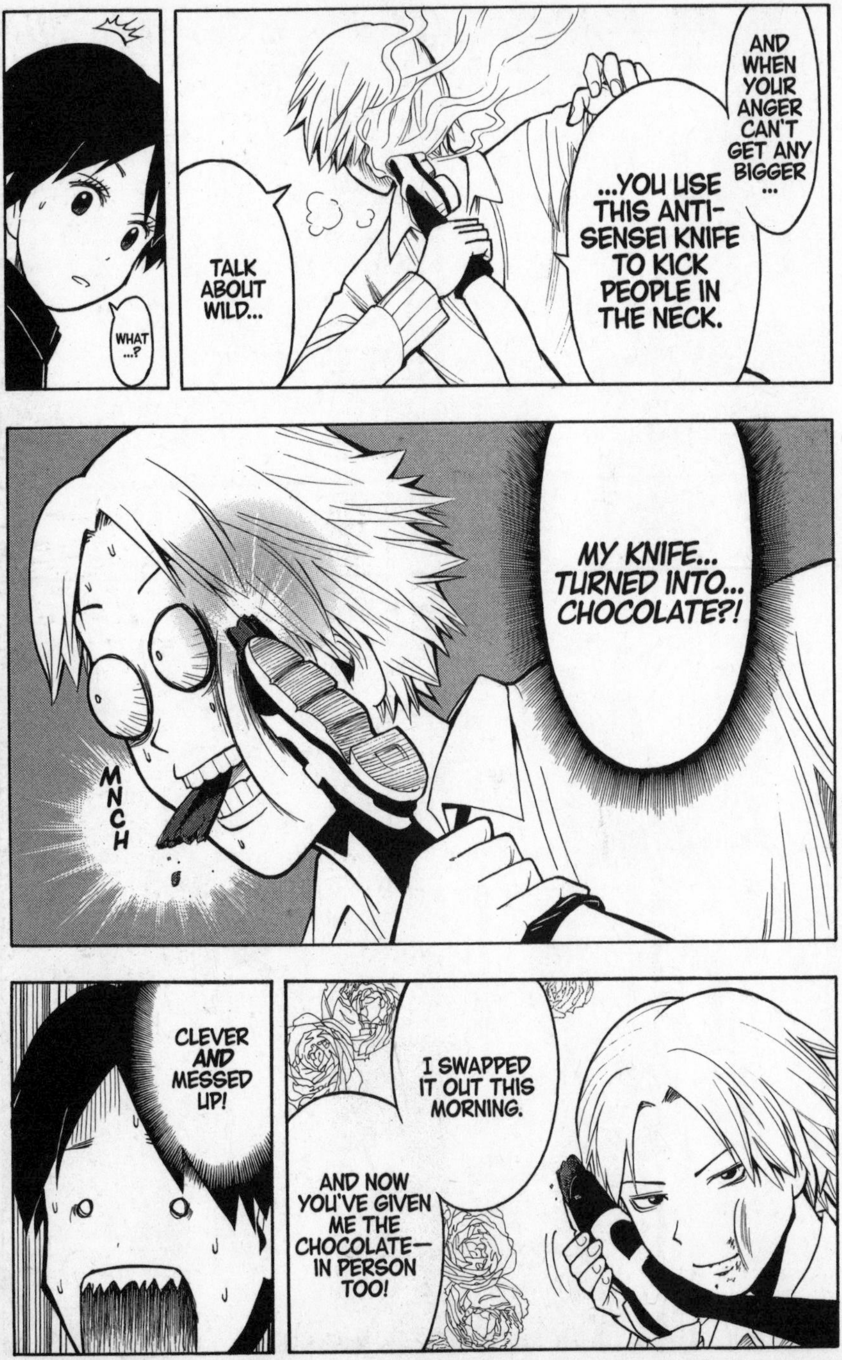
AND WHEN YOUR ANGER CAN'T GET ANY BIGGER ...
...YOU USE THIS ANTI-SENSEI KNIFE TO KICK PEOPLE IN THE NECK.
TALK ABOUT WILD...
WHAT ...?
MY KNIFE... TURNED INTO... CHOCOLATE?!
MNCH
I SWAPPED IT OUT THIS MORNING.
AND NOW YOU'VE GIVEN ME THE CHOCOLATE— IN PERSON TOO!
CLEVER AND MESSED UP!

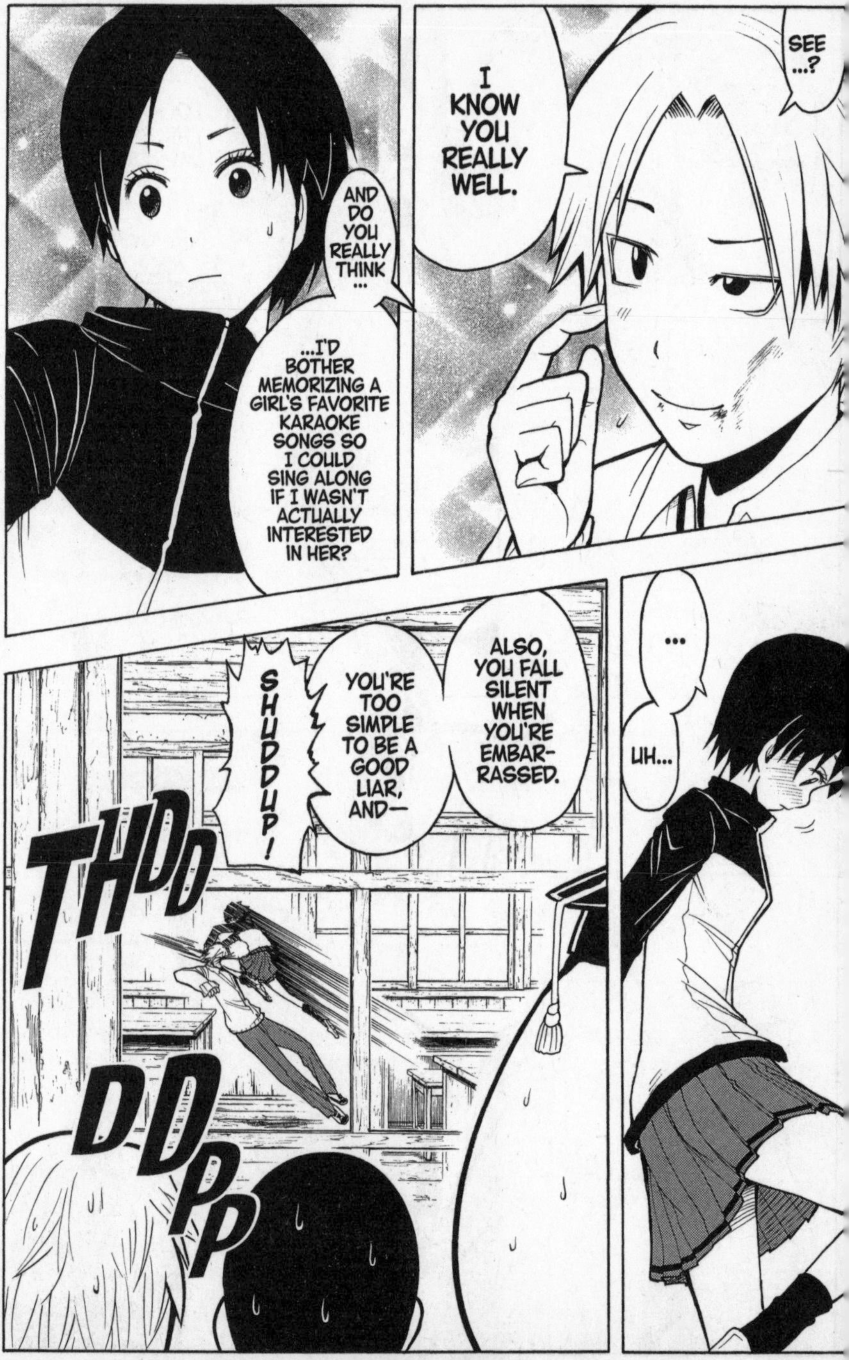

SEE ...?
I KNOW YOU REALLY WELL.
AND DO YOU REALLY THINK ...
...I'D BOTHER MEMORIZING A GIRL'S FAVORITE KARAOKE SONGS SO I COULD SING ALONG IF I WASN'T ACTUALLY INTERESTED IN HER?
...
UH...
ALSO, YOU FALL SILENT WHEN YOU'RE EMBARRASSED.
YOU'RE TOO SIMPLE TO BE A GOOD LIAR, AND—
SHUDDUP!
THDD DDPP

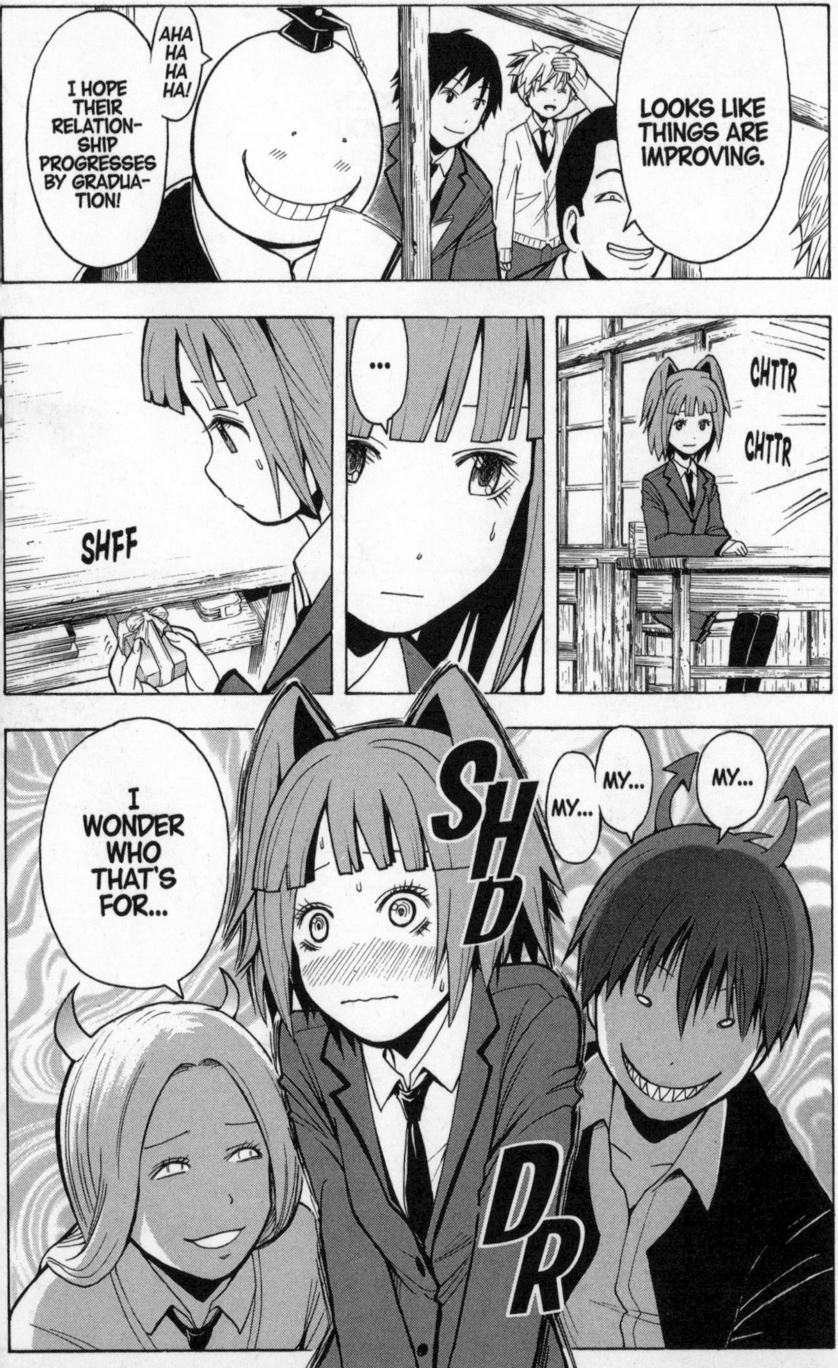
LOOKS LIKE THINGS ARE IMPROVING.
AHA HA HA HA!
I HOPE THEIR RELATION-SHIP PROGRESSES BY GRADUA-TION!
CHTTR
CHTTR
...
SHFF
MY...
MY...
MY...
SHD
DR
I WONDER WHO THAT'S FOR...

Spasmodic Funnies
"She's a brute! I knew it!"

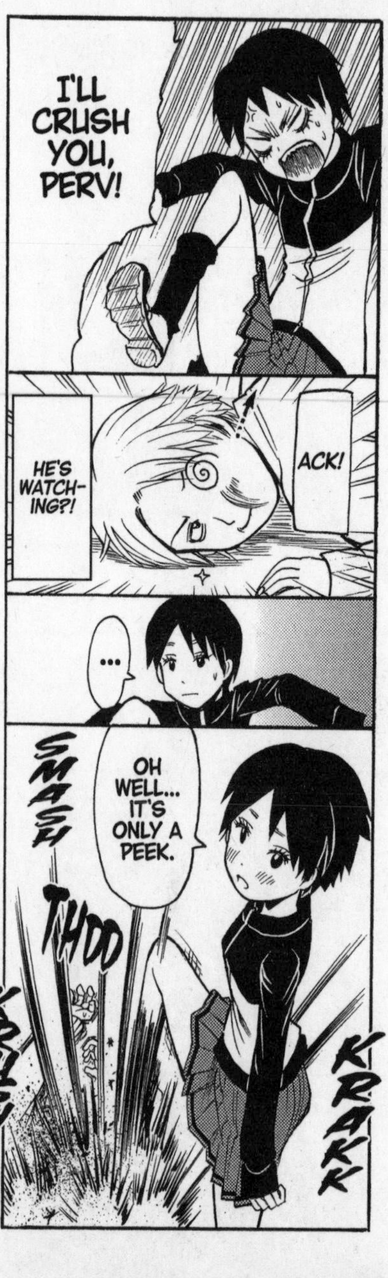
I'LL CRUSH YOU, PERV!
ACK!
HE'S WATCHING?!
...
OH WELL... IT'S ONLY A PEEK.
SMASH
THOO
KRAKK
KRUSH

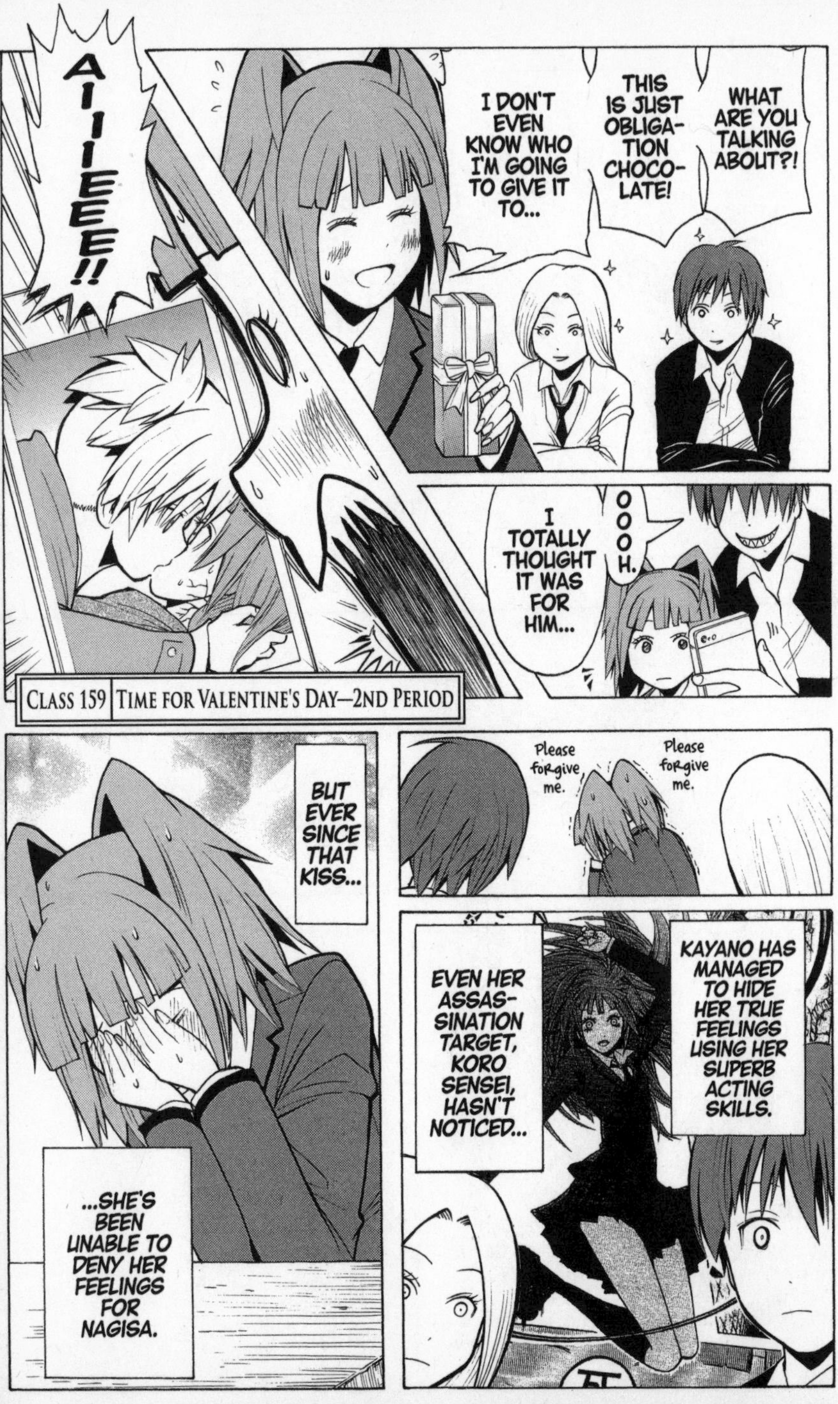
WHAT ARE YOU TALKING ABOUT?!
THIS IS JUST OBLIGATION CHOCOLATE!
I DON'T EVEN KNOW WHO I'M GOING TO GIVE IT TO...
OOOH.
I TOTALLY THOUGHT IT WAS FOR HIM...
AIIIEEEE!!
CLASS 159 TIME FOR VALENTINE'S DAY—2ND PERIOD
Please forgive me.
Please forgive me.
KAYANO HAS MANAGED TO HIDE HER TRUE FEELINGS USING HER SUPERB ACTING SKILLS.
EVEN HER ASSASSINATION TARGET, KORO SENSEI, HASN'T NOTICED...
BUT EVER SINCE THAT KISS...
...SHE'S BEEN UNABLE TO DENY HER FEELINGS FOR NAGISA.

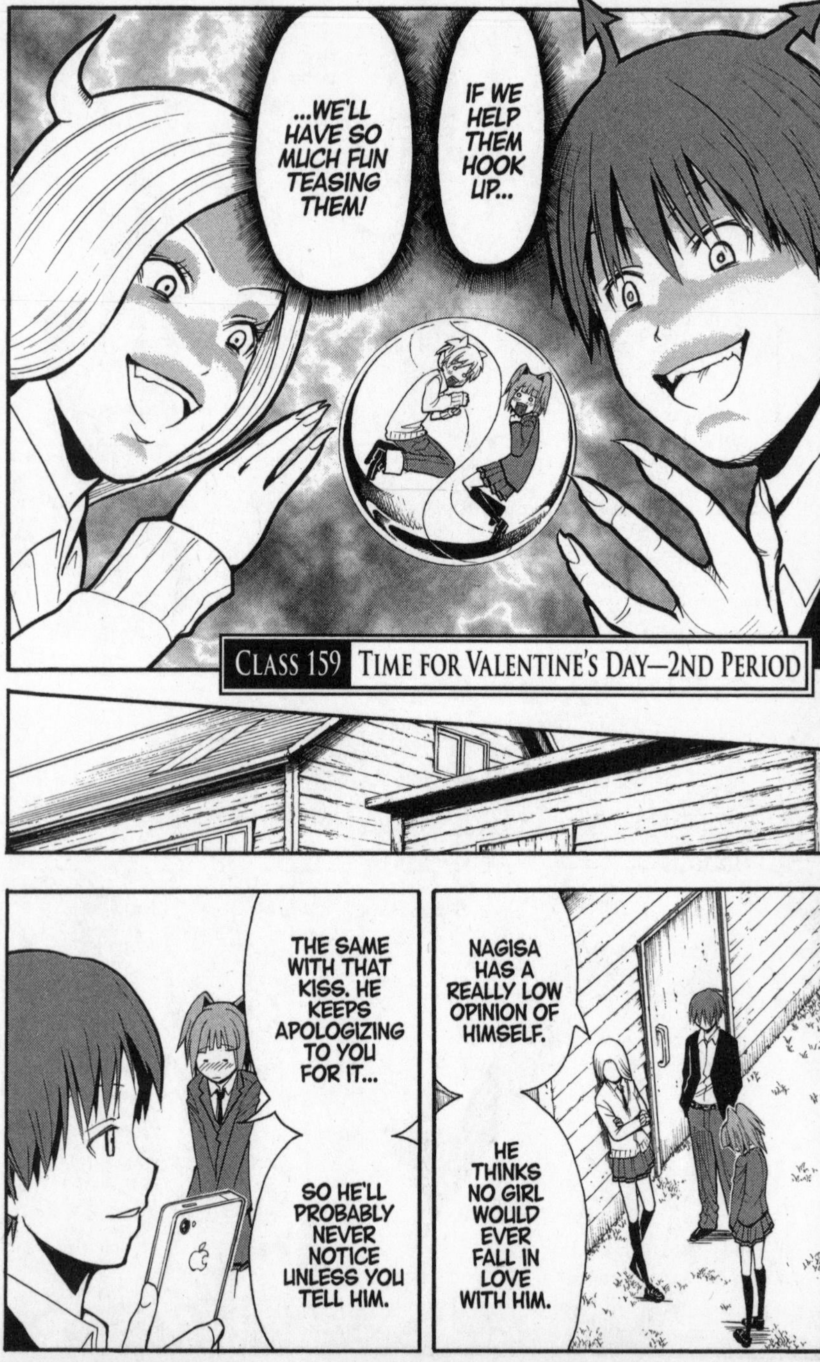
IF WE HELP THEM HOOK UP...
...WE'LL HAVE SO MUCH FUN TEASING THEM!
CLASS 159 TIME FOR VALENTINE'S DAY—2ND PERIOD
NAGISA HAS A REALLY LOW OPINION OF HIMSELF.
HE THINKS NO GIRL WOULD EVER FALL IN LOVE WITH HIM.
THE SAME WITH THAT KISS. HE KEEPS APOLOGIZING TO YOU FOR IT...
SO HE'LL PROBABLY NEVER NOTICE UNLESS YOU TELL HIM.

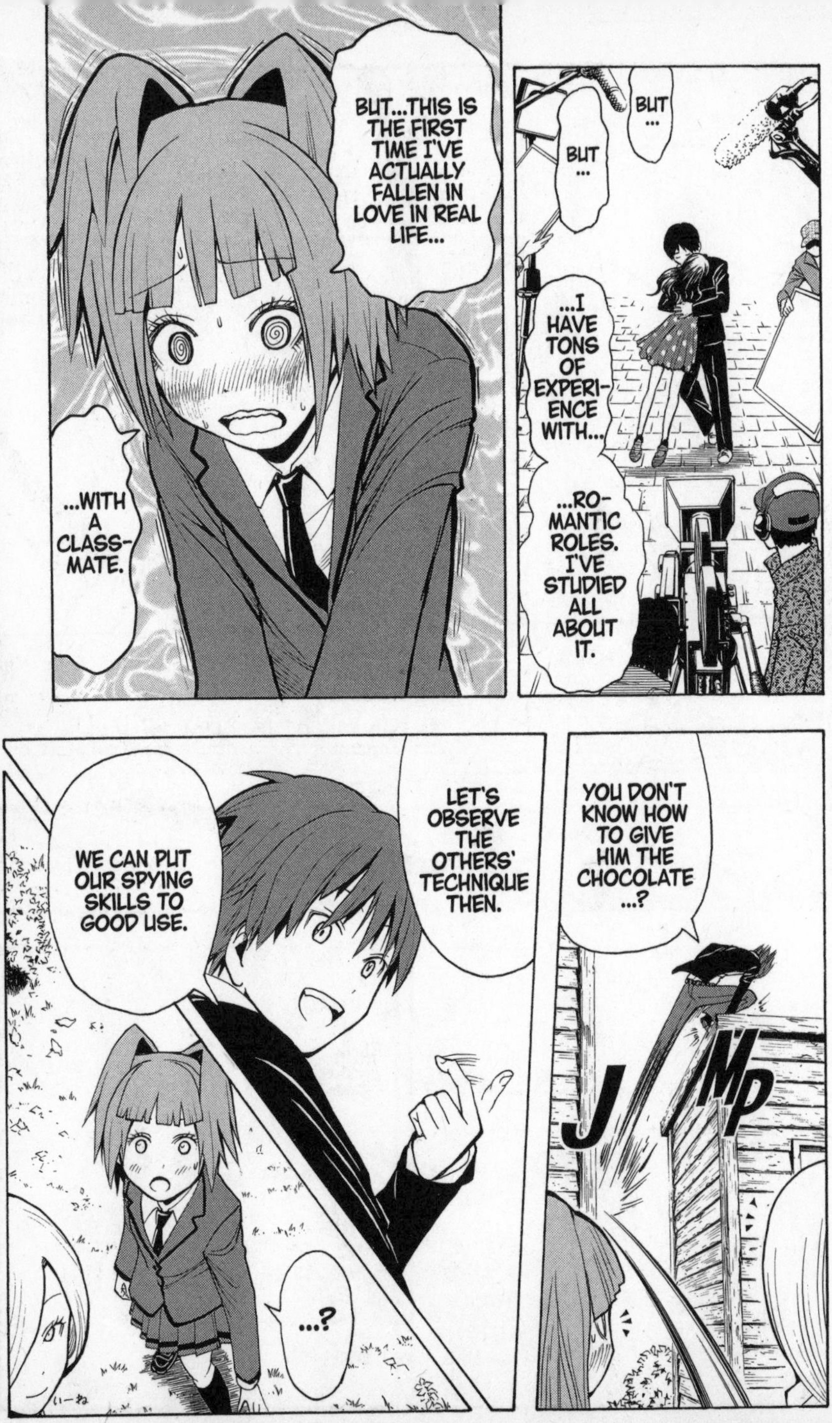
BUT ...
BUT ...
...I HAVE TONS OF EXPERIENCE WITH...
...ROMANTIC ROLES. I'VE STUDIED ALL ABOUT IT.
BUT...THIS IS THE FIRST TIME I'VE ACTUALLY FALLEN IN LOVE IN REAL LIFE...
...WITH A CLASSMATE.
YOU DON'T KNOW HOW TO GIVE HIM THE CHOCOLATE ...?
JUMP
LET'S OBSERVE THE OTHERS' TECHNIQUE THEN.
WE CAN PUT OUR SPYING SKILLS TO GOOD USE.
...?

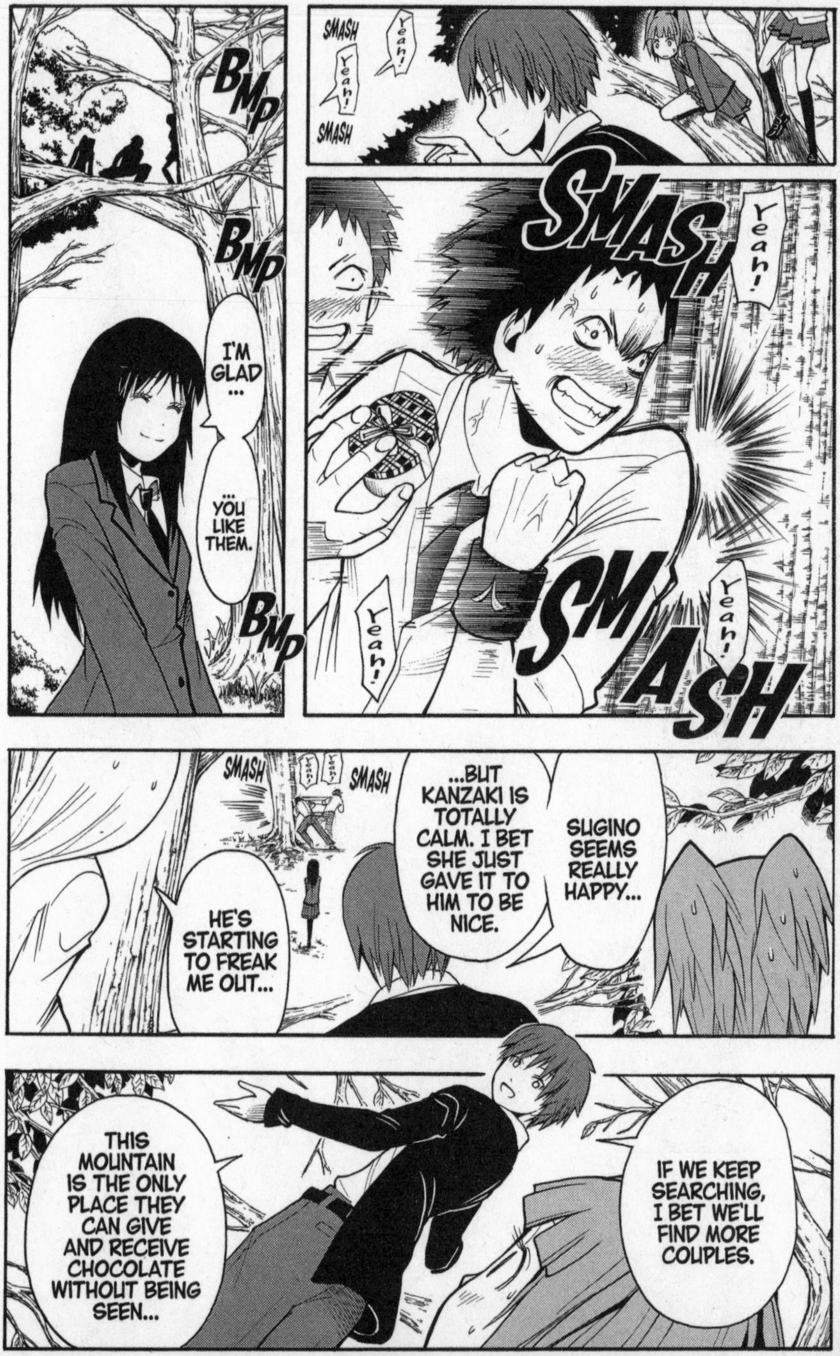
Yeah!
SMASH
Yeah!
SMASH
SMASH
Yeah!
Yeah!
SMASH
Yeah!
BMP
BMP
I'M GLAD...
...YOU LIKE THEM.
BMP
SUGINO SEEMS REALLY HAPPY...
...BUT KANZAKI IS TOTALLY CALM. I BET SHE JUST GAVE IT TO HIM TO BE NICE.
SMASH
Yeah!
Yeah!
SMASH
HE'S STARTING TO FREAK ME OUT...
IF WE KEEP SEARCHING, I BET WE'LL FIND MORE COUPLES.
THIS MOUNTAIN IS THE ONLY PLACE THEY CAN GIVE AND RECEIVE CHOCOLATE WITHOUT BEING SEEN...

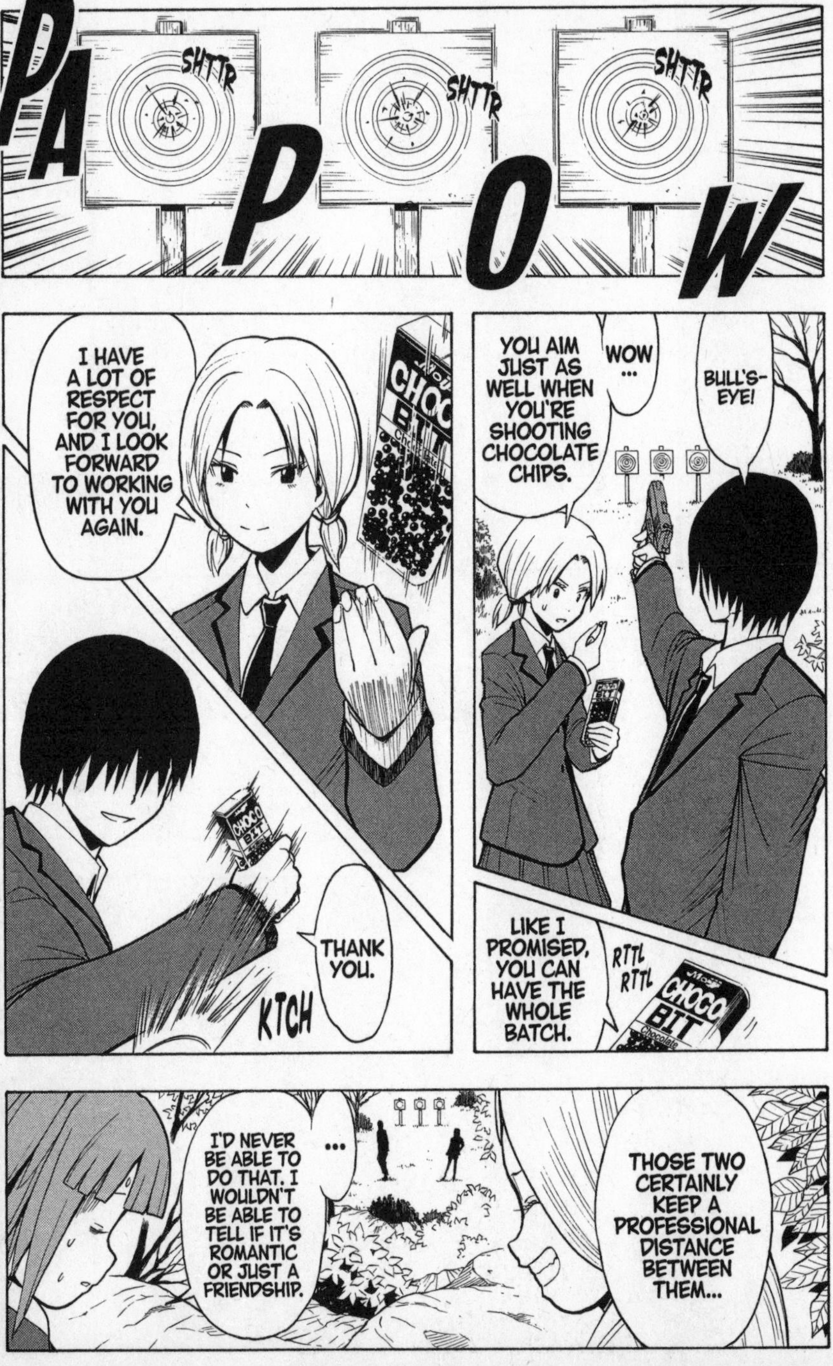
SHTTR
SHTTR
SHTTR
PAPOW
BULL'S-EYE!
WOW ...
YOU AIM JUST AS WELL WHEN YOU'RE SHOOTING CHOCOLATE CHIPS.
LIKE I PROMISED, YOU CAN HAVE THE WHOLE BATCH.
RTTL RTTL
CHOCO BIT
Chocolate
I HAVE A LOT OF RESPECT FOR YOU, AND I LOOK FORWARD TO WORKING WITH YOU AGAIN.
CHOCO BIT
THANK YOU.
KTCH
THOSE TWO CERTAINLY KEEP A PROFESSIONAL DISTANCE BETWEEN THEM...
...
I'D NEVER BE ABLE TO DO THAT. I WOULDN'T BE ABLE TO TELL IF IT'S ROMANTIC OR JUST A FRIENDSHIP.

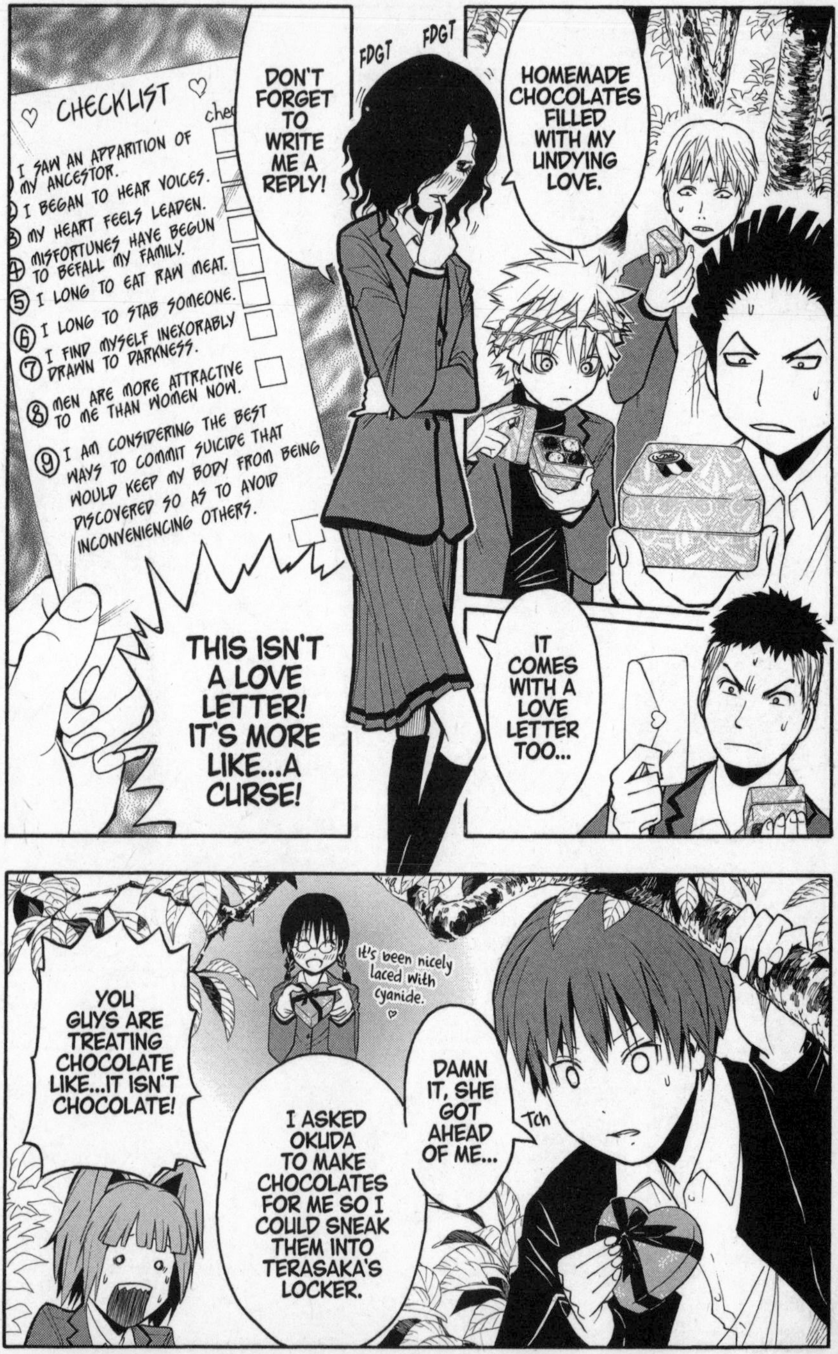
HOMEMADE CHOCOLATES FILLED WITH MY UNDYING LOVE.
FDGT
FDGT
DON'T FORGET TO WRITE ME A REPLY!
IT COMES WITH A LOVE LETTER TOO...
CHECKLIST
1 I SAW AN APPARITION OF MY ANCESTOR.
2 I BEGAN TO HEAR VOICES.
3 MY HEART FEELS LEADEN.
4 MISFORTUNES HAVE BEGUN TO BEFALL MY FAMILY.
5 I LONG TO EAT RAW MEAT.
6 I LONG TO STAB SOMEONE.
7 I FIND MYSELF INEXORABLY DRAWN TO DARKNESS.
8 MEN ARE MORE ATTRACTIVE TO ME THAN WOMEN NOW.
9 I AM CONSIDERING THE BEST WAYS TO COMMIT SUICIDE THAT WOULD KEEP MY BODY FROM BEING DISCOVERED SO AS TO AVOID INCONVENIENCING OTHERS.
THIS ISN'T A LOVE LETTER! IT'S MORE LIKE...A CURSE!
DAMN IT, SHE GOT AHEAD OF ME...
Tch
I ASKED OKUDA TO MAKE CHOCOLATES FOR ME SO I COULD SNEAK THEM INTO TERASAKA'S LOCKER.
It's been nicely laced with cyanide.
YOU GUYS ARE TREATING CHOCOLATE LIKE...IT ISN'T CHOCOLATE!

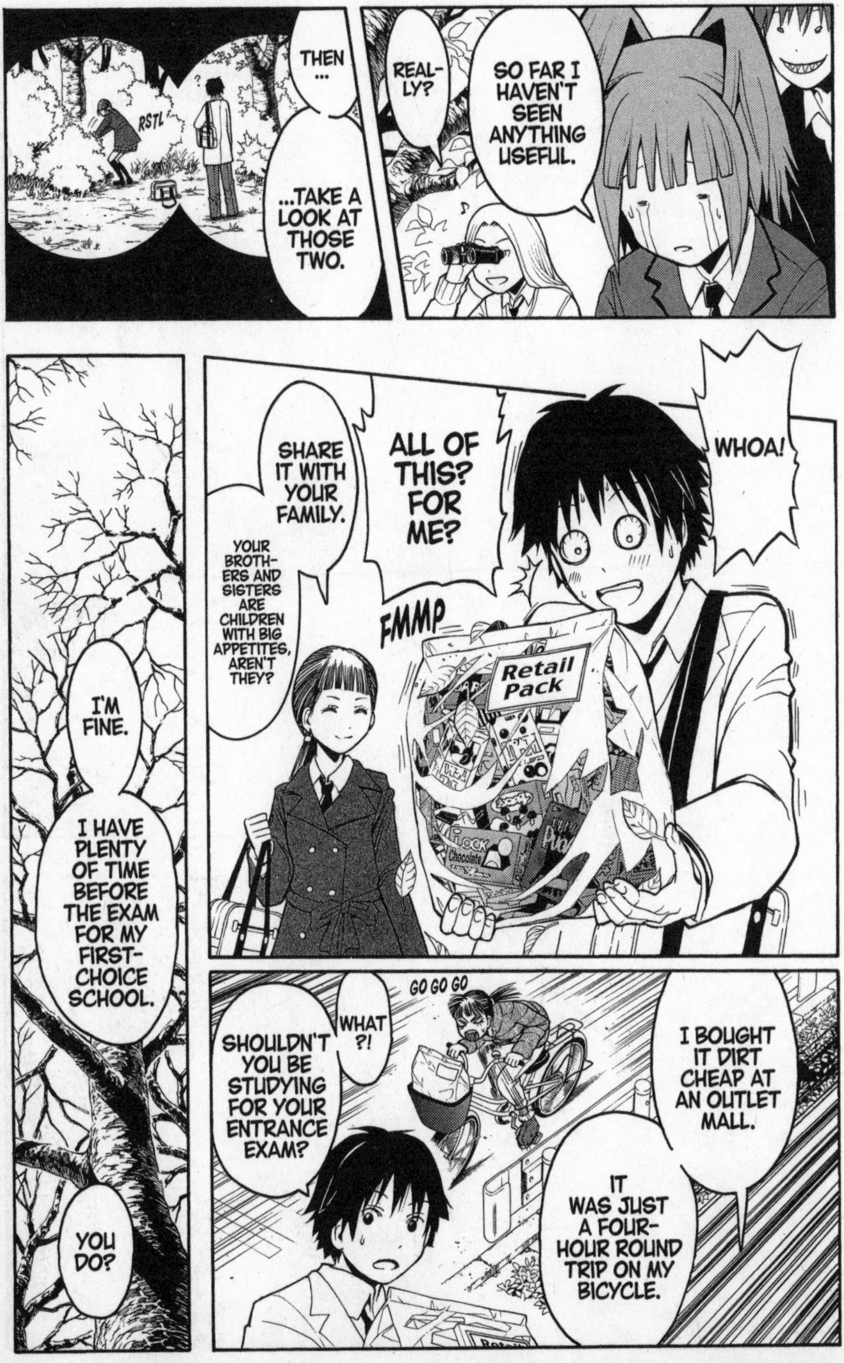
SO FAR I HAVEN'T SEEN ANYTHING USEFUL.
REAL-LY?
THEN ...
...TAKE A LOOK AT THOSE TWO.
?
RSTL
WHOA!
ALL OF THIS? FOR ME?
SHARE IT WITH YOUR FAMILY.
YOUR BROTH-ERS AND SISTERS ARE CHILDREN WITH BIG APPETITES, AREN'T THEY?
FMMP
Retail Pack
I BOUGHT IT DIRT CHEAP AT AN OUTLET MALL.
IT WAS JUST A FOUR-HOUR ROUND TRIP ON MY BICYCLE.
GO GO GO
WHAT ?!
SHOULDN'T YOU BE STUDYING FOR YOUR ENTRANCE EXAM?
I'M FINE.
I HAVE PLENTY OF TIME BEFORE THE EXAM FOR MY FIRST-CHOICE SCHOOL.
YOU DO?

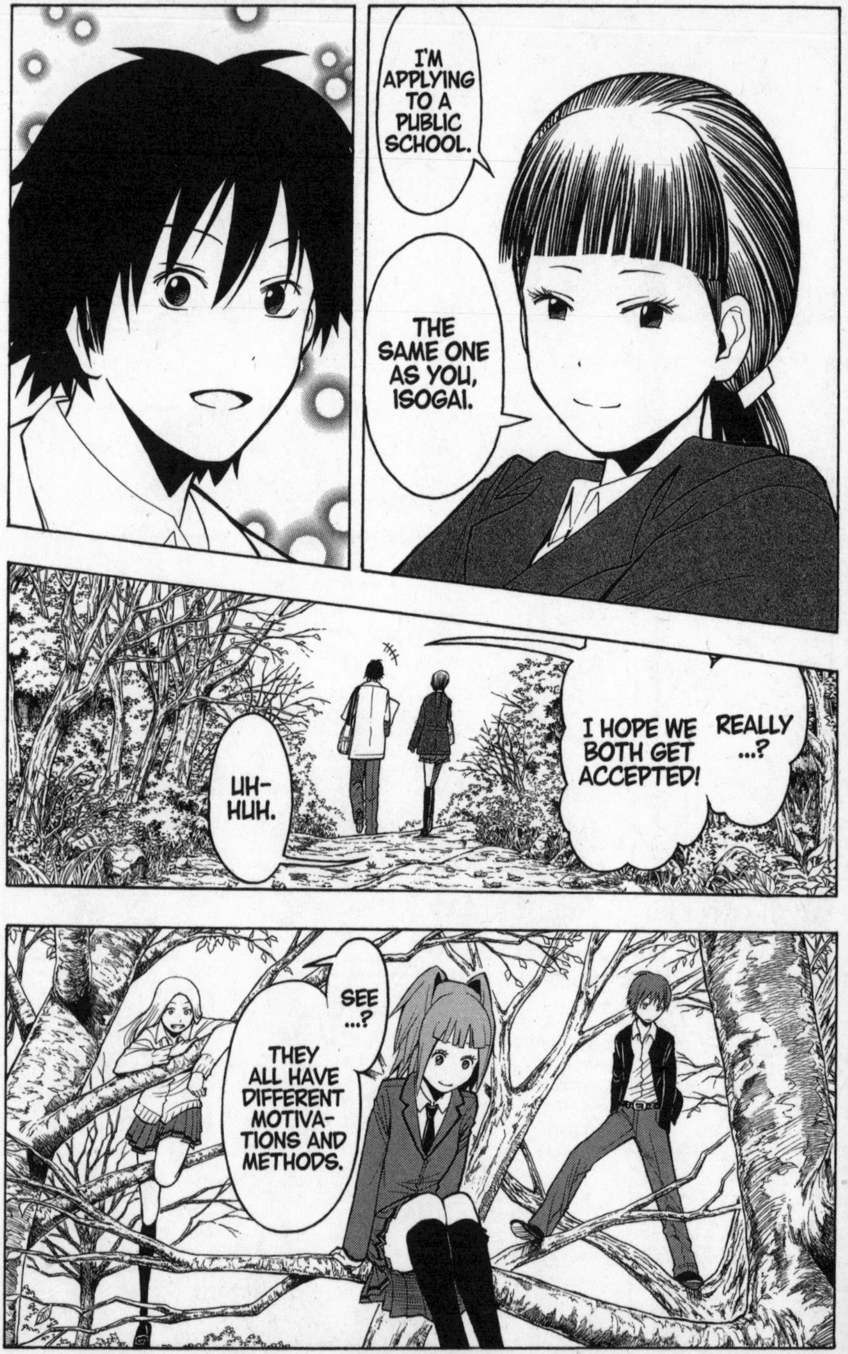
I'M APPLYING TO A PUBLIC SCHOOL.
THE SAME ONE AS YOU, ISOGAI.
I HOPE WE BOTH GET ACCEPTED!
REALLY ...?
UH-HUH.
SEE ...?
THEY ALL HAVE DIFFERENT MOTIVATIONS AND METHODS.

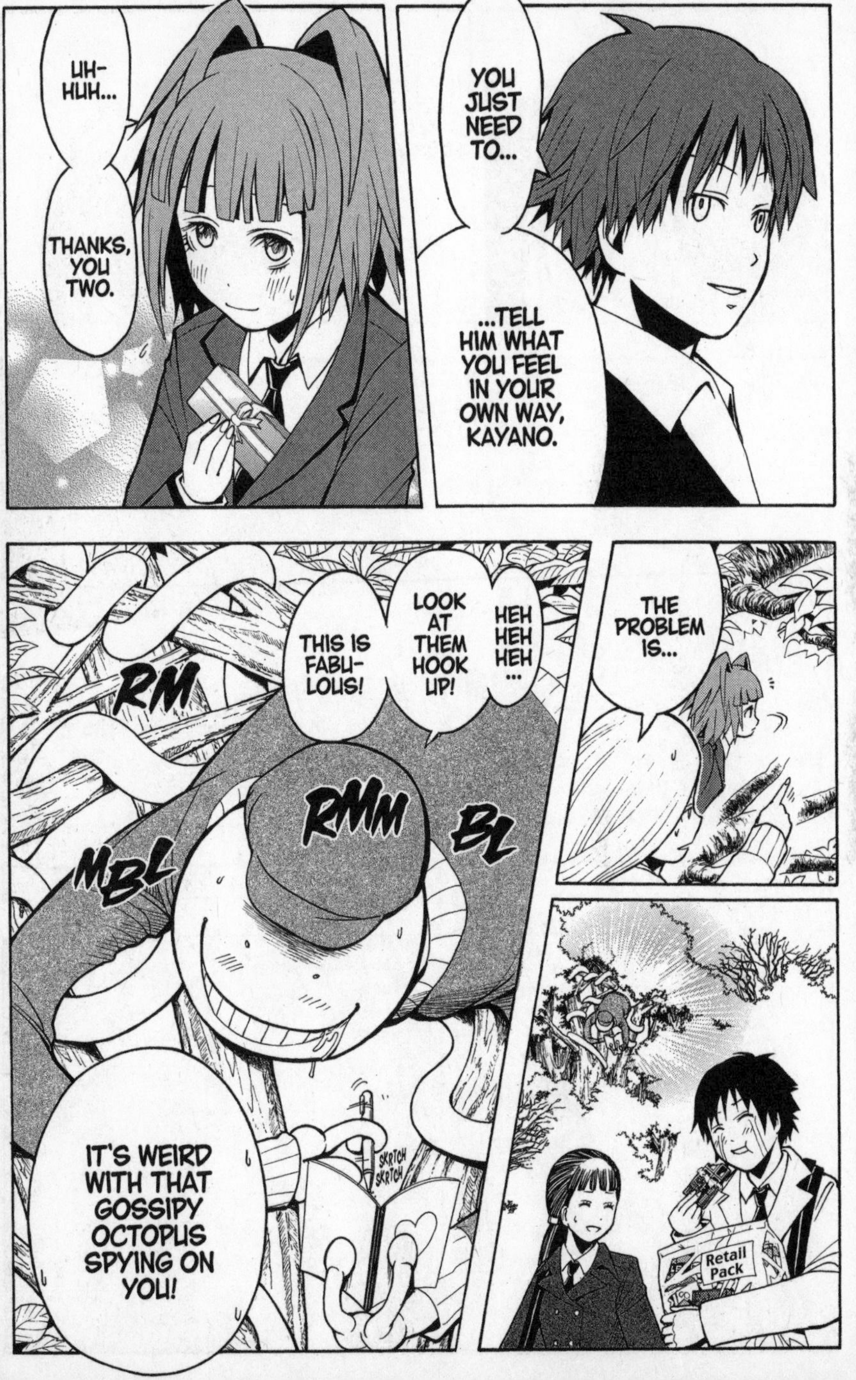
YOU JUST NEED TO...
...TELL HIM WHAT YOU FEEL IN YOUR OWN WAY, KAYANO.
UH-HUH...
THANKS, YOU TWO.
THE PROBLEM IS...
Retail Pack
HEH HEH HEH...
LOOK AT THEM HOOK UP!
THIS IS FABU-LOUS!
RM
RMM
BL
MBL
SKRTCH SKRTCH
IT'S WEIRD WITH THAT GOSSIPY OCTOPUS SPYING ON YOU!

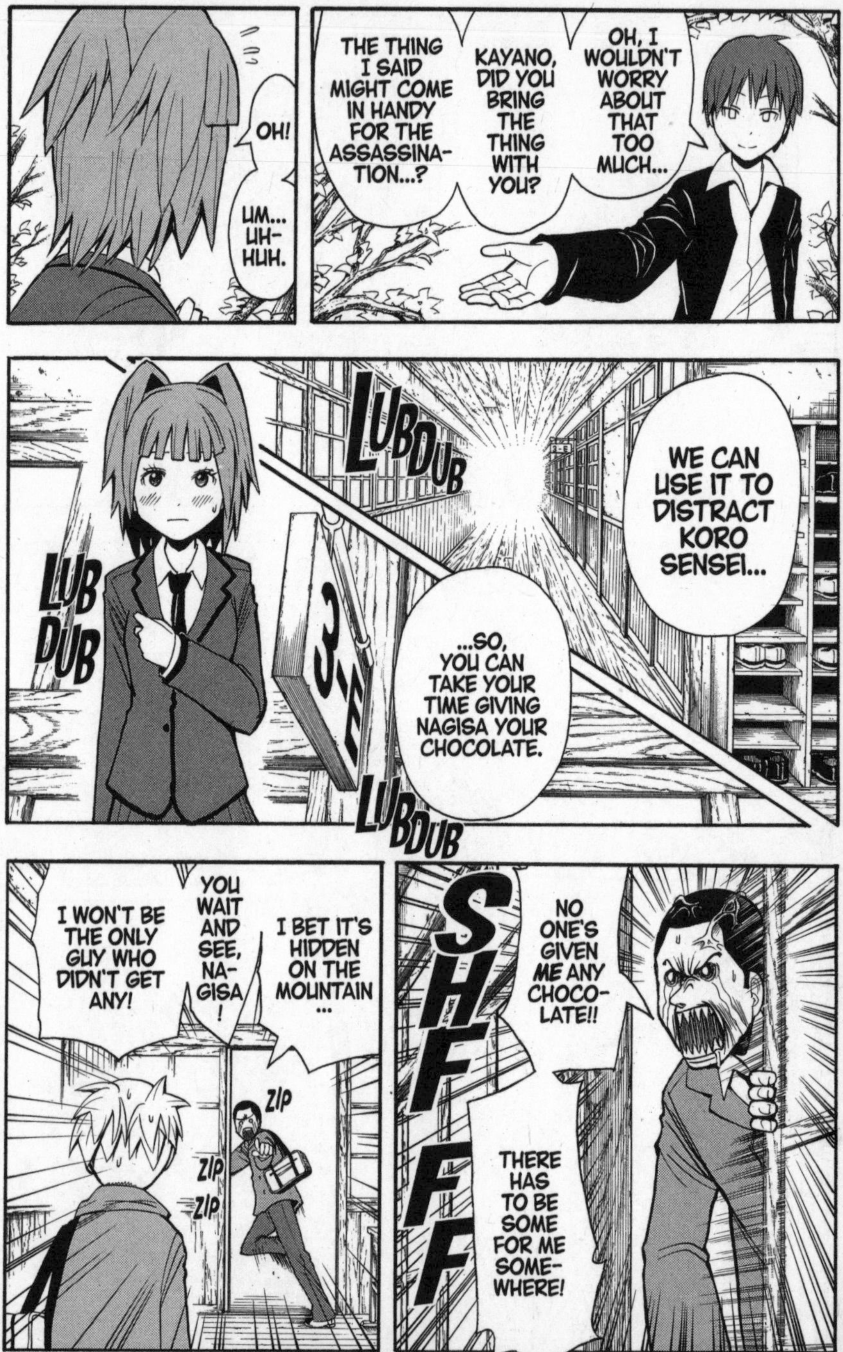
OH, I WOULDN'T WORRY ABOUT THAT TOO MUCH...
KAYANO, DID YOU BRING THE THING WITH YOU?
THE THING I SAID MIGHT COME IN HANDY FOR THE ASSASSINATION...?
OH!
UM... UH-HUH.
LUBDUB
WE CAN USE IT TO DISTRACT KORO SENSEI...
...SO, YOU CAN TAKE YOUR TIME GIVING NAGISA YOUR CHOCOLATE.
LUB DUB
LUBDUB
SHFFFF
NO ONE'S GIVEN ME ANY CHOCOLATE!!
THERE HAS TO BE SOME FOR ME SOME-WHERE!
I BET IT'S HIDDEN ON THE MOUNTAIN...
YOU WAIT AND SEE, NA-GISA!
I WON'T BE THE ONLY GUY WHO DIDN'T GET ANY!
ZIP
ZIP
ZIP

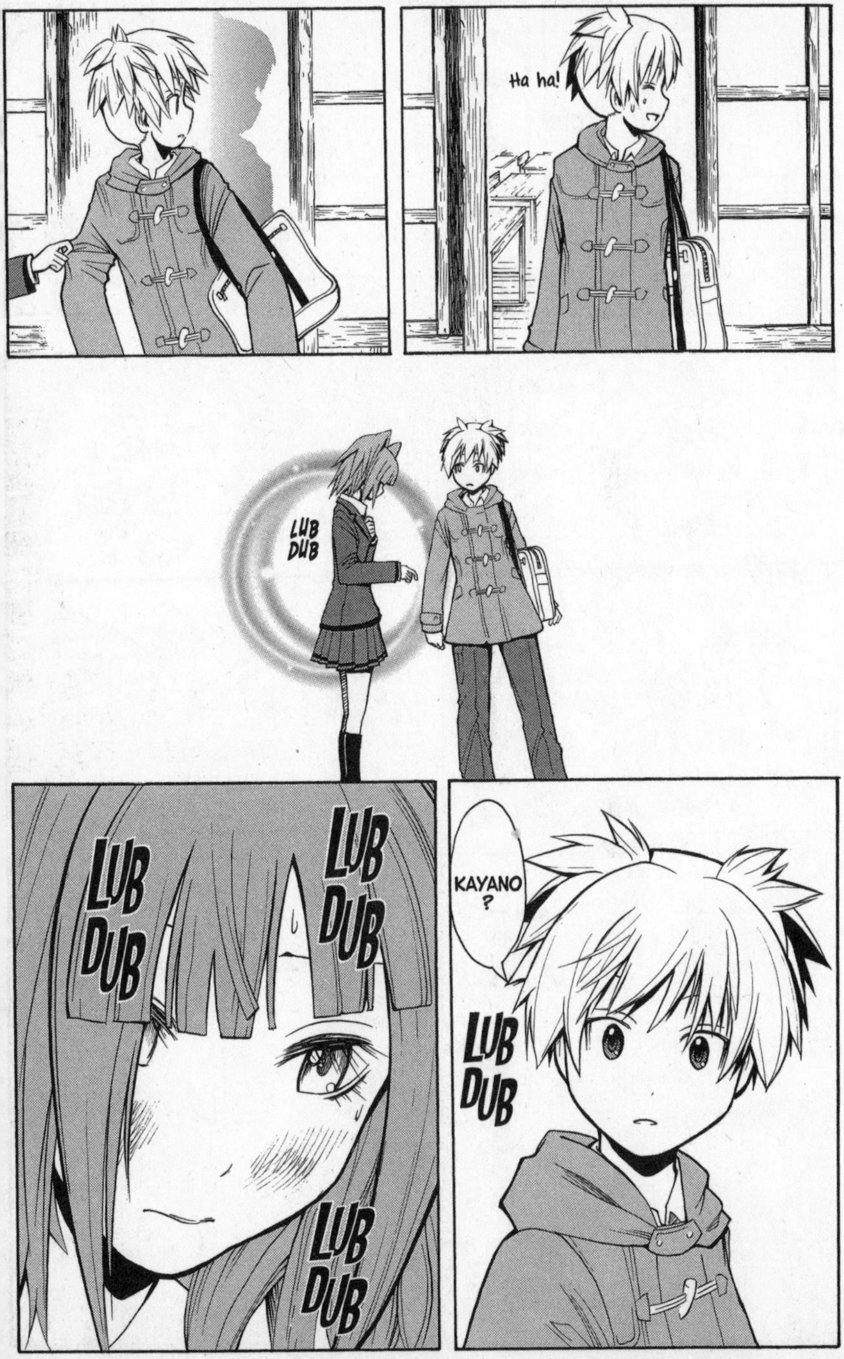
Ha ha!
LUB
DUB
KAYANO
?
LUB
DUB
LUB
DUB
LUB
DUB
LUB
DUB

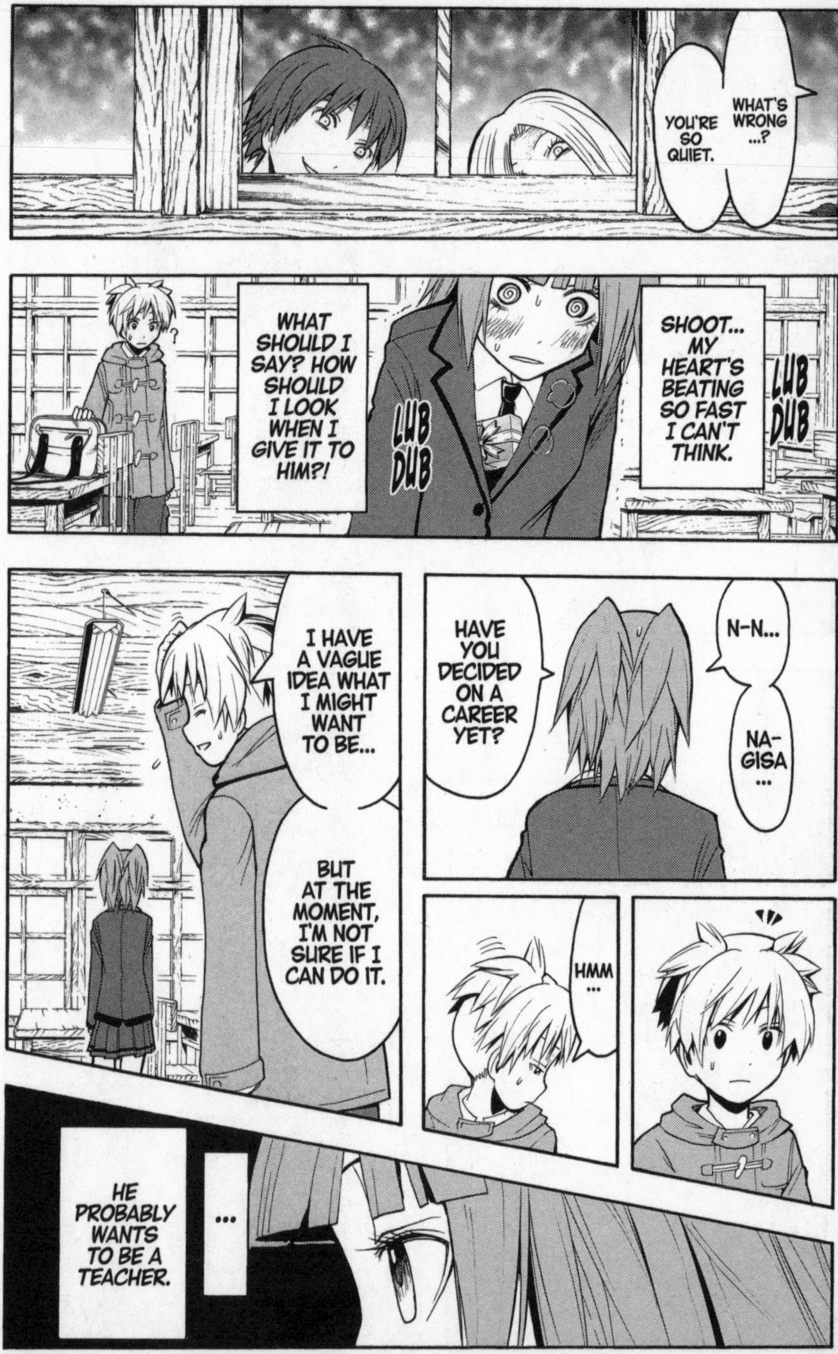
WHAT'S WRONG ...?
YOU'RE SO QUIET.
SHOOT... MY HEART'S BEATING SO FAST I CAN'T THINK.
LUB DUB
LUB DUB
WHAT SHOULD I SAY? HOW SHOULD I LOOK WHEN I GIVE IT TO HIM?!
N-N...
NA-GISA ...
HAVE YOU DECIDED ON A CAREER YET?
HMM ...
I HAVE A VAGUE IDEA WHAT I MIGHT WANT TO BE...
BUT AT THE MOMENT, I'M NOT SURE IF I CAN DO IT.
...
HE PROBABLY WANTS TO BE A TEACHER.

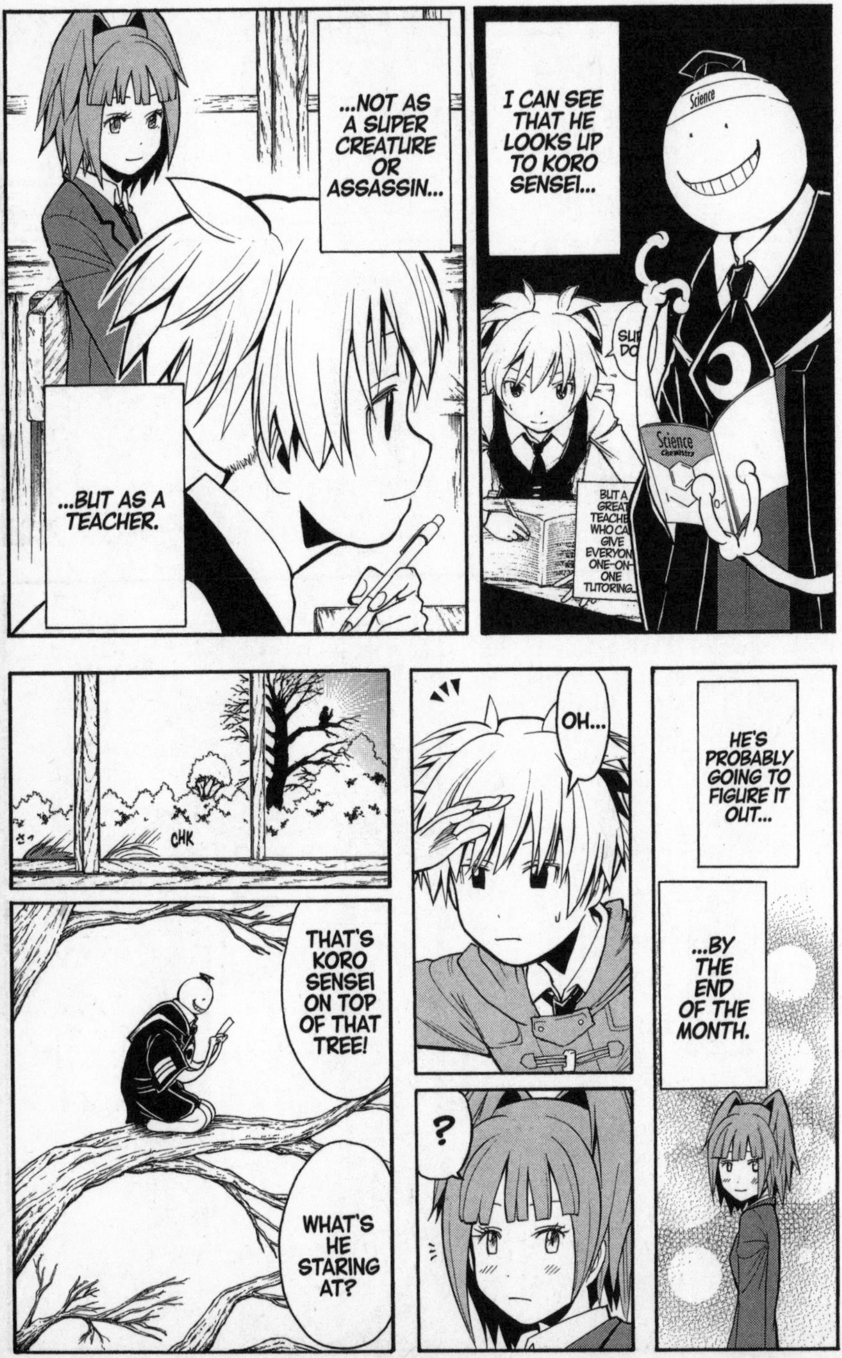
I CAN SEE THAT HE LOOKS UP TO KORO SENSEI...
Science
BUT A GREAT TEACHE WHO CA GIVE EVERYON ONE-ON-ONE TUTORING...
Science
...NOT AS A SUPER CREATURE OR ASSASSIN...
...BUT AS A TEACHER.
HE'S PROBABLY GOING TO FIGURE IT OUT...
...BY THE END OF THE MONTH.
OH...
?
CHK
THAT'S KORO SENSEI ON TOP OF THAT TREE!
WHAT'S HE STARING AT?

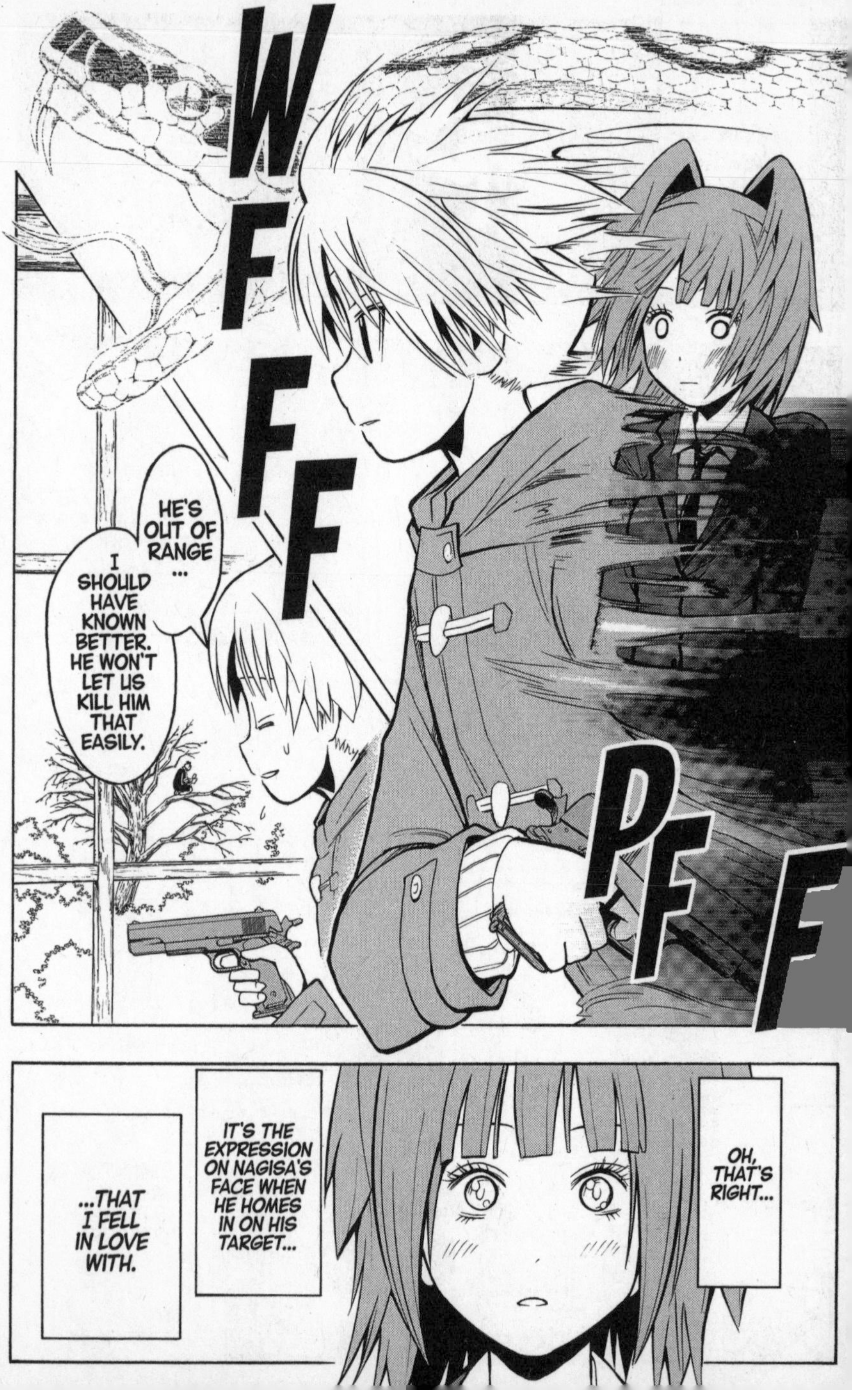
WFFF
HE'S OUT OF RANGE...
I SHOULD HAVE KNOWN BETTER. HE WON'T LET US KILL HIM THAT EASILY.
PFFF
OH, THAT'S RIGHT...
IT'S THE EXPRESSION ON NAGISA'S FACE WHEN HE HOMES IN ON HIS TARGET...
...THAT I FELL IN LOVE WITH.

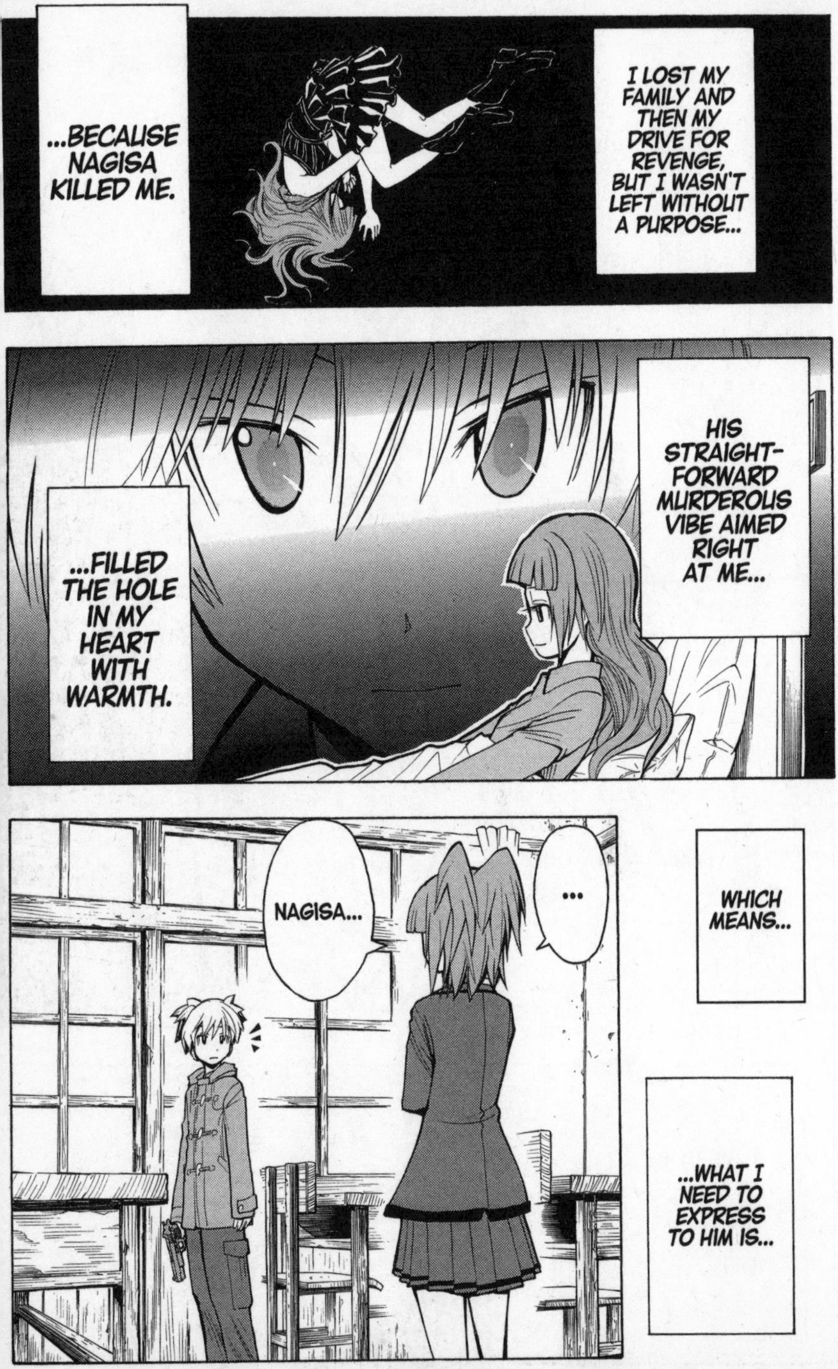
I LOST MY FAMILY AND THEN MY DRIVE FOR REVENGE, BUT I WASN'T LEFT WITHOUT A PURPOSE...
...BECAUSE NAGISA KILLED ME.
HIS STRAIGHT-FORWARD MURDEROUS VIBE AIMED RIGHT AT ME...
...FILLED THE HOLE IN MY HEART WITH WARMTH.
WHICH MEANS...
...WHAT I NEED TO EXPRESS TO HIM IS...
...
NAGISA...

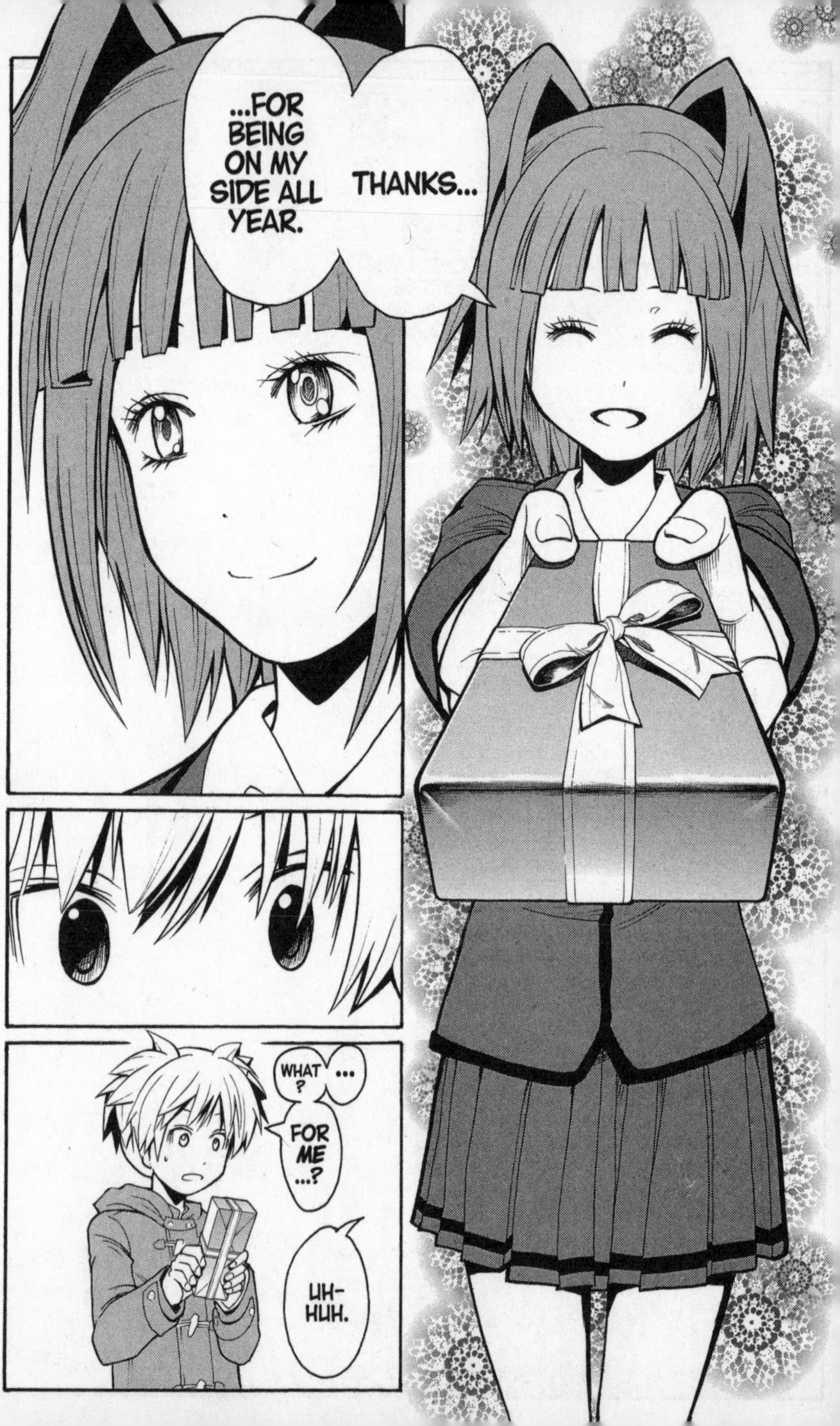
THANKS...
...FOR BEING ON MY SIDE ALL YEAR.
...
WHAT?
FOR ME...?
UH-HUH.

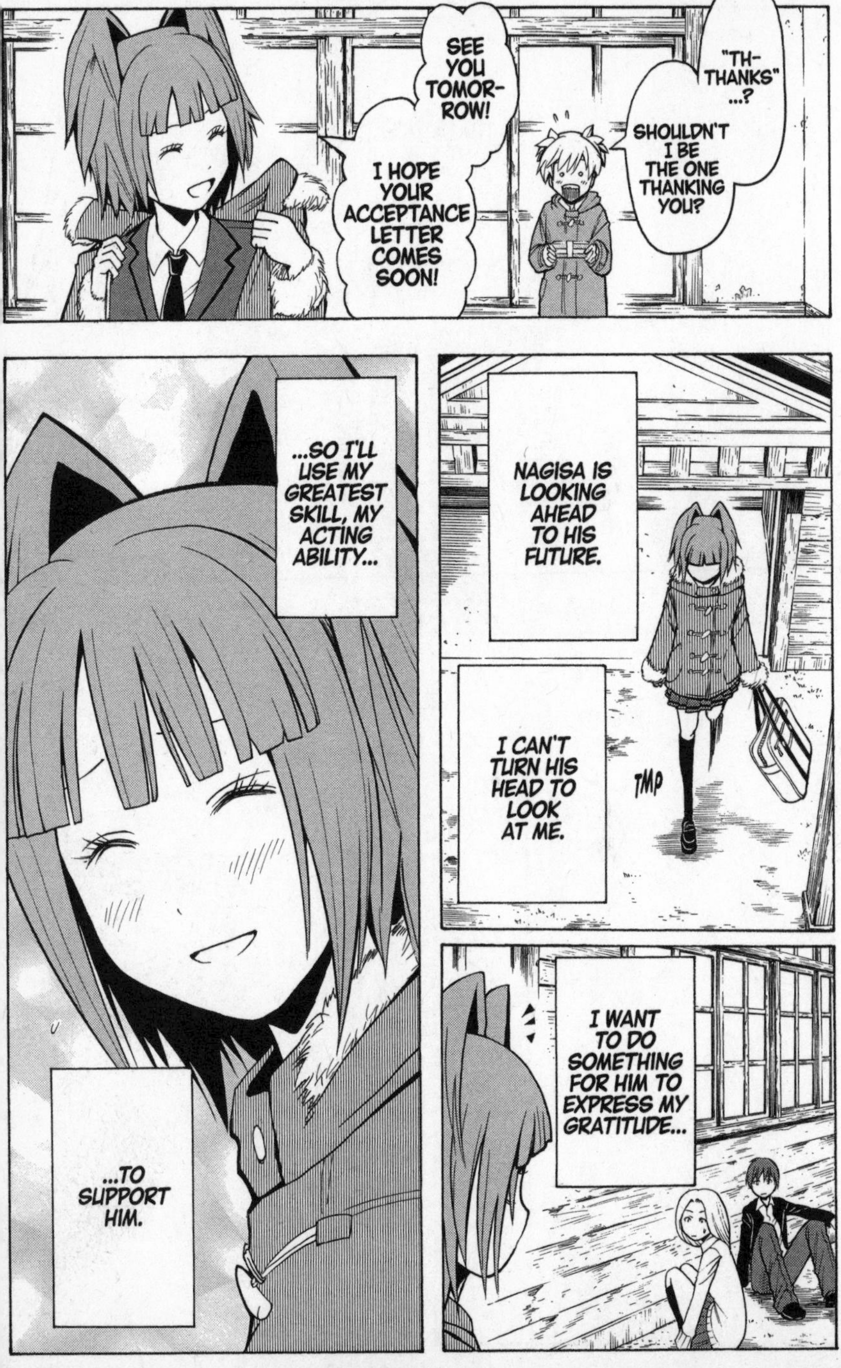
"TH-THANKS" ...?
SHOULDN'T I BE THE ONE THANKING YOU?
SEE YOU TOMORROW!
I HOPE YOUR ACCEPTANCE LETTER COMES SOON!
NAGISA IS LOOKING AHEAD TO HIS FUTURE.
I CAN'T TURN HIS HEAD TO LOOK AT ME.
TMP
I WANT TO DO SOMETHING FOR HIM TO EXPRESS MY GRATITUDE...
...SO I'LL USE MY GREATEST SKILL, MY ACTING ABILITY...
...TO SUPPORT HIM.

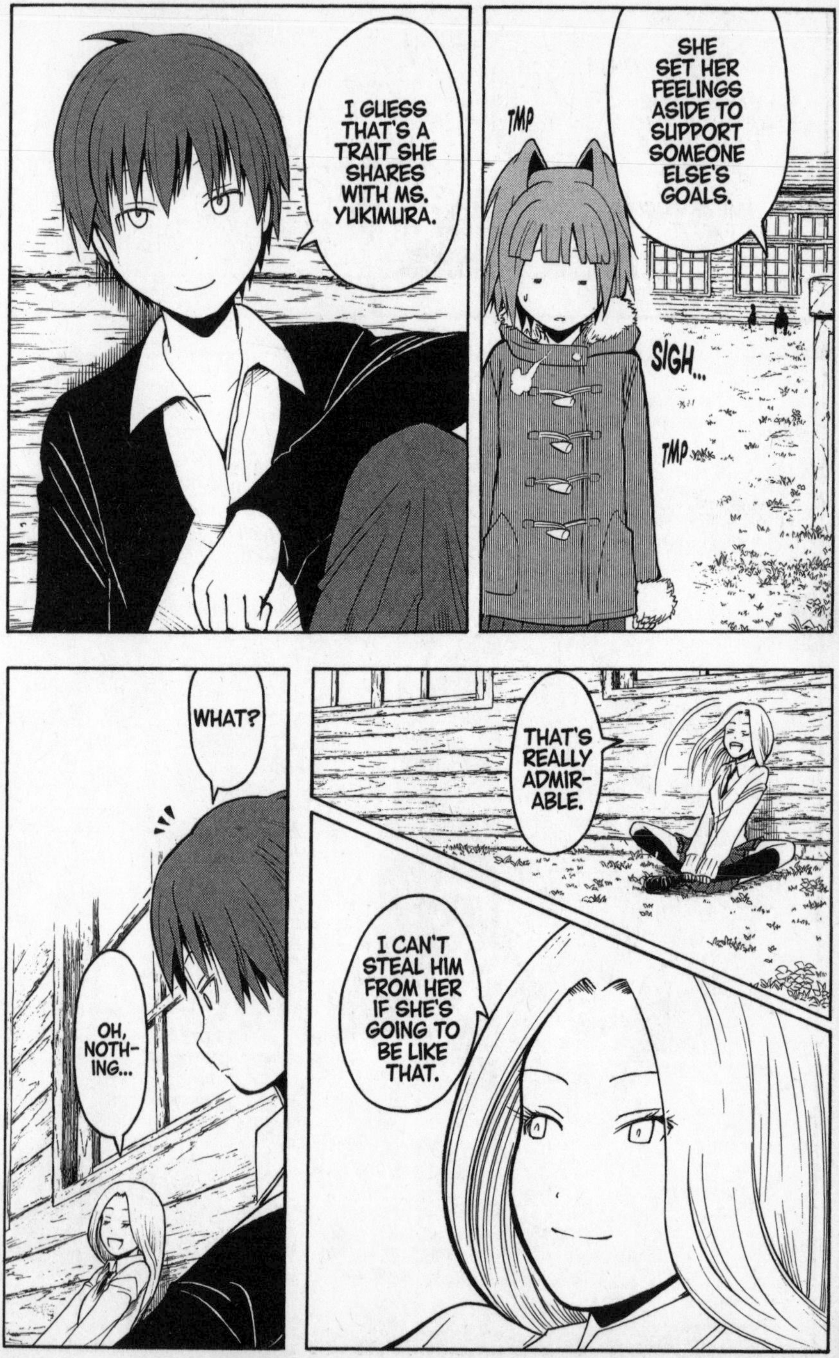
TMP
SHE SET HER FEELINGS ASIDE TO SUPPORT SOMEONE ELSE'S GOALS.
SIGH...
TMP
I GUESS THAT'S A TRAIT SHE SHARES WITH MS. YUKIMURA.
THAT'S REALLY ADMIR-ABLE.
I CAN'T STEAL HIM FROM HER IF SHE'S GOING TO BE LIKE THAT.
WHAT?
OH, NOTH-ING...

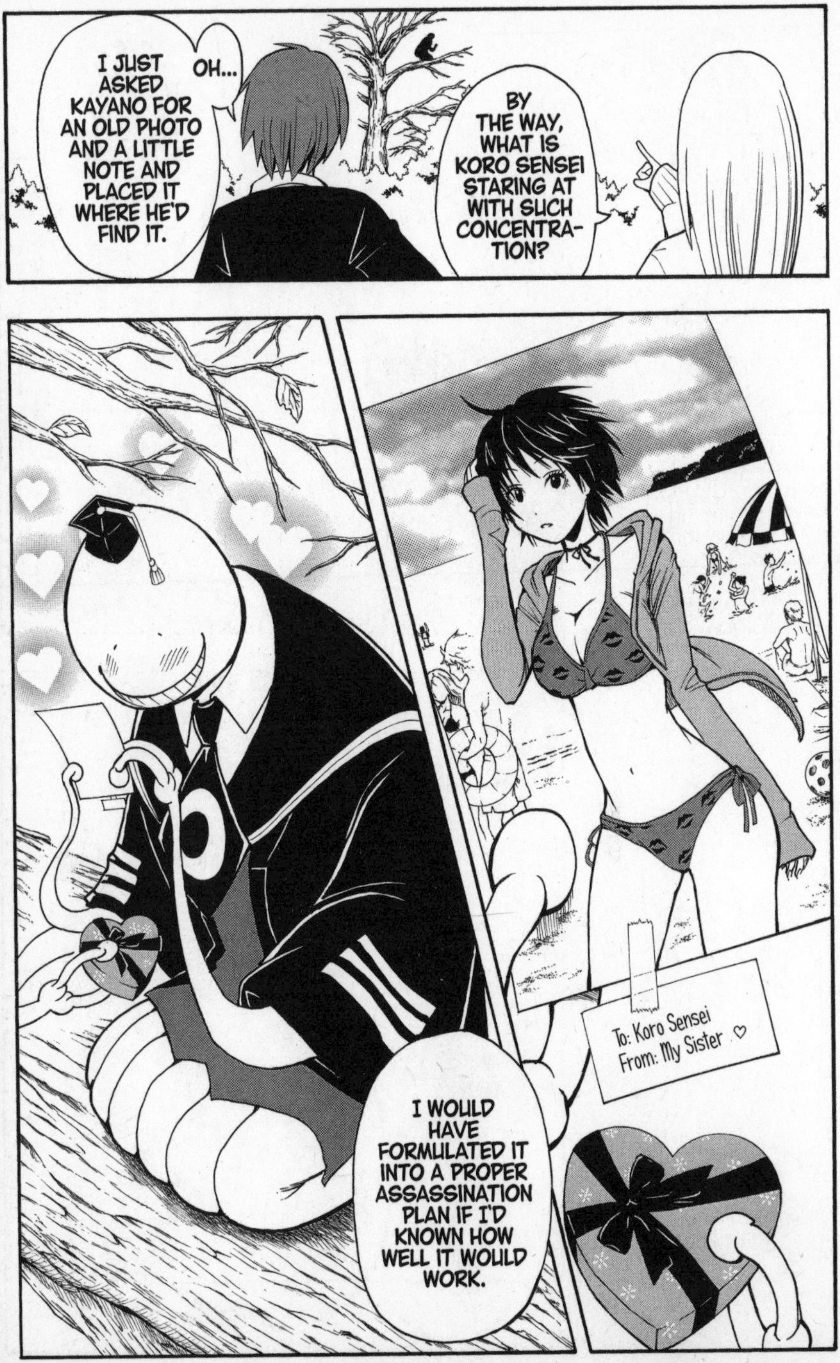
BY THE WAY, WHAT IS KORO SENSEI STARING AT WITH SUCH CONCENTRATION?
OH...
I JUST ASKED KAYANO FOR AN OLD PHOTO AND A LITTLE NOTE AND PLACED IT WHERE HE'D FIND IT.
To: Koro Sensei
From: My Sister ♡
I WOULD HAVE FORMULATED IT INTO A PROPER ASSASSINATION PLAN IF I'D KNOWN HOW WELL IT WOULD WORK.

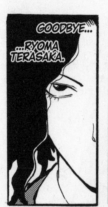

NO, I'VE GOT NOTHING TO SAY TO YOU.
GOODBYE...
...RYOMA TERASAKA.

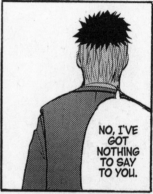

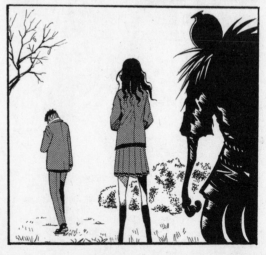

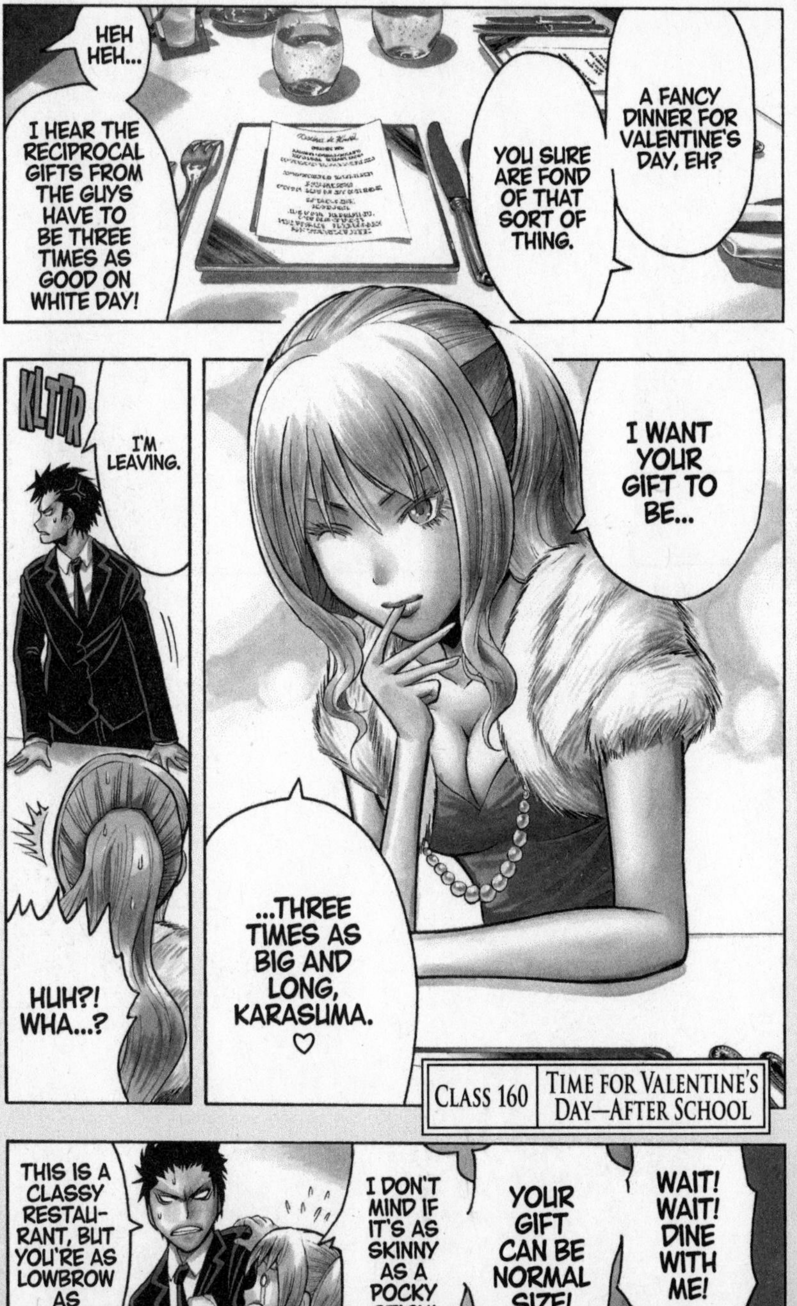
A FANCY DINNER FOR VALENTINE'S DAY, EH?
YOU SURE ARE FOND OF THAT SORT OF THING.
HEH HEH...
I HEAR THE RECIPROCAL GIFTS FROM THE GUYS HAVE TO BE THREE TIMES AS GOOD ON WHITE DAY!
I WANT YOUR GIFT TO BE...
...THREE TIMES AS BIG AND LONG, KARASUMA. ♡
CLASS 160 TIME FOR VALENTINE'S DAY—AFTER SCHOOL
KLTTR
I'M LEAVING.
HUH?! WHA...?
WAIT! WAIT! DINE WITH ME!
YOUR GIFT CAN BE NORMAL SIZE!
I DON'T MIND IF IT'S AS SKINNY AS A POCKY STICK!
THIS IS A CLASSY RESTAURANT, BUT YOU'RE AS LOWBROW AS ALWAYS...

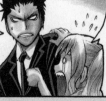

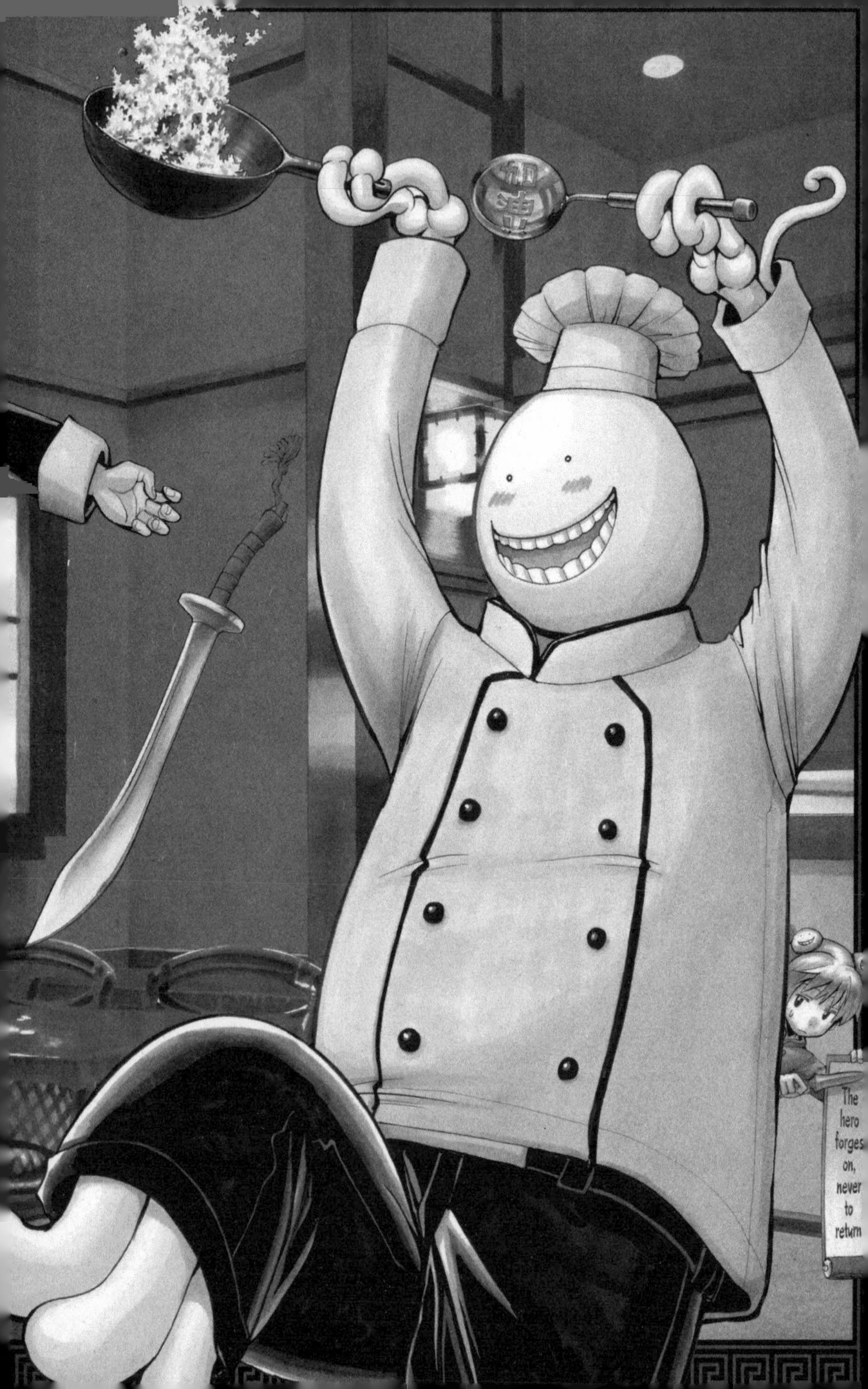
The hero forges on, never to return

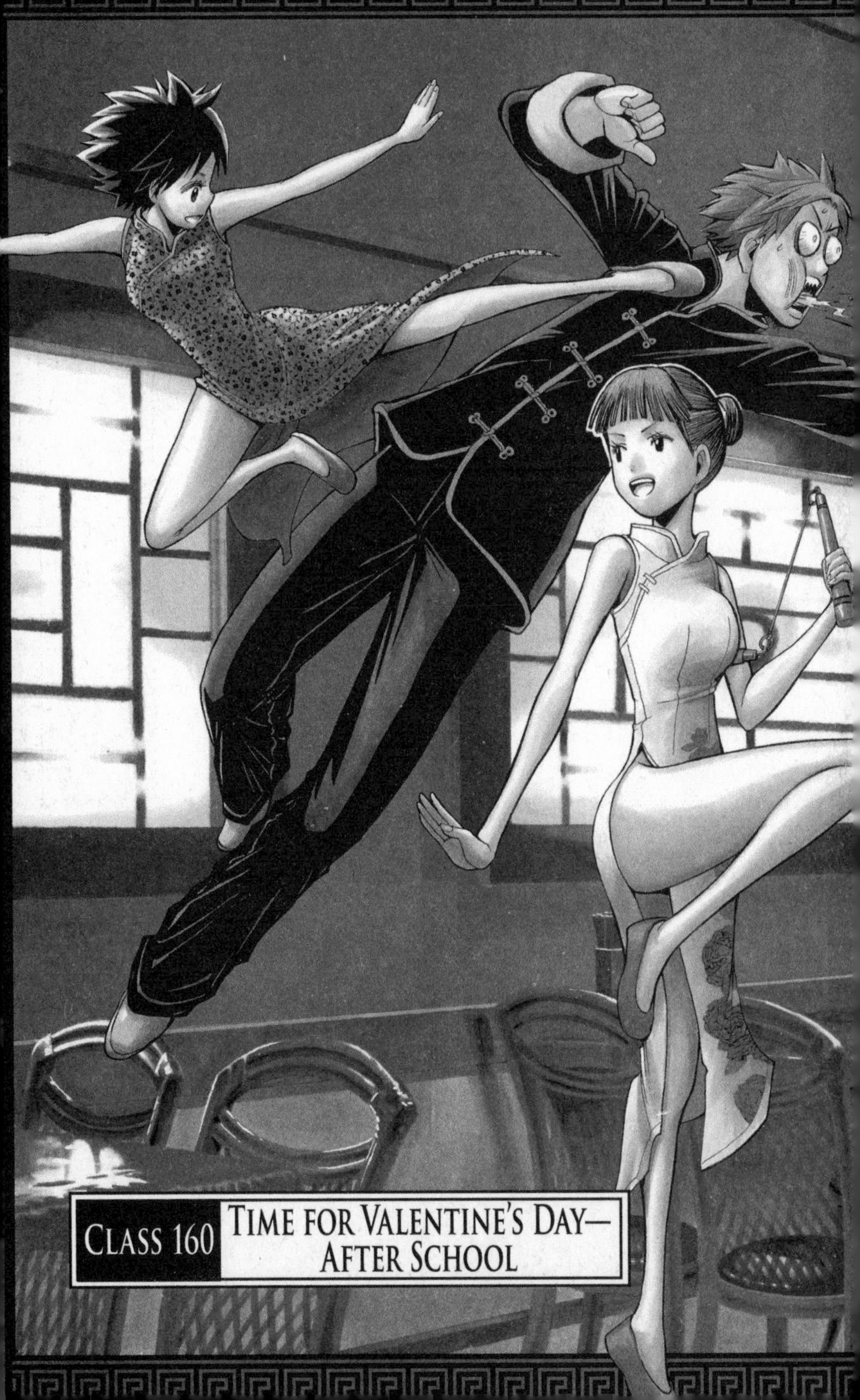
Class 160
Time for Valentine's Day—After School

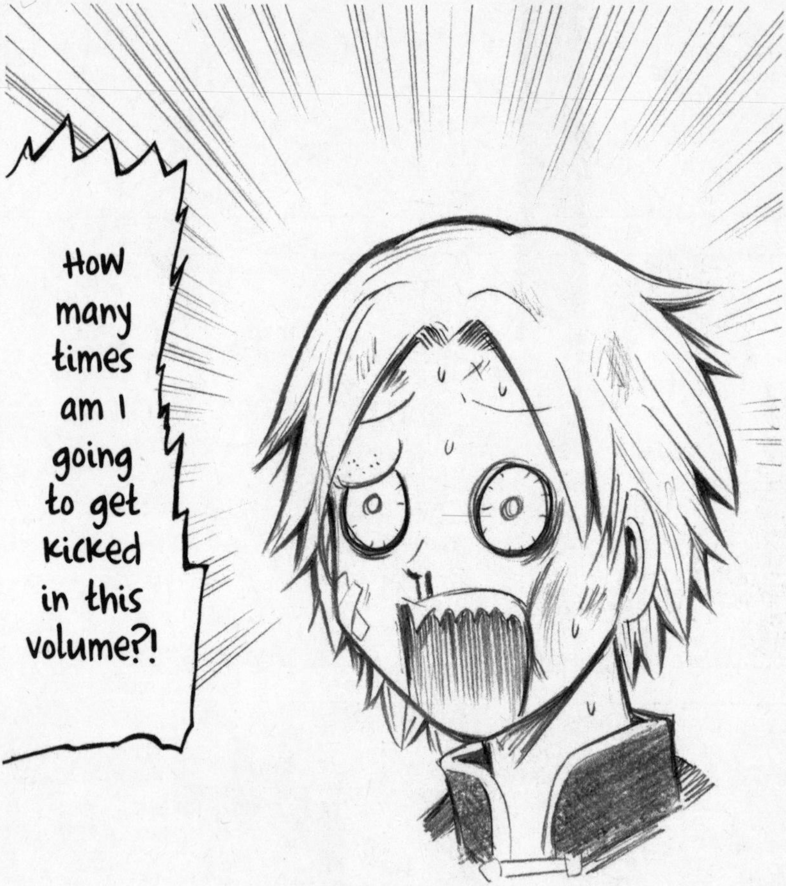
How many times am I going to get kicked in this volume?!

You're a convenient fall guy.

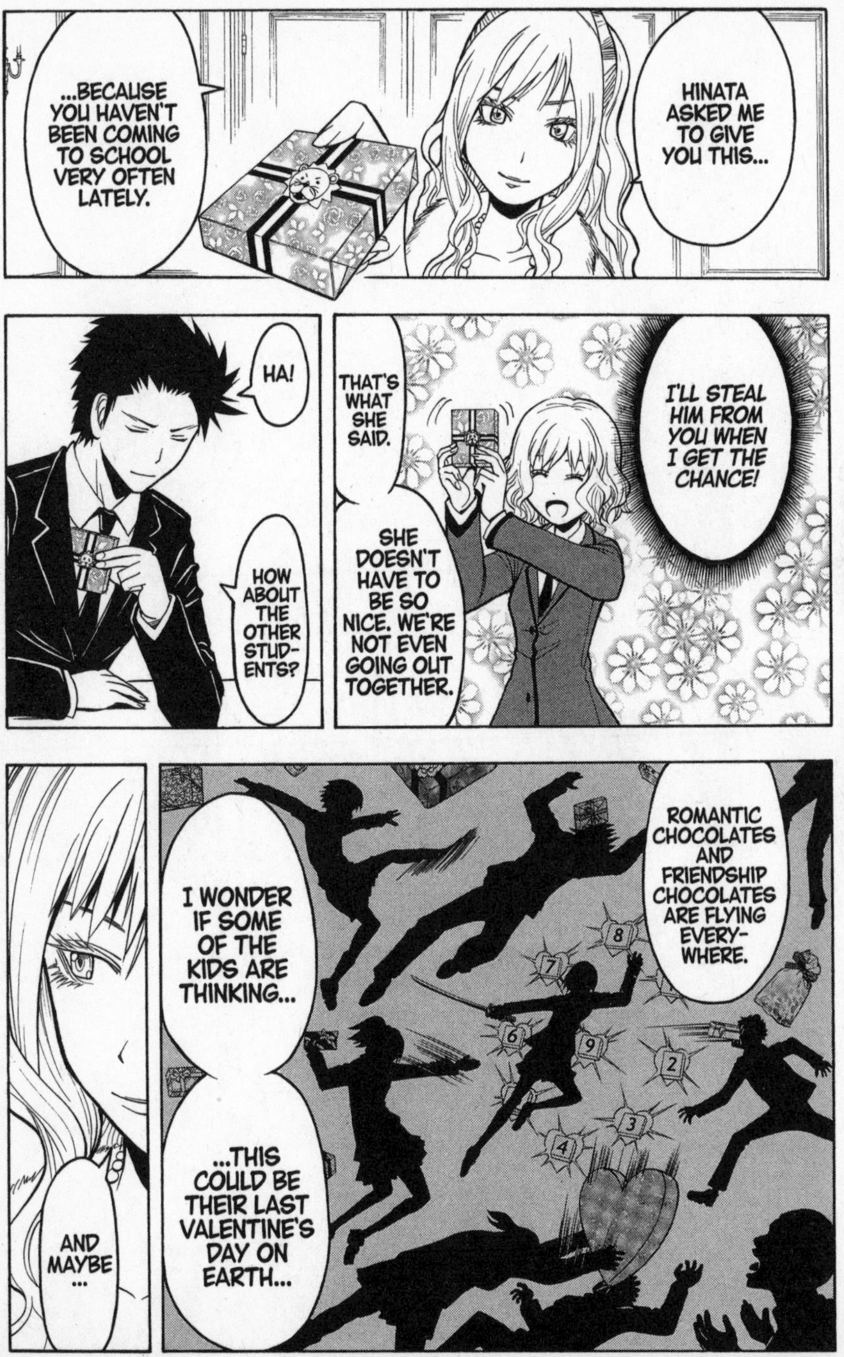
HINATA ASKED ME TO GIVE YOU THIS...
...BECAUSE YOU HAVEN'T BEEN COMING TO SCHOOL VERY OFTEN LATELY.
I'LL STEAL HIM FROM YOU WHEN I GET THE CHANCE!
THAT'S WHAT SHE SAID.
SHE DOESN'T HAVE TO BE SO NICE. WE'RE NOT EVEN GOING OUT TOGETHER.
HA!
HOW ABOUT THE OTHER STUDENTS?
ROMANTIC CHOCOLATES AND FRIENDSHIP CHOCOLATES ARE FLYING EVERY-WHERE.
I WONDER IF SOME OF THE KIDS ARE THINKING...
...THIS COULD BE THEIR LAST VALENTINE'S DAY ON EARTH...
AND MAYBE ...

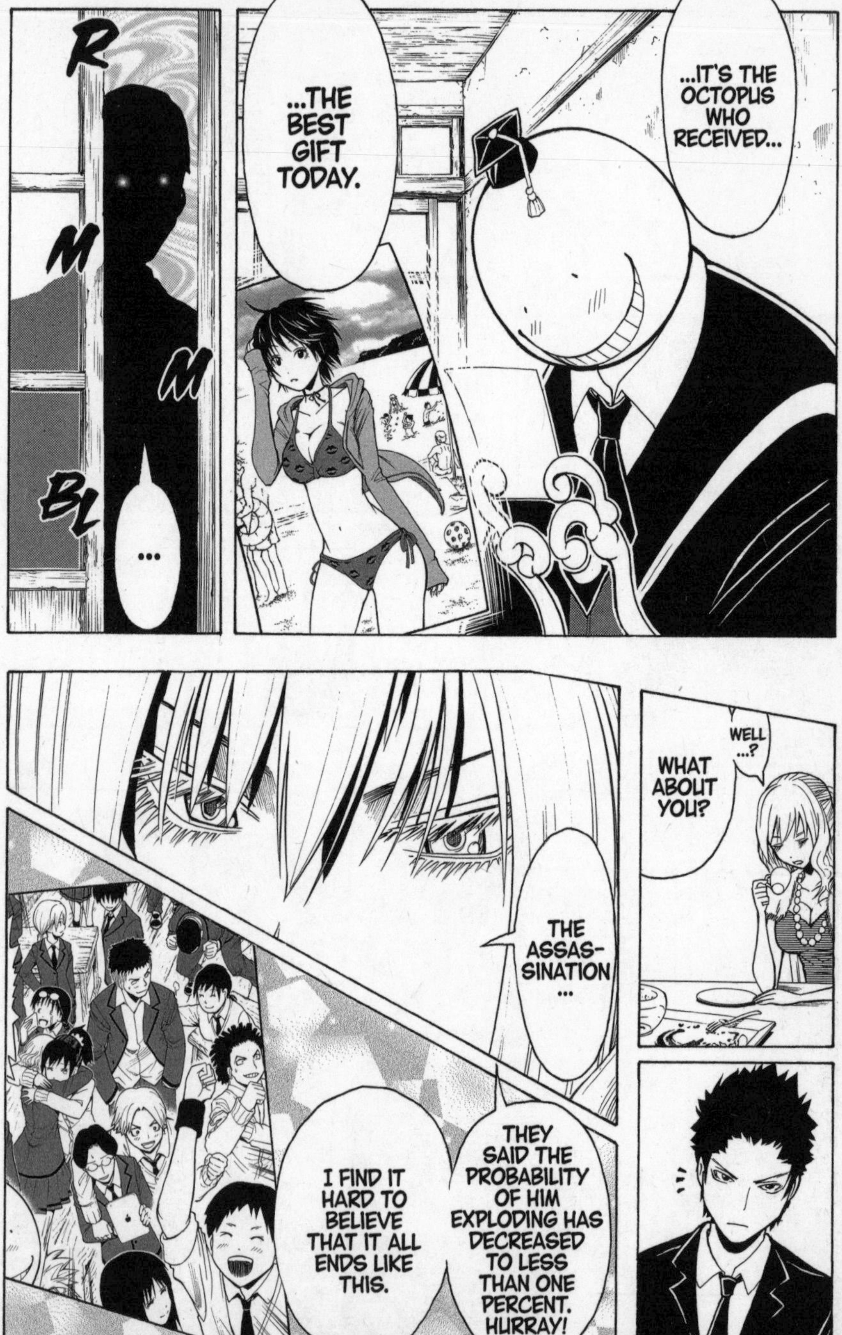
...IT'S THE OCTOPUS WHO RECEIVED...
...THE BEST GIFT TODAY.
RMMBL
...
WELL ...?
WHAT ABOUT YOU?
THE ASSAS-SINATION ...
THEY SAID THE PROBABILITY OF HIM EXPLODING HAS DECREASED TO LESS THAN ONE PERCENT. HURRAY!
I FIND IT HARD TO BELIEVE THAT IT ALL ENDS LIKE THIS.

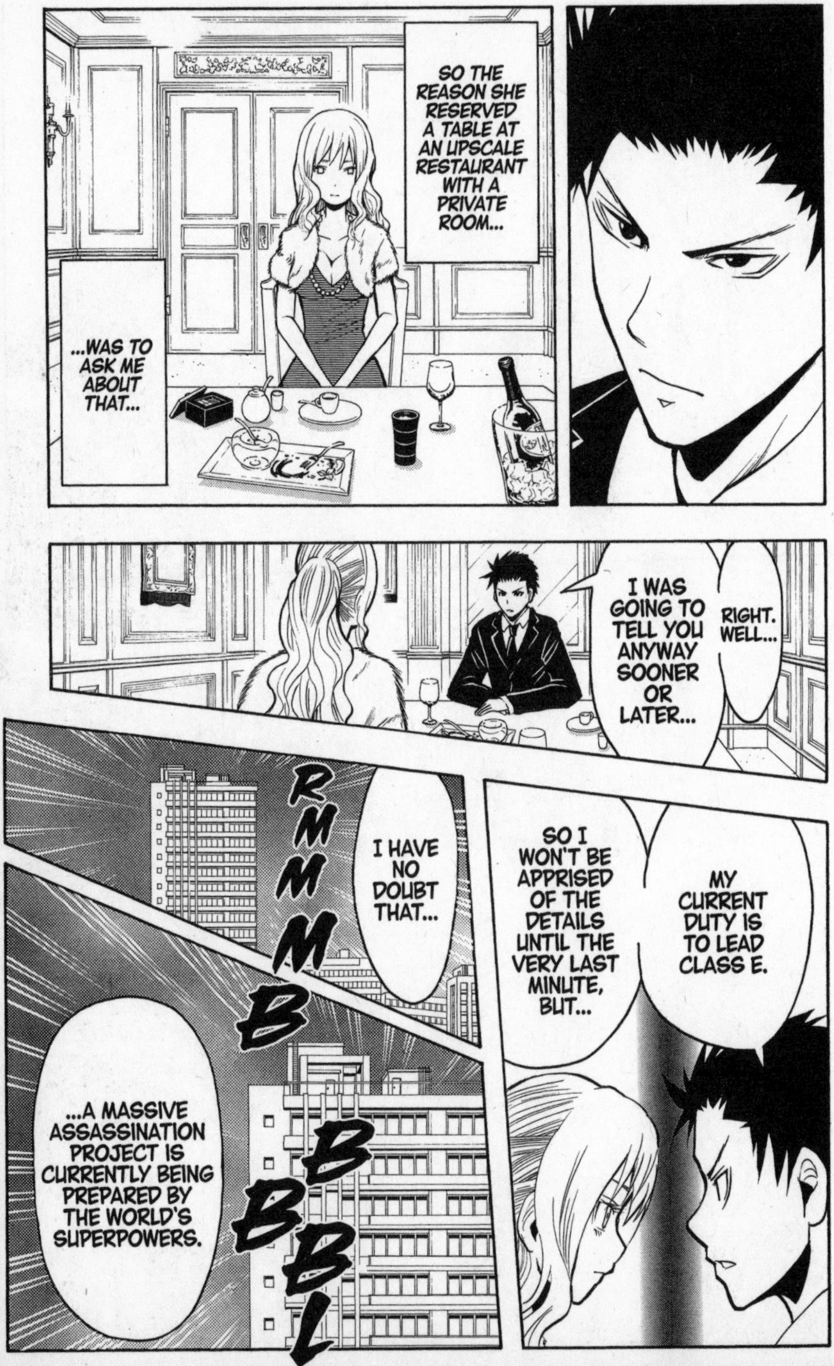
SO THE REASON SHE RESERVED A TABLE AT AN UPSCALE RESTAURANT WITH A PRIVATE ROOM...
...WAS TO ASK ME ABOUT THAT...
RIGHT. WELL...
I WAS GOING TO TELL YOU ANYWAY SOONER OR LATER...
MY CURRENT DUTY IS TO LEAD CLASS E.
SO I WON'T BE APPRISED OF THE DETAILS UNTIL THE VERY LAST MINUTE, BUT...
I HAVE NO DOUBT THAT...
RMMMBBBBL
...A MASSIVE ASSASSINATION PROJECT IS CURRENTLY BEING PREPARED BY THE WORLD'S SUPERPOWERS.

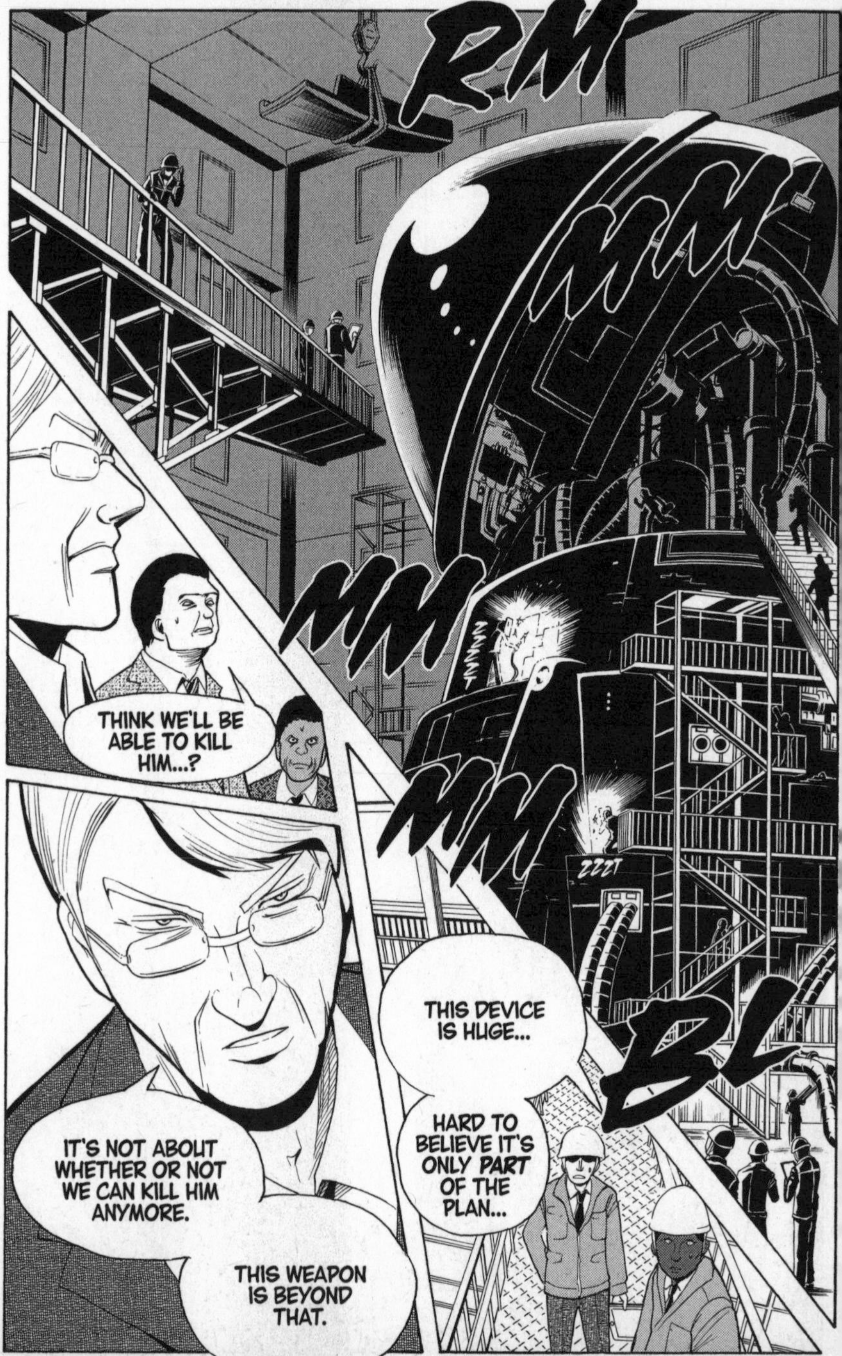

RM
MMM
MMM
MMM
ZZZT
ZZZT
BL
THIS DEVICE IS HUGE...
HARD TO BELIEVE IT'S ONLY PART OF THE PLAN...
THINK WE'LL BE ABLE TO KILL HIM...?
IT'S NOT ABOUT WHETHER OR NOT WE CAN KILL HIM ANYMORE.
THIS WEAPON IS BEYOND THAT.

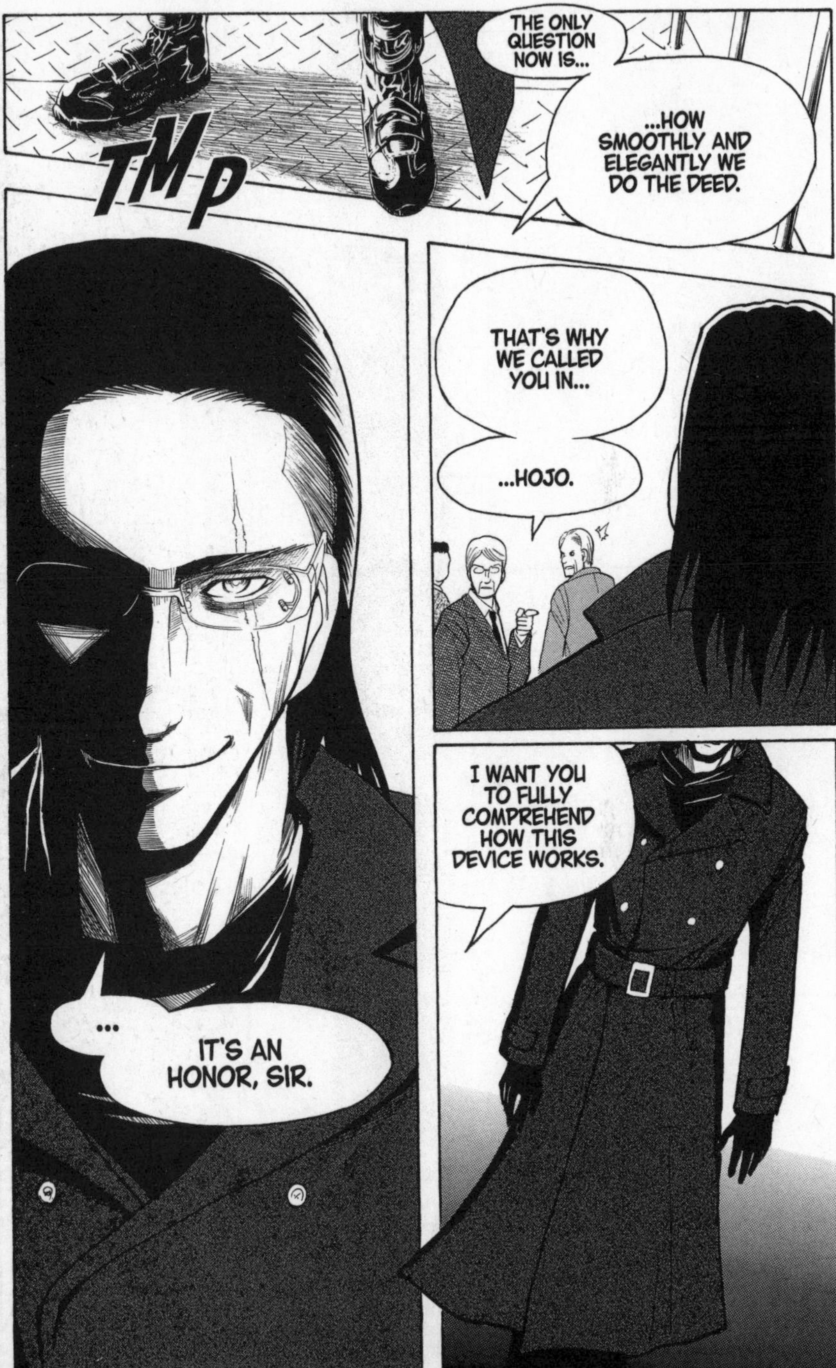
THE ONLY QUESTION NOW IS...
...HOW SMOOTHLY AND ELEGANTLY WE DO THE DEED.
TMP
THAT'S WHY WE CALLED YOU IN...
...HOJO.
I WANT YOU TO FULLY COMPREHEND HOW THIS DEVICE WORKS.
... IT'S AN HONOR, SIR.

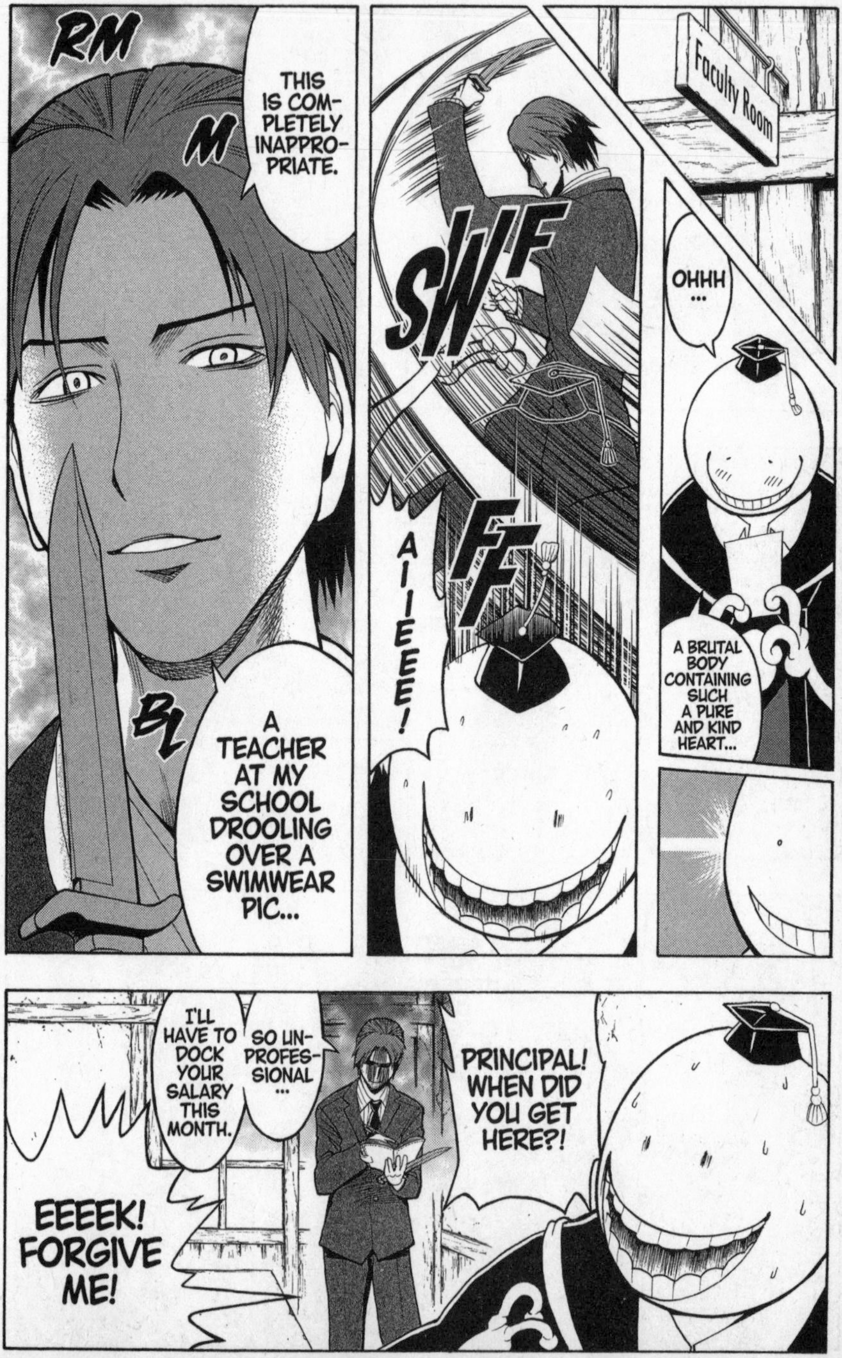
Faculty Room
OHHH...
A BRUTAL BODY CONTAINING SUCH A PURE AND KIND HEART...
SWF
FF
AIIEEEE!
RM
M
THIS IS COM-PLETELY INAPPRO-PRIATE.
BL
A TEACHER AT MY SCHOOL DROOLING OVER A SWIMWEAR PIC...
PRINCIPAL! WHEN DID YOU GET HERE?!
SO UN-PROFES-SIONAL...
I'LL HAVE TO DOCK YOUR SALARY THIS MONTH.
RM
EEEEK! FORGIVE ME!

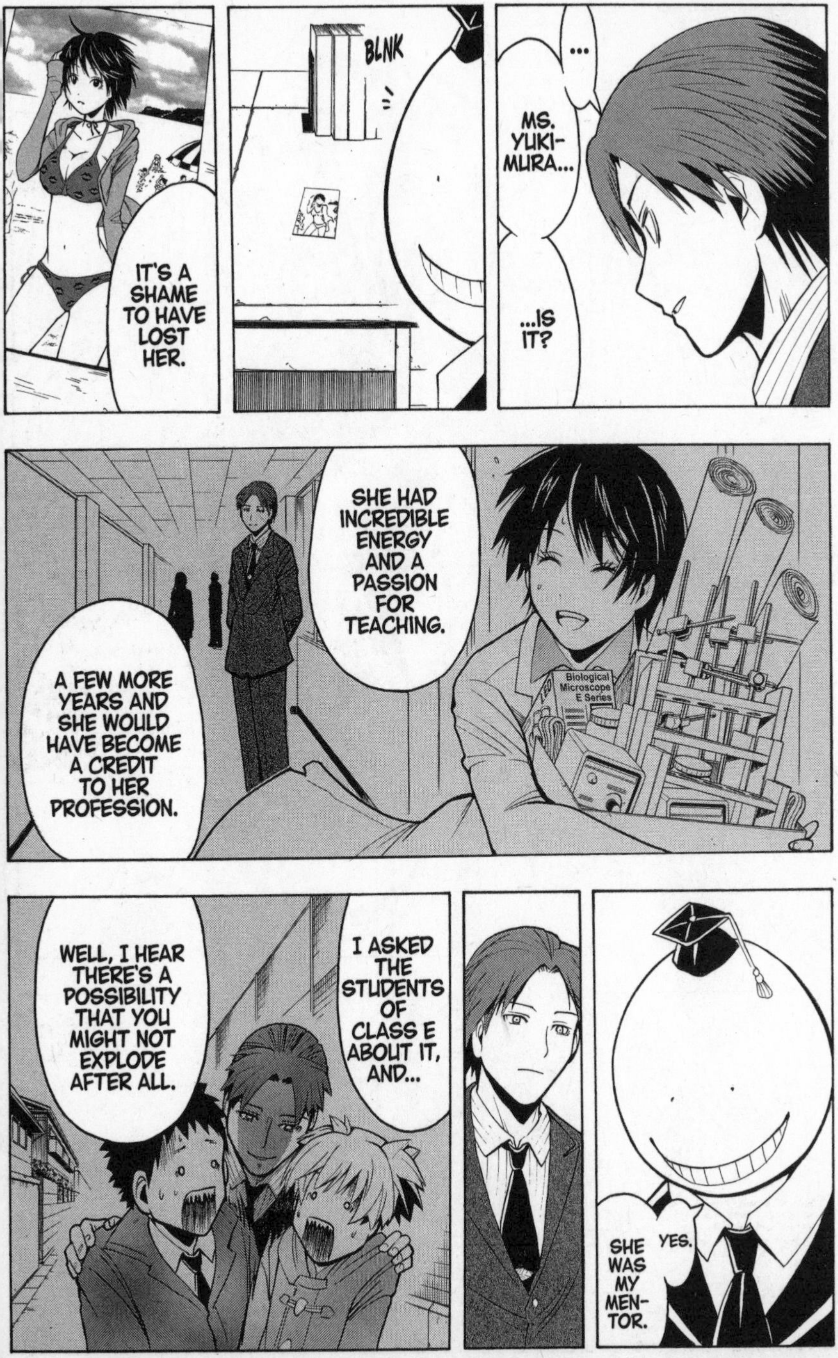
...
MS. YUKIMURA...
...IS IT?
BLNK
IT'S A SHAME TO HAVE LOST HER.
SHE HAD INCREDIBLE ENERGY AND A PASSION FOR TEACHING.
Biological Microscope E Series
A FEW MORE YEARS AND SHE WOULD HAVE BECOME A CREDIT TO HER PROFESSION.
YES.
SHE WAS MY MENTOR.
I ASKED THE STUDENTS OF CLASS E ABOUT IT, AND...
WELL, I HEAR THERE'S A POSSIBILITY THAT YOU MIGHT NOT EXPLODE AFTER ALL.

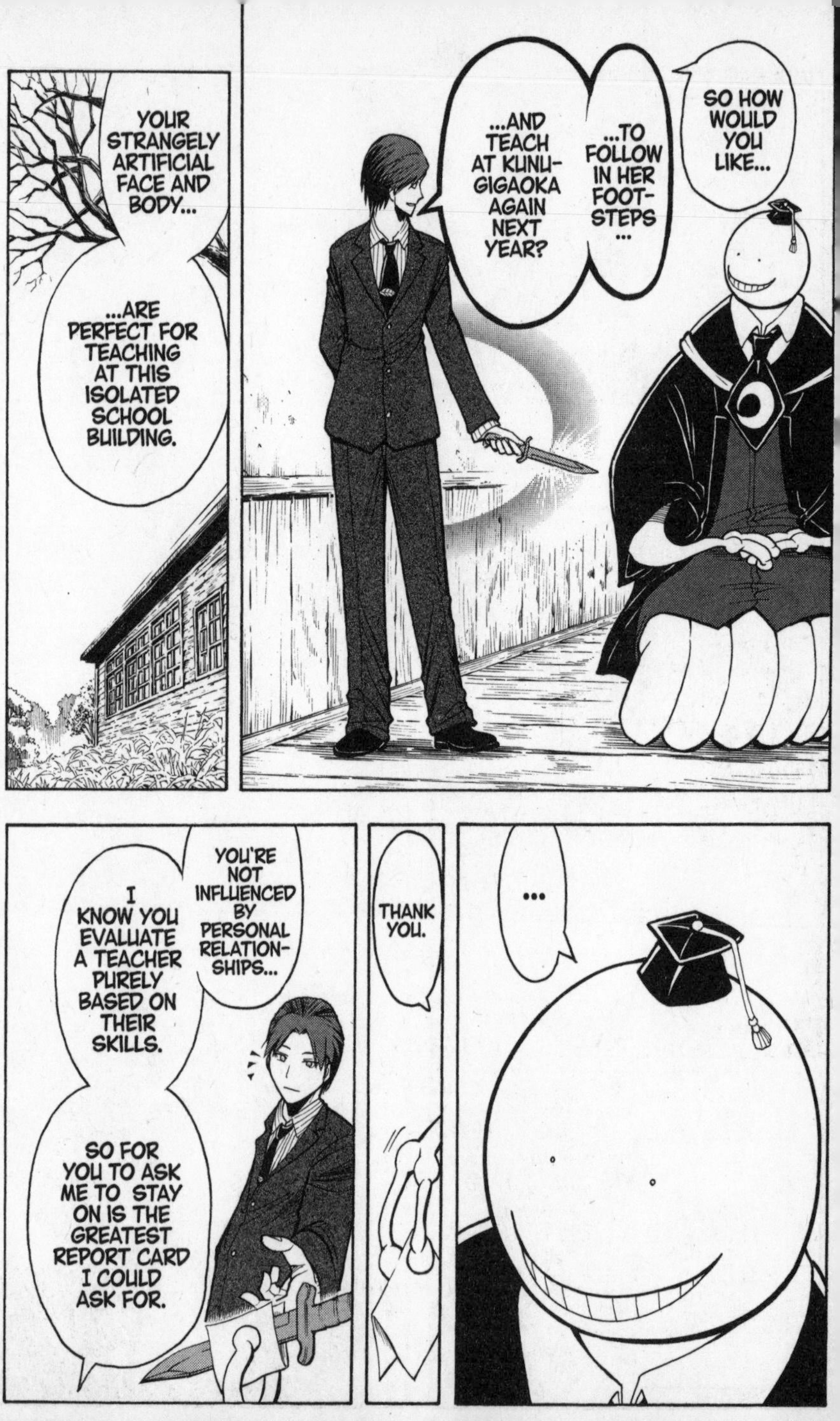
SO HOW WOULD YOU LIKE...
...TO FOLLOW IN HER FOOTSTEPS...
...AND TEACH AT KUNUGIGAOKA AGAIN NEXT YEAR?
YOUR STRANGELY ARTIFICIAL FACE AND BODY...
...ARE PERFECT FOR TEACHING AT THIS ISOLATED SCHOOL BUILDING.
...
THANK YOU.
YOU'RE NOT INFLUENCED BY PERSONAL RELATIONSHIPS...
I KNOW YOU EVALUATE A TEACHER PURELY BASED ON THEIR SKILLS.
SO FOR YOU TO ASK ME TO STAY ON IS THE GREATEST REPORT CARD I COULD ASK FOR.

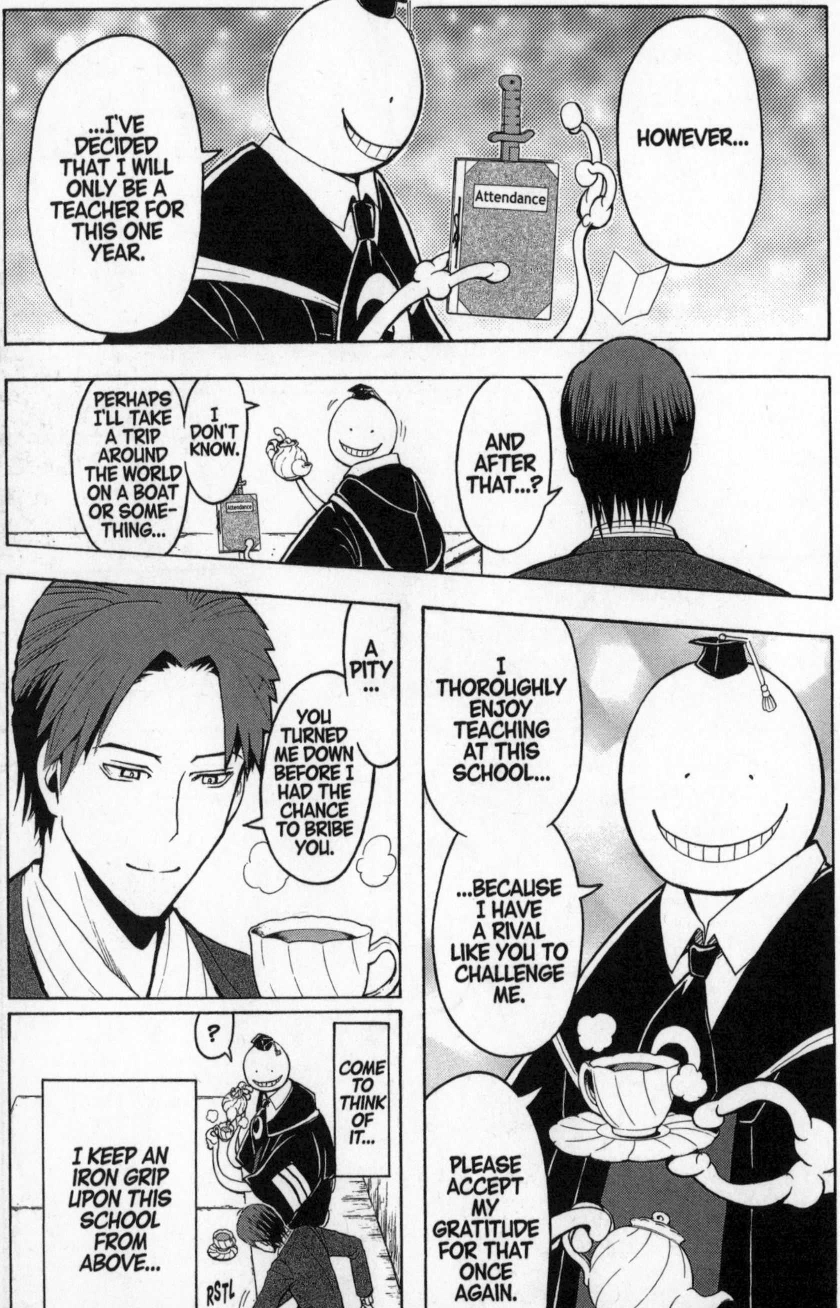
HOWEVER...
...I'VE DECIDED THAT I WILL ONLY BE A TEACHER FOR THIS ONE YEAR.
Attendance
AND AFTER THAT...?
I DON'T KNOW.
PERHAPS I'LL TAKE A TRIP AROUND THE WORLD ON A BOAT OR SOME-THING...
Attendance
I THOROUGHLY ENJOY TEACHING AT THIS SCHOOL...
...BECAUSE I HAVE A RIVAL LIKE YOU TO CHALLENGE ME.
PLEASE ACCEPT MY GRATITUDE FOR THAT ONCE AGAIN.
A PITY...
YOU TURNED ME DOWN BEFORE I HAD THE CHANCE TO BRIBE YOU.
?
COME TO THINK OF IT...
I KEEP AN IRON GRIP UPON THIS SCHOOL FROM ABOVE...
RSTL

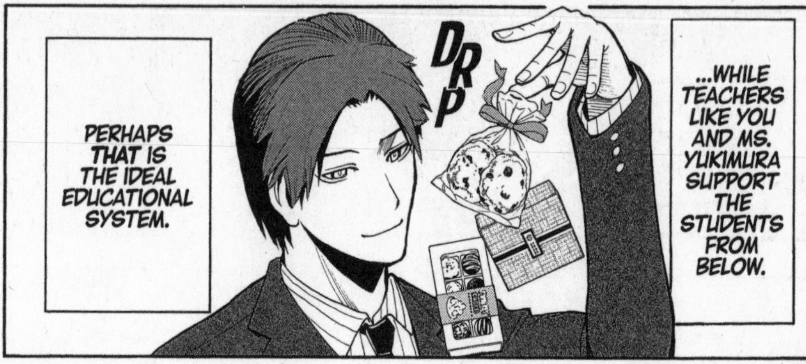
...WHILE TEACHERS LIKE YOU AND MS. YUKIMURA SUPPORT THE STUDENTS FROM BELOW.
DRP
PERHAPS THAT IS THE IDEAL EDUCATIONAL SYSTEM.

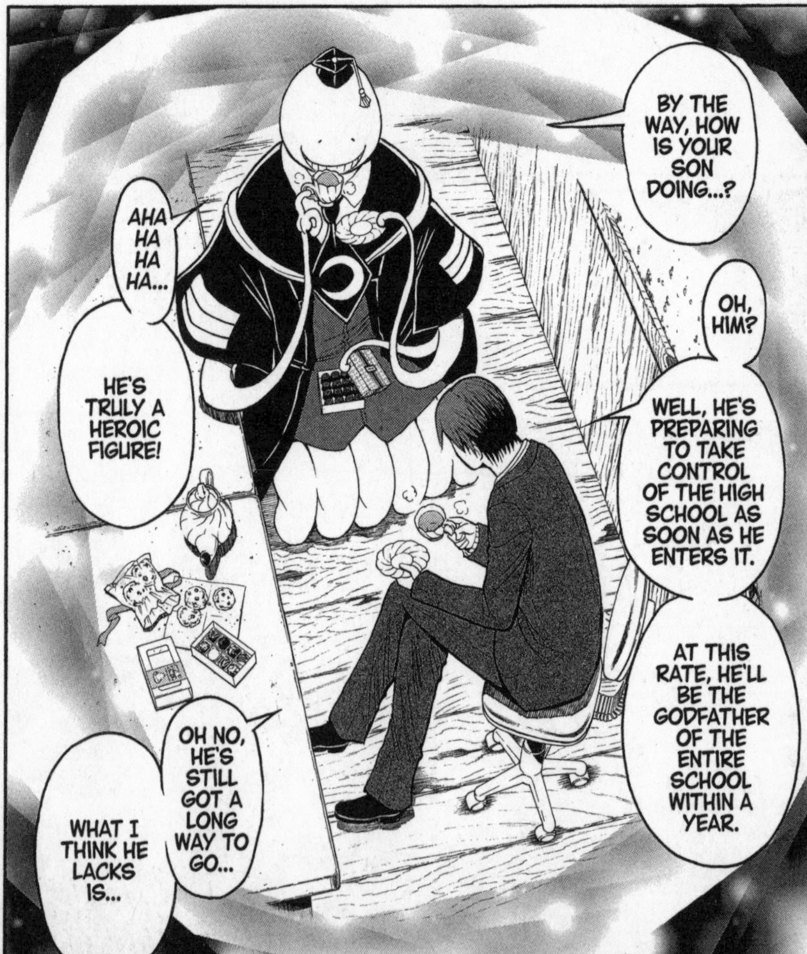
BY THE WAY, HOW IS YOUR SON DOING...?
OH, HIM?
WELL, HE'S PREPARING TO TAKE CONTROL OF THE HIGH SCHOOL AS SOON AS HE ENTERS IT.
AT THIS RATE, HE'LL BE THE GODFATHER OF THE ENTIRE SCHOOL WITHIN A YEAR.
AHA HA HA HA...
HE'S TRULY A HEROIC FIGURE!
OH NO, HE'S STILL GOT A LONG WAY TO GO...
WHAT I THINK HE LACKS IS...

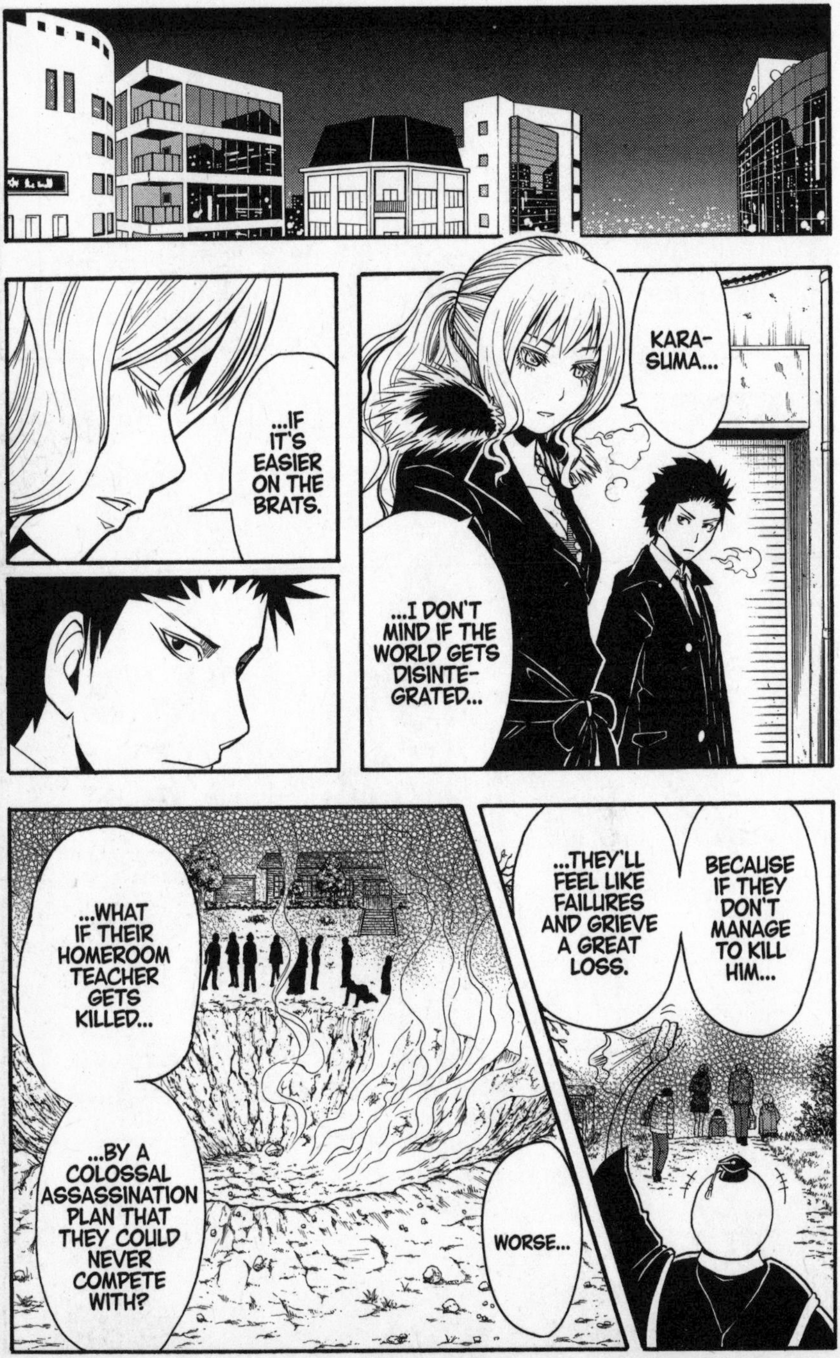
KARA-SUMA...
...I DON'T MIND IF THE WORLD GETS DISINTE-GRATED...
...IF IT'S EASIER ON THE BRATS.
BECAUSE IF THEY DON'T MANAGE TO KILL HIM...
...THEY'LL FEEL LIKE FAILURES AND GRIEVE A GREAT LOSS.
WORSE...
...WHAT IF THEIR HOMEROOM TEACHER GETS KILLED...
...BY A COLOSSAL ASSASSINATION PLAN THAT THEY COULD NEVER COMPETE WITH?

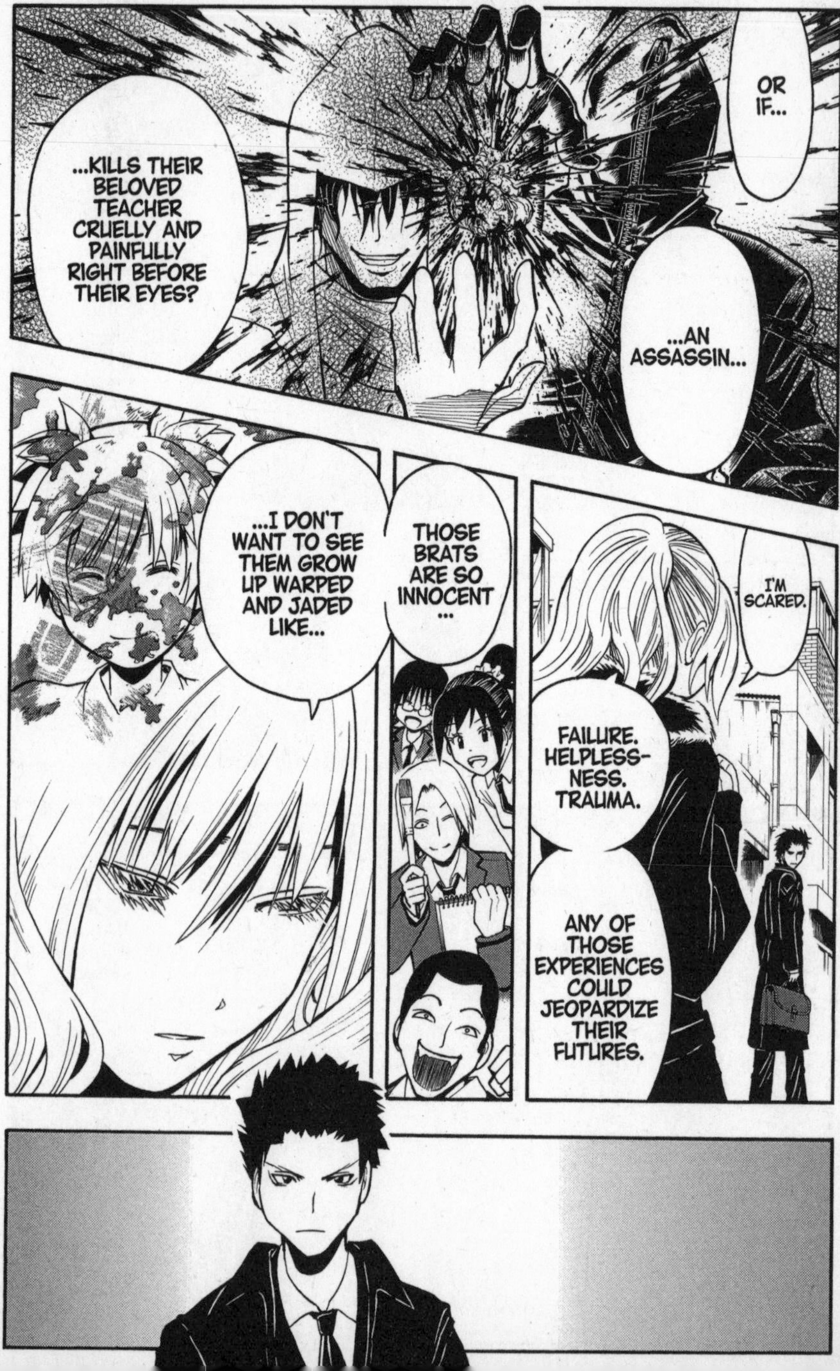
OR IF...
...AN ASSASSIN...
...KILLS THEIR BELOVED TEACHER CRUELLY AND PAINFULLY RIGHT BEFORE THEIR EYES?
I'M SCARED.
FAILURE. HELPLESS-NESS. TRAUMA.
ANY OF THOSE EXPERIENCES COULD JEOPARDIZE THEIR FUTURES.
THOSE BRATS ARE SO INNOCENT...
...I DON'T WANT TO SEE THEM GROW UP WARPED AND JADED LIKE...

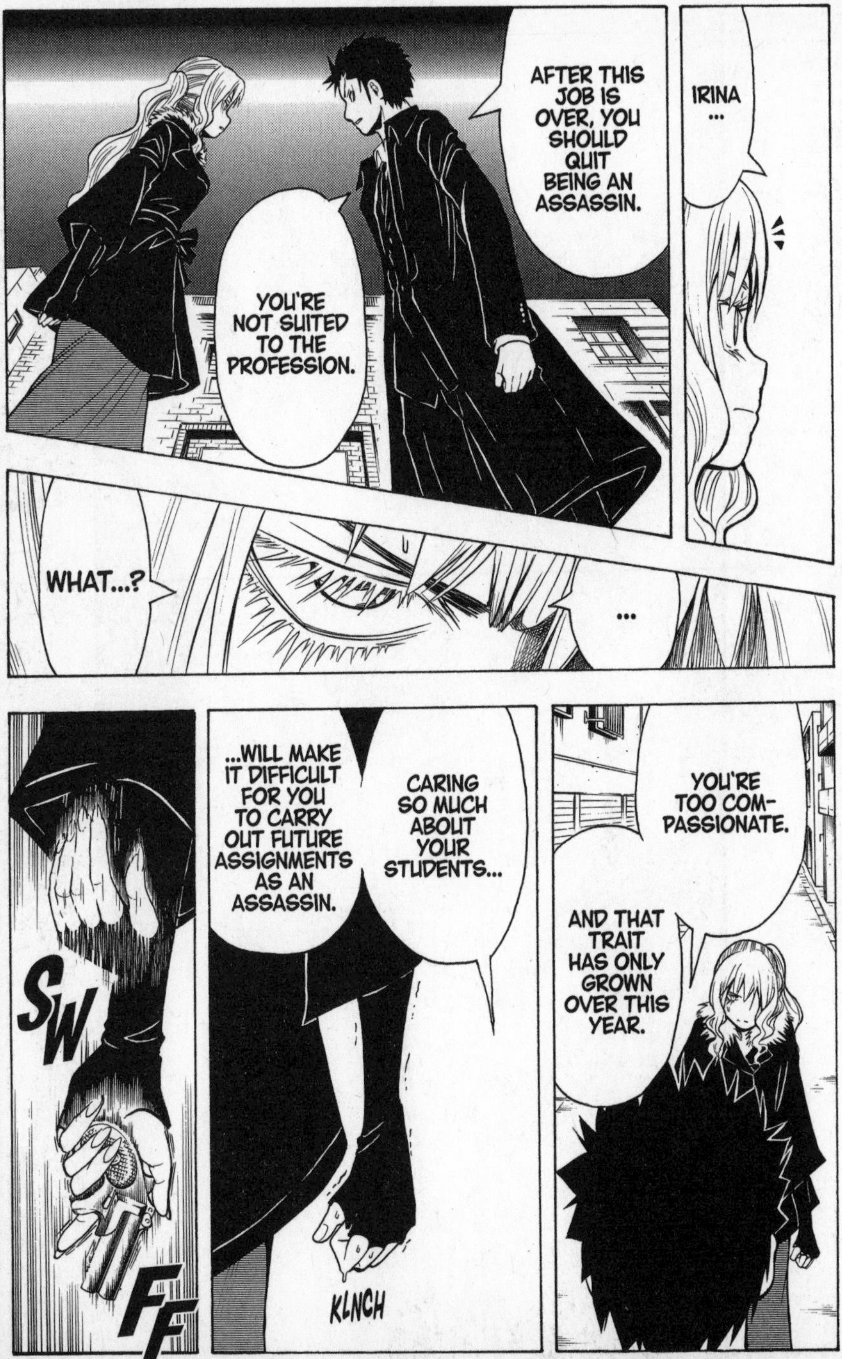
IRINA ...
AFTER THIS JOB IS OVER, YOU SHOULD QUIT BEING AN ASSASSIN.
YOU'RE NOT SUITED TO THE PROFESSION.
...
WHAT...?
YOU'RE TOO COM-PASSIONATE.
AND THAT TRAIT HAS ONLY GROWN OVER THIS YEAR.
CARING SO MUCH ABOUT YOUR STUDENTS...
...WILL MAKE IT DIFFICULT FOR YOU TO CARRY OUT FUTURE ASSIGNMENTS AS AN ASSASSIN.
KLNCH
SWFF

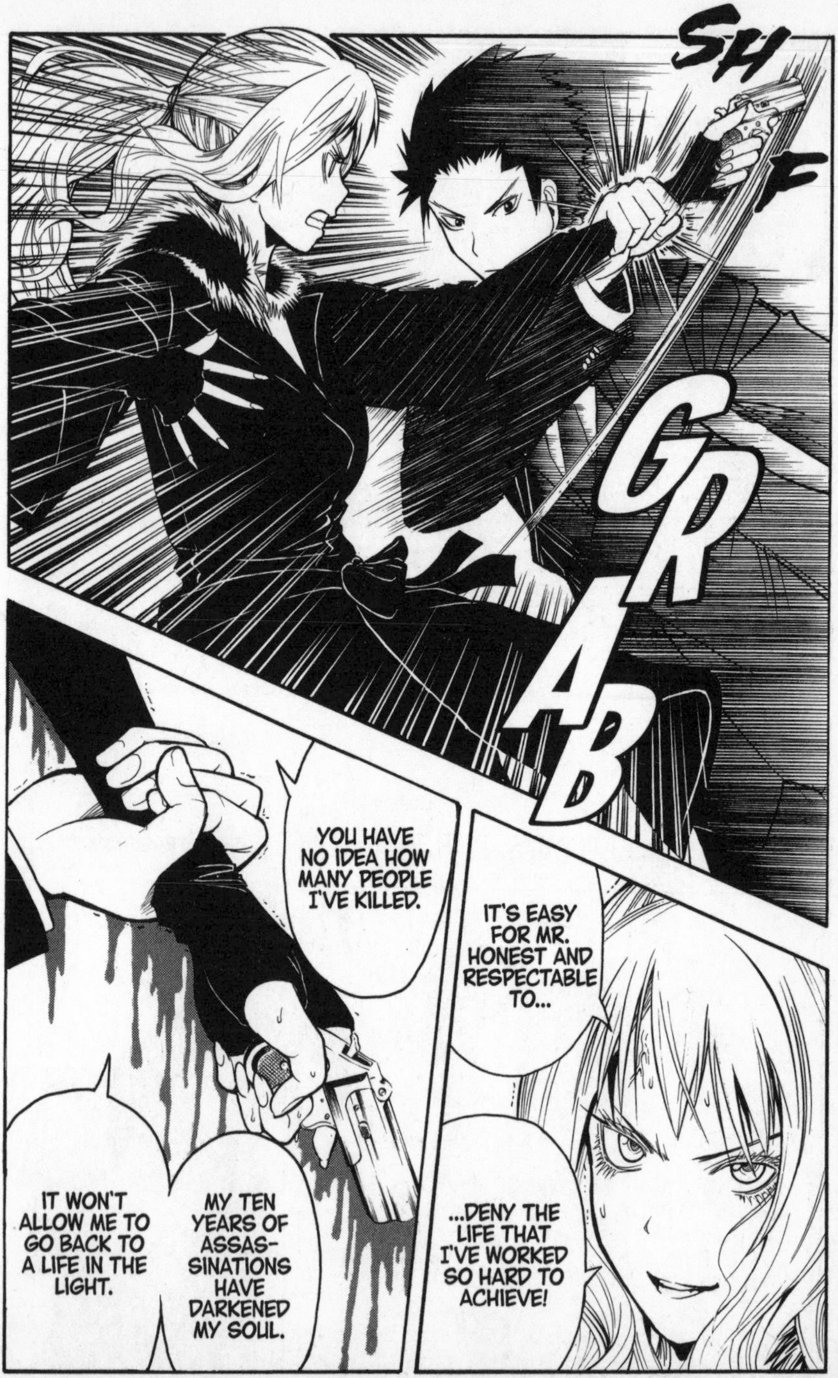
SHF
GRAB
IT'S EASY FOR MR. HONEST AND RESPECTABLE TO...
...DENY THE LIFE THAT I'VE WORKED SO HARD TO ACHIEVE!
YOU HAVE NO IDEA HOW MANY PEOPLE I'VE KILLED.
MY TEN YEARS OF ASSAS-SINATIONS HAVE DARKENED MY SOUL.
IT WON'T ALLOW ME TO GO BACK TO A LIFE IN THE LIGHT.

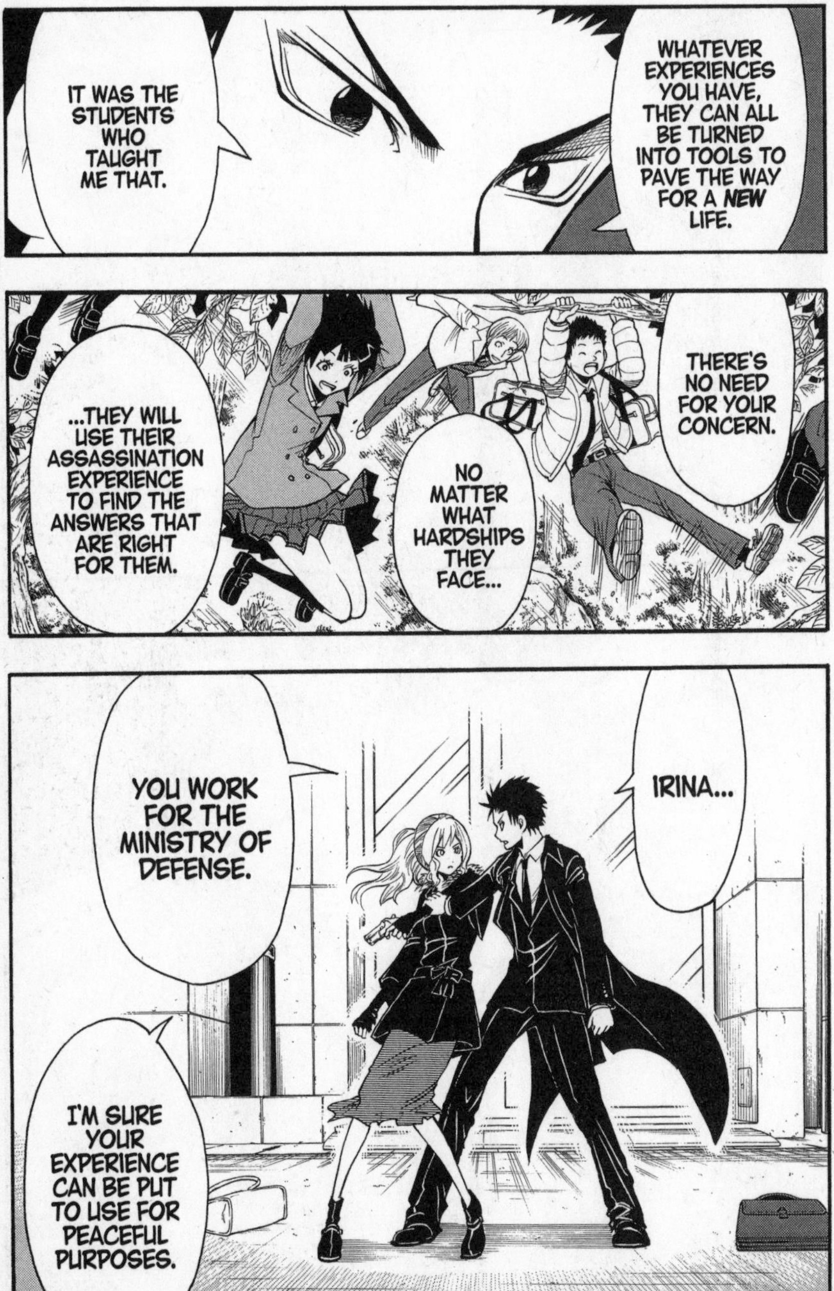
WHATEVER EXPERIENCES YOU HAVE, THEY CAN ALL BE TURNED INTO TOOLS TO PAVE THE WAY FOR A *NEW* LIFE.
IT WAS THE STUDENTS WHO TAUGHT ME THAT.
THERE'S NO NEED FOR YOUR CONCERN.
NO MATTER WHAT HARDSHIPS THEY FACE...
...THEY WILL USE THEIR ASSASSINATION EXPERIENCE TO FIND THE ANSWERS THAT ARE RIGHT FOR THEM.
IRINA...
YOU WORK FOR THE MINISTRY OF DEFENSE.
I'M SURE YOUR EXPERIENCE CAN BE PUT TO USE FOR PEACEFUL PURPOSES.

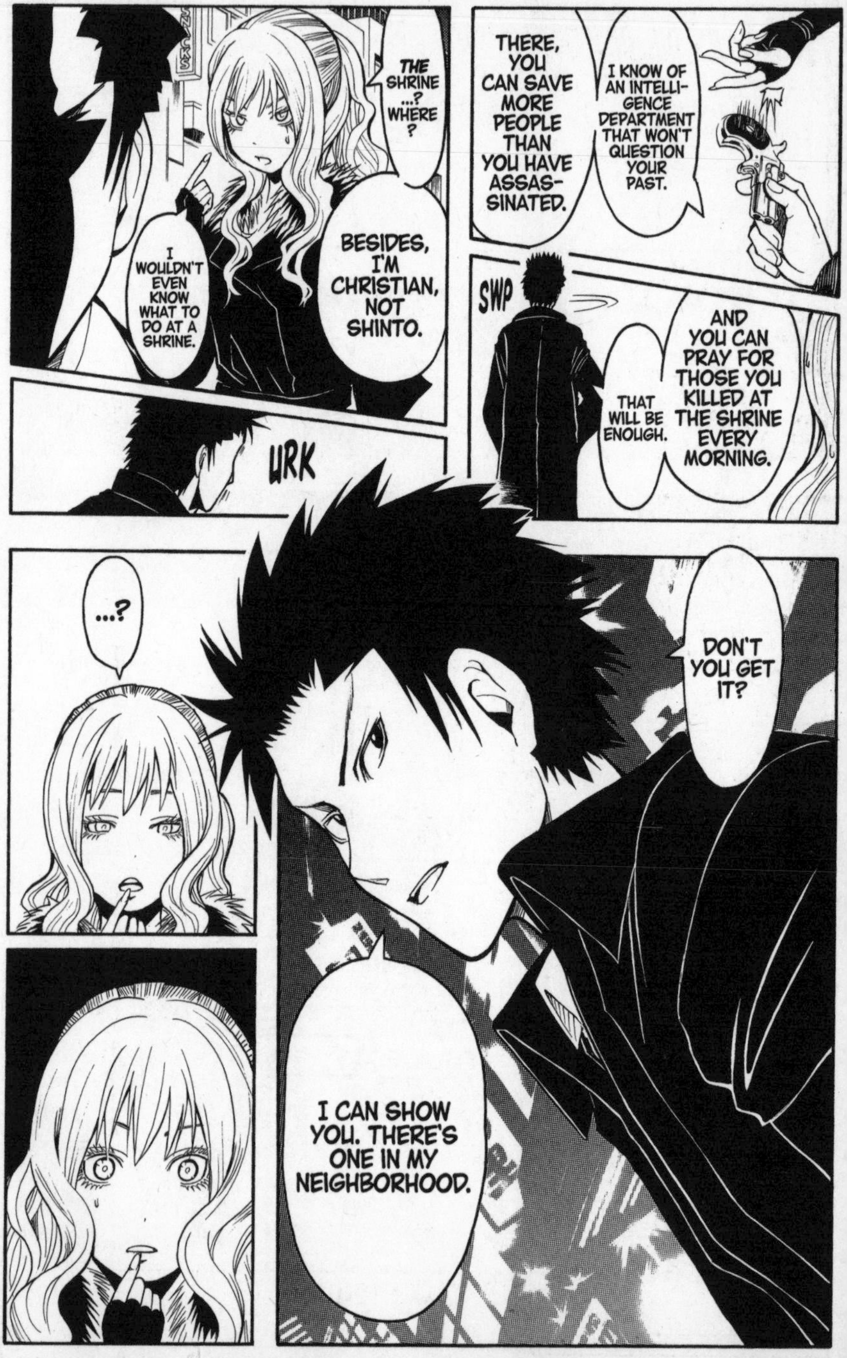
I KNOW OF AN INTELLIGENCE DEPARTMENT THAT WON'T QUESTION YOUR PAST.
THERE, YOU CAN SAVE MORE PEOPLE THAN YOU HAVE ASSASSINATED.
SWP
AND YOU CAN PRAY FOR THOSE YOU KILLED AT THE SHRINE EVERY MORNING.
THAT WILL BE ENOUGH.
THE SHRINE ...? WHERE?
BESIDES, I'M CHRISTIAN, NOT SHINTO.
I WOULDN'T EVEN KNOW WHAT TO DO AT A SHRINE.
URK
DON'T YOU GET IT?
I CAN SHOW YOU. THERE'S ONE IN MY NEIGHBORHOOD.
...?

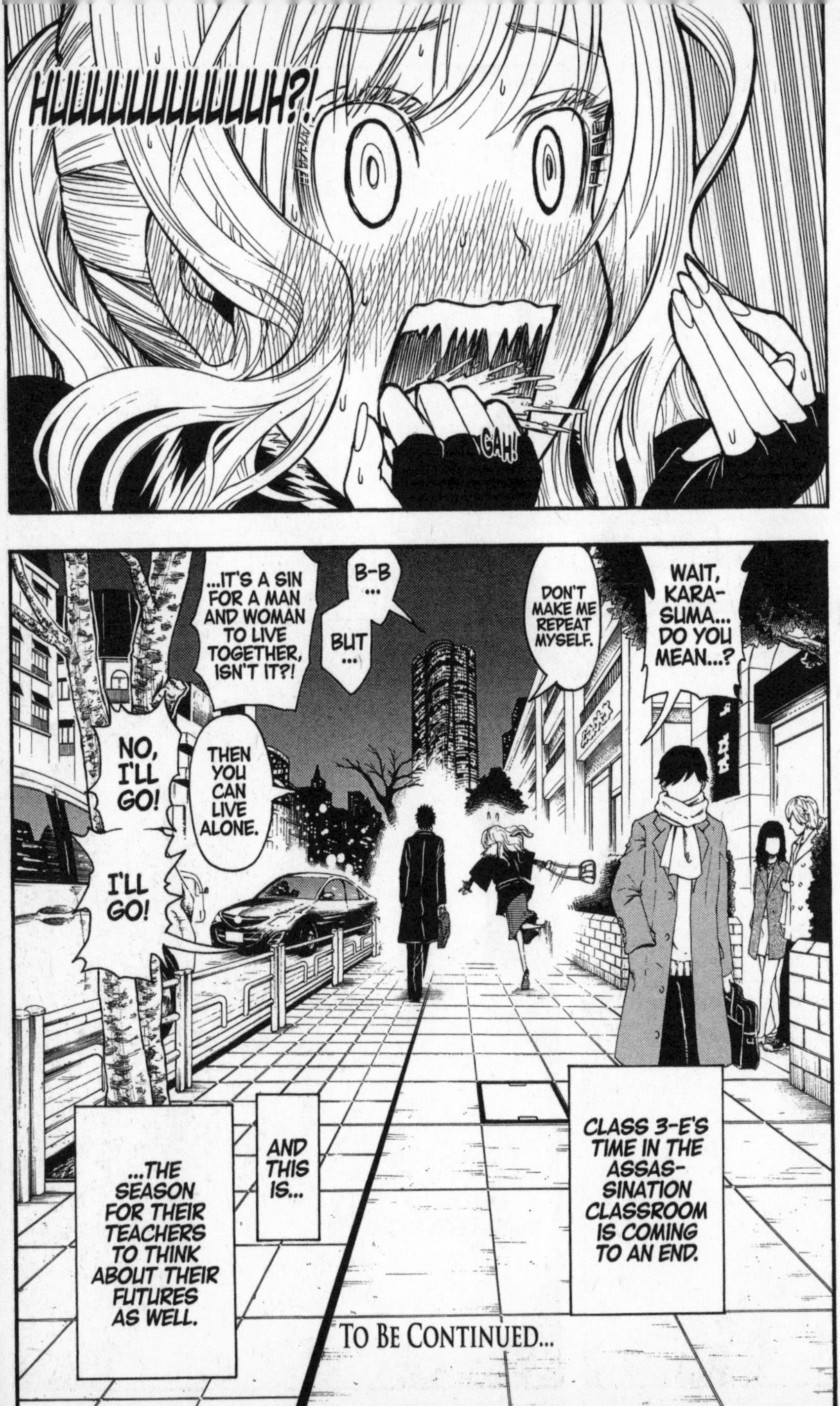
HUUUUUUUUUUUH?!
GAH!
WAIT, KARASUMA... DO YOU MEAN...?
DON'T MAKE ME REPEAT MYSELF.
B-B... BUT...
...IT'S A SIN FOR A MAN AND WOMAN TO LIVE TOGETHER, ISN'T IT?!
THEN YOU CAN LIVE ALONE.
NO, I'LL GO!
I'LL GO!
CLASS 3-E'S TIME IN THE ASSASSINATION CLASSROOM IS COMING TO AN END.
AND THIS IS...
...THE SEASON FOR THEIR TEACHERS TO THINK ABOUT THEIR FUTURES AS WELL.
TO BE CONTINUED...

Hi!

\\|//

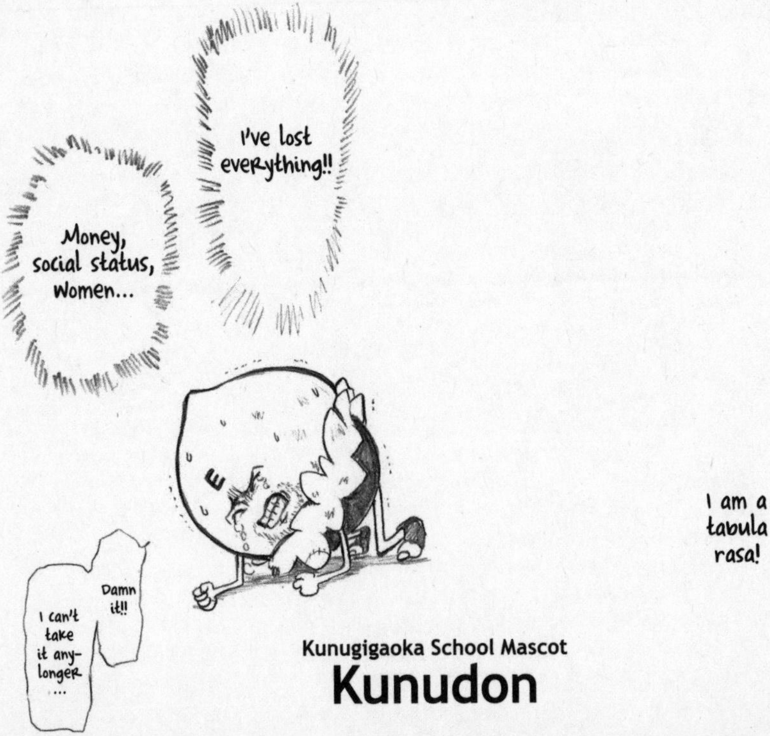
I've lost everything!!
Money, social status, women...
I am a tabula rasa!
Damn it!!
I can't take it any-longer...

Kunugigaoka School Mascot
Kunudon

In my previous series, *Neuro*, I aimed to wrap up the manga properly, but my goal for *Assassination Classroom* is to wrap up everyone's story arc properly.

The ending is the most important part of this manga, so I handed the storyline to the people working on the anime and the live—action movie so that we could all bring the curtain down on the series with the same ending.

Shortly after this volume comes out [in Japan], the series will end in the magazine, the anime will enter its climax and the live—action movie *Assassination Classroom: Graduation* will be released in theaters.

I'd like you to enjoy the art form that you prefer, but it would be great if you could enjoy and compare *Assassination Classroom* in all its formats.

The various staff and I have put a lot of effort into our respective art forms to create the one—and—only *Assassination Classroom* together!

—Yusei Matsui

Yusei Matsui was born on the last day of January in Saitama Prefecture, Japan. He has been drawing manga since elementary school. Some of his favorite manga series are *Bobobo—bo Bo-bobo*, *JoJo's Bizarre Adventure* and *Ultimate Muscle*. Matsui learned his trade working as an assistant to manga artist Yoshio Sawai, creator of *Bobobo—bo Bo-bobo*. In 2005, Matsui debuted his original manga *Neuro: Supernatural Detective* in *Weekly Shonen Jump*. In 2007, *Neuro* was adapted into an anime. In 2012, *Assassination Classroom* began serialization in *Weekly Shonen Jump*.

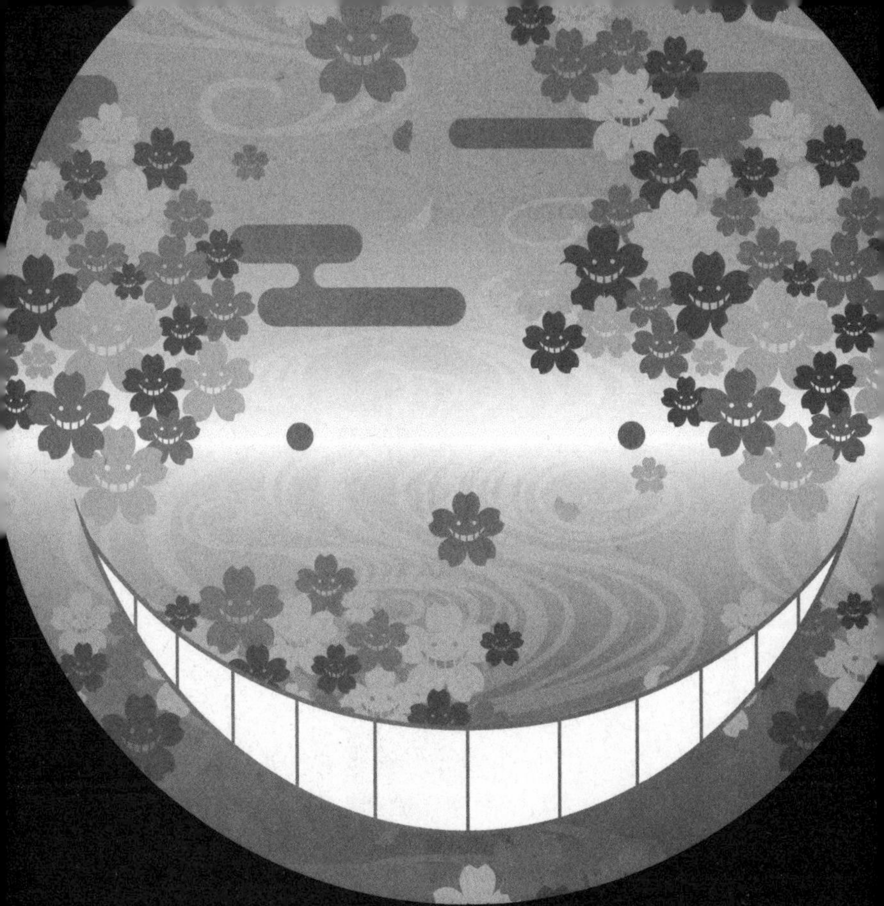

How do you like this new pattern? The falling cherry blossoms in this "Koro Blossom Shower" should bring out the tender Japanese heart inside of you. The other patterns for this cherry blossom motif that we didn't choose were brilliant too; I hope I'll get the chance to show them to you somewhere someday...

ASSASSINATION CLASSROOM

YUSEI MATSUI

18

TIME FOR VALENTINE'S DAY

A MOMENT OF TENTACLE ZEN

That's one small step for man,
one giant tentacle for mankind.

– Captain Koro

ASSASSINATION CLASSROOM

Volume 18
SHONEN JUMP ADVANCED Manga Edition

Story and Art by YUSEI MATSUI

Translation/Tetsuichiro Miyaki
English Adaptation/Bryant Turnage
Touch-up Art & Lettering/Stephen Dutro
Cover & Interior Design/Sam Elzway
Editor/Annette Roman

ANSATSU KYOSHITSU © 2012 by Yusei Matsui
All rights reserved.
First published in Japan in 2012 by SHUEISHA Inc., Tokyo.
English translation rights arranged by SHUEISHA Inc.

Printed in the U.S.A.

Published by VIZ Media, LLC
P.O. Box 77010
San Francisco, CA 94107

10 9 8 7 6 5 4 3 2 1
First printing, October 2017

www.viz.com

Syllabus for
Assassination Classroom, Vol. 19

Koro Sensei's lessons in verbal defense are put to the test when Karma must use his brains instead of his brawn to rescue a classmate. Then things finally begin to go smoothly for the students of 3–E. Everyone receives some good news about their futures and Nagisa settles on a career goal. But the peace is broken when the world's nations miraculously manage to coordinate their efforts long enough to launch a plan to assassinate Koro Sensei with the aid of the strongest mercenary in the world and an ultimate weapon! Will anyone break ranks to protect everyone's favorite tentacled teacher…?

Available December 2017!